Favorite Recipes of America

SALADS

including appetizers

FAVORITE RECIPES PRESS,
Louisville, Kentucky

Contents

Introduction 3
Salad Terms and Definitions 4
Variety Adds Interest to Salads 5
Tossed Green Salad 6
The Salad Bowl 7
Add Gourmet Touch 8
How to Make a Good Salad 9
Salad Calorie Chart 10
Abbreviations Used in This Book 16
Salad Dressings 17
Fruit Salads 43
Congealed Fruit Salads 65
Vegetable Salads 91
Congealed Vegetable Salads 119
Mixed Fruit and Vegetable Salads 137
Meat and Poultry Salads 153
Seafood Salads 177
Cereal and Pasta Salads 203
Egg and Cheese Salads 223
Frozen Salads 245
Party and Dessert Salads 271
Foreign Salads 295
Appetizers 313
Index 379
Acknowledgments 384

© Favorite Recipes Press, 1968
Post Office Box 18324
Louisville, Kentucky
Library of Congress Catalog Card No. 68-25331

Introduction

Americans love salads. In fact, many wouldn't think of serving a meal without a salad. Salads can be a meal in themselves, one course of a meal, or a little side dish. They are not only lovely to look at but are an important part of the diet.

Salads seem to be the perfect natural food for weight-conscious Americans—even though some salads can be rich and hearty. Salads are usually easy to prepare. So they are the natural answer for the homemaker on days when she is busy and doesn't have much time to devote to preparing a meal.

In this collection you will find salads galore. The pages are packed with recipes of fruit, vegetable, meat, green and molded salads—plus those from foreign lands.

Roman emperors dined on dressed lettuce. The common folk dipped their chicory and lettuce in salt; so from salata, *the Latin word for salted,* came salad.

The custom of mixing greens with oils and herbs quickly traveled from Italy and early Greece to Spain and France, where the people lovingly adopted it. In time, the French and Spaniards introduced salads to America.

The recipes in the "Salads" edition of *FAVORITE RECIPES OF AMERICA* were selected from the more than 100,000 recipes in my files to represent regional cookery at its very best. Recipes have been collected from every part of the United States.

Each of these favorite American recipes was home tested by cooks across the nation just like you. Every homemaker endorsed her own favorite recipe. Her name appears under her personal recipe. You'll treasure the many recipes in this collection which will become your favorites.

Mary Anne Richards
Staff Home Economist
Favorite Recipes Press, Inc.

SALAD TERMS
AND DEFINITIONS

Antipasto	Italian appetizer assortment.
Aspic	A clear, savory jelly used in molds or to garnish cold dishes.
Bienfatique	French term. A salad of greens tossed until limp, or with a hot dressing.
Blanch	To parboil in water for a minute; or to pour water over food and then drain it almost immediately.
Canapé	A small appetizer of bread or toast topped with a savory mixture.
Chapon	A small cube of stale French bread rubbed with garlic and tossed with the salad greens to add a hint of flavor.
Chill	To keep in a refrigerator until cold but not frozen.
Chop	To cut into small pieces.
Cube	To cut into small dice.
Cut	To chop or slice.
Dice	Cut into small squares.
Flake	To break into small pieces with a fork.
Garnish	To decorate a dish by adding small amounts of food or herbs for color or flavor.
Grate	To reduce to particles by rubbing on or grinding in a grater.
Hors d' oeuvres	French appetizer course. An assortment of small portions of meat, fish, egg or vegetables.
Julienne	Food cut in long thin strips.
Mince	To chop finely or put through a mincer or press.
Mold	To shape in a mold. A gelatin-stiffened mixture set in a mold.
Pare	To remove the skin of fruit or vegetables with a knife or parer.
Pit	To remove kernel of fruit.
Toss	To mix with light strokes, lifting with a fork and spoon. To flip in the air.

VARIETY ADDS INTEREST
TO SALADS

ESCAROLE

FRENCH OR
BELGIUM ENDIVE

ROMAINE COS

BIBB LETTUCE

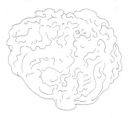

BOSTON LETTUCE

ICEBURG LETTUCE

CHICORY OR CURLY
ENDIVE

LEAF LETTUCE

CHINESE OR
CELERY CABBAGE

SPINICH LEAVES

WATERCRESS

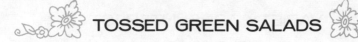 # TOSSED GREEN SALADS

The most classic salad is the simplest.

Rub the bowl with a clove of garlic or toss a chapon with the salad. (A chapon is a small piece of bread rubbed with a cut clove of garlic.)

Prepare a variety of salad greens. Dry gently and thoroughly so that no drops of water cling to them. Tear in bite-size pieces with the fingers and heap in the salad bowl. Pour French dressing over the greens and toss lightly with a fork and spoon until the dressing has coated all the parts, or sprinkle the salad lightly with olive oil, turning the leaves over and over until each glistens. Put salt and pepper in vinegar (about ¼ as much as oil) and mix lightly with greens.

Ways to Improvise

Add any of these to greens:

1. Artichokes, cut small
2. Avocado, in thin slices
3. Carrot, grated raw
4. Cauliflowerets, raw
5. Cheese, crumbled
6. Cucumber slices or sticks
7. Ham, in slivers
8. Mushrooms, (uncooked) in thin slices
9. Radish slices
10. Red onion rings
11. Shrimp, whole or broken
12. Tiny cheese balls.

GREEN SALAD VARIATIONS

Chef's Salad   Add julienne-shaped pieces of ham, chicken, turkey and cheese separately or in combination, or use bits of sardine or anchovies.

Herb Salad   Add 1 tablespoon of finely cut fresh herbs before adding dressing. Use any of the following alone or in combination: anise, basil, borage, bunet, chervil, chives, mint, rue, sorrel, or tarragon. Herbs can be overdone so be careful.

There are appetizer salads, dinner or with-the-meal salads, main dish or salad plates or dessert salads—choose one to fit in each menu.

Salad bowls are made of many different materials. You may choose from wood, silver, ceramic, stainless steel, clear glass, plastic, china, aluminum, pottery or ovenproof.

No matter what type of bowl you use, each type needs a little extra care. Nothing is more elegant than silver for special occasions but you must protect your bowl by using a glass liner. First toss your salad in the glass liner; then place it in the silver bowl for serving.

For a cheerful family dinner or just for everyday, ceramic bowls are a favorite. They have one drawback—they require very careful handling to prevent chipping. Ceramic bowls seem well worth it because they are so gay and colorful.

Stainless steel bowls are sleek and modern looking. It's never necessary to polish these bowls and they may be used for all types of salads.

Clear glass salad bowls are perfect for showing off a fresh fruit salad, but they become unpleasantly smudged with oils for tossed salad. Ovenproof bowls are essential for hot salads. Hearty, delicious hot salads may be prepared, heated and served in these stainproof bowls. For an added touch slip the bowl into a decorative holder before putting it on the table.

The wooden salad bowl is the choice of most people. Wash your wooden bowl with a damp cloth—no soap—and dry at once. But by all means, wash it!

Wilted Greens

This is a green salad with a twist. Bacon drippings give the hot sweet-sour dressing a very special flavor.

6 slices bacon	½ teaspoon salt
½ cup sliced green onion	8 cups leaf lettuce, torn
¼ cup vinegar	6 radishes, thinly sliced
¼ cup water	1 hard-cooked egg, chopped
4 teaspoons sugar	

Place lettuce in large salad bowl. Pour hot dressing over lettuce; toss until well coated. Garnish with radish slices and chopped egg. Serve at once.

ADD GOURMET TOUCH
Herbs and Cheese

HERBS:	USE WITH
Basil	Tomato salads, fresh tomato slices
Caraway	Coleslaw, beet salads
Dill Seed	Coleslaw, potato salad
Marjoram	French dressing, fresh tomato slices, meat salads
Oregano	Potato or tuna salads
Rosemary	French dressing or mayonnaise for chicken or potato salads
Savory	Tossed salads
Thyme	French dressing marinade for diced chicken

SPICES:	USE WITH
Allspice	Fruit salads, fruit salad dressings
Cinnamon	Tomatoes, cottage cheese garnishes
Ginger	Pear salads
Mace	Whipped cream dressings for fruit salads
Mustard	Mixed with water for commercial mayonnaise or French dressing
Paprika	Add to oil and vinegar for additional color
Cayenne Pepper	Salad dressings, meat, fish and vegetable salads

BLENDS:	USE WITH
Seasoning Salt	Substitute for salt in oil and vinegar dressings
Italian Dressing	French dressing, tossed green salads
Apple Pie Spice	Waldorf salad
Curry Powder	French dressing for chicken salad
Salad Lift	Add to oil and vinegar for French dressing or stir into prepared salad dressing
Pickling Spice	Beet salads
Herb Seasoning	Sliced cucumbers, sliced tomatoes, French dressing

CHEESE	USE WITH
Amer. Cheddar	Tossed salads, dressings, appetizers
Bleu (Blue)	Tossed salads, dressings, appetizer spreads
Brick	Salads, appetizers
Camembert	Fruit salads, appetizer spreads
Cottage	Fruit, vegetable salads
Cream	Fruit, vegetable salads, dressings, appetizer spreads
Gorgonzola	Salads, dressings
Gouda	Appetizers
Muenster	Raw vegetable appetizers
Provolone	Appetizers
Roquefort	Dressings, appetizers
Ricotta	Salads, appetizers
Swiss	Fruit, vegetable salads

HOW TO
MAKE A GOOD SALAD

1. Choose the appropriate salad.
   a. Light salad with hearty meal.
   b. Tart salad with fish.
   c. Hearty or hot salad for main course.
   d. Fruit salad as appetizer, dessert, or meat accompaniment.
2. Good combinations with contrast in color, texture, form and flavor are a must.
3. Prepare salad greens with care.
   a. Store unwashed in tightly-covered container or plastic bag in refrigerator.
   b. Wash as needed to avoid "rusting."
4. Choose correct dressing.
5. Toss ingredients lightly. Do not bruise or crush greens. Use minimum amount of dressing.
6. Arrange attractively but avoid a "fixed" appearance. Salads must be simple and casual. Use a large enough plate so salad does not extend over edge.
7. Cold . . . Crisp . . . Cold—these are key words.

Head Lettuce

To wash iceburg lettuce, cut out the core. Hold the lettuce, core side up, under the running water; run cold water into the opening. Shake off excess water and dry thoroughly.

Leaf Lettuce, Endive, Spinach, etc.

Swish each leaf in water separately. Allow water to drain off. Roll up in clean towel to absorb excess moisture. Store, wrapped, in refrigerator until ready to use.

Salad Etiquette

Q: Where would I place individual salads?
A: First course salads should be in the center of each place, for formal serving on a large plate. Main course salads should be placed at left of dinner plate. If the table is crowded, place directly above forks. In this case the bread and butter plate should be omitted.
Q: Is it proper to have salad on the table at the beginning of the meal?
A: Yes. Place your salad just before seating your guest.
Q: How should I serve a platter of salad or a bowl of mixed greens?
A: It may be passed provided it is easy to handle and servings can be easily removed. It is permissible for the hostess to serve individual salad plates and pass them around.
Q: Should dressing always be passed?
A: Pass your dressing if none has already been added to the salad.
Q: Is a salad fork always necessary?
A: A dinner salad may be eaten with the same fork as the main course.
Q: Where does the salad fork appear in the table setting?
A: This depends on when the salad is to be served during the meal: for the first course, the fork is at the extreme left. If with the main course or following it, the fork is inside the dinner fork just at left of the dinner plate.

SALAD CALORIE CHART

FOOD	AMOUNT	CALORIES
CHEESE		
Blue mold (Roquefort type)	1 oz.	105
Cheddar or American		
Ungrated	1 1-in. cube	70
Grated	1 c.	455
Cheddar, process	1 oz.	105
Cheddar cheese foods	1 oz.	28
Cottage cheese (from skim milk)		
Creamed	1 oz.	30
Uncreamed	1 oz.	25
Creamed	1 c.	240
Uncreamed	1 c.	195
Cream cheese	1 c.	105
	1 tbsp.	55
Swiss	1 oz.	105
MEAT, POULTRY, FISH, SHELL-FISH, RELATED PRODUCTS		
Bacon, broiled or fried crisp	2 slices	95
Chicken, cooked		
Flesh and skin, broiled, boneless	3 oz.	185
Canned, boneless	3 oz.	170
Pork, cured, cooked		
Ham, smoked, lean and fat	3 oz.	290
Luncheon meat		
Cooked ham, sliced	2 oz.	170
Canned, spiced or unspiced	2 oz.	165
Crab meat, canned or cooked	3 oz.	90
Salmon, pink, canned	3 oz.	120
Shrimp, canned, meat only	3 oz.	110
Tuna, canned in oil, drained, solids	3 oz.	170
NUTS, PEANUTS, RELATED PRODUCTS		
Almonds, shelled	1 c.	850
Brazil nuts, broken pieces	1 c.	905
Cashew nuts, roasted	1 c.	770
Coconut		
Fresh or shredded	1 c.	330
Dried, shredded, sweetened	1 c.	345
Peanuts, roasted, shelled		
Halves	1 c.	840
Chopped	1 tbsp.	50

FOOD	AMOUNT	CALORIES
Peanut butter	1 tbsp.	90
Pecans		
Halves	c.	740
Chopped	1 tbsp.	50
Walnuts, shelled		
Black or native, chopped	1 c.	790
English or Persian, halves	1 c.	650
English or Persian, chopped	1 tbsp.	50

VEGETABLES AND VEGETABLE PRODUCTS

FOOD	AMOUNT	CALORIES
Beans		
Lima, immature, cooked	1 c.	150
Snap, green, cooked in small amount of water	1 c.	25
Snap, green, canned, solids and liquids	1 c.	45
Beets, cooked, diced	1 c.	70
Cabbage		
Raw, finely shredded	1 c.	25
Raw, coleslaw	1 c.	100
Cooked	1 c.	40
Cabbage, celery or Chinese		
Raw, leaves and stem, 1-in. pieces	1 c.	15
Cooked	1 c.	25
Carrots		
Raw, whole, 5½ x 1 in.	1 carrot	20
Grated	1 c.	45
Cooked, diced	1 c.	45
Cauliflower, cooked, flower buds	1 c.	30
Celery, raw		
Stalk, large outer, 8 x 1½ in. at root end	1 stalk	5
Pieces, diced	1 c.	20
Cucumber, 10 oz., 7½ x 2 in.		
Raw, pared	1 cucumber	25
Raw, pared, center slice, 1/8-in. thick	6 slices	5
Endive, curly (including escarole)	2 oz.	10
Lettuce, headed, raw		
Head, loose leaf, 4-in. diameter	1 head	30
Head, compact, 4¾-in. diameter, 1 lb.	1 head	70
Leaves	2 large or 4 small	5
Mushrooms, canned, solids and liquids	1 c.	30

FOOD	AMOUNT	CALORIES

Onions
- Mature, raw 2½-in. diameter .... 1 onion 50
- Mature, cooked .... 1 c. 80
- Young, green, small, without tops.... 6 onions 25

Parsley, raw, chopped .... 1 tbsp. 1

Peas, green
- Cooked .... 1 c. 110
- Canned, solids and liquids .... 1 c. 170
- Canned, strained .... 1 oz. 10

Peppers, sweet, raw, about 6 per lb.
- Green pod without stem and seeds.... 1 pod 15
- Red pod without stem and seeds...... 1 pod 20
- Canned, pimentos, medium .... 1 pod 10

Potatoes, medium, about 3 per lb.
- Peeled after boiling .... 1 potato 105
- Peeled before boiling .... 1 potato 90

Potato chips, medium, 2-in. diameter..10 chips 110

Radishes, raw, small, without tops ...... 4 radishes 10

Sauerkraut, canned, drained, solids .... 1 c. 30

Tomatoes, raw, about 3 per lb. .... 1 tomato 30

Tomato juice, canned .... 1 c. 50

Tomato catsup .... 1 tbsp. 15

FRUIT AND FRUIT PRODUCTS

Apples, raw, 2½-in. diameter, about
- 3 per lb. .... 1 apple 70

Apple juice, fresh or canned .... 1 c. 125

Applesauce, canned
- Sweetened .... 1 c. 185
- Unsweetened .... 1 c. 100

Apricots
- Raw, about 12 per lb. .... 3 apricots 55
- Canned, in heavy syrup, halves and syrup .... 1 c. 220
- Dried, uncooked, 40 small halves .... 1 c. 390
- Dried, cooked, unsweetened, fruit and liquid .... 1 c. 240

Avocados, raw
- California varieties, 10 oz. 3 1/3 x 4¼ in., peeled and pitted .... ½ avocado 185
- Florida varieties, 13 oz., 4 x 3 in., peeled and pitted .... ½ avocado 160
- ½-in. cubes .... 1 c. 195

Bananas, raw, 6 x 1½ in. .... 1 banana 85

FOOD	AMOUNT	CALORIES
Blackberries or blueberries, raw	1 c.	85
Cantaloupe, raw, about 1 2/3 lb.	½ melon	40
Cherries		
Raw, sour, sweet hybrid	1 c.	65
Canned, sour, red, pitted	1 c.	105
Cranberry sauce, sweetened, canned or cooked	1 c.	550
Cranberry juice cocktail, canned	1 c.	140
Dates, pitted, cut	1 c.	505
Figs		
Raw, small, about 12 per lb.	3 figs	90
Dried, large, 2 x 1 in.	1 fig	60
Fruit cocktail, canned in heavy syrup, solids and liquids	1 c.	195
Grapefruit, raw, medium, 4¼-in. diameter		
White	½ grapefruit	50
Pink or red	½ grapefruit	55
Grapefruit sections, raw, white	1 c.	75
Grapefruit juice		
Fresh	1 c.	95
Canned, unsweetened	1 c.	100
Canned, sweetened	1 c.	130
Grapes, raw		
American type (slip skin)	1 c.	70
European type (adherent skin)	1 c.	100
Grape juice, bottled	1 c.	165
Lemons, raw, medium, 2 1/5-in. diameter	1 lemon	20
Lemon juice		
Fresh	1 c.	60
	1 tbsp.	5
Canned, unsweetened	1 c.	60
Lemonade concentrate, frozen, sweetened		
Undiluted, 6-oz. can	1 can	430
Water added	1 c.	110
Lime juice, fresh or canned	1 c.	65
Oranges, raw		
Navel, California (winter) 2 4/5-in. diameter	1 orange	60
Other varieties, 3-in. diameter	1 orange	70
Orange juice, fresh		
California, Valencia, summer	1 c.	120

| --- | --- | --- |
Florida varieties	1 c.	110
Orange juice, canned, unsweetened	1 c.	120
Orange juice concentrate, frozen		
Undiluted 6-oz. can	1 can	330
Water added	1 c.	110
Orange and grapefruit juice, frozen concentrate		
Undiluted 6-oz. can	1 can	330
Water added	1 c.	110
Papayas, raw, ½-in. cubes	1 c.	70
Peaches		
Raw, whole, about 4 per lb.	1 peach	35
Raw, sliced	1 c.	65
Canned, yellow fleshed, solids and liquids	1 c.	65
Canned, syrup pack, heavy, halves or slices	1 c.	200
Dried, uncooked	1 c.	420
Dried, cooked, unsweetened, 10-12 halves and 6 tbsp. liquid	1 c.	220
Frozen, 12-oz. carton	1 carton	265
Peach nectar, canned	1 c.	115
Pears		
Raw, 3 x 2½-in. diameter	1 pear	100
Canned, solids and liquids, heavy syrup	1 c.	195
Pear nectar, canned	1 c.	130
Pineapple		
Raw, diced	1 c.	75
Canned, syrup pack, solids and liquid		
Crushed	1 c.	205
Sliced, slices and juice	2 sm. or 1 lge. and 2 tbsp. juice	95
Pineapple juice, canned	1 c.	120
Raisins, dried	1 c.	460
Raspberries, red		
Raw	1 c.	70
Frozen, 10-oz. carton	1 carton	280
Strawberries		
Raw, capped	1 c.	55
Frozen, 10-oz. carton	1 carton	300
Frozen, 16-oz. can	1 can	485
Watermelon, raw, wedge 4 x 8-in.	1 wedge	120

GRAIN PRODUCTS

Macaroni, cooked until tender	1 c.	155
Noodles, egg, cooked	1 c.	200
Rice, cooked		
Parboiled	1 c.	205
White	1 c.	200
Spaghetti, cooked until tender	1 c.	155

FATS AND OILS

Oils, salad or cooking		
Corn	1 tbsp.	125
Cottonseed	1 tbsp.	125
Olive	1 tbsp.	125
Soybean	1 tbsp.	125
Salad dressings		
Bleu cheese	1 tbsp.	90
Commercial, plain, mayonnaise type	1 tbsp.	60
French	1 tbsp.	60
Home cooked, boiled	1 tbsp.	30
Mayonnaise	1 tbsp.	110
Thousand Island	1 tbsp.	75

MISCELLANEOUS ITEMS

Beverages, carbonated		
Ginger ale	1 c.	80
Cola type	1 c.	105
Gelatin, dry:		
Plain	1 tbsp.	35
Dessert powder, 3-oz. pkg.	½ c.	325
Gelatin dessert salad, ready to eat:		
Plain	1 c.	155
With fruit	1 c.	170
Olives, pickled:		
Green	7 jumbo	65
Ripe	7 jumbo	85
Pickles, cucumber:		
Dill, large, 4 x 1¾-in.	1 pickle	15
Sweet, 2¾ x ¾-in.	1 pickle	20
Sherbet, factory packed	1 c.	235
Vinegar	1 tbsp.	2

 # ABBREVIATIONS

Teaspoon	tsp.	Large	lge.
Tablespoon	tbsp.	Package	pkg.
Cup	c.	Square	sq.
Pound	lb.	Dozen	doz.
Ounce	oz.	Pint	pt.
Medium	med.	Quart	qt.

MEASUREMENTS

3 tsp. = 1 tbsp.
2 tbsp. = ⅛ c.
4 tbsp. = ¼ c.
8 tbsp. = ½ c.
16 tbsp. = 1 c.
5 tbsp. + 1 tsp. = 1/3 c.
12 tbsp. = ¾ c.
4 oz. = ½ c.
8 oz. = 1 c.
16 oz. = 1 lb.
1 oz. = 2 tbsp. fat or liquid

2 c. fat = 1 lb.
2 c. = 1 pt.
2 c. sugar = 1 lb.
⅝ c. = ½ c. + 2 tbsp.
7/8 c. = ¾ c. + 2 tbsp.
2 pt. = 1 qt.
1 qt. = 4 c.
A few grains = Less than ⅛ tsp.
Pinch = As much as can be taken
   between tip of finger and thumb
Speck = Less than ⅛ tsp.

CAN CONTENTS

Average Contents   *Can Size*

1 c.	8 oz.
1¾ c.	No. 300
2 c.	No. 1 tall
2½ c.	No. 2
3½ c.	No. 2½
4 c.	No. 3

Salad Dressings

MAKE YOUR OWN DRESSING

A light French dressing (oil, vinegar or lemon juice and seasonings) is appropriate for almost any salad. Mayonnaise, whipped cream, or cooked dressing should be used according to your own taste. According to the ingredients, vary the seasoning. Don't be afraid to experiment— you may create something special.

BASIC INGREDIENTS

Here are some supplies needed to make a good dressing. Study them, taste them, and make your own personal choice.

Oils

Some people prefer fruity Italian oil; others like the more delicate French type. Vegetable oils—made from corn, cotton seed, peanuts and soybeans—are good and richer in food value than the more widely used olive oil. No matter what type you use top quality is essential.

Vinegar

Strength in vinegars varies so much that a little at a time should be added until the desired taste is reached. Old-fashioned vinegar has a mild, sweet taste. For a distinctive taste in your dressing, add tarragon, wine, pear, garlic or other specially seasoned vinegar.

Seasoning

Use regular table salt; it won't cake. Black pepper is at its best when freshly ground. To add garlic flavor—add minced fresh garlic, garlic salt or powdered dry garlic. Use dried or fresh herbs sparingly; remember with herbs a little goes a long way.

Other Salad Staples

Keep these on hand—garlic, celery salt, onion salt, minced onion and onion juice.

Horseradish, pickle relish, caraway, sesame, celery and mustard seeds add distinctive flavor to both salads and salad dressings. Don't overlook fresh and dried herbs, such as sage, mint, chives, basil, oregano, chervil (like parsley but slightly peppery) and dill. Use sharp table steak sauce and red pepper sauce for zesty tang. Crunchy nuts and raisins give a pleasing texture and taste contrast to fish, meat and fruit salads and aspics.

All-Purpose Dressing

2 eggs
4 tbsp. vinegar
4 tbsp. water
4 tbsp. sugar
⅛ tsp. salt
⅛ tsp. black pepper

Combine all ingredients in top of double boiler. Cook, beating constantly with rotary beater until light and fluffy. Will keep for a week in refrigerator. For fruit salad substitute 4 tablespoons pineapple juice for water in basic dressing. For potato salad marinate potatoes with dressing combined with 2 teaspoons mustard and 2 tablespoons mayonnaise. Yield: 2 cups.

Virginia Lewis Sullivan, Home Economics Teacher, St. Charles, Va.

 ## Amish Dressing

1 tsp. salt
2 tbsp. dry mustard
1 c. sugar
4 tbsp. flour
1 tsp. onion powder
2 eggs, beaten
2 c. milk
1 c. vinegar
1 tbsp. melted butter

Mix dry ingredients well with eggs; gradually add milk and vinegar. Cook, stirring, until thickened. Stir in butter. Refrigerate. Yield: 1 quart dressing.

Mrs. James L. Harrison, Hon. Pres. Coast Guard Officers' Wives' Club,
Traverse City, Mich.

Avocado Salad Dressing

1 3-oz. pkg. cream cheese, softened
1 clove of garlic, mashed
½ green pepper, chopped
1 or 2 avocados, chopped
½ to 1 pt. sour cream
Salt and pepper to taste
2 tbsp. mayonnaise

Mash cream cheese; mix in garlic and green pepper. Add remaining ingredients; mix well. Chill before serving. Yield: 4-6 servings.

Mrs. William P. Schellhase, Officers' Wives' Club, Guam, Marianas Islands

Bacon-Mayonnaise Dressing

6 slices bacon
5 tbsp. vinegar
5 tbsp. sugar
2 eggs, beaten
4 tbsp. mayonnaise

Cut bacon into small pieces; fry until crisp. Add vinegar and sugar to eggs; combine with bacon. Bring to boiling point. Boil for 1 minute. Remove from heat. Set aside. At serving time, add mayonnaise; stir well. Serve on lettuce.

Mrs. Robert J. Nolan, Bangor, Maine

 ### Pennsylvania Dutch Hot Bacon Dressing

3 slices bacon
1 tbsp. flour
2 tbsp. sugar
1 egg, beaten
¼ c. vinegar
1 c. water

Cut bacon into small pieces; fry until crisp. Remove bacon from drippings. Mix flour with sugar; add egg, vinegar and water. Stir until well blended. Cook in bacon drippings until thickened. Pour over lettuce, endive, spinach or dandelion greens. Garnish with the bacon bits and hard-cooked egg.

Mrs. Frank R. More, Hon. Pres. Officers' Wives' Club, Morocco

Blue Cheese Dressing

1 c. olive oil
½ c. vinegar
1 4-oz. pkg. blue cheese, crumbled
1 tbsp. sugar
1 ½ tsp. salt
½ tsp. pepper
½ tsp. dry mustard
2 tsp. angostura aromatic bitters

Combine all ingredients in screw-top jar. Shake vigorously. Store in refrigerator and shake before using. Yield: 1 pint.

Photograph for this recipe on page 17.

Bleu Cheese Chef's Dressing

3 oz. bleu cheese, crumbled
2 tbsp. vinegar
1 tsp. anchovy paste
Dash of steak sauce
1 tbsp. lemon juice
½ c. olive oil
½ clove of garlic, minced
Salt and pepper

Combine all ingredients thoroughly; mix in blender. Yield: 1 cup.

Mrs. Denis Lohman, Dugway, Utah

Bleu Cheese-Cottage Cheese Dressing

1 pt. cottage cheese
1 4-oz. pkg. bleu cheese
Juice of 1 lemon
1 c. mayonnaise
1 c. half and half
½ tsp. salt
¼ tsp. black pepper
Dash of cayenne pepper
2 cloves of garlic, crushed
3 or 4 drops of Tabasco sauce

Place half of both cheeses in blender. Reserve remaining cheese. Add remaining ingredients and blend well. Remove from blender. Add remaining crumbled cheeses. Cover. Store in refrigerator. If smooth consistency is desired, place all the cheeses in blender. May be thinned with additional half and half, if desired. Yield: 1 quart.

Judy Hoskins, Sioux City, Iowa, Favorite Recipes Food Fair

Creamy Bleu Cheese Dressing

1 qt. mayonnaise
1 tsp. garlic powder
1 3-oz. pkg. bleu cheese
½ c. whipping cream
½ c. buttermilk

Beat all ingredients together until smooth. Cover and refrigerate. Yield: 5 cups.

Judith M. Unze, Home Economics Teacher, Appleton, Minn.

21

Buttermilk Dressing

½ c. sugar
1 tsp. dry mustard
1 tsp. salt
¼ tsp. celery seed
1 tbsp. flour
½ c. vinegar
1 c. buttermilk
1 tbsp. butter
2 beaten eggs

Mix sugar, mustard, salt, celery seed and flour. Add vinegar, buttermilk and butter. Cook in double boiler until thickened. Pour thick mixture over beaten eggs. Return to double boiler; cook until mixture reaches consistency of soft custard. Cool. Use with fruit salads or coleslaw.

Ruth C. Peabody, Home Economics Teacher, Sunnyside, Wash.

Cabbage Dressing

½ c. water
1 c. sugar
1 c. vinegar
1 tsp. celery seed
1 tsp. mustard seed

Combine all ingredients. Boil for 3 minutes. Refrigerate. Yield: 1 pint.

Sharron Mallin, Home Economics Teacher, Buhl, Minn.

Barbara's Coleslaw Dressing

5 tbsp. sugar
1 tbsp. plus 1 tsp. flour
1 tsp. dry mustard
Pinch of salt
1 egg, beaten
¼ c. vinegar
¾ c. water
Butter size of walnut
1 c. salad dressing

Thoroughly mix sugar, flour, mustard, salt and egg; set aside. Combine vinegar, water and butter; bring to boil. Add first mixture and cook for a few minutes. Remove from heat; beat well. Add salad dressing and beat again. Dressing will keep for several weeks in refrigerator.

Mrs. Barbara Hinegardner, Home Economics Teacher, Bel Air, Md.

22

Caesar Salad Dressing

   1 egg
   ¾ c. salad oil
   ¼ c. lemon juice
   1 tsp. salt
   ½ tsp. pepper
   1 tsp. Worcestershire sauce
   ¼ c. grated Parmesan cheese

Cook egg in boiling water for 1 minute. Break egg into bowl and whip. Slowly add oil, beating at high speed. Reduce speed; add remaining ingredients. Yield: 1¼ cups.

Mrs. Joseph Goode, Reno, Nev., Favorite Recipes Food Fair

 ### Catalina Dressing

   ¼ tsp. black pepper
   ¼ c. vinegar
   ½ c. catsup
   1 small onion, grated
   ½ tsp. salt
   ½ c. sugar
   1 c. salad oil

Using a rotary beater, mix all ingredients except oil in order listed. Gradually add oil while beating. Refrigerate. Yield: 1 pint.

Mrs. Ina Luadtke, Home Economics Teacher, Fisher, Minn.

Celery Seed Dressing

   ½ c. sugar
   1 tsp. dry mustard
   1 tsp. salt
   1 tsp or more onion, grated or onion juice (opt.)
   ¼ to ⅓ c. vinegar
   ⅔ to 1 c. salad oil
   1 tsp. to 1 tbsp. celery seed
   1 tsp. paprika (opt.)

Mix sugar, mustard, salt and onion. Alternately add vinegar and oil a little at a time, beginning with vinegar. Beat well. Add celery seed and paprika. Cover and store in refrigerator. Serve on fruit or fresh vegetable salads.

Mrs. Margaret Cepelka, Home Economics Teacher, Berryville, Va.

Chiffonade Dressing

⅓ c. vinegar
1 c. corn oil
1 clove of garlic
1 ½ tsp. salt
1 tsp. sugar
½ tsp. paprika
½ tsp. dry mustard
1 hard-cooked egg, chopped
2 tbsp. chopped green pepper
2 tbsp. chopped pimento
2 tsp. chopped parsley

Combine all ingredients in jar; cover and shake well. Chill for several hours; remove garlic. Pour over sliced tomatoes and cucumbers, if desired. Refrigerate for at least 30 minutes.

Mrs. Carl S. Leidy, Lathrop, Cal., Favorite Recipes Food Fair

Condensed Milk Dressing

2 eggs
¾ c. vinegar
2 to 3 tbsp. water
1 can condensed milk
½ tsp. prepared mustard

Beat eggs until thick. Add 1 tablespoon vinegar-water mixture to eggs and beat. Add 1 to 2 tablespoons milk; beat. Repeat additions of vinegar and milk, beating after each. Blend in mustard. Store, tightly covered, in refrigerator. Serve on tomato, chopped cabbage or fruit salad.

Thelma Huff, Home Economics Teacher, Pelahatchie, Miss.

Low Calorie Dressing

1 c. cottage cheese
1 10½-oz. can condensed tomato soup
1 tbsp. India or sweet pickle relish
1 tbsp. lemon juice
Grated rind of 1 lemon (opt.)

Blend all ingredients; chill. Stir well and serve over crisp salad greens. Two tablespoons dressing contains 25 calories. Yield: 2 cups.

Dora Hoover, Macon, Ga., Favorite Recipes Food Fair

 ## Dill Dressing

   1 tbsp. dill seed
   1 ½ tsp. dry mustard
   1 tsp. salt
   1 tbsp. sugar
   Coarsely ground pepper
   2 tbsp. tarragon vinegar
   6 tbsp. salad oil

Mash dill seed well in palm of hand; add to dry mustard, salt, sugar and pepper. Mix thoroughly. Add vinegar; stir until sugar is completely dissolved. Add oil; stir well. Serve. Yield: 6 servings.

Mrs. John W. White, Albuquerque, N. M., Favorite Recipes Food Fair

Favorite French Dressing

   1 c. salad oil
   ⅔ c. catsup
   ¼ c. sugar
   Juice of 1 to 2 lemons
   1 tsp. Worcestershire sauce
   1 tsp. dry mustard (opt.)
   1 tsp. paprika
   ½ to 1 tsp. salt
   ½ c. vinegar
   1 clove garlic (opt.)

Mix all ingredients except vinegar and garlic with a rotary beater. Add vinegar. If desired, float a clove of garlic on top of dressing.

Mrs. Lenda B. Edwards, Home Economics Teacher, Bennettsville, S. C.

French Dressing

    Garlic salt or garlic clove
1 *c. vinegar*
1 ⅔ *c. oil*
1 *c. sugar*
4 *tsp. salt*
1 *tsp. pepper*
1 *tsp. paprika*
¼ *tsp. celery salt*

Mix all ingredients by beating or shaking in a jar.

Mrs. Mary B. Pattberg, Home Economics Teacher, Falls Village, Conn.

Low-Calorie French Dressing

1 *clove garlic, sliced*
¼ *c. vinegar*
¾ *tsp. salt*
⅛ *tsp. pepper*
¼ *tsp. paprika*
2 *tsp. sugar*
½ *c. tomato juice*
2 *tbsp. water*
2 *tbsp. salad oil*

Add garlic to vinegar; let stand 20 minutes. Strain. Combine salt, pepper, paprika and sugar in jar. Add tomato juice, water, vinegar and oil. Cover and shake vigorously. Store in refrigerator. Shake again before using. Yield: 1 cup.

Ann Friends Huh, Home Economics Teacher, Caledonia, Minn.

Tangy French Dressing

1 *10½-oz. can tomato soup*
⅓ *c. honey*
2 *tsp. prepared mustard*
2 *tbsp. vinegar*
2 *tsp. Worcestershire sauce*
1 *tsp. salt*
1 *tsp. paprika*
½ *c. lemon juice*
1 *tbsp. grated onion*
¾ *c. oil*

Combine all ingredients; beat at medium speed until well blended. Pour into jar. Two garlic cloves may be added to jar. Refrigerate until ready for use.

Mrs. Helen W. Thompson, Valentine, Neb., Favorite Recipes Food Fair

Chutney Fruit Dressing

¾ c. powdered sugar
1 tsp. paprika
Salt and pepper to taste
Juice of 1 lemon
¼ tsp. dry mustard
1 tsp. vinegar
2 tbsp. catsup
½ c. salad oil
1 tbsp. Worcestershire sauce
½ c. chutney

Place all ingredients in pint jar; shake well. Cover. Store in refrigerator. Keeps indefinitely.

Mrs. Ralph L. Hoehne, Officers' Wives' Club, Taiwan, Republic of China

 ## Cranberry Dressing

1 c. jellied cranberry sauce
1 c. mayonnaise
2 tbsp. lime or lemon juice
1 c. whipped cream (opt.)

Blend cranberry sauce and mayonnaise with electric mixer. Add juice. For a richer dressing, fold in whipped cream.

Mrs. Thelma Hause, Home Economics Teacher, Claremont, N. H.

Dressing For Grapefruit Salad

⅓ c. (scant) sugar
¾ tsp. salt
1 tsp. (heaping) celery salt
1 tsp. paprika
1 tsp. dry mustard
1 tbsp. lemon juice
1 tsp. onion juice
4 tbsp. vinegar
1 c. corn oil

Mix sugar, salt, celery salt, paprika and mustard; add lemon juice, onion juice, vinegar and oil. Chill. Serve over grapefruit and orange sections.

Mrs. Kenneth L. McLean, Albuquerque, N. M., Favorite Recipes Food Fair

Cream Dressing

    1 3-oz. pkg. cream cheese
½ c. heavy cream
    6 lge. marshmallows, quartered

Cream the cheese with the cream. Add marshmallows; mix well. Let stand overnight. Beat well before serving.

Marval Klecker, Home Economics Teacher, Viroqua, Wis.

 ### Cream Cheese Dressing

    1 8-oz. pkg. cream cheese, softened
⅛ tsp. salt
1 tbsp. lemon juice
2 to 3 tbsp. mayonnaise

Cream the cheese with electric mixer. Add remaining ingredients; mix well. Serve on fruit halves or lettuce.

Mrs. Deanna Patin Roy, Home Economics Teacher, Marksville, La.

 ### Fruit Fluff

    2 tbsp. flour
½ c. sugar
    2 egg yolks, well beaten
⅓ c. lemon juice
⅔ c. pineapple juice
    8 lge. marshmallows, finely chopped
⅔ c. almonds, chopped
½ pt. whipped cream

Combine flour and sugar. Add egg yolks, lemon juice and pineapple juice. Cook until thickened. Add marshmallows and almonds. Cool. Fold in whipped cream. Dressing will keep a week in refrigerator. Yield: 3½-4 cups.

Mrs. Martha B. Overby, Home Economics Teacher, Norlina, N. C.

Fruit Salad Dressing

½ c. lemon juice
    2 eggs, beaten
¾ c. sugar
    Whipped cream to taste

(Continued on next page)

Mix lemon juice, eggs and sugar in small saucepan. Cook over low heat, stirring constantly, until mixture is consistency of custard. Cool and refrigerate in covered dish. When ready to use, mix desired amount of whipped cream with lemon juice mixture. It must be used same day lemon and cream are mixed; it will not keep.

Mrs. Carl Ekstrom, Home Economics Teacher, New Carlisle, Ind.

Fruited Dressing

1 pkg. vanilla pudding mix
1 16-oz. can fruit cocktail, drained
Milk
2 c. miniature marshmallows
1 pt. whipped cream

Prepare vanilla pudding according to package directions using juice from fruit cocktail plus enough milk to make 2 cups liquid. Fold in fruit cocktail and marshmallows. Cool. Add whipped cream before serving.

Mrs. Muriel Hyden, Home Economics Teacher, Appleton, Minn.

Honey Creme Dressing

1 3-oz. pkg. cream cheese
¼ tsp. salt
2 tbsp. honey
¼ c. sour cream

Whip or mash cream cheese with salt, honey and sour cream in small bowl. Serve with salad.

Janet Thomas, Tampa, Fla., Favorite Recipes Food Fair

Honey-Lime Dressing

3 tbsp. fresh lime juice
3 tbsp. honey
6 tbsp. salad oil

Combine ingredients in small mixing bowl. Beat at medium speed with electric mixer until creamy. Serve on fruit salads.

Mrs. W. E. Hill, Tulsa, Okla.

Ginger Cream Dressing

    1 c. pineapple juice
    3 tbsp. lemon juice
    4 tsp. sugar
    1 tbsp. cornstarch
  ¾ tsp. salt
    1 egg, well beaten
  ½ c. miniature marshmallows
    4 tbsp. candied ginger, finely chopped
    1 c. 40% cream, stiffly whipped

Bring first 5 ingredients to boiling point; remove from heat and pour slowly on egg, beating well. Return to heat and cook in double boiler until thick. When cold, stir in marshmallows and candied ginger. Fold in whipped cream.

Mrs. Myrtle Menefee, Home Economics Teacher, Clint, Tex.

Lemonade Dressing

  ⅓ c. undiluted frozen lemonade concentrate
  ⅓ c. honey
  ⅓ c. salad oil
    1 tsp. celery seed

Combine ingredients; beat with rotary beater until smooth. Serve with fruit salads.

Helene Fanberg, Home Economics Teacher, Whitehall, Mich.

Rum Creme Dressing

    1 3-oz. pkg. cream cheese
    2 tbsp. sugar
    1 tbsp. rum
    1 tbsp. lemon juice
  ¼ tsp. grated lemon rind
    Dash of salt
  ½ c. whipped cream

Blend cream cheese and sugar. Add rum, lemon juice, lemon rind and salt. Blend until smooth. Fold in whipped cream. Serve on fruit. Yield: 1 cup dressing.

Mrs. Albert H. Wunderlich, Officers' Wives' Club,
Prestwick MOA Sta., Scotland

Sherried Fruit Dressing

    4 tbsp. fresh lemon juice
    ⅛ tsp. salt
    4 tbsp. sugar
    2 tbsp. Sherry

Combine all ingredients; stir until sugar is dissolved. Serve on jellied fruit salad. Yield: 6 servings.

Mrs. James D. Craik, New Orleans, La.

Green Goddess Salad Dressing

    1 c. mayonnaise
    2 tbsp. tarragon vinegar
    1 tbsp. lemon juice
    1 clove of garlic, pressed
    ¼ c. chopped chives
    2 tbsp. minced parsley
    ½ c. sour cream
    1 2-oz. can anchovies, well mashed or 10 in. tube anchovy
       paste

Place ingredients in bowl in order given, mixing and blending well as each ingredient is added. Cover and refrigerate for 24 hours. Yield: 1 pint.

Mrs. R. H. Northwood, Dayton, Ohio, Favorite Recipes Food Fair

Greek Salad Dressing

    ¾ c. olive oil
    ¼ c. red wine vinegar
    ⅛ tsp. dry mustard
    ½ tsp. salt
    ¼ tsp. pepper

Place all ingredients in small jar; shake thoroughly. Chill before serving. Yield: 6-8 servings.

Mrs. H. L. Hillyard, Hon. Pres. WANAF JUSMAGG, Athens, Greece

Horseradish Cream

    1 c. whipping cream
    1 tsp. sugar

(Continued on next page)

⅛ tsp. salt
1 tbsp. vinegar
4 tbsp. prepared horseradish, drained

Whip cream until stiff. Fold in remaining ingredients. This is especially good with baked ham.

Bernice E. Kirkeby, Home Economics Teacher, Willow Lake, S. D.

 ## Imperial Dressing

¼ c. brown sugar
1 ½ tsp. salt
⅛ tsp. freshly ground pepper
1 tsp. onion salt
½ tsp. celery seed
2 or 3 drops of Tabasco sauce
1 tsp. paprika
½ tsp. dill
½ c. red wine vinegar
1 c. catsup
1 c. olive oil
3 tbsp. capers and juice
1 tsp. Worcestershire sauce
1 or 2 cloves of garlic

Combine sugar, salt, pepper, onion salt, celery seed, Tabasco sauce, paprika, dill and vinegar. Simmer. Cool for 10 minutes. Blend in catsup, olive oil, capers and juice and Worcestershire sauce. Add garlic; cool dressing at room temperature for 1 hour. Refrigerate until ready to use. Shake well before using. Yield: 2¾ cups.

Mrs. Allen K. Rosson, Granite City, Ill.

 ## Italian Salad Dressing

¼ c. olive oil
2 tbsp. lemon juice
1 tsp. lemon rind, grated
Salt to taste
½ tsp. oregano or thyme
1 clove garlic, minced
1 tbsp. Parmesan cheese, grated
½ tsp. black pepper, freshly ground

Combine all ingredients; mix well. Chill. Mix again before using.

Angela D'Gerolamo, Home Economics Teacher, New Orleans, La.

Mayfair Dressing

1 tbsp. pepper
1 tbsp. monosodium glutamate
3 eggs
1 tbsp. anchovy paste or 1 2-oz. can anchovy fillets
4 tbsp. horeradish mustard
1 stalk celery, chopped
½ med. onion, minced
2 c. salad oil

Place all ingredients except oil in blender; blend well. Gradually add oil, ¼ cup at a time. Pour into 1-quart jar. Keeps for 2 weeks in refrigerator. Yield: 1 quart dressing.

Mrs. James M. Howarton, Las Vegas, Nev., Favorite Recipes Food Fair

Basic Mayonnaise

2 egg yolks
1 c. salad oil
Juice of 1 lemon

Beat egg yolks until lemon colored. Continue beating and add salad oil, 1 drop at a time. Slowly add lemon juice, beating constantly. Store in covered container in refrigerator. Yield: 1 cup.

Mrs. James Britt, Rochester, N. Y.

One-Minute Mayonnaise

1 c. salad oil
1 tbsp. vinegar
1 tbsp. lemon juice
1 egg
½ tsp. salt
⅛ tsp. paprika
¼ tsp. dry mustard
Dash of cayenne

Pour ¼ cup oil into electric blender. Add vinegar, lemon juice, egg and seasonings. Cover and blend 5 seconds. While blender is running, remove cover; add remaining oil in steady stream. Turn off blender immediately after adding oil. Yield: 1½ cups.

Josephine L. Grissette, Home Economics Teacher, Montgomery, Ala.

Soy Mayonnaise

½ c. Soyalac
1 c. water
1 c. oil
½ tsp. salt
Juice of 1 lemon

Mix Soyalac and water in blender. Add oil, salt and lemon juice gradually. Season with onion, garlic or paprika, if desired. Yield: 2½ cups.

Grace Smith, Home Economics Teacher, Dalton, Ga.

 ### Mom's Dressing

¾ c. mayonnaise
¼ c. vinegar
½ tsp. sugar
1 tbsp. celery seed

Combine all ingredients until well-mixed. Serve over green tossed salad. Yield: 1 cup.

Mrs. Carolene Wood, Home Economics Teacher, Perkins, Okla.

 ### Onion Dressing

1 c. sugar
1 tsp. salt
1 tsp. paprika
¼ c. onion juice
½ tsp. mustard
½ c. cider vinegar
1 ¼ c. corn oil
1 tbsp. celery seed

Dissolve first 5 ingredients in vinegar and boil 1 minute. Cool to lukewarm; beat until thick. Gradually add oil, beating constantly. When stiff, fold in celery seed. Yield: 2 cups.

Mrs. Virginia Boyle, Home Economics Teacher, Ashland, Ill.

 ### Parmesan Salad Dressing

1 clove of garlic, mashed
½ c. salad oil
¼ c. lemon juice
¼ c. grated Parmesan cheese

(Continued on next page)

Place garlic in bottom of wooden salad bowl; add remaining ingredients. Yield: 10 servings.

Mrs. Tarleton Watkins, Officers' Wives' Club, Taipei, Taiwan

 ### Paprika Dressing, Low Calorie

½ med. onion, pureed or chopped
1 c. vinegar
2 tbsp. paprika
2 tbsp. salt
15 ¼-grain sugar substitute tablets
¼ tsp. dry mustard
3 c. corn oil

Combine all ingredients except oil; gradually add oil, blending until oil is finely dispersed. Shake well before serving if dressing separates on standing.

Mrs. Ronald S. Whitehead, Winston-Salem, N. C.

 ### Plantation Salad Dressing

1 pt. mayonnaise
½ pt. French dressing
3 oz. Parmesan cheese
1 clove of garlic, crushed
2 tbsp. anchovy paste

Combine all ingredients. Store in refrigerator. Serve on tossed lettuce and croutons.

Mrs. Craig Selden, Tucson, Ariz., Favorite Recipes Food Fair

 ### Potato Salad Dressing

1 tbsp. mayonnaise
1 tbsp. salad dressing
½ pt. whipping cream
1 tbsp. brown sugar
2 tbsp. sweet pickle relish

Cream mayonnaise and salad dressing. Gradually add whipping cream. Add brown sugar and pickle relish; combine with salad.

Yvonne Elzinga, Home Economics Teacher, Payson, Utah

Uncooked Potato Salad Dressing

    4 hard-cooked eggs
    3 heaping tbsp. mayonnaise
    1 heaping tbsp. prepared mustard
    ⅔ c. vinegar
    4 to 6 tbsp. sugar
    ¼ tsp. salt
    ⅛ tsp. ground pepper
    ¼ tsp. celery seed

Reserve 1 egg for garnish. Mash 3 egg yolks, mayonnaise and mustard together. Combine vinegar, sugar, salt, pepper and celery seed; add to egg yolk mixture. Mix thoroughly. Chop and add 3 egg whites. Chill. Garnish with remaining egg.

Madge G. Young, Home Economics Teacher, Annapolis, Md.

Garlic Roquefort Dressing

    1 c. sour cream
    1 c. mayonnaise
    Juice of 1 lemon
    2 tbsp. vinegar
    1 tbsp. garlic salt
    ½ tsp. prepared mustard
    ½ tsp. monosodium glutamate
    ½ tsp. paprika
    3 oz. Roquefort cheese, crumbled

Combine all ingredients except cheese, mixing well; add cheese. Let stand for several hours before serving.

Mrs. Willard C. Wiggins, Pres. Officers' Wives' Club, Hof AFS, Germany

Gourmet Salad Dressing

    3 oz. Roquefort cheese
    1 3-oz. pkg. cream cheese, softened
    1 c. thick sour cream
    ¼ c. Sherry
    1 tbsp. grated onion
    ½ tsp. salt
    ¼ tsp. paprika
    2 drops of Tabasco sauce

Crumble Roquefort cheese into bowl; blend in cream cheese until smooth. Add remaining ingredients, blending until creamy. Cover and store in refrigerator.

Mrs. Floyd W. Baker, Fort Campbell, Ky., Favorite Recipes Food Fair

Quick Roquefort Dressing

½ c. French dressing
¼ c. crumbled Roquefort cheese
 Salt and pepper

Combine French dressing and cheese in jar; shake well. Add salt and pepper to taste. Yield: 2/3 cup.

Audrey Rohrer, Home Economics Teacher, Belle Fourche, S. D.

 ## Roquefort-Curry Salad Dressing

2 c. mayonnaise
½ lb. Roquefort cheese, crumbled
½ tsp. curry powder

Combine all ingredients; mix well. Keep refrigerated.

Mrs. Clyde Hester, Baton Rouge, La.

Roquefort Dressing

¼ lb. Roquefort cheese
3 tbsp. light cream
⅓ c. salad oil
¼ c. wine vinegar
½ c. mayonnaise
¼ tsp. freshly ground pepper

Break cheese; place all ingredients in blender. Blend at low speed for 10 seconds. Serve over salad greens. Yield: 1 cup.

Mrs. John H. Mascali, Pres. Officers' Wives' Club, Moffett Field, Cal.

 ## Quick Russian Dressing

½ c. mayonnaise
¼ c. chili sauce
½ tsp. lemon juice

Combine ingredients; mix well. Chill.

Mrs. DeLaura Jones, Home Economics Teacher, Newport News, Va.

Russian Dressing

1 c. water
1 c. sugar
Juice of 2 lemons
2 c. salad oil
1 c. catsup
2 tsp. Worcestershire sauce
2 tbsp. onion, grated
1 tsp. celery salt
1 tsp. paprika
Pinch of red pepper

Boil water and sugar. Cool. Add remaining ingredients and mix thoroughly. Chill.

Carol Van Sickle, Home Economics Teacher, Wells, Minn.

Cooked Salad Dressing

2 eggs
½ tsp. salt
¼ c. vinegar
¾ c. water
½ c. sugar
2 tbsp. cornstarch
½ tsp. mustard

Beat eggs in small saucepan. Add remaining ingredients in order given, combining sugar and cornstarch. Cook over low heat, stirring constantly until thick. Yield: 1 pint.

Mrs. Carol Brann, Jr., Home Economics Teacher, Mifflinburg, Pa.

Creamy Salad Dressing

8 egg yolks
½ tsp. dry mustard, dissolved in 1 tbsp. boiling water
1 c. sugar
2 tbsp. flour
½ tsp. salt
½ c. sour cream
1 c. hot vinegar

Beat egg yolks until light and lemon colored. Add mustard, sugar, flour, salt and sour cream, beating constantly. Add vinegar. Cook in double boiler until thick. Remove from heat and beat well until creamy, using rotary beater or electric mixer. Use for potato, egg or cabbage salad.

Mrs. LaVera Kraig, Home Economics Teacher, Aberdeen, S. D.

Crab Dressing

¼ c. salad oil
½ c. spinach
½ c. parsley
1 clove of garlic
2 tbsp. chives
1 ¼ c. mayonnaise

Blend all ingredients except mayonnaise in blender until finely chopped Add mayonnaise. Serve with crab salad. Yield: 6 servings.

Mrs. Roy Dennison, Charleston, S. C., Favorite Recipes Food Fair

 ### Crab Louis Dressing

1 c. mayonnaise
¼ c. sour cream
¼ c. chili sauce
¼ c. green onion, chopped
1 tsp. lemon juice
Salt

Combine mayonnaise, sour cream, chili sauce, onion and lemon juice. Salt to taste. Chill. Yield: 2 cups.

Betty Ann McCullough, Home Economics Teacher, Conneaut Lake, Pa.

Seafood Salad Dressing

2 c. mayonnaise
¼ c. catsup
¼ c. green onions, chopped
¼ c. dill pickles, chopped
2 hard cooked eggs, chopped
½ tsp. black pepper
1 clove garlic (split and stuck on toothpick)
1 can shrimp
1 can crab

Mix mayonnaise and catsup; fold in onion, pickles, eggs and pepper. Add garlic. Cover and place in refrigerator for several hours. When ready to serve, remove garlic and fold in shrimp and crab. Pour over chopped lettuce, tomatoes and avocado or salad greens.

Mrs. Evelyn H. Duke, Home Economics Teacher, Columbia, La.

Zippy Seafood Dressing

1 c. mayonnaise
¼ c. French dressing
¼ c. chili sauce or catsup
½ tsp. salt
Pepper
1 tsp. prepared horseradish
1 tsp. Worcestershire sauce

Combine all ingredients. Toss salad with enough dressing to bind.

Ada Bell Norman, Commerce City, Colo.

Sour Cream Dressing

1 c. thick sour cream
2 tbsp. white vinegar
1 tbsp. onion, minced
¼ tsp. sugar
¼ tsp. salt
Dash of black pepper

Combine all ingredients. Serve on green salad or slaw.

Mrs. Celia Williams, Home Economics Teacher, Mt. Pleasant, Ark.

Sweet Mustard Dressing

1 c. mayonnaise
¼ c. mustard
¼ c. sugar
¼ medium onion, finely grated

Combine mayonnaise, mustard and sugar. Add onion; mix well. Dressing keeps indefinitely in refrigerator. Serve on tossed salad, lettuce wedges, hamburgers, hot dogs or bread.

Esther H. Collier, Home Economics Teacher, Evergreen, N. C.

Sweet Pickle Dressing

½ c. catsup
½ c. mayonnaise
½ c. sweet pickles, finely chopped

Blend catsup and mayonnaise; add chopped pickles. Chill. Serve over green vegetable salads. Yield: 1¼ cups.

Mrs. Yvonne T. Napp, Home Economics Teacher, Butler, Ala.

Thousand Island Dressing

1 egg yolk
1 tsp. dry mustard
1 tsp. confectioner's sugar
½ tsp. salt
Dash of cayenne pepper
1 c. salad oil
1 tbsp. lemon juice or vinegar
4 tbsp. chili sauce
4 tbsp. chopped stuffed olives
1 tbsp. chopped chives
1 hard-cooked egg, chopped
½ tsp. paprika

Beat together egg yolk, mustard, sugar, salt and pepper. Continue beating while adding a third of the oil a drop at a time; add remaining oil more rapidly. Thin from time to time with lemon juice or vinegar. Add chili sauce, olives, chives, eggs and paprika; mix thoroughly. Chill. Yield: 2¾ cups.

Virginia Boxley, Home Economics Teacher, Berryville, Ark.

 ### Vinegar And Oil (Vinaigrette)

1 tbsp. vinegar
3 tbsp. olive oil
Salt and pepper to taste

Mix all ingredients well; pour over vegetable salad just before serving. Lemon juice may be substituted for vinegar.

Marjorie Hallman, Montgomery, Ala.

 ### Mrs. Smith's Vinaigrette Dressing

⅓ c. vinegar
⅔ c. salad oil
6 chopped scallions
¼ c. chopped capers
1 tbsp. chopped chives or parsley
¼ tsp. ground pepper
½ tsp. salt
Dash garlic juice

Mix and blend all ingredients well. Pour over sliced tomatoes, asparagus tips, string beans or other vegetables; marinate several hours in refrigerator. This is also very good with Kentucky bibb lettuce.

Mrs. Hulett C. Smith, Wife of Governor of West Virginia, Charleston

Waldorf Salad Dressing

2 c. sugar
2 tbsp. flour
4 eggs
2 c. cream, Milnot or milk
1 ½ c. vinegar

Combine sugar, flour and eggs; cream well. Add cream and a small amount of water; stir well. Add vinegar. Bring to boil over low heat; boil for 5 minutes. Cool; pour into quart jar. Refrigerate. Yield: 1 quart.

Mrs. Howard Derr, Officers' Wives' Club, Duluth, Minn.

Watercress Salad Dressing

2 eggs
2 c. salad oil
2 tbsp. horseradish
¼ c. catsup
2 tbsp. grated onion
1 tsp. salt
⅓ c. vinegar
2 tbsp. paprika
1 tsp. Worcestershire sauce
Dash of Tabasco sauce

Place all ingredients in quart jar; shake vigorously. Dressing will keep for several weeks. Serve over watercress topped with chopped onion and crumbled bacon. Yield: 1 quart.

Mrs. John G. Zierdt, Hon. Pres. Officers' Wives' Club, Redstone Arsenal, Ala.

Zippy Dressing For Vegetable Salad

¼ c. honey
⅔ c. undiluted evaporated milk
¼ c. lemon juice
½ tsp. salt
½ tsp. dry mustard
1 tsp. paprika

Combine all ingredients. Beat until creamy smooth. Refrigerate until thick.

Mrs. Gwen Bayer, Home Economics Teacher, Tuolumne, Cal.

Fruit Salads

FAVORITE
FRUIT COMBINATIONS

1. Avocado slices, grapefruit sections and a sprinkling of pomegranate seeds.

2. Diced fresh pineapple, strawberries and a sprinkling of finely-minced mint.

3. Banana slices topped with peanut butter and peanuts.

4. Prunes or apricots stuffed with cream or cottage cheese.

5. Orange or grapefruit sections, avocado slices, red apples.

6. Avocado cubes or slices and melon balls.

7. Cut-up apples, oranges, bananas, grapes, marshmallows, and nuts blended with mayonnaise and whipped cream.

8. Pineapple slices or peach or pear halves topped with cottage or cream cheese.

9. Pear halves stuffed with cream cheese and stuck with salted almonds or other salted nuts.

10. Fresh or canned pineapple, strawberries and halves of blue plums.

Special Fruit Hints

Brighten up the edges of lettuce leaves or pineapple rings by dipping them in paprika.

Use the fruit juices from the fruits used in the salads to mix with mayonnaise for a dressing.

Give a festive touch to your fruit salad by decorating with candied fruit.

Substitute orange for vinegar in mint sauce and serve with fruit salad.

To prevent discoloration of fruit, slice with stainless steel knife at the last moment, or sprinkle with lemon juice or powdered ascorbic or citric acid preparations (may be purchased in drug store), and store in refrigerator until serving time.

Stuffed Apple Salad

1 ½ c. sugar
2 c. water
Red cinnamon candies
Red food coloring
6 apples
2 pkg. cream cheese, softened
½ c. chopped walnuts

Combine sugar, water, cinnamon candies and a few drops of red food coloring; bring to a boil. Core and peel apples. Cook apples in syrup until tender but still firm; apples should be a rosy pink when done. Remove apples from syrup; drain and cool. Beat cheese well; add nuts. Stuff apples. Serve on watercress or crisp lettuce. Yield: 6 servings.

Mrs. Ernest Moore, Officers' Wives' Club, Clark AFB, Philippine Islands

 Avocado Salad With Rum Dressing

3 ripe avocados
⅓ c. light rum
⅔ c. salad oil
⅛ tsp. white pepper
Lettuce leaves

Chill avocados. Cut into halves; remove seed. Beat rum, salad oil and pepper until slightly thickened. Place avocado halves on bed of lettuce; fill cavity with dressing. Yield: 6 servings.

Mrs. H. A. Snyder, Officers' Wives' Club, Honolulu, Hawaii

French Avocado Salad

2 med. ripe avocados
3 strips bacon
½ c. French dressing
4 leaves romaine

Cut avocados into halves; remove seed and peel. Fry bacon until crisp; drain and mince. Add bacon to French dressing. Pour dressing into cavity of each avocado. Serve cold on romaine leaves. Yield: 4 servings.

Mrs. Thomas Place, Winston-Salem, N. C., Favorite Recipes Food Fair

Banana-Nut Salad

> 6 or 8 bananas
> ½ c. nuts, chopped
> 1 c. sugar
> ¾ c. water
> 1 egg, well beaten
> 2 tbsp. butter, melted
> ¼ c. mild vinegar
> 2 tbsp. flour

Combine sugar and flour; add egg and mix thoroughly. Add butter, vinegar and water. Mix thoroughly. Cook over hot water, stirring constantly until thick and smooth. Cool. Dip bananas in cool dressing and roll in nuts. Yield: 6-8 servings.

Jean Cline, Home Economics Teacher, Morehead, Ky.

Banana-Peanut Salad

> 1 c. brown sugar
> 1 ½ tbsp. vinegar
> 3 tbsp. water
> 1 egg
> Butter
> 5 ripe bananas
> ½ c. ground or chopped salted peanuts

Beat brown sugar with vinegar, water, egg and a lump of butter the size of an egg; boil for 1 to 2 minutes. Cool slightly. Slice bananas lengthwise onto large flat dish; pour boiled dressing over bananas. Sprinkle peanuts over all. Yield: 10 servings.

Mrs. Wilfred L. Sterzik, Officers' Wives' Club, Atlanta Army Dep., Ga.

Banana-Coconut Salad

> 4 bananas
> Lemon juice
> ½ c. mayonnaise
> ½ c. whipped cream (opt.)
> 1 c. toasted coconut or chopped nuts

Cut bananas lengthwise in half and then crosswise in half. To prevent discoloring, prepare salad just before serving and coat bananas immediately with

(Continued on next page)

lemon juice. Combine mayonnaise and whipped cream if desired. Roll bananas in mayonnaise mixture, then in coconut or chopped nuts. Serve on crisp salad greens. Yield: 4 servings.

Mrs. Shirley Leslie, Home Economics Teacher, Magazine, Ark.

Mandarin Salad

 1 can Mandarin orange slices, drained
 ½ jar pineapple cheese spread or equivalent whipped cream
 ⅓ c. pecans, chopped
 1 c. miniature marshmallows or coconut
 2 tbsp. mayonnaise

Combine ingredients well. Serve on lettuce leaf. Yield: 6 servings.

Mrs. James N. Kelly, Home Economics Teacher, Mansfield, La.

Stuffed Peach Salad

 6 peach halves
 1 3-oz. pkg. cream cheese
 ¼ c. Maraschino cherries
 ½ c. pecans, chopped
 ½ c. mayonnaise
 1 c. whipped cream
 Red food coloring
 Whole cloves

Cream the cheese with nuts and cherries. Fill the centers of each peach half with cheese mixture. Place a half peach on top of the cheese center, making a whole peach. Dilute a small bit of red coloring with water and brush over one corner of the peach to produce a blush. Stick a clove in one end for the stem. Yield: 6 servings.

Mrs. Willie Fay Spurlock, Home Economics Teacher, Hazard, Ky.

Pear Salad

 1 15-oz. can pear halves, drained
 4 lettuce leaves
 4 tbsp. mint jelly
 Mayonnaise
 4 cherries

(Continued on next page)

Place pear halves on lettuce; fill centers with mint jelly. Top with ¼ teaspoon mayonnaise and cherries.

Mrs. Chester L. Holland, Officers' Wives' Club, Ft. Rucker, Ala.

 ### Marinated Pear Salad Delight

> 3 fresh Bartlett pears
> 1 c. salad oil
> ¼ c. white wine vinegar
> ½ tsp. salt
> 2 tbsp. chopped parsley
> 4 tsp. chopped pimento
> ½ tsp. basil
> 6 pitted dates
> ¼ c. tangy cheese spread
> Lettuce

Halve and core pears. Combine all remaining ingredients except dates, cheese spread and lettuce in a jar. Cover and shake well. Place pear halves, cut sides down, in shallow bowl; pour oil-vinegar dressing over them. Cover; let stand 1 to 1½ hours. Stuff dates with cheese spread. Arrange pears, cut sides up, on lettuce-lined serving plate; garnish with dates. Spoon remaining dressing over pears. Yield: 6 servings.

Photograph for this recipe below.

Cranberry-Pineapple Salad

    1 can cranberry sauce
    1 can pineapple rings, well drained
    1 box cottage cheese
    8 Maraschino cherries

Place sliced cranberry sauce on lettuce cups and lay a ring of pineapple over sauce. Place a tablespoon of cottage cheese in center of pineapple. Place a cherry on top of cheese. Yield: 8 servings.

Mrs. Janice P. Cabler, Home Economics Teacher, Nashville, Tenn.

 ### Quick Pineapple And Lettuce Salad

    1 crisp lettuce leaf
    2 slices pineapple
    2 tbsp. grated Velveeta cheese
    1 tsp. (heaping) mayonnaise
    Dash of paprika

Place lettuce leaf on salad plate; place overlapping slices of pineapple on lettuce. Spread cheese over pineapple. Top with mayonnaise; sprinkle with paprika. Yield: 1 serving.

Mrs. George P. Ward, Officers' Wives' Club, Zweibrucken, Germany

Ambrosia Salad

    1 qt. grated coconut
    6 oranges, peeled, sectioned and halved
    4 bananas, sliced
    1 pt. sliced pineapple, cut into strips
    1 pt. strawberries, cut into halves
    Sugar
    1 c. sherry
    Whole strawberries

Drain fruits, reserving juices. Sprinkle bottom of a large salad bowl with coconut; add a layer of fruit. Sprinkle with sugar. Continue alternating fruits, sugar and coconut layers, ending with layer of coconut. Combine reserved juices and sherry; pour over all. Garnish with whole strawberries; chill thoroughly. Bottled cherries may be substituted for strawberries. If so, use liquid from cherries and omit sherry. Yield: 10-12 servings.

Mrs. E. E. McBride, Pres. Officers' Wives' Club, Goeppingen, Germany

Angel Salad

1 lge. can pineapple chunks
2 eggs, beaten
½ c. sugar
Juice of 1 lemon
1 8-oz. pkg. cream cheese
½ pt. heavy cream, whipped
1 sm. bottle Maraschino cherries, cut up
1 can pitted white cherries, drained
1 lge. can fruit cocktail, drained
½ lb. marshmallows
½ c. English walnuts

Drain pineapple, reserving 1/3 cup juice. Place eggs, reserved pineapple juice, sugar and lemon juice in double boiler. Cook until thick; cool. Blend in cheese. Fold cream into cooked dressing. Combine fruits. Pour dressing over fruits; mix well. Add marshmallows and nuts. Chill for 24 hours before serving.

Mrs. Lawrence J. Anderson, Ocean City, N. J., Favorite Recipes Food Fair

Banana Fruit Salad

2 c. diced bananas
1 c. chopped apples
1 c. fruit cocktail
¼ c. raisins
¼ c. sour cream

Combine fruits; toss lightly with sour cream. Serve on lettuce leaves. Yield: 4-6 servings.

Mrs. Donald Sims, Roanoke, Va.

Barbara's Salad

1 small can crushed pineapple, drained
1 tbsp. flour
1 tbsp. butter
1 c. cheese, grated
2 apples, diced
¼ pkg. miniature marshmallows

Combine pineapple juice, flour and butter; cook until thick. Combine remaining ingredients; add to juice mixture. Mix well. Yield: 8 servings.

Barbara Pou, Home Economics Teacher, Greenville, S. C.

Best-Ever Summer Salad

½ *watermelon*
1 *cantaloupe*
Honeydew melon balls
Chunk pineapple, grapes and strawberries (opt.)

Scoop out inside of melons with scoop. Serve in peeled melon rings on cupped lettuce, or as center piece in watermelon shell on large bed of lettuce or other greens.

DRESSING FOR MELON BALLS:

½ *c. sugar*
⅓ *c. water*
1 *tbsp. grated lemon rind*
1 *tbsp. grated orange rind*
3 *tbsp. lemon juice*
2 *tbsp. lime juice*

Combine ingredients; boil 5 minutes. Cool; pour over melon balls, let stand for few hours in refrigerator. Yield: 10-15 servings.

Mary Jo Thompson, Home Economics Teacher, Ardmore, Ala.

Cantaloupe Salad

1 *yellow, firm cantaloupe, diced*
6 *fresh peaches, diced*
1 *lb. seedless grapes*
1 *small bag marshmallows, cut in pieces*
Mayonnaise to taste

Combine fruits and marshmallows. Mix with desired amount of mayonnaise. Chill. Yield: 12 servings.

Mrs. A. C. Jones, Jr., Home Economics Teacher, Kingsville, Tex.

Cherries And Sour Cream Salad

2 *1-lb. cans red water-packed cherries, well drained*
1 *13½-oz. can pineaple chunks, well drained*
1 *3½-oz. can flaked coconut*
1 *c. miniature marshmallows*
¾ *c. confectioners' sugar*
½ *tsp. salt*
2 *c. sour cream*
Salad greens

(Continued on next page)

Combine fruits, coconut, marshmallows, sugar and salt. Fold sour cream carefully into mixture. Cover and refrigerate overnight or for several hours. Garnish with salad greens. Red dessert cherries may be substituted for water-packed cherries. Omit confectioners' sugar. Yield: 6-8 servings.

Mrs. Francis A. Mikulis, Officers' Wives' Club, Pease AFB, N. H.

 ### Citrus Salad With Lemon Mayonnaise Dressing

2 grapefruit or 1 No. 303 can grapefruit sections
3 oranges
1 avocado
1 persimmon

Peel, section and remove membranes from citrus fruits. Peel avocado and slice lengthwise. Cut peeled persimmon into bite-sized pieces. Arrange fruits attractively on lettuce. Serve with lemon mayonnaise.

LEMON MAYONNAISE:

1 egg
¼ c. lemon juice
1 tsp. mustard
1 tsp. salt
1 tsp. sugar
¼ tsp. paprika
1 pt. salad oil

Combine all ingredients except salad oil. Slowly beat in salad oil. Continue beating until thick. Yield: 2½ cups mayonnaise. Yield: 6 servings.

Margarette C. Weeks, Home Economics Teacher, Highland, Cal.

 ### Clara's Grape Salad

2 egg yolks
Juice of 1 lemon
¼ tsp. dry mustard
¼ tsp. salt
½ pt. heavy cream, whipped
1 lb. grapes, seeded
½ lb. marshmallows, cut up
1 No. 2 can pineapple slices, diced

Cook yolks, lemon juice, mustard and salt until thick; cool. Stir whipped cream into egg mixture. Pour over grapes, marshmallows and pineapple. Chill for 24 hours.

Marian L. Downing, Brunswick, Me.

Cold Light Delight

> 1 pkg. frozen melon balls
> 1 pkg. frozen raspberries
> 1 pkg. frozen mixed fruit
> 1 c. small seedless green grapes
> 2 bananas, sliced

Empty frozen fruit packages into serving dish. Do not break up fruit. Allow to sit at room temperature for 4 hours. Refrigerate grapes until ready to serve. Gently separate fruit; add grapes and bananas. Yield: 8-12 servings.

Mrs. R. J. Bell, Officers' Wives' Club, Seattle, Wash.

 ### Colorful Quick Fruit & Melon Salad

> 1 can fruit cocktail or jar of fruits for salad, drained
> ½ c. whipped cream
> 1 cantalope or honeydew melon pared and sliced ½ in. thick
> ¼ tsp. vanilla
> 2 tbsp. sugar
> Various fresh fruits: apples, bananas, grapes
> Maraschino cherries

Add vanilla and sugar to cream. Fold into fruit mixture. Place slice of melon on lettuce leaf. Fill hole with fruit mixture; top with a cherry. Yield: 6-8 servings.

Mrs. Geneva Gill Cooper, Home Economics Teacher, Monticello, Ky.

Cranberry Fluff Salad

> 2 c. raw ground cranberries
> 3 c. miniature marshmallows
> ¾ c. sugar
> 2 c. diced unpared tart apples
> ½ to 1 c. seedless green grapes
> ¼ tsp. salt
> 1 c. heavy cream, whipped

Combine cranberries, marshmallows and sugar. Cover; chill overnight. Add apples, grapes, walnuts and salt. Fold in cream; chill. Yield: 8-10 servings.

Mrs. Harvey H. Reese, Officers' Wives' Club, Norton AFB, Cal.

Cranberry-Orange Relish

1 pkg. cranberries, ground
2 oranges, seeds removed and ground
2 c. sugar

Add sugar to ground cranberries and oranges. Store in refrigerator several hours before serving. Yield: 6-8 servings.

Mrs. Mae Van Petett, Home Economics Teacher, Tompkinsville, Ky.

 ### Cranberry Salad Supreme

1 c. raw cranberries, chopped
1 c. sugar
2 c. seedless or Tokay grapes, chilled
½ c. canned pineapple, diced and chilled (opt.)
1 c. whipped cream
½ to 2 c. walnuts or pecans, chopped
½ c. marshmallows, quartered (opt.)

Combine cranberries and sugar. Blend. Refrigerate overnight. Drain off liquid. Combine grapes, pineapple, nuts and whipped cream. Fold into cranberry mixture. Add marshmallows and stir until evenly distributed. Yield: 10-12 servings.

Nancy Lee, Home Economics Teacher, Cleburne, Tex.

Fix-Ahead Fruit Salad

3 oranges
2 to 3 tbsp. mayonnaise
1 No. 303 can fruit salad, drained
1 No. 303 can apricots, drained and sliced
1 No. 303 can peaches, drained and sliced
1 to 2 c. miniature marshmallows
Tangerine sections (opt.)
Sliced bananas (opt.)
Royal Anne cherries (opt.)

Cut oranges into halves; scoop out and reserve pulp and juice. Blend mayonnaise and reserved pulp and juice from oranges. Add remaining ingredients. Mix well; chill thoroughly. Yield: 6-8 servings.

Mrs. Robert C. McElveen, Savannah, Ga.

Florida Salad

> 4 c. thickly sliced avocado
> 1 c. fresh pineapple wedges
> ⅓ c. salad oil
> ⅓ c. vinegar
> 1 clove garlic, finely minced
> Salt and pepper

Toss avocado and pineapple. Combine remaining ingredients and pour over avocado mixture. Chill, turning occasionally. Serve on lettuce. Yield: 6 servings.

Anna Sprow, North Miami Beach, Fla.

 French Pineapple Salad

> 1 lge. pineapple
> 1 lge. orange, sectioned and peeled
> 2 peaches, sliced
> 1 banana, slant sliced
> 1 apple, sliced
> 1 pt. strawberries, hulled and sweetened
> 1 c. pecan halves

Cut pineapple in half lengthwise, remove fruit and cut into cubes. Dust cubes lightly with sugar. Combine all ingredients. Chill for 30 minutes. Lightly pile fruit mixture into pineapple shells. Yield: 6-8 servings.

Mrs. Marvel E. Wax, El Paso, Tex.

 Fresh Fruit Salad

> 1 c. sliced strawberries
> 2 peaches, diced
> 10 plums, quartered
> 3 oranges, sliced
> 1 pineapple, cubed
> 2 pears, cubed
> Mayonnaise (opt.)
> Lettuce leaves or parsley

Drain fruits, reserving juice. Combine fruits, mixing carefully. Thin a small amount of mayonnaise with reserved juice; pour over fruits. Garnish with lettuce. Yield: 6 servings.

Mrs. John M. Cragin, Officers' Wives' Club, Fort Clayton, Canal Zone

Fruit Cocktail-Marshmallow Whip

1 No. 303 can fruit cocktail
¼ lb. marshmallows, cut into eighths
1 tsp. lemon juice
1 tbsp. grated lemon peel
1 c. heavy cream, whipped

Reserve ¼ cup fruit cocktail for garnish. Combine remaining fruit cocktail with marshmallows. Refrigerate for 1 hour. Drain; add lemon juice and grated lemon peel. Fold in whipped cream. Garnish each serving with remaining fruit. Yield: 6 servings.

Mrs. William L. Nellans, Officers' Wives' Club, Toul Rosieres AB, France

 ### Fruit Medley Supreme

1 No. 2½ can fruit cocktail, drained
1 No. 13½-oz. can pineapple tidbits, drained
1 No. 16 oz. can Mandarin orange sections
1 ½ c. miniature marshmallows
1 8-oz. pkg. Neufchatel cheese
2 tbsp. sour or sweet cream or evaporated milk

Combine fruits and marshmallows. Soften cheese with cream or milk; fold into fruit mixture. Chill. Yield: 10 servings.

Jean Beaman Walker, Home Economics Teacher, Knoxville, Tenn.

 ### Fruit Salad In Avocado Boats

3 med. ripe avocados
3 tsp. fresh lime juice
1 c. fresh grapefruit sections
1 c. fresh pineapple wedges
¼ c. olive or salad oil
1 tbsp. vinegar
½ tsp. salt
⅛ tsp. ground pepper
½ tsp. ground cumin seed

Wash avocados; cut into halves and remove seed. Brush with 2 teaspoons lime juice to prevent discoloration. Fill cavities with grapefruit sections and pineapple wedges. Combine remaining ingredients; beat with rotary beater. Serve over salad. Yield: 6 servings.

Janice McLain, Hattiesburg, Miss.

Fruit Plate And Dressing

> *Pear halves*
> *Peach halves*
> *Cantaloupe slices*
> *Pineapple rings*
> *Bananas*

Arrange fruits on platter. Pour dressing over all fruit.

DRESSING:

> *2 eggs*
> *3 tbsp. sugar*
> *1 tbsp. cream*
> *3 tsp. dry mustard*
> *½ tsp. salt*
> *3 tbsp. lemon juice*
> *1 pt. whipped cream*
> *1 c. marshmallows, diced*
> *1 c. pecans, chopped*

Combine eggs, sugar, cream, mustard, salt and lemon juice. Cook in double boiler until thick. Cool. Fold in remaining ingredients. Yield: 10 servings.

> *Mrs. Frances Morton, Home Economics Teacher, Tallulah, La.*

Fruit Salad With Boiled Dressing

> *1 can fruit cocktail, drained*
> *1 can pitted white cherries, drained*
> *1 can sliced peaches, drained and diced*
> *1 can pineapple chunks, drained*
> *3 or 4 bananas, sliced*
> *2 or 3 oranges, sectioned*
> *1 c. miniature marshmallows*

Combine all ingredients.

BOILED DRESSING:

> *2 eggs*
> *2 tbsp. sugar*
> *4 tbsp. vinegar*
> *½ tsp. salt*
> *2 tbsp. butter*
> *1 c. heavy cream, whipped*

Combine eggs, sugar, vinegar and salt; cook in double boiler until thick. Add butter; cool. Fold in cream. Mix fruit and dressing just before serving.

> *Mrs. James A. Wiley, Officers' Wives' Club, Fort Greely, Alaska*

Grape, Banana, And Cottage Cheese Salad

½ c. seedless green grapes, halved
2 bananas, diced
½ pt. small curd cottage cheese
¼ c. pecans, chopped (opt.)
  Maraschino cherries (opt.)

Combine all ingredients. A little cream may be added to make salad creamier. Serve on lettuce leaves; top with Maraschino cherries. Yield: 4-6 servings.

Mrs. Irene Miller Byrom, Home Economics Teacher, Brenham, Tex.

 ### Gumdrop Salad

1 No. 2½ can cubed pineapple
½ lb. miniature marshmallows
½ lb. small gumdrops
½ c. chopped pecans
1 lb. white grapes, halved
1 small bottle Maraschino cherries, drained and chopped

Drain pineapple, reserving ¼ cup juice for dressing. Combine all salad ingredients. Do not use spiced gumdrops.

DRESSING:

2 eggs, beaten
¼ c. sugar
¼ c. lemon juice
¼ c. reserved pineapple juice

Combine all ingredients; cook, stirring constantly, until the consistency of salad dressing. Serve over salad. Yield: 12 servings.

Mrs. Wm. C. Apgar, Officers' Wives' Club, Essex, England

Holiday Salad

1 lb. chopped cranberries
1 c. sugar
1 c. chopped nuts
2 c. quartered and seeded Tokay grapes
½ pt. heavy cream

Combine cranberries and sugar; refrigerate overnight. Add remaining ingredients before serving. Yield: 8 servings.

Phoebe W. Lambertz, El Paso, Tex.

 ### Hawaiian Papaya Salad

1 med. papaya, peeled and diced
1 very ripe pineapple, peeled and diced
3 bananas, diced
2 oranges, peeled and diced
3 red apples, diced
6 walnuts, chopped
1 c. marshmallows (opt.)
Grated fresh coconut
4 tbsp. honey

Combine all ingredients; chill well. Serve on lettuce or ti leaves topped with additional coconut. Yield: 8 servings.

Mrs. Eugene Lash, Long Island, N. Y.

 ### Heavenly Hash

1 egg
¼ c. cornstarch
½ c. sugar
1 c. pineapple juice
2 No. 2 cans pineapple chunks, drained
1 pkg. marshmallows, cut up
½ c. nuts (opt.)
1 c. whipped cream

Cook egg, cornstarch, sugar and pineapple juice until thick. Cool. Mix pineapple chunks, marshmallows and nuts together; add to the egg mixture. Fold in whipped cream. Refrigerate. Yield: 6 servings.

Mrs. Bonnie Jackson, Home Economics Teacher, Stanton, Ky.

Low-Calorie Fruit Salad

1 c. cantaloupe balls or cubes
½ c. orange sections, diced
2 bananas, diced
1 c. lettuce, chopped
2 tbsp. low-calorie dressing

Chill all ingredients. Lightly toss together just before serving. Yield: 6 servings.

Ruth L. Auge, Home Economics Teacher, Belen, N. M.

 ### Mandarin Orange And Grape Salad

6 tbsp. salad oil
3 tbsp. wine vinegar
½ tsp. salt
Freshly ground pepper
Pinch of basil
1 tsp. grated onion
Crisp lettuce leaves
1 ½ c. seedless white grapes
1 can Mandarin oranges, drained
Avocado slices (opt.)

Combine all ingredients except lettuce and fruits. Chill all ingredients thoroughly. Arrange grapes, orange sections and avocado on lettuce leaves; add a small amount of dressing. Yield: 4-6 servings.

Mrs. Rudolph Dale Rasmusson, Pres. Officers' Wives' Club, Clovis, N. M.

 ### Old Fashioned Fruit Salad

4 canned pineapple slices, cut up
1 lge. red apple, diced
2 bananas, sliced
½ c. chopped walnuts
⅓ c. heavy cream, whipped
2 tbsp. lemon juice
2 tbsp. sugar
Pinch of salt

Combine fruits and nuts. Blend together whipped cream, lemon juice, sugar and salt. Pour over fruits; mix lightly. Yield: 4-6 servings.

Mrs. Twila Dismukes, Mount Dora, Fla.

Orange And Avocado Salad

Lettuce leaves
4 lge. oranges, peeled and sectioned
2 med. avocados, peeled and sliced
Watercress sprigs
¼ c. salad dressing
¼ c. catsup
2 tbsp. sugar
3 tbsp. salad oil
2 tbsp. cider vinegar

Arrange lettuce and fruits on individual plates; garnish with watercress. Combine salad dressing, catsup, sugar, oil and vinegar in shaker; pour over salad. If fruits are mixed thoroughly with dressing, the salad will remain fresh for several hours in refrigerator. Yield: 8 servings.

Mrs. George W. Rhyne, Hon. Pres. Officers' Wives' Club, Ft. Ritchie, Md.

Orange-Peanut Butter Salad

8 Florida oranges
¼ c. mayonnaise
¼ c. peanut butter
1 ½ c. thinly sliced celery
½ c. peanuts
2 bananas, sliced

Cut slices from top of oranges; cut off peel spiral fashion. Go over fruit again, removing any remaining white membrane. Slice about ¼ inch thick; dice coarsely. Measure to make 3 cups diced oranges. Blend mayonnaise into peanut butter until smooth. Combine with diced oranges, celery, peanuts and banana slices; toss lightly. Serve on crisp greens; garnish with cream cheese balls and Florida orange slices. Yield: 6 servings.

Photograph for this recipe on page 43.

Pear-Avocado Salad

1 No. 2½ can Bartlett pear halves, chilled
2 avocados, peeled and halved
Candied ginger, diced
Lettuce

For each serving arrange 2 pear halves and 1 avocado half on a lettuce leaf. Place 2 or 3 pieces of ginger in each piece of pear and avocado. Serve with poppy seed dressing.

Mildred Williams, Home Economics Teacher, El Paso, Tex.

Pear And Grape Salad

Milk
1 8-oz. pkg. cream cheese
2 lge. ripe pears, peeled and halved
Lettuce
Halved seedless green grapes

Mix a small amount of milk with cream cheese for easy spreading consistency. Place pear halves on lettuce leaves, cut side down; frost generously with cream cheese. Press grapes, cut side down, onto pears, covering pears completely. Yield: 4 servings.

Mrs. Charles K. Townsend, Officers' Wives' Club, Washington, D. C.

 Pineapple Sandwich Salad

4 tsp. Maraschino cherry juice
1 6-oz. pkg. cream cheese
4 tsp. Maraschino cherries, chopped
8 pineapple slices
Bibb lettuce
Maraschino cherry wedges

Combine cherry juice and cream cheese; blend until smooth. Add chopped cherries and mix well. For each serving place a slice of pineapple on lettuce; spread with cream cheese mixture and cover with a second slice of pineapple. Place a spoonful of the cream cheese mixture in the center of the pineapple and garnish with cherry wedges. Yield: 4 servings.

Mrs. Myrtle Deranger, Home Economics Teacher, Sunset, La.

Six Cup Salad

1 c. sour cream
1 c. shredded coconut
1 c. miniature marshmallows
1 c. Mandarin oranges
1 c. crushed pineapple
1 c. finely chopped pecans
8 Maraschino cherries

Combine all ingredients except cherries in 1½ or 2-quart bowl. Refrigerate for at least 24 hours. Cut into individual servings. Garnish each serving with a cherry. Yield: 8 servings.

Mrs. Alvin S. Transeau, Officers' Wives' Club, Corpus Christi, Tex.

Simdau Fruit Salad

1 grapefruit, sectioned
3 oranges, sectioned
3 bananas, sliced
3 tart apples, diced
1 c. miniature marshmallows
½ c. chopped pecans
½ c. mayonnaise
¼ c. slightly thawed orange juice

Combine fruits, marshmallows and nuts. Mix mayonnaise and orange juice; add to fruit mixture. Chill for at least 1 hour before serving. Toss lightly just before serving. Spoon into lettuce-lined bowl and garnish with Maraschino cherries and mint leaves, if desired. Yield: 6-8 servings.

Mrs. William P. Riley, Jr., Tucson, Ariz.

 ### Stuffed Cranberry-Pear Salad

4 c. fresh cranberries
1 whole orange, quartered and seeded
½ small grapefruit, sectioned and seeded
2 c. sugar or 1 c. sugar and 1 c. syrup
Pear halves

Put cranberries, oranges and grapefruit through food chopper. Add sugar and syrup. Mix well. Chill a few hours before serving. This relish will keep several days in refrigerator. Fill pear half with this mixture at serving time.

Mrs. Zella H. Mills, Home Economics Teacher, Sneedville, Tenn.

Stuffed Honeydews

3 honeydew melons
1 c. watermelon balls
1 c. cantaloupe balls
1 c. honeydew balls
1 c. pineapple chunks
1 c. fresh or Mandarin orange slices
1 ½ c. Port or Rose wine

Cut 1 inch off top of each melon; scoop out seed. Combine fruits; fill melons with fruit mixture. Pour ½ cup of wine into each fruit-filled melon; replace tops of melons. Chill for 2 to 3 hours. Cut melons into halves; serve. Yield: 6 servings.

Mrs. Robert Wellener, Pres. Officers' Wives' Club, Olathe NAS, Kansas

Summer Fruit Toss

    1 cantaloupe, made into balls
    1 bunch white seedless grapes
    1 small can pineapple chunks, drained
    2 lge. bananas, chunked

Toss fruits together. Pour Honey Dressing over salad just before serving.

HONEY DRESSING:
    ¼ *c. honey*
    ⅛ *c. real lime juice*
    Dash of salt

Beat ingredients until completely combined. Yield: 4 servings.

Mrs. Cilicia H. Burden, Morgantown, Ky.

 ### Thanksgiving Salad

    4 firm red apples, diced
    ½ *c. pomegranate seeds*
    ½ *c. seedless raisins*
    Mayonnaise or salad dressing

Combine apples, pomegranate seeds and raisins; mix. Add mayonnaise or salad dressing. Yield: 6-8 servings.

Mrs. Myrtle Burnham, Lee, Me.

Utopia Salad

    ½ *lge. cantaloupe, cubed*
    1 c. fresh peaches, diced
    2 or 3 plums, diced

Combine fruit and add salad dressing.

SALAD DRESSING:
    1 tbsp. sugar
    1 tsp. prepared mustard
    ¼ *c. salad dressing*
    ⅛ *c. evaporated milk*

Mix sugar, mustard and salad dressing. Add enough evaporated milk to form salad dressing. Yield: 6 servings.

Mrs. Frances Hicks, Utopia, Tex., Favorite Recipes Food Fair

Congealed Fruit Salads

HINTS FOR
MOLDED MASTERPIECES

Avoid diluting the gelatin mixture, drain frozen or canned fruits thoroughly before adding. Or, substitute syrup from the fruits as a part of the liquid for added flavor.

Chill gelatin until it is the consistency of unbeaten egg whites before adding fruits and vegetables. If they are added to the gelatin mixture before it is this consistency, they will sink to the bottom of the mold and won't be distributed throughout the gelatin.

Carefully fold the fruits and vegetables into the thickened gelatin to distribute them evenly.

To mold different flavors or colors in layers, chill each layer until set before adding the next one.

For a stay-put garnish in a molded salad, arrange the design, such as a ring of cucumber slices on a layer of partially set gelatin. Chill, then pour another layer of gelatin over the design. Chill until firm.

To keep bubbles in a carbonated beverage that is used as the liquid in a gelatin salad, pour the beverage down the side of the bowl. Stir with an up and down motion.

Unmolding Gelatin Salads

To unmold salads molded in conventional molds, dip the mold in warm but not hot water to the depth of the gelatin. Loosen around the edge with the tip of a paring knife.

Rinse the serving dish with cold water. Don't dry the plate so the gelatin will slide easily if it needs to be centered on the plate. Place the serving dish on top of the mold and turn upside down. Shake gently, holding serving dish tightly to the mold. Remove mold carefully.

If gelatin does not unmold rapidly, repeat the process.

Apricot Ring

1 ½ c. apricot juice
½ c. water
2 pkg. lemon or 1 lemon pkg. and 1 orange pkg. gelatin
Juice of 2 lemons
Juice of 1 orange
1 No. 2½ can apricot halves, drained and sieved
2 3-oz. pkg. cream cheese, diced
1 c. pecans, broken

Heat apricot juice and water. Add gelatin; stir until dissolved. Add enough water to lemon and orange juice to make 1 cup liquid. Add to the gelatin mixture. Add apricots. Chill until mixture begins to thicken. Add cream cheese and nuts. Chill until firm. Yield: 10-12 servings.

Mrs. Imogene Spring, Seymour, Tex.

 Avocado Mousse

1 tbsp. unflavored gelatin
2 tbsp. cold water
1 pkg. lime gelatin
2 c. hot water
1 c. ripe avocado, mashed
½ c. mayonnaise
½ c. whipped cream

Soften unflavored gelatin in cold water. Dissolve both gelatins in hot water. Chill until partially set. Stir in remaining ingredients. Pour into a mold greased with mayonnaise. Chill until firm. Unmold on crisp salad greens. Garnish with fruit and mint sprigs if desired. Yield: 8 servings.

Mrs. Blazita G. Flores, Home Economics Teacher, Ben Bolt, Tex.

 Avocado Salad

1 pkg. lime gelatin
1 c. hot water
2 c. avocado, mashed
½ small onion, grated
½ c. mayonnaise
Juice of 1 lemon
½ tsp. salt
¾ c. whipped cream

Dissolve gelatin in hot water; cool until syrupy. Add avocado, onion, mayonnaise, lemon and salt. Fold in whipped cream. Mold.

Mrs. Susan R. Salter, Montgomery, Ala., Favorite Recipes Food Fair

Blackberry Delight

1 blackberry gelatin
1 c. sugar
1 c. boiling water
1 3-oz. pkg. cream cheese
1 carton frozen blackberries
¼ c. nuts, chopped

Dissolve gelatin and sugar in boiling water. Soften cheese in 4 tablespoons of the hot mixture. Cool remaining gelatin mixture. Add frozen blackberries, nuts and cheese mixture to cooled gelatin. Refrigerate until firm. Yield: 8 servings.

Mrs. Clarice I. Snider, Erwin, Tenn.

Bing Cherry Congealed Salad

1 pkg. cherry gelatin
1 c. hot cherry juice
1 c. cold water
1 8-oz. pkg. cream cheese
1 sm. pkg. pecans, almonds or walnuts
1 No. 2 can Bing cherries

Dissolve gelatin in boiling cherry juice. Add cold water. Cool. Cream the cheese until soft. Add nuts. Stir into thickened gelatin. Add cherries. Chill until firm. Yield: 6 servings.

Mrs. Grace Hunt, Home Economics Teacher, Starkville, Miss.

Bing Cherry Salad

1 No. 2 can Bing cherries, pitted
1 pkg. lemon gelatin
1 ¼ c. grape juice
½ c. pecans, broken (opt.)
1 pkg. cream cheese
½ c. mayonnaise

Heat juice from cherries; add gelatin and stir until dissolved. Add enough grape juice to make 2 cups liquid; chill. When slightly congealed, add cherries and nuts. Chill until firm. Serve with a dressing made by blending the cream cheese and mayonnaise. Yield: 8-10 servings.

Mrs. E. T. Parker, Waco, Tex.

Molded Cranberry Salad

2 c. cranberries
1 ¼ c. cold water
1 c. sugar
1 envelope unflavored gelatin
½ c. chopped celery
½ c. chopped nuts
½ tsp. salt

Cook cranberries in 1 cup water for 20 minutes. Stir in sugar; cook for 5 minutes longer. Soften gelatin in remaining ¼ cup cold water; add to hot cranberries. Stir until dissolved. Set aside to cool. When mixture begins to thicken, add celery, nuts and salt. Rinse mold with cold water; pour cranberry mixture into mold. Chill until firm. Unmold onto serving plate; garnish with salad greens, if desired. Yield: 6 servings.

Mrs. Lyndon B. Johnson

Mint-Melon Souffle Mold

1 c. hot water
1 3-oz. pkg. lemon gelatin
2 or 3 sprigs fresh mint
½ c. cold water
2 tbsp. lemon juice
½ c. mayonnaise
½ tsp. salt
1 c. honeydew melon, diced
1 c. cantaloupe, diced
¼ c. toasted and blanched almonds, slivered

Pour hot water over gelatin and mint sprigs; stir until gelatin is dissolved. Let steep for 5 minutes. Remove mint; add cold water, lemon juice, mayonnaise and salt. Blend well with electric or rotary beater. Pour into refrigerator tray; quick-chill in freezer for 15 to 20 minutes or until firm about 1 inch from edge, but soft in center. Beat until fluffy. Fold in remaining ingredients. Chill until firm. Yield: 4-6 servings.

Mrs. Barbara Rawdon, Columbus, Ga.

Watermelon Delight

1 pkg. cherry gelatin
2 c. watermelon balls

Prepare gelatin as directed on package, omitting ¼ cup of water. Refrigerate until mixture reaches the consistency of egg white. Add watermelon balls. Chill until firm. Yield: 5 servings.

Mrs. Marilee Steward, Ionia, Mich.

Mandarin Orange Salad

2 c. juice from Mandarin oranges and frozen orange juice
1 pkg. peach gelatin
1 can Mandarin orange sections, drained
1 can water chestnuts, thinly sliced
1 c. (heaping) miniature marshmallows

Heat orange juice; add gelatin and stir until dissolved. Let cool until thickened. Add remaining ingredients. Chill until firm. Yield: 10 servings.

Mrs. Eugene S. Turner, Lexington, Tenn., Favorite Recipes Food Fair

Molded Orange Salad

1 3-oz. pkg. orange gelatin
1 c. boiling water
1 c. orange juice
1 11-oz. can mandarin orange sections, drained
¼ c. slivered almonds, blanched and toasted
2 c. creamed cottage cheese

Dissolve gelatin in boiling water; stir until gelatin is dissolved. Cool. Add orange juice and chill in refrigerator until mixture is consistency of unbeaten egg whites. Gently fold in drained mandarin orange sections and toasted almonds. Pour into 4-cup ring mold. Chill until well set. Unmold on crisp lettuce; fill center with cottage cheese. Yield: 6 servings.

Photograph for this recipe on page 65.

Peach Whip

1 pkg. orange gelatin
1 c. hot water

(Continued on next page)

70

1 c. peach juice
1 c. mashed peaches
½ pt. heavy cream, whipped

Dissolve gelatin in hot water; cool. Add peach juice; chill until slightly thickened. Whip until foamy; fold in peaches and whipped cream. Pour into mold; chill until firm. Yield: 6-8 servings.

Mrs. James I. Johnson, Officers' Wives' Club, Argentia, Newfoundland

 Pear Salad

1 lge. can pears, drained
1 c. pear juice
1 pkg. lime gelatin
1 8-oz. pkg. cream cheese
½ pt. whipping cream
Blanched chopped almonds
Whole almonds

Puree pears; set aside. Bring pear juice to a boil; add gelatin, stirring until dissolved. Add pears and cream cheese; beat until smooth. Add more pear juice if too thick. Cool completely; fold in cream. Chill; fold in chopped almonds. Top with whole almonds; place in shallow mold. Chill until firm. Yield: 6 servings.

Gladys Lewis, Grass Valley, Cal.

 Lime Molded Salad

1 pkg. lime gelatin
1 c. marshmallow pieces
1 c. boiling water
Pinch of salt
2 tsp. lemon juice
¼ c. cottage cheese
½ pt. cream, whipped
1 sm. can crushed pineapple
1 sm. pkg. pecans

Dissolve gelatin and marshmallows in water; add salt and lemon juice. Let set until mixture begins to congeal; add remaining ingredients. Chill until firm. Yield: 10 servings.

Bobby Noland, Irvine, Ky.

Pineapple-Cheese Salad

> 1 box lemon gelatin
> 1 c. hot water
> 1 8-oz. can pineapple
> ¼ c. sugar
> ½ tsp. salt
> Juice of 1 lemon
> 1 c. cubed American cheese
> ½ c. chopped walnuts
> ¼ c. chopped pimento
> 1 c. dessert topping mix, whipped

Dissolve gelatin in hot water; chill until partially set in 8½ x 8½-inch pan. Fold remaining ingredients into whipped topping; add to gelatin. Chill until firm. Yield: 8 servings.

Mamie Van Campen, Colby, Kan.

Pineapple-Cream Cheese Salad

> 1 pkg. lime or lemon gelatin
> 1 c. boiling water
> 1 3-oz. pkg. cream cheese
> 1 c. half and half
> 1 c. crushed pineapple, drained
> ½ c. nuts, chopped

Dissolve gelatin in boiling water; chill until partially set. Blend cheese and half and half until smooth. Add pineapple and nuts to cheese mixture. Fold into gelatin and refrigerate until firm. Yield: 8 servings.

Helen Phillips, Metamora, Ohio

Pineapple-Cream Salad

> 1 small can crushed pineapple, undrained
> 1 box strawberry gelatin
> 1 small carton cottage cheese
> 1 c. nuts, chopped
> 1 c. whipped cream

Boil pineapple and gelatin together for 3 minutes. Add cottage cheese and nuts. Fold in sweetened whipped cream. Chill until firm. Yield: 6 servings.

Shelby H. Morris, Home Economics Teacher, Antioch, Tenn.

Pineapple Delight

1 pkg. cream cheese
1 sm. box lime gelatin
1 sm. can pineapple chunks, drained
1 c. chopped pecans

Bring cream cheese to room temperature. Prepare gelatin according to package directions; pour into cream cheese. Blend in pineapple; add nuts. Chill until firm. Yield: 15-20 servings.

Louise Treece, Belmont, N. C.

Pink Pineapple Salad

1 med. can crushed pineapple
2 c. sugar
2 tbsp. lemon juice
2 pkg. cherry gelatin
1 c. cold water
2 c. grated American cheese
½ pt. cream, whipped

Combine pineapple, sugar and lemon juice; heat to a boil. Pour over gelatin; stir until dissolved. Add cold water; chill until partially set. Add cheese; fold in whipped cream. Chill until firm. Yield: 10-12 servings.

Jean Carloss, Lebanon, Tenn., Favorite Recipes Food Fair

Red And White Salad

1 pkg. lemon gelatin
10 marshmallows
1 sm. can crushed pineapple
1 sm. pkg. cream cheese, softened
¼ c. salad dressing
1 c. whipping cream, whipped
¼ to ½ c. chopped nuts
1 pkg. strawberry gelatin

Prepare lemon gelatin according to package instructions; add marshmallows while gelatin is hot. Cool; add pineapple, cream cheese, salad dressing, cream, and nuts. Pour into mold; chill until firm. Prepare strawberry gelatin according to package directions; pour over top of firm gelatin. Chill until firm. Yield: 9-12 servings.

Mrs. Martin Messersmith, Gering, Neb.

Raspberry Bavarian Salad

1 pkg. raspberry gelatin
1 c. boiling water
1 pkg. frozen raspberries
1 c. miniature marshmallows
½ c. whipped cream

Dissolve gelatin in boiling water. Add raspberries and marshmallows. Refrigerate until mixture starts to jell. Whip. Combine whipped cream and whipped gelatin mixture. Put into individual molds and chill. Yield: 8 servings.

Sylvia Benson, Home Economics Teacher, John Day, Ore.

Amber Fruit Salad

1 pkg. apple gelatin
½ tsp. salt
1 c. hot water
⅓ c. pineapple juice
⅔ c. cold water
1 tbsp. lemon juice
½ c. apple, diced
½ c. banana slices
¾ c. crushed pineapple, drained

Dissolve gelatin and salt in hot water. Add pineapple juice, cold water and lemon juice. Chill until slightly thickened. Fold in apple, banana slices and pineapple. Pour into 1-quart mold. Chill until firm. Unmold and garnish with watercress and apple slices. Yield: 6 servings.

Mrs. Gertrude H. McRae, Rockingham, N. C.

Applesauce-Pineapple Salad

3 3-oz. pkg. lime gelatin
2 c. boiling water
1 No. 2 can crushed pineapple, undrained
1 can applesauce
½ c. nuts, chopped

Dissolve gelatin in boiling water. Cool. Add remaining ingredients and pour into 1 large or 10 individual molds. Chill until firm.

Mrs. Robert Borders, Bangor, Maine

Apricot Salad

> 2 pkg. orange gelatin
> 2 c. boiling water
> 1 lge. can apricots, drained and mashed
> 1 c. pineapple and apricot juice
> 1 lge. can diced pineapple, drained
> 1 c. fruit juice
> 1 tbsp. butter
> 2 tbsp. (heaping) flour
> ½ c. sugar
> 1 egg, beaten
> 1 c. whipped cream
> Grated American cheese
> Miniature marshmallows

Dissolve gelatin in boiling water; add apricots, pineapple juice mixture and pineapple. Pour into mold; chill until firm. Combine fruit juice, butter, flour, sugar and egg; cook until thick and smooth. Cool; add whipped cream. Spread over mold; sprinkle with cheese. Top with marshmallows. Yield: 12-15 servings.

Deborah Long, Worthington, Minn.

 ### Avocado Salad

> ½ c. boiling water
> 1 pkg. lime gelatin
> 1 No. 2 can crushed pineapple
> ½ tsp. salt
> 2 tbsp. lemon juice
> ½ c. mayonnaise
> ½ pt. heavy cream
> 1 avocado, diced

Pour water over gelatin to dissolve; add all remaining ingredients. Pour into mold; chill until firm. Yield: 4-6 servings.

Mrs. Gerald Kilburn, Officers' Wives' Club, Staten Island, N. Y.

 ### Banana-Pineapple Salad

> 2 pkg. lemon gelatin
> 1 No. 2½ can crushed pineapple, drained
> 4 bananas, sliced
> 2 c. miniature marshmallows

(Continued on next page)

1 c. pineapple syrup
1 egg
¾ c. sugar
½ tsp. salt
3 tbsp. flour
½ pt. whipped cream

Dissolve gelatin according to package directions; cool until slightly thickened. Add fruit and marshmallows; chill until firm. Combine remaining ingredients except whipped cream. Cook slowly until thickened. Cool; fold in whipped cream. Spread over gelatin; chill. Yield: 12-14 servings.

Iva Bringhurst, Cedar City, Utah

 ### Black Cherry Salad

1 ½ pkg. cherry gelatin
1 No. 2 can black cherries, drained
1 c. grape juice
1 small can crushed pineapple, drained
1 c. nuts

Dissolve gelatin in hot cherry and pineapple juice. Add grape juice. When almost set, stir in pineapple, cherries, and nuts. Yield: 8-10 servings.

Mrs. George G. Walker, Flora, Miss.

 ### Blueberry Salad

1 can blueberries, drained
1 can crushed pineapple, drained
1 pkg. black raspberry gelatin
1 c. pecans, chopped

Bring combined juices to a boil. Add gelatin; stir until dissolved. Add blueberries, pineapple and nuts. Chill until set.

Mrs. Matha L. Taylor, Home Economics Teacher, Dothan, Ala.

 ### Cherry Coke Salad

1 pkg. cherry gelatin
1 sm. can crushed pineapple, drained
1 sm. bottle Maraschino cherries, drained
1 3-oz. pkg. cream cheese
1 6-oz. bottle Coca-Cola
½ c. pecans, chopped

(Continued on next page)

Dissolve gelatin in heated pineapple and cherry juice. Stir in cream cheese until smooth. Chill until very thick. Add remaining ingredients and pour into a 1-quart mold. Chill until firm. Lime gelatin and 7-up may be substituted for cherry gelatin and Coca-Cola if a green salad is desired. Cheese may be folded in last instead of melted in hot juice.

Lurleen B. Wallace, Governor of Alabama, Montgomery

Cheese-Top Gelatin Salad

2 pkg. lemon gelatin
2 c. hot water
2 c. cold water
1 can pineapple chunks, drained
4 bananas, sliced
1 c. miniature marshmallows
1 c. pecans
½ c. halved white grapes

Dissolve gelatin in hot water; add cold water. Cool until thickened; fold in remaining ingredients. Chill in 9 x 12-inch pan until firm.

DRESSING:

1 c. pineapple juice
2 tbsp. butter
2 tbsp. flour
1 egg, beaten
1 c. whipped cream
Grated cheddar cheese

Combine all ingredients except whipped cream and cheese; cook over low heat. Cool; fold in whipped cream. Spread over salad. Top with cheese.

Agatha Johnson, Mitchell, S. D., Favorite Recipes Food Fair

 ### Citrus Salad

1 pkg. lemon gelatin
1 pkg. orange gelatin
1 No. 303 can citrus salad fruit, undrained
1 No. 303 can grapefruit sections, undrained
1 c. crushed or chunk pineapple, undrained
2 c. boiling water

Dissolve gelatins in boiling water. Add citrus salad fruit and grapefruit sections. Add pineapple; stir well. Pour into large loaf pan. Chill until firm. Yield: 12-15 servings.

Nancy M. Riley, McConnelsville, Ohio

Cranberry Delight

1 pkg. raw cranberries, ground
1 ½ c. sugar
1 pkg. strawberry gelatin
1 ¼ c. hot water
1 small can crushed pineapple
1 c. marshmallows, diced
1 c. nuts, chopped
½ c. flaked coconut

Combine ground cranberries and sugar. Chill overnight. Next morning, dissolve strawberry gelatin in hot water. Add to cranberries. Fold in pineapple, marshmallows and nuts. Mix well. Pour into molds; sprinkle with coconut. Chill until set. Yield: 10-12 servings.

Mrs. Margaret Kemp, Home Economics Teacher, Mountain View. Ark.

Cranberry-Gelatin Salad

1 pkg. cranberries, washed
2 pkg. orange gelatin
1 ½ c. granulated sugar
1 lge. can crushed pineapple, undrained
1 c. celery, diced
½ c. walnuts

Cook cranberries in water until soft. Drain and press through sieve. Bring sieved mixture to boil. Add gelatin and sugar; stir until dissolved. Add pineapple. Cool until thickened. Stir in celery and walnuts. Chill. Yield: 12-15 servings.

Jeanette Weiss, Ovid, Colo.

Cranberry-Orange Molds

1 pkg. fresh cranberries
1 orange
2 c. sugar
1 c. chopped pecans
1 c. chopped celery
2 pkg. lemon gelatin

Grind berries and orange; add sugar and let stand. Dissolve gelatin in 3 cups hot water and cool. Combine all ingredients; put in molds and chill until firm.

Mrs. Mills E. Godwin, Jr., Wife of Governor of Virginia, Richmond

Cranberry-Strawberry Salad

2 3-oz. pkg. strawberry gelatin
2 c. boiling water
1 lb. pkg. frozen strawberries
1 10-oz. pkg. frozen cranberry relish
2 8-oz. cans crushed pineapple

Dissolve the gelatin in the boiling water. Add the frozen strawberries and cranberry relish. Stir until they are melted and mixed. Add the crushed pineapple. Chill until firm. Yield: 12 servings.

Betty Huey, Home Economics Teacher, Marysville, Kan.

Fresh Strawberry Salad

2 pkg. strawberry gelatin
1 ½ c. boiling water
1 lge. can crushed pineapple
2 boxes strawberries, partially thawed
1 carton sour cream

Dissolve gelatin in water; cool. Mix pineapple and strawberries; add to gelatin. Pour half of mixture into bowl; chill for 1 hour. Let sour cream set at room temperature for 1 hour; spread over chilled mixture. Cover with remaining gelatin; chill until firm.

Sibyl Bateman, New Orleans, La.

Ginger-Fruit Molds

Pineapple juice plus water to make 1¼ c. liquid
2 3-oz. pkg. lemon gelatin
1 ½ c. ginger ale
1 8-oz. can pineapple tidbits, drained
½ c. chopped pecans
1 banana, diced
1 can seedless green grapes
1 can Mandarin oranges, drained
2 tbsp. minced candied ginger

Heat juice-water mixture to boiling; dissolve gelatin in hot mixture. Cool to room temperature; add remaining ingredients. Turn into molds; chill until firm. Unmold onto lettuce. Yield: 10 servings.

Mary H. Coble, Boston, Mass.

Gooseberry-Banana Salad

1 c. sugar
1 pt. gooseberries, drained
1 pkg. lemon gelatin
3 bananas
1 pt. boiling water
½ c. nuts
1 c. marshmallows, finely cut
Salt

Add sugar to gooseberries; heat slowly and stir until sugar dissolves. Cool. Dissolve gelatin in boiling water. Chill until it starts to jell. Combine all ingredients. Chill until firm.

Mrs. Austin Noblitt, Home Economics Teacher, Rockville, Ind.

 ### Gooseberry Salad

2 pkg. lemon gelatin
2 c. hot water
1 c. miniature marshmallows
Juice and grated rind of 1 orange
Gooseberry juice
1 c. finely chopped celery
1 No. 2 can gooseberries, drained
⅔ c. sugar

Dissolve gelatin in water; add marshmallows, stirring to melt. Combine orange and gooseberry juice with enough water to make 2 cups; add to gelatin mixture. Cool until partially set. Add rind, celery, gooseberries and sugar; pour into 9 x 12-inch pan. Chill until firm. Yield: 12 servings.

Mrs. Opal York, Fredonia, Kan.

Honeydew Surprise

1 pkg. lime gelatin
1 c. boiling water
1 c. chunk pineapple, drained
1 c. Mandarin oranges
1 medium honeydew melon
Salad greens
Cottage cheese
French dressing

(Continued on next page)

Dissolve gelatin in boiling water; cool until partially set. Add pineapple and oranges. Peel whole melon. Cut a slice from one end; remove seeds. Fill center with fruit gelatin. Wrap in cellophane; refrigerate until gelatin is firm. Slice; place on bed of greens. Spoon cottage cheese on top. Serve with French dressing. Yield: 8 servings.

Rhoda M. Grushkin, Home Economics Teacher, Union, N. J.

Lemon-Cheese Salad

1 pkg. lemon gelatin
1 c. boiling water
1 lge. pkg. cream cheese
1 sm. can crushed pineapple
1 tsp. sugar
1 tsp. vanilla flavoring
Few drops of green food coloring
½ c. chopped pecans
1 12-oz. bottle 7-Up

Dissolve gelatin in hot water; add gradually to cheese. Beat until smooth. Stir in pineapple, sugar, vanilla, food coloring and nuts. Stir in 7-Up; pour into mold. Chill until thickened; stir. Chill until firm. Yield: 8 servings.

Mrs. M. W. Lassen, Officers' Wives' Club, Lexington, Ky.

Lime Fruit Salad

1 pkg. lime gelatin
¾ c. boiling water
1 3-oz. pkg. cream cheese
14 marshmallows
½ c. crushed pineapple
½ c. evaporated milk
⅓ c. mayonnaise
1 tsp. lemon juice
½ c. pineapple juice
½ c. pecans, chopped
2 bananas (opt.)

Combine gelatin, boiling water, cream cheese and marshmallows. Stir over low heat until gelatin is thoroughly dissolved. Cool. Add pineapple, evaporated milk, mayonnaise, lemon juice, pineapple juice, pecans and bananas. Refrigerate until firm. Yield: 6-8 servings.

Cecile Foxworth, Home Economics Teacher, St. Petersburg, Fla.

Mixed Fruit Mold

1 lge. can crushed pineapple, drained
Juice of 1 lemon
1 can dark sweet cherries, drained
Cooking sherry to taste
Frozen orange juice
1 box cherry gelatin
1 box raspberry gelatin
3 bananas, sliced
2 lge. apples, chopped
1 c. chopped pecans and English walnuts
Salt

Combine juices from pineapple, lemon, cherries, sherry and orange juice to make 4 cups liquid. Bring 2 cups liquid to a boil; pour over gelatins. Stir until dissolved; add cold juice and remaining ingredients. Chill until firm. Yield: 12 servings.

Jacque Wimbish, Greenville, S. C., Favorite Recipes Food Fair

Molded Fruit Medley

2 envelopes unflavored gelatin
1 c. cold water
2 c. hot water
⅔ c. sugar
⅛ tsp. salt
½ c. lemon juice
4 c. mixed fresh, frozen or canned fruit

Sprinkle gelatin on cold water to soften; dissolve thoroughly in very hot water. Add sugar, salt and lemon juice; stir until sugar is dissolved. Chill until mixture is consistency of unbeaten egg white; fold in fruit. Turn into a 6-cup mold; chill until firm. Blueberries, peach slices, halved white grapes, sliced bananas or cantaloupe pieces may be used for fruit. Yield: 10-12 servings.

Susan Brandt, Tallahassee, Fla.

Molded Grape Supreme

1 envelope unflavored gelatin
¼ c. cold water
1 c. boiling water
½ c. sugar

(Continued on next page)

Dash of salt
1 6-oz. can frozen grape juice concentrate
3 tbsp. lemon juice
¾ c. seedless grapes, halved
2 medium bananas, diced
¼ c. nuts, chopped

Sprinkle gelatin over cold water to soften. Add boiling water, sugar and salt; stir until dissolved. Stir in grape and lemon juice. Refrigerate until partially thickened. Fold in fruits and nuts. Pour into 1-quart mold. Refrigerate until firm. Yield: 6 servings.

Mrs. Beth Jones, Nashville, Tenn.

 Molded Fruit Swirl

1 ½ c. boiling water
1 pkg. cherry gelatin
1 c. raw cranberries, ground
¾ c. sugar
1 c. crushed pineapple
½ c. celery, diced
½ c. apple, diced
½ c. walnuts, chopped (opt.)

Dissolve gelatin in water. Cool. Refrigerate until thickened. Add sugar to cranberries. Add all ingredients to gelatin. Refrigerate until set. Serve with salad dressing or whipped cream. Yield: 8 servings.

Nancy McCormack, Bancroft, Idaho

 Molded Grapefruit Salad

1 envelope unflavored gelatin
¼ c. cold water
½ c. hot water
½ c. sugar
Pinch of salt
1 c. unpared apples, diced
2 ½ c. grapefruit, undrained
½ c. walnuts, broken

Soften gelatin in cold water; Dissolve in hot water. Add sugar and salt. Cool. Add apples and grapefruit. Chill until partially set. Add nuts. Chill until firm. Yield: 6 servings.

Mrs. Sarah S. Steffey, Home Econimocs Teacher, Greenville, Pa.

Molded Fruit Salad

    1 pkg. lemon gelatin
    1 c. hot water
    ½ c. cold water
    1 c. whipping cream, whipped
    1 c. Mandarin orange sections
    1 c. sliced peaches
    1 c. diced pineapple
    1 c. light sweet cherries
    1 c. dark sweet cherries

Dissolve gelatin in water; add cold water. Chill until thickened. Blend in whipped cream; add fruits. Pour into mold; chill until firm. Yield 12 servings.

Mrs. Elizabeth Benson, Coldwater, Mich.

Orange Molded Salad

    1 pkg. orange gelatin
    1 c. boiling water
  16 marshmallows, quartered
    1 c. fresh orange juice, heated
    1 c. crushed pineapple
    1 c. bananas, sliced
    ¼ c. Maraschino cherries, quartered
    1 c. sugar
    ¼ c. lemon juice
    ⅓ c. orange juice
    ¼ c. pineapple juice
    2 eggs, beaten
    1 c. whipped cream

Dissolve gelatin in boiling water. Melt marshmallows in heated orange juice; add to the gelatin mixture. Chill until mixture begins to set; add pineapple, bananas and cherries. Mix lightly. Chill until firm. Combine sugar, lemon juice, orange juice, pineapple juice and eggs. Cook until thickened; cool. Fold in whipped cream; serve with gelatin mixture. Yield: 8 servings.

Mrs. Dorothy Nelson, Idaho Falls, Idaho

Orange-Peach Salad

    1 pkg. orange gelatin
    1 c. boiling water
    ⅔ c. pineapple juice
    4 fresh peaches, peeled and diced
    1 c. pineapple, drained and diced
    ½ c. seedless green grapes

(Continued on next page)

Dissolve gelatin in boiling water; add pineapple juice. Refrigerate until mixture begins to thicken. Fold in remaining ingredients. Cover with Saran wrap; chill. Yield: 4-6 servings.

Dorothy G. Scothorn, Home Economics Teacher, Kennedy, Minn.

Orange-Pineapple Salad

Juice from oranges
Juice from pineapple
1 pkg. orange gelatin
1 sm. can frozen orange juice
1 can Mandarin oranges, drained
1 sm. can crushed pineapple, drained
1 lge. banana, sliced

Combine juice from oranges and pineapple with enough water to make 1 cup liquid; bring to a boil. Pour over gelatin; stir until dissolved. Add frozen orange juice and fruits; pour in mold. Chill until firm. Yield: 8 servings.

Clara Rhodes, Beatrice, Neb.

Orange-Tangerine Salad

½ c. boiling water
1 pkg. orange gelatin
1 ½ c. frozen orange juice, diluted
1 can Mandarin oranges
1 sm. can pineapple chunks
1 3-oz. pkg. cream cheese, cut in cubes
40 miniature marshmallows
2 egg yolks
¼ c. butter
½ c. sugar
½ tsp. dry mustard
½ tbsp. vinegar
¼ pt. whipping cream

Pour water over gelatin; add orange juice. Let set until thickened. Fold in fruits, cream cheese and marshmallows; place in ring mold. Chill until firm. Cook remaining ingredients, except cream, until thick in double boiler. Add cream; simmer until mixed. Yield: 8 servings.

Elsie Anderson, Pasco, Wash., Favorite Recipes Food Fair

Peach Pickle Salad Mold

2 pkg. orange or lemon gelatin
2 ½ c. boiling peach juice
2 lge. jars or cans spiced peaches, drained and diced
2 cans white seedless grapes, drained
1 No. 2 can pineapple tidbits, well-drained
1 c. almonds or pecans, chopped

Dissolve gelatin in boiling peach juice. Let cool. Combine peaches, grapes and pineapple. Add to gelatin. Add nuts. Chill until firm. Yield: 10-12 servings.

Myrtis L. McAlhany, St. George, S. C.

 ### Pineapple-Cranberry Mold

1 No. 2 can crushed pineapple and water
2 pkg. lemon gelatin
½ c. lemon juice
⅓ c. walnuts, chopped
3 tbsp. orange peel, shredded or chopped
3 c. whole cranberry sauce

Drain syrup from pineapple and add enough water to make 1½ c. liquid. Heat to boiling and pour over gelatin. Stir until completely dissolved. Stir in pineapple and remaining ingredients. Turn into mold. Chill until firm. To unmold, dip into hot water about 15 seconds; invert. Yield: 8-10 servings.

Maggie Beth Watts, Home Economics Teacher, Era, Tex.

Raw Cranberry Salad

1 lb. cranberries, washed
2 unpeeled oranges
1 ½ c. sugar
3 pkg. lemon gelatin
4 ½ c. water
1 ½ c. chopped celery
½ c. chopped nuts

Grind cranberries and oranges; soak with sugar for 1 hour. Prepare gelatin according to package directions using the 4½ cups water. Combine all ingredients;

(Continued on next page)

pour into 8½ x 14-inch dish or individual molds. Chill until firm. Serve with mixture of equal portions of mayonnaise and whipping cream. Yield: 15-18 servings.

Catherine H. Hall, Urbana, Ill.

Walnut Jewel Salad

 1 *pkg. pineapple gelatin*
 1 *c. hot water*
 ½ *tsp. salt*
 1 *c. chopped raw cranberries*
 ½ *c. canned crushed pineapple, drained*
 ½ *c. diced celery*
 ½ *c. chopped walnuts*

Dissolve gelatin in hot water; add salt. Combine water with drained pineapple juice to make 1 cup liquid; add to gelatin. Chill until slightly thickened. Fold in remaining ingredients. Turn into a 1-quart mold or into 8 individual molds. Chill until firm. Unmold onto bed of crisp lettuce; decorate with additional walnut halves and serve with honey creme salad dressing.

Photograph for this recipe below.

Raspberry Gelatin Salad

> 1 3-oz. pkg. raspberry gelatin
> ¾ c. boiling water
> 1 sm. pkg .frozen red raspberries
> 1 sm. can crushed pineapple with juice
> ½ pt. sour cream

Dissolve gelatin in boiling water; add frozen raspberries. Stir; add pineapple with juice. Place half of mixture in an 8-inch square pan. Chill until thickened. Spoon sour cream over gelatin; cover with remaining gelatin mixture. Chill until firm. Yield: 6 servings.

Mrs. Claude Harding, Officers' Wives' Club, Lexington, Ky.

 Raspberry-Melon Ring

> 2 envelopes unflavored gelatin
> ½ c. lemon juice
> 1 ¼ c. boiling water
> ¾ c. sugar
> ¼ tsp. salt
> 2 c. raspberry syrup
> ¾ c. melon balls
> 3 10-oz. pkg. frozen raspberries, thawed and drained

Soften gelatin in lemon juice; dissolve in boiling water. Stir in sugar, salt and raspberry syrup. Chill until partially set. Add melon balls and raspberries. Chill until firm. Yield: 5 servings.

Mrs. Ruth L. West, Home Economics Teacher, Laurel, Miss.

Raspberry Surprise Gelatin

> 1 c. applesauce
> 1 pkg. raspberry gelatin
> 1 7-oz. bottle 7-Up
> 1 No. 9 can crushed pineapple, drained
> ⅓ c. pecans, chopped

Heat applesauce; add gelatin. Stir until gelatin is dissolved. Cool mixture to lukewarm. Stir in the 7-Up. Add pineapple and pecans. Mix thoroughly. Chill until firm. Yield: 4-6 servings.

Mrs. Stenson Terry, Home Economics Teacher, San Perlita, Tex.

Strawberry-Banana Salad

 2 pkg. strawberry gelatin
 1 c. boiling water
 2 10-oz. pkg. frozen sliced strawberries, thawed
 1 1-lb. 4-oz. can crushed pineapple, drained
 3 med. bananas, mashed
 1 c. coarsely chopped walnuts
 1 pt. sour cream

Dissolve gelatin in water; add all ingredients except sour cream. Mix well; pour half of gelatin mixture in 12 x 8 x 2-inch baking dish. Chill until firm; spread sour cream evenly over mixture. Cover with remaining gelatin mixture; chill until firm. Yield: 12 servings.

Jeraldine W. Dowdy, Midland, Mich.

Strawberry-Grapefruit Mold

 1 pkg. strawberry gelatin
 1 pkg. unflavored gelatin
 10-oz. pkg. frozen strawberries, thawed
 1 can grapefruit sections, drained

Dissolve strawberry gelatin according to package directions. Add dissolved unflavored gelatin; cool. Stir in strawberries; add grapefruit sections. Mold as desired. Chill until firm. Yield: 6 servings.

Mrs. Evelyn R. Sheets, Home Economics Teacher, Yatesville, Ga.

Strawberry Surprise

 2 6-oz. pkgs. strawberry or cherry gelatin
 3 c. hot water
 1 No. 2½ can applesauce
 3 10-oz. pkg. frozen strawberries, thawed
 Sour cream or whipped cream

Dissolve gelatin in hot water; cool until mixture is consistency of egg whites. Add applesauce and strawberries; chill until firm. Top with sour cream or whipped cream. Yield: 18 servings.

Mrs. Louella Pence, Macon, Ill.

Summer Salad

1 pkg. lime or lemon gelatin
2 c. strawberries
1 sm. can Mandarin oranges
1 sm. can crushed pineapple, drained
1 pt. cottage cheese
1 8-oz. pkg. cream cheese
¼ c. milk

Prepare gelatin according to directions on package; cool until slightly thickened. Add fruits and cottage cheese; chill until firm. Beat cream cheese until soft; thin to spreading consistency with milk. Spread over salad. Yield: 8 servings.

Frances Harper, St. Helens, Ore.

Thanksgiving Cranberry Salad

1 orange
1 qt. cranberries
2 pkg. lemon gelatin
2 c. hot water
2 c. sugar
½ c. chopped nuts

Peel orange, reserving peel; section and chop pulp. Grind cranberries and orange rind in food chopper. Dissolve gelatin in hot water; add sugar. Stir until dissolved. Chill gelatin mixture until thickened. Add cranberries, orange rind, nuts and orange. Place in 9 x 11-inch pan; chill until firm.

Mrs. Robert Blickenstaff, Officers' Wives' Club, Athens, Greece

Wedding Ring Salad

1 6-oz. pkg. lemon gelatin
2 c. hot water
1 lb. Thompson green grapes
1 11-oz. can Mandarin orange sections, drained
1 c. pecans, chopped
2 medium cantaloupes, peeled
Juice drained from oranges plus enough water to make 1 c.
   liquid

Dissolve gelatin in hot water; cool. Add juice-water mixture. Cool until gelatin mixture thickens. Add grapes, oranges and nuts. Remove stem ends of cantaloupes; carefully scoop out seeds. Fill cavity with gelatin mixture. Let set 12 to 24 hours or until congealed. Slice cantaloupe into ½ to ¾-inch circles to serve. Yield: 8-10 servings.

Lorene Featherstone, Jackson, Tenn., Favorite Recipes Food Fair

Vegetable Salads

EASY VEGETABLE SALADS

1. Diced celery and grated raw carrots mixed with raisins or nuts.
2. On a slice of lettuce place asparagus tips sprinkled with grated cheese.
3. Little cherry tomatoes, yellow plum tomatoes with unpared cucumber slices, and sliced spring onions.
4. Sliced cucumbers and minced parsley.
5. Sliced tomatoes covered with cucumber slices, and onion rings or slices.
6. Thinly sliced radishes, slices of raw turnips (cut very thin) and raw cauliflowerets.
7. Mound of cottage cheese with diced green or red pepper, cucumber, and onions.
8. Stuff small tomatoes with cottage cheese, sprinkle with minced chives, parsley, or toasted almonds; or stuffed with grated cabbage and minced mint; or stuffed with cream cheese mixed with minced onion, green pepper and stuffed olives.

BEAN SALAD IDEAS

These bean salads are hearty enough to serve as a main dish.

Caesar Style

Mixed marinated large white beans into green salad just before serving. Drizzel on an oil and vinegar garlic-flavored dressing. Add a raw egg. Garnish with anchovy strips and small bread cubes browned in garlic-flavored butter or oil. Dust with grated Parmesan cheese.

Red Bean Salad

While beans are still hot, combine 2½ cups cooked beans with 1½ cups coarsely cut celery, 1 cup sliced, on the bias, sweet Spanish onions, ½ cup sliced sweet pickles, and ½ cup small cubes sharp Cheddar Cheese if desired. Add 1 tablespoon sweet pickle liquid and ½ cup or more oil and vinegar dressing. Allow to stand in refrigerator several hours or overnight. Garnish with rings of onion or green pepper or hard-cooked egg slices.

Great Northern Salad

Place hot, drained beans in salad bowl rubbed with garlic. Lightly mix in just enough oil and vinegar dressing to coat the beans. Cover; chill several hours or overnight. An hour or so before ready to serve, fold lightly into the beans ¼ cup minced onions, ½ cup each celery and dill or sweet pickles, and enough mayonnaise to moisten well. Season as desired. Add to this as you would your favorite potato salad. Chill before serving.

Artichoke Salad Bowl

>   1 9-oz. pkg. frozen artichoke hearts
>   8 c. broken mixed salad greens
> ½ c. sliced radishes
>   2 tbsp. herb-seasoned croutons
> ⅓ c. buttermilk
>   3 tbsp. mayonnaise
> ½ c. finely diced pared cucumber
>   1 tbsp. lemon juice
> ½ tsp. garlic salt
> ½ tsp. sugar
> ⅛ tsp. pepper

Cook artichoke hearts according to package directions; drain. Chill. Place greens in a large bowl; arrange artichoke hearts and radish slices on top. Sprinkle with croutons. Blend buttermilk and mayonnaise until smooth; stir in cucumber and lemon juice. Add remaining ingredients. Just before serving, drizzle half the dressing over salad. Toss lightly to mix. Serve salad with remaining dressing.

Mrs. Roland C. Meeks, Hon. V. Pres. Officers' Wives' Club,
Hof Air Sta., Germany

 ### Bay Ranch Salad

>   2 jars marinated artichoke hearts
>   1 bunch romaine lettuce
>   1 sm. head lettuce, torn
>   4 oz. fresh or canned crab meat
>   2 whole green onions, chopped
>   2 hard-cooked eggs
>   2 tbsp. (heaping) mayonnaise
> Salt and pepper

Drain artichoke hearts, reserving marinade. Line salad bowl with romaine lettuce. Combine 1 jar of artichoke hearts, half the crab meat, 1 onion, 1 chopped egg, and mayonnaise mixed with reserved marinade. Season to taste with salt and pepper. Toss lightly with torn lettuce. Garnish with remaining artichoke hearts, crab meat and sliced egg. Yield: 8 servings.

Mrs. John E. Kennedy, Norfolk, Va.

Green Salad With Marinated Artichoke Hearts

>   1 can artichoke hearts
> ¼ c. salad oil

(Continued on next page)

⅔ c. wine vinegar
½ tsp. salt
Dash of Worcestershire sauce
Dash of Tabasco sauce
1 tsp. salad herbs
Pinch of dill
Salad greens
Chopped tomatoes
Chopped green peppers
Croutons

Combine artichoke hearts, salad oil, vinegar, and seasonings. Marinate, refrigerated, for several hours. Combine salad greens, tomatoes and green peppers. Toss with artichoke hearts and dressing. Add croutons; serve. Do not use frozen artichokes. Yield: 6-8 servings.

Mrs. Daniel P. Shadrach, Pres. Officers' Wives' Club, Robins AFB, Ga.

 ## Asparagus Vinaigrette

1 tsp. sugar
1 ½ tsp. salt
⅛ tsp. cayenne pepper
¼ tsp. paprika
Few drops of garlic juice
⅓ c. vinegar
1 c. salad oil
3 tbsp. chopped green onion
4 tbsp. sweet pickle relish
2 tbsp. chopped parsley
4 tbsp. chopped green pepper
2 tbsp. chopped pimento
1 tbsp. capers
2 lge. cans asparagus, drained

Combine sugar, salt, cayenne pepper, paprika and garlic juice. Add vinegar and salad oil slowly, beating thoroughly. Add onion, relish, parsley, green pepper, pimento and capers to oil mixture. Pour vinaigrette sauce over asparagus. Marinate, refrigerated, overnight or longer. Yield: 4-6 servings.

Mrs. Max Y. Harris, Officers' Wives' Club, Wichita, Kan.

 ## Asparagus-Radish Salad

3 tbsp. olive oil
1 tbsp. vinegar
1 tsp. salt

(Continued on next page)

Freshly ground black pepper
1 small clove garlic, crushed
Green asparagus, cooked and chilled
20 to 25 radishes, thinly sliced
Salad greens

Mix oil, vinegar, salt, pepper and garlic. Add radishes and marinate for 2 to 3 hours. Place asparagus on salad greens. Arrange the radishes on top. Pour remaining marinade over radishes. Yield: 4 servings.

Mrs. Aussie A. Miller, Home Economics Teacher, Newton, Tex.

 ## Green Asparagus Salad

3 cans whole green asparagus
1 bottle Italian dressing
½ c. tarragon vinegar
1 tsp. tarragon leaves (dried)
1 tsp. garlic salt
Fresh ground black pepper

Drain asparagus well. Place in layers on shallow pan; sprinkle each layer with a little dry tarragon, fresh ground black pepper and garlic salt. Pour salad dressing and vinegar over layers; let stand overnight at room temperature Chill and serve on lettuce leaves, topped with mayonnaise flavored with a little of the marinade.

Mrs. Winthrop Rockefeller, Wife of Governor of Arkansas, Little Rock

Bean Salad

1 med. can slender green beans, drained
1 med. can yellow wax beans, drained
1 med. can sm. green lima beans, drained
1 med. can kidney beans, drained
1 c. diced celery
2 med. onions, sliced in rings
½ c. chopped green pepper or 1 green pepper, sliced
1 to 2 c. cauliflower buds
2 ½ c. cider vinegar
2 ½ c. sugar
1 tsp. salt

Combine vegetables; mix well. Combine remaining ingredients; bring to boil. Pour over vegetables; marinate 24 to 48 hours.

Beatrice E. Warner, Cuyahoga Falls, Ohio

Green And Red Salad

4 tbsp. salad oil
1 c. wine vinegar
1 c. sugar
2 lge. cans French-style green beans
1 can pimentos, chopped
1 small head cauliflower, cut in small pieces
1 c. whole almonds
Salt and pepper to taste
Rosemary to taste
Basil to taste
Bay leaf to taste

Mix oil, vinegar and sugar together. Stir until sugar dissolves. Add remaining ingredients. Refrigerate for 24 hours. Will keep for 1 week if refrigerated. Yield: 8 servings.

Ellen Morgan Schenck, Home Economics Teacher, West Lawn, Pa.

 ### Combination Bean Salad

1 9-oz. pkg. frozen green beans with toasted almonds
1 10-oz. pkg. frozen corn and peas with tomatoes
4 tbsp. salad oil
¼ c. vinegar
2 tbsp. sugar
¼ tsp. dry mustard
Lettuce leaves
1 15-oz. can red kidney beans, drained

Prepare vegetables separately as directed on packages, reserving bag of almonds from green beans and substituting 1 tablespoon salad oil for butter in cooking each vegetable. Do not drain. Cool. Combine remaining salad oil with vinegar, sugar and mustard. Stir until blended. Line salad bowl with lettuce. Arrange green beans, corn and kidney beans in 3 separate sections in bowl. Chill. Just before serving, sprinkle salad oil mixture over salad; sprinkle with reserved almonds. Yield: 8 servings.

Photograph for this recipe on page 91.

 ### Patio Salad

4 15-oz. cans kidney beans, drained
8 hard-cooked eggs, diced
1 c. onion, chopped
2 c. celery, diced

(Continued on next page)

What's in a salad? Practically everything. A salad may be a main dish, a side dish, an appetizer or a dessert. No matter what salad you choose, its success will depend to a large extent on your choice of dressing. It's the dressing that gives a salad character and personality.

SILHOUETTE SALAD DRESSING

1⅔ c. evaporated milk
⅓ c. vinegar
1 pkg. desired salad dressing mix
1 tsp. sugar

Put milk in 1-quart container. Gradually add vinegar, stirring constantly. Add mix and sugar; shake or stir until blended. Refrigerate. Serve over mixed greens, vegetables, seafood, meat, poultry, fruit salads or with cabbage for coleslaw. Yield: 2 cups dressing.

CURRY SALAD DRESSING

1⅔ c. evaporated milk
½ c. salad oil
½ c. lemon juice
4 tsp. curry powder
1 tsp. each sugar and salt
¼ tsp. ginger
2 tbsp. chopped chutney (opt.)

Beat evaporated milk and oil until blended. Beat in lemon juice until smooth. Mix in remaining ingredients. Refrigerate. Serve over fruit, poultry or seafood salads. Yield: 2½ cups dressing.

MONTEREY SALAD DRESSING

1⅔ c. evaporated milk
½ c. vinegar
1 pkg. dehydrated onion soup mix
½ c. catsup or chili sauce
1 tsp. Worcestershire sauce

Put evaporated milk in 1-quart container. Gradually add vinegar, stirring constantly. Add remaining ingredients; shake or stir until blended. Chill. Serve over mixed greens, vegetable, meat or seafood salads. Yield: 2½ cups dressing.

STEAK HOUSE SALAD DRESSING

¾ c. evaporated milk
½ c. salad oil
3 tbsp. vinegar or lime juice
1 pkg. Bleu cheese salad dressing mix

Beat milk and oil until blended. Add vinegar or lime juice; beat smooth. Stir in mix. Refrigerate. Serve over mixed greens, vegetables, meat, poultry or seafood salads or toss with cabbage for coleslaw. Yield: 1½ cups dressing.

See photograph on reverse page.

1 ⅓ c. pickle relish
2 c. sharp cheddar cheese, shredded
2 c. sour cream

Mix beans, eggs, onion, celery, pickle relish and cheese. Add sour cream; toss lightly. Serve on lettuce; garnish with additional hard-cooked egg if desired. Yield: 20 servings.

Mrs. Mary Frances B. Wilson, Centre, Ala.

Low Calorie Pickled Green Bean Salad

2 pkg. frozen green beans
1 c. dietetic pickle relish

Cook green beans according to package directions; drain and cool. Combine green beans and relish; chill and serve. Yield: 6 servings.

Mrs. Esther Green, Casey, Ill.

A Man's Salad

Lettuce
Pickled beets, sliced
Hard-boiled eggs, sliced
Bermuda or red onions, thinly sliced
Mayonnaise

Make bed of crisp, very green lettuce. Place slices of pickled beets on lettuce, adding slices of hard-boiled eggs and onion rings. Top with mayonnaise. Lemon juice may be substituted for mayonnaise and asparagus for beets.

Mrs. S. A. Hunt, Jr., Columbia, S. C., Favorite Recipes Food Fair

Broccoli Vinaigrette

2 10-oz. pkg. frozen chopped broccoli
1 bottle Italian salad dressing
2 hard-cooked eggs, chopped
1 2-oz. jar pimento, chopped
8 black olives, chopped

(Continued on next page)

Cook broccoli according to package directions; drain and chill. Just before serving moisten broccoli with Italian dressing and garnish with combined eggs, pimento and olives. Yield: 6 servings.

Dorothy L. Anderson, Home Economics Teacher, Princeton, Minn.

 ### Golden West Salad

> 3 c. carrots, grated
> 6 soda crackers, rolled
> 3 hard-cooked eggs, diced
> ½ tsp. salt
> ½ c. celery, chopped
> 3 tbsp. lemon juice
> 1 tbsp. onion juice or 1 onion, grated
> ¾ c. salad dressing
> ½ c. peanuts, ground

Combine all ingredients except salad dressing and peanuts. Make a paste with salad dressing and peanuts. Add to carrot mixture; mix lightly. Yield: 8 servings.

Agnes Kowitz Boulger, Bradley, Ill.

Luncheon Salad

> 6 fresh carrots, washed and scraped
> 6 hard-cooked eggs
> 1 c. pecans
> 1 sm. onion
> Salt to taste
> Mayonnaise
> 6 soda crackers, crumbled
> 6 lettuce leaves

(Continued on next page)

Put carrots, eggs, pecans and onion through food chopper using medium blade. Combine ground ingredients with salt and enough mayonnaise to hold mixture together in salad bowl. Add crackers just before serving. Serve on lettuce leaves. Egg yolks may be mashed instead of ground. Yield: 6 servings.

Mrs. Georgia M. Grissom, Cincinnati, Ohio

Cabbage-Tomato-Pepper Slaw

½ *medium head cabbage, shredded*
2 *medium tomatoes, pared and chopped*
½ *medium green pepper, chopped*
1 *tsp. celery seed*
½ *c. salad dressing*
1 *tsp. mustard*
1 *tbsp. milk*
Salt and pepper to taste

Combine cabbage, tomatoes and green pepper. Mix lightly with celery seed. Combine salad dressing, mustard, milk, salt and pepper. Add dressing to vegetables; mix lightly. Chill before serving. Yield: 6 servings.

Linda Lee Benson, Home Economics Teacher, Tampico, Ill.

Confetti Salad

2 *to 3 tbsp. bacon drippings*
2 *tsp. flour*
2 *tsp. sugar*
½ *tsp. salt*
1 *tsp. dry mustard*
Dash of cayenne pepper
1 *egg*
¼ *c. vinegar*
¼ *c. milk*
1 *c. sour cream*
3 *c. green cabbage, finely shredded*
3 *c. red cabbage, finely shredded*
¾ *c. green onions, thinly sliced*
6 *strips bacon, crisply fried and crushed*

Blend bacon drippings, flour, sugar, salt, dry mustard and pepper. Beat egg and vinegar together; add to mixture in skillet. Cook over low heat until smooth and thick; stir constantly. Combine milk and sour cream. Stir into thickened mixture. Chill thoroughly. Pour over cabbage, onions and bacon. Yield: 8-10 servings.

Mrs. Arva Nell Needham, Home Economics Teacher, La Grange, Tex.

Favorite Alaskan Vegetable Salad

2 c. raw cabbage, chopped
½ c. raw spinach, cut with scissors or torn
⅓ c. parsley, cut
Onion to taste
Salt and pepper to taste
Mayonnaise

Combine all ingredients. Toss lightly with a fork. Yield: 6 servings.

Mary Lou Tucker, Home Economics Teacher, Palmer, Alaska

Green Cabbage Salad

2 c. sugar
½ c. water
1 c. vinegar
1 lge. head cabbage, shredded
1 tbsp. salt
½ bunch celery, chopped
½ tsp. celery seed
½ tsp. mustard seed
1 green pepper, chopped
1 red pepper, chopped

Boil sugar, water and vinegar for 2 minutes. Let cool. Mix cabbage with salt; let stand for 1 hour. Squeeze out all juice. Add remaining ingredients. Mix cabbage mixture with boiled mixture. Yield: 10-12 servings.

Mrs. Ladonna Nelson, Marietta, Minn.

Old Fashion Peanut-Cabbage Salad

2 tbsp. flour
¾ c. sugar
Salt and pepper to taste
2 beaten eggs
1 ½ c. water
½ c. vinegar
3 tbsp. mustard
1 lge. head cabbage, shredded
½ c. peanuts, broken

Sift together flour, sugar, salt and pepper. Combine eggs, water, vinegar and mustard. Mix well. Add to dry mixture. Cook until mixture becomes a sauce. Cool. Pour sauce over cabbage and peanuts; mix well. Yield: 10 servings.

Katie B. Whorton, Home Economics Teacher, Cabot, Ark.

Red Cabbage Slaw

3 c. red cabbage, shredded
¼ c. parsley, chopped
2 tbsp. garlic vinegar
1 tsp. sugar
½ tsp. salt
2 tbsp. capers
1 tbsp. onion
½ c. sour cream

Combine all ingredients. Mix well. Yield: 6-8 servings.

Nelda L. Roark, Olla, La.

Slaw

1 head cabbage
2 to 4 onions
Salt to taste
¾ to 1 c. plus 2 tbsp. sugar
1 c. vinegar
1 c. oil
1 tsp. dry or prepared mustard
1 tsp. celery salt or seed (opt.)

Make layer of cabbage, onions and salt to taste. Sprinkle ¾ to 1 cup sugar over cabbage. Combine vinegar, remaining sugar, oil and mustard; bring to a boil. Pour over cabbage and onions; let stand overnight in refrigerator. Yield: 8 servings.

Boverda Rudolph, Favorite Recipes Food Fair, Sharpe, Ky.

Buffet Salad

1 small head cauliflowerets, sliced crosswise
1 medium onion, cut in rings
½ c. stuffed olives, sliced
½ to ⅔ c. French dressing
1 small head lettuce, broken in pieces
¼ to ½ c. Bleu or Roquefort cheese, crumbled

Combine cauliflowerets, onion, olives and French dressing. Let stand for 30 minutes. Just before serving add lettuce and cheese. Toss lightly. Yield: 6-8 servings.

Mrs. Fern Gordon, Home Economics Teacher, Cheboygan, Mich.

Cauli-Slaw

½ head fresh cauliflower, finely grated
¼ c. carrots, grated
¼ c. celery, finely chopped
¼ c. green pepper, finely chopped
¼ tsp. vinegar
¼ tsp. sugar
  Salt and pepper to taste
  Mayonnaise

Combine all ingredients; mix well. Chill. Sprinkle with paprika or garnish with hard-cooked egg slices arranged in petal fashion if desired. Yield: 6 servings.

Carol Jean McConnell, Fredericktown, Pa.

 ### Raw Cauliflower Salad

1 small head cauliflower, chopped
3 tbsp. onion, diced
1 lge. tomato, diced
¼ green pepper, chopped

SOUR CREAM DRESSING

½ c. sour cream
4 tsp. white vinegar
1 tbsp. sugar
Dash of salt

Mix cauliflower, onion, tomato and pepper. Stir sour cream and vinegar together; add sugar and salt. Add to cauliflower mixture. Yield: 4 servings.

Julie Gorman, Home Economics Teacher, Mound City, Kan.

 ### Celery Rings

3 tbsp. butter
1 3-oz. pkg. cream cheese
3 tbsp. tomato paste
Salt and red pepper to taste
1 bunch celery

Cream butter; add cheese and tomato paste. Mix well. Add salt and red pepper. Stuff celery stalks with mixture. Put celery hearts together; place remaining pieces of celery around to make the stalk into its original shape. Wrap in waxed paper; chill. Slice into rings. Yield: 8 servings.

Evelyn Ford, Home Economics Teacher, Berryville, Va.

Celery Slaw

1 tsp. salt
1 ½ tsp. sugar
⅛ tsp. pepper
Dash of paprika
⅓ c. salad oil
2 tbsp. vinegar
¼ c. sweet or sour cream
2 c. celery, thinly sliced
2 tbsp. pimento, slivered
Salad greens
Green pepper rings

Combine salt, sugar, pepper, paprika, oil and vinegar. Beat with a rotary beater. Add cream; continue beating until smooth. Marinate celery in dressing for a few minutes. Add pimento; toss. Place greens in salad bowl; pile celery mixture in center. Garnish with green pepper rings. Yield: 6 servings.

Mrs. Dorothy Maxwell, Westville, Ill.

 ### Cucumber Cooler

¼ c. vinegar
1 tbsp. lemon juice
1 tsp. celery seed
2 tbsp. sugar
1 tsp. salt
⅛ tsp. pepper
¼ tsp. Accent
¼ c. onion, chopped
2 tbsp. parsley, chopped
3 medium cucumbers, thinly sliced

Mix all ingredients except cucumbers in jar or plastic container. Add cucumbers; toss to coat with dressing. Chill thoroughly. Turn or shake container several times while chilling. Yield: 4-6 servings.

Mrs. Emily Sundbeck, Home Economics Teacher, Manor, Tex.

Cucumber In Sour Cream

1 medium cucumber, sliced
1 tsp. salt
3 tbsp. cultured sour cream
1 tsp. vinegar
1 tsp. sugar
¼ tsp. dill weed

(Continued on next page)

Sprinkle cucumber with salt; cover with water. Soak. Combine sour cream, vinegar, sugar and dill weed. Drain cucumber; add dressing. If dressing is too thick, add a small amount of milk or cream. Yield: 3 servings.

Mrs. Carol S. Johnson, Home Economics Teacher, Alexandria, Minn.

Cucumber Salad

        3 to 4 lge. cucumbers, sliced
        2 lge. tomatoes, cubed
        1 pkg. Swiss cheese, diced
        1 lge. onion, chopped
        2 No. 303 cans mixed carrots and peas, drained
        ¾ bottle Italian dressing
        ⅔ c. milk
        ⅔ c. sugar
        1 pt. mayonnaise
        Garlic salt to taste
        1 to 2 c. cooked shrimp or ham, diced (opt.)

Combine cucumbers, tomatoes, cheese, onion, carrots and peas. Combine Italian dressing and milk; add sugar. Cook and stir over low heat until sugar is dissolved. Cool. Add mayonnaise and garlic salt; blend thoroughly. Add to vegetable mixture. Add shrimp or ham if desired. Yield: 8 servings.

Mrs. Ella Jo Adams, Allen, Tex.

Corn Relish Salad

DRESSING:

        ⅔ c. salad oil
        2 ½ tbsp. vinegar
        2 ½ tsp. salt
        ½ tsp. pepper
        1 ¼ tsp. dry mustard

Combine all ingredients.

        1 No. 2 can whole kernel corn
        ½ green pepper, chopped
        2 ½ tsp. pimento, diced
        5 small stalks celery, diced
        1 medium onion, chopped

Mix vegetables; add dressing. Refrigerate for 24 hours. Yield: 8-10 servings.

Jessie Chambers, Home Economics Teacher, Cheyenne, Wyo.

Corn Salad

    1 No. 2 can whole kernel corn, drained
    1 pimento, chopped
    1 small onion, chopped
    1 small green pepper, chopped
    1 small cucumber, chopped
    ½ c. French dressing

Combine all ingredients. Serve on lettuce cups. If desired, mayonnaise may be substituted for French dressing and the salad used for stuffing tomatoes. Yield: 4 servings.

Mrs. Judy Brumley, Kyle, Tex.

 ### Scrumptious Corn Salad

    2 12-oz. cans whole kernel corn, drained
    ¾ c. diced unpared cucumber
    ¼ c. diced onion
    2 sm. tomatoes, chopped
    ¼ c. sour cream
    2 tbsp. mayonnaise
    1 tbsp. vinegar
    ½ tsp. salt
    ¼ tsp. dry mustard
    ¼ tsp. celery seed

Combine corn, cucumber, onion and tomatoes in salad bowl. Blend sour cream with mayonnaise; add remaining ingredients. Add sour cream mixture to corn mixture; toss gently to coat vegetables. Chill thoroughly. Spoon into lettuce cups. Yield: 6-8 servings.

Mrs. Ollie Giltner, Ludlow, Ky.

 ### Dandelion Salad (Pennsylvania Dutch)

    Young, tender dandelion greens
    4 thick slices bacon, cubed
    ½ c. salad dressing
    1 egg
    1 tsp. salt
    1 tbsp. flour
    2 tbsp. sugar
    4 tbsp. vinegar
    1 c. water
    2 hard-cooked eggs, sliced

(Continued on next page)

Wash dandelion greens; roll in cloth and pat dry. Put into a salad bowl. Fry bacon; pour over dandelion greens. Blend salad dressing, egg, salt, flour, sugar, vinegar and water. Pour into skillet in which bacon was fried and cook until mixture boils and is quite thick. Pour hot mixture over greens; stir well. Garnish with egg slices. Serve immediately. Yield: 6 servings.

Mrs. Doris G. Howerten, Home Economics Teacher, Kutztown, Pa.

Bouquet Salad

> 1 head crisp lettuce
> 2 to 3 tomatoes, sliced
> 3 hard-cooked eggs, sliced
> 1 small cucumber, sliced
> ½ green pepper, sliced
> 6 to 8 red radishes, sliced
> 1 carrot, cut in slivers
> 3 stalks celery, cut in slivers
> 1 to 2 slices Swiss cheese, cut in slivers
> 5 strips bacon, fried and crumbled
> ½ c. olives, chopped
> Garlic clove
> French dressing
> Salt and pepper to taste

Rub wooden salad bowl with garlic clove. Toss all ingredients together. French dressing may be served separately. Yield: 8 servings.

Dianne J. MacPherson, New Holland, Pa., Favorite Recipes Food Fair

Caesar Salad

> 3 or 4 cloves of garlic, diced
> 1 c. olive oil
> 2 c. crisp croutons
> 3 qts. salad greens
> ½ c. unseasoned salad oil
> ½ c. Parmesan cheese, grated
> ¼ c. bleu cheese
> 1 tbsp. Worcestershire sauce
> ½ tsp. dry mustard
> Salt and pepper to taste
> 2 hard cooked eggs, chopped
> ½ c. fresh lemon juice

Combine garlic and olive oil; let stand at room temperature for several hours. Toast croutons until brown at 250 degrees. Combine salad greens, salad oil,

(Continued on next page)

Parmesan and bleu cheese. Add Worcestershire sauce, dry mustard, salt, and pepper. Scatter eggs over greens. Pour in fresh lemon juice. Toss very thoroughly. Dip croutons into garlic-oil mixture. Add to salad. Serve while croutons are crunchy. Yield: 6-8 servings.

Mrs. Mildred H. Beck, Home Economics Teacher, Fairhope, Ala.

 ## Caesar Salad

2 cloves garlic, sliced
1 ½ oz. olive oil
⅔ lb. romaine lettuce, chilled and cut in 1-inch strips
1 ½ oz. lemon juice
1 tbsp. mashed anchovies
2 eggs
½ tsp. dry mustard
¼ tsp. white pepper
1 tbsp. Worcestershire sauce
6 drops Tabasco sauce
Parmesan cheese
1 c. bacon-flavored croutons
Pimento strips (opt.)

Combine 1 garlic clove and olive oil; let stand overnight. Rub wooden salad bowl with remaining garlic clove; add lettuce. Combine lemon juice and anchovies; blend well. Add garlic-oil mixture; blend. Add eggs; blend. Pour over lettuce; toss until all leaves are covered. Add mustard, pepper, Worcestershire and Tabasco sauce; toss after each addition. Sprinkle with Parmesan cheese; toss. Add croutons and pimento; toss. Serve immediately in wooden salad bowls. Yield: 2 servings.

Marjorie B. Brice, Home Economics Teacher, Ottawa Lake, Mich.

Caesar Salad

1 clove garlic, mashed
½ c. salad oil
1 head lettuce or ½ head lettuce and 1 bunch curly endive
1 2-oz. can anchovy fillets (opt.)
3 to 4 tomatoes, diced
1 c. croutons
¼ c. lemon juice
1 beaten egg
½ c. Parmesan cheese, grated
¼ c. bleu cheese, finely crumbled
1 tsp. Worcestershire sauce
½ tsp. pepper
½ tsp. salt

(Continued on next page)

Combine garlic and salad oil; let stand. Combine lettuce, tomatoes, croutons and anchovies, if desired. Strain oil-garlic mixture. Pour over vegetables. Combine remaining ingredients; beat well. Pour over salad; toss lightly. Garnish with sliced tomatoes. Yield: 6 servings.

Shirley Ann Murray, Winchester, Va.

 ### Lettuce Salad With Hot Dressing

> 1 sm. head lettuce, shredded
> 2 to 3 tbsp. chopped onion
> 4 slices bacon
> 1 tbsp. (heaping) flour
> ¼ c. vinegar
> 2 tbsp. sugar
> 1 tsp. mustard
> 1 egg, beaten
> Salt and pepper to taste

Combine lettuce and onion. Fry bacon until done; remove from pan. Blend flour into bacon grease; add crumbled bacon. Add enough warm water to vinegar to make 1 cup; stir in sugar and mustard. Slowly add mixture to egg, being careful not to cook egg. Add to bacon mixture and cook, stirring constantly, until thickened. Season lettuce and cover with hot dressing.

Mrs. Dorothy A. Stocking, Indianapolis, Ind.

Original Caesar Salad

> 6 cloves of garlic, quartered lengthwise
> 1 c. olive or salad oil
> Bread slices
> Grated Parmesan cheese
> 3 med. heads romaine lettuce
> 2 to 3 tbsp. wine vinegar
> Juice of 1 lemon
> 1 or 2 eggs
> Salt
> Dash of Worcestershire sauce
> Pepper

Place garlic in olive oil; let stand for 1 to several days. Cut enough bread, to make 1 cup, into 5 strips lengthwise; cut each strip crosswise 5 times to make squares. Spread on cookie sheet. Pour a small amount of garlic-olive oil over bread. Bake at 225 degrees for 2 hours. Sprinkle with cheese. Place in jar in refrigerator. Place lettuce in chilled salad bowl, just before serving. Sprinkle

(Continued on next page)

with remaining garlic-olive oil; sprinkle with vinegar. Add lemon juice. Cook eggs for 1 minute. Break into salad; season with salt and Worcestershire sauce. Sprinkle with pepper and cheese. Toss 6 or 7 times or until dressing is well combined and every leaf is coated. Add croutons; toss 1 or 2 times. Serve on chilled dinner plates. Garnish with rolled anchovies, if desired. Yield: 6 servings.

Mrs. Claudia Ashley McLemore, Garland, N. C.

Pennsylvania Dutch Cold Lettuce

¼ c. sugar
2 tbsp. mayonnaise
1 ½ tbsp. cream or evaporated milk
¼ c. vinegar (scant)
Salt to taste
1 medium size head of lettuce, torn in small pieces

Mix sugar and mayonnaise; blend in cream or evaporated milk. Add vinegar and salt. Immediately before serving, pour the dressing over lettuce. Toss so that every piece of lettuce is well-coated. Yield: 6 servings.

Jane E. Spangler, Home Economics Teacher, Shippensburg, Pa.

Poker Club Salad

1 head lettuce, shredded
1 c. shredded spinach
1 c. shredded endive
2 tomatoes, chopped
½ c. crumbled bleu cheese
1 green pepper, minced

Combine all ingredients; toss lightly.

DRESSING:

1 tbsp. Worcestershire sauce
1 tbsp. steak sauce
⅓ tsp. curry powder
⅓ tsp. celery salt
¼ clove of garlic, crushed
¼ tsp. dry mustard
⅓ tsp. pepper
1 pt. French dressing

Combine all ingredients; serve with salad.

Beth B. Beach, Miami, Fla.

Spring Salad Bowl

1 bunch leaf lettuce, torn in bite-size pieces
½ bunch watercress
1 ½ c. tiny spinach leaves
24 carrot curls
4 green onions with tops, chopped
12 ripe olives, pitted
12 almonds, blanched and toasted
Italian dressing

Combine greens, carrot curls and and onions. Stuff olives with almonds. Add to greens. Toss with Italian dressing. Yield: 6 servings.

Mrs. Verna Eberhart, Cavalier, N. D.

Stuffed Chilled Lettuce

1 3-oz. pkg. cream cheese
2 tbsp. Roquefort cheese
2 tbsp. grated carrots
1 tbsp. minced green pepper
2 tbsp. diced tomatoes
⅛ tsp. pepper
⅛ tsp. salt
1 tsp. minced onion
1 head iceberg lettuce, cored

Combine all ingredients except lettuce; mix well. Stuff lettuce; wrap in cloth. Chill until firm; slice crosswise.

Mrs. Mildred W. Schubert, Williamstown, N. J.

Okra Salad

1 can cut okra
1 No. 1 can tomatoes or 2 tomatoes, sliced
1 tsp. lemon juice
½ tsp. salt
1 tsp. chopped parsley
½ tsp. chili powder
¼ tsp. white pepper
Swiss chard
1 hard-boiled egg, grated

Mix okra and tomatoes in salad bowl with lemon juice, salt, parsley, chili powder and pepper. Serve on Swiss chard and garnish with hard-boiled egg.

Kathryn S. Johnson, St. Petersburg, Fla., Favorite Recipes Food Fair

Okra Salad With Chive Dressing

1 lb. whole young okra
1 c. salad oil
⅓ c. lemon juice
1 tbsp. chopped chives
½ tsp. salt
⅛ tsp. pepper
Lettuce
Tomatoes, thinly sliced

Cook okra until it is tender but still retains shape and texture. Drain thoroughly and chill. Combine next 5 ingredients. Serve okra on lettuce with dressing and tomatoes as garnish.

Mrs. Pat C. Holland, Huntsville, Ala.

Italian Onion Salad

Italian onions
Oil-vinegar dressing
Anchovies
Salt and pepper to taste

Cut Italian onions in very thin slices; soak in oil-vinegar dressing 30 minutes. Toss with anchovies and additional dressing. Add salt and pepper to taste. Serve cold.

Mrs. H. W. Brooker, Maitland, Fla.

 ### Mock Crab Salad

3 c. raw parsnips, shredded
1 ½ c. celery, finely cut
1 pimento, finely cut
½ c. olives
1 tsp. horseradish
½ tsp. salt
¼ tsp. pepper
½ c. mayonnaise
Lettuce

Combine all ingredients; toss. Serve on lettuce. Yield: 6 servings.

Mrs. Mari Hurley, Home Economics Teacher, El Centro, Cal.

Surprise Salad Bowl

2 c. coarsely ground parsnips
1 c. thinly sliced celery
1 tsp. grated onion
2 tbsp. diced sweet pickle
1 hard-cooked egg, coarsely chopped
Salt and pepper
½ c. mayonnaise or salad dressing

Place parsnips in bowl with celery, onion, pickle and egg. Sprinkle with salt and pepper. Mix with mayonnaise. May be served on lettuce if desired. Yield: 8 servings.

Leontine Giraud, Madison, S. D.

 ### Winter Salad Bowl

½ c. raw parsnip, grated
2 tbsp. sweet onion, chopped
¼ c. celery, chopped
4 stuffed olives, chopped
¼ tsp. salt
French dressing
⅓ med. head lettuce, torn in bite-size pieces
2 tbsp. mayonnaise

Marinate parsnip, onion, celery, olives and salt in French dressing for 1 to 2 hours. Just before serving, add lettuce. Toss lightly with mayonnaise. Yield: 2-3 servings.

Mrs. Bettie Lou Snapp, Home Economics Teacher, Albuquerque, N. M.

English Pea Salad

1 can English peas, drained
1 sm. onion or several green onions, chopped
1 dill pickle, chopped
½ c. diced cheddar cheese
½ c. chopped celery (opt.)
Salt and pepper to taste
½ c. mayonnaise or salad dressing
Bell pepper (opt.)
Pimento (opt.)
Olives (opt.)
Paprika

(Continued on next page)

Mix all ingredients together. Top with sprinkling of paprika. Chill 15 to 30 minutes or longer. Yield: 4-6 servings.

Mrs. John Whitt, Alice, Tex.

Green Peas And Zucchini Salad

1 lb. small zucchini, thinly sliced
2 c. boiling salted water
1 10-oz. pkg. frozen green peas and pearl onions
1 envelope Italian salad dressing mix
2 tbsp. wine or cider vinegar
Crisp salad greens

Cook zucchini in boiling water for 1 minute. Drain. Cook peas and onions as directed on package. Prepare salad dressing mix as directed on envelope. Combine vegetables with ½ cup salad dressing and wine vinegar. Cover and chill at least 4 hours. Gently stir once or twice. To serve, line a chilled bowl with salad greens. Spoon in marinated vegetables. Serve with remaining salad dressing. Yield: 7-8 servings.

Photograph for this recipe below.

113

English Pea Salad

1 No. 2 can drained peas
1 c. finely chopped celery
1 c. chopped green onions
2 hard-boiled eggs
½ c. chopped pickles
Lettuce
Mayonnaise

Mix together first 5 ingredients; serve on lettuce with mayonnaise.

Mrs. Helen Knowles, Reidsville, N. C.

 ### English Pea And Cheese Salad

1 No. 2 can English peas, drained
1 medium tomato, diced
1 c. mild cheddar cheese, cubed
1 tbsp. pimentos, chopped
4 tbsp. salad dressing or mayonnaise
Dash of seasoned salt
6 lettuce leaves
Dash paprika

Combine English peas, tomato, cheese, pimentos, salad dressing or mayonnaise and seasoned salt. Toss just enough to mix lightly. Serve on lettuce leaf; garnish with paprika. Yield: 6 servings.

Mrs. Winnie McQueen, Home Economics Teacher, Santa Anna, Tex.

Pea Salad

1 medium can peas, drained
3 sweet pickles, diced
½ small onion, diced
1 hard cooked egg, diced (opt.)
1 raw egg
1 ½ tsp. sugar
1 ½ tsp. pickle vinegar
2 tbsp. half and half cream
Dash of salt
1 tbsp. peanut butter

Combine raw egg, sugar, vinegar, cream and salt. Cook over low heat until thickened, stirring constantly. Add peanut butter; mix. Pour cooked mixture over peas, pickles, onion and hard-cooked egg. Toss lightly. Yield: 6 servings.

Nevaleen Joy Selmat, Home Economics Teacher, Wakita, Okla.

German Sour Cream Potato Salad

2 strips bacon
3 green onions, chopped
1 c. chopped celery
1 tsp. flour
½ tsp. dry mustard
1 ¼ tsp. salt
⅓ c. California sauterne
1 tbsp. white wine vinegar
2 c. diced boiled potatoes
6 hard-cooked eggs, diced
2 tbsp. chopped parsley
2 tbsp. chopped pimento
1 c. grated cheddar cheese

Cook bacon until crisp. Remove bacon; crumble and set aside. Cook onions and celery in bacon fat until soft but not browned; stir in flour, mustard, salt and wine. Cook, stirring constantly until mixture boils. Blend in wine vinegar. Pour over potatoes and eggs; add bacon, parsley and pimento. Mix lightly. Pour into shallow baking dish; top with cheese. Bake at 375 degrees for 15-20 minutes until salad is heated and cheese is melted. Yield: 4-6 servings.

Gladys B. Harrison, San Pablo, Cal., Favorite Recipes Food Fair

Hot Potato Salad

3 c. sliced potatoes
Salt
4 to 6 slices bacon
¼ c. chopped celery
¼ c. chopped onion
1 tbsp. flour
¾ tsp. mustard
⅛ tsp. pepper
1 tbsp. sugar
⅓ c. vinegar
1 egg, beaten
2 hard-cooked eggs, sliced
⅓ c. salad dressing

Cook potatoes in boiling salted water until tender, but not done. Drain; keep hot. Cook bacon in frying pan until crisp, reserving 2 tablespoonfuls fat. Remove from pan; break into pieces. Cook celery and onion in reserved bacon fat until tender. Blend in flour, mustard, ½ teaspoonful salt, pepper and sugar. Stir in 1/3 cup water and vinegar. Add beaten egg. Cook, stirring for 2 minutes. Pour over hot potatoes mixed with hard-cooked eggs and bacon. Mix carefully with salad dressing. Yield: 4 servings.

Edna Alsup, Traverse City, Mich.

Olive-Potato Salad

6 medium potatoes
2 hard-cooked eggs, chopped
1 c. stuffed olives, quartered
¼ c. celery, diced
2 tbsp. onion, finely diced
⅓ c. thick cream
¼ c. vinegar
Salt

Boil potatoes until tender; drain and cool. Peel and cube. Add olives, eggs, celery and onion. Mix cream and vinegar; scald. Add to potato mixture; mix well. Salt to taste. Yield: 8 servings.

Ida Vivian Hrncir, Home Economics Teacher, Hallettsville, Tex.

 ### Kraut Salad

1 lge. can sauerkraut
2 med. onions, chopped
1 green pepper, chopped
1 c. chopped celery
1 sm. can pimentos, chopped
Salt to taste
½ c. sugar
½ c. white vinegar

Rinse sauerkraut; drain. Add all ingredients except sugar and vinegar. Boil sugar and vinegar; pour over mixture. Chill. Yield: 8 servings.

Ruby Dowdy, Brownfield, Tex.

Jane's Spinach Salad

1 lb. fresh spinach
4 hard-cooked eggs, chopped
8 sl. bacon, fried and crumbled
¼ c. green onions, chopped
½ c. Italian salad dressing
Salt to taste

Remove large veins from spinach; tear leaves into small pieces. Combine spinach, eggs and bacon. Add onions; toss lightly. Just before serving add dressing and salt. Yield: 6 servings.

Mrs. Jane Davis, Home Economics Teacher, Corpus Christi, Tex.

Quick Tomato Slaw

¼ c. salad dressing
1 tbsp. prepared mustard
2 c. cabbage, coarsely shredded
1 c. tomatoes, diced
¼ c. green pepper, chopped
¼ c. cucumber, sliced
1 tsp. salt

Combine salad dressing and mustard. Add remaining ingredients. Chill for 30 minutes. Yield: 6 servings.

Patsy K. Myers, Home Economics Teacher, Hopkinsville, Ky.

 ### Stuffed Tomato Salad

6 firm tomatoes
Heart of 1 head lettuce, chopped
1 stalk celery, chopped
1 small bottle stuffed olives, chopped
1 green pepper, chopped
¼ c. mayonnaise
French dressing

Cut off stem ends of tomatoes. Scoop out the inside of the tomatoes. Combine tomato pulp, lettuce, celery, olives and green pepper. Add mayonnaise. Put mixture into tomato cups. Pour French dressing over each tomato cup. Yield: 6 servings.

Mrs. Lois Farrington, Home Economics Teacher, Mesick, Mich.

 ### Summertime Delight

2 lge. tomatoes
1 medium onion, chopped
1 medium banana pepper, chopped
½ tsp. salt
1 tsp. sugar
1 tbsp. vinegar

Combine tomatoes, onion, and banana pepper. Add salt, sugar and vinegar. Mix. Yield: 4 to 6 servings.

Mrs. Ray Mofield, Home Economics Teacher, Benton, Ky.

Tomato And Onion Salad

1 garlic clove, minced
1 tsp. salt
1 tsp. sugar
¼ tsp. pepper
2 tsp. prepared mustard
¼ c. olive or salad oil
2 tbsp. tarragon vinegar
6 firm tomatoes, sliced
1 onion, thinly sliced
Chopped parsley

Combine garlic and salt; mash with a spoon. Stir in sugar, pepper, mustard, oil and vinegar. Pour over tomato and onion slices. Sprinkle with parsley. Chill. Serve without dressing. Yield: 6 to 8 servings.

Mrs. Pat Ashbrook, Home Economics Teacher, LaGrange, Ky.

Tomato And Pepper Surprise Salad

2 lge. tomatoes, diced
1 lge. bell pepper, diced
1 medium onion, diced
¼ lge. box soda crackers, crumbled
Salt and pepper to taste
2 tbsp. (heaping) mayonnaise

Combine all ingredients. Toss lightly. Yield: 6 servings.

Anne G. Rollins, Home Economics Teacher, Coward, S. C

Zucchini And Onion Salad

2 lb. zucchini, cut into thin slices
2 lge. sweet onions, thinly sliced
⅓ c. chili sauce
⅓ c. olive oil
¼ c. wine vinegar
½ tsp. garlic salt
⅛ tsp. pepper

Cover zucchini with boiling water; bring to a boil over moderate heat. Drain; place in a large shallow pan. Add onions. Combine remaining ingredients; pour over vegetables. Chill for several hours. Drain; arrange on lettuce. Yield: 8 servings.

Mrs. LeRoy Erickson, Officers' Wives' Club, RAF Welford, Newbury, England

Congealed Vegetable Salads

Jellied Artichoke Salad

1 can consomme
1 envelope unflavored gelatin
⅓ c. water
1 tsp. lemon juice
⅛ tsp. salt
1 box frozen artichoke hearts, cooked
½ pt. sour cream

Heat consomme. Soak gelatin in water; add consomme, lemon juice and salt. Quarter artichoke hearts; arrange around sides of eight small cup salad molds. Fill three-fourths full with gelatin mixture. Chill until almost set. Fill each mold with sour cream. Chill until firm. Invert on lettuce leaf and top with dab of mayonnaise, if desired. Yield: 8 servings.

Mrs. Frank M. Kyes, Hon. Pres. Dental Naval Officers' Wives' Club, Washington, D. C.

Asparagus Or Broccoli Mold

1 tbsp. unflavored gelatin
1 can asparagus or 1 pkg. frozen broccoli, cooked
¼ c. cold water
½ c. whipped cream
½ c. mayonnaise
1 tsp. salt
2 to 4 tbsp. lemon juice
1 c. almonds

Dissolve gelatin in cold water; let stand until partially set. Drain hot liquid from vegetables and add enough water to make 1 cup liquid. Combine liquid and gelatin mixture. Fold in whipped cream, mayonnaise, salt and lemon juice. Add vegetables and almonds. Congeal. Serve with mayonnaise whipped with a small amount of lemon juice. Yield: 8-10 servings.

Mrs. J. W. Gant, Home Economics Teacher, Sparta, Tenn.

Congealed Asparagus Salad

1 box lime gelatin
1 c. boiling water
1 c. mayonnaise
½ c. milk
¼ tsp. salt
½ c. cheese, grated
1 tbsp. onion, grated

(Continued on next page)

1 tbsp. vinegar
Dash of red pepper or a few drops Tabasco sauce
1 No. 300 can green cut asparagus, drained

Dissolve gelatin in boiling water. Cool until syrupy. Mix mayonnaise, milk, salt, cheese, onion, vinegar and pepper. Fold into thickened gelatin. Add asparagus. Turn into oiled mold. Congeal. Yield: 6 servings.

Elizabeth Heard, Home Economics Teacher, Jackson, Miss.

Molded Kidney Bean Salad

2 tbsp. lemon juice
2 tbsp. water
1 envelope unflavored gelatin
1 1-lb. can kidney beans, drained
½ c. chopped celery
½ c. sweet pickle relish
2 hard-cooked eggs, chopped
½ c. mayonnaise
1 tbsp. grated onion
¼ tsp. salt
1 c. evaporated milk

Place lemon juice and water in custard cup. Sprinkle gelatin over top; let stand for 5 minutes to soften. Place custard cup in small saucepan with small amount of water. Place over low heat; heat until gelatin is dissolved. Mix beans with remaining ingredients except milk. Stir in gelatin; blend in evaporated milk. Ladle into 5-cup oiled ring mold. Chill until firm. Yield: 6-8 servings.

Photograph for this recipe on page 119.

Congealed Beet Salad

1 No. 2 can shoestring beets
1 pkg. lemon gelatin
1 ½ tbsp. vinegar
1 tsp. salt
1 ½ tbsp. grated onion
¼ c. sliced stuffed olives
2 tbsp. horseradish
1 ¼ c. chopped celery
½ c. nuts (opt.)

Drain beets, reserving juice; add enough water to make 1½ cups juice. Heat water-beet juice mixture to boiling; add gelatin. Stir until clear. Add vinegar and salt. Chill until partially set. Stir in remaining ingredients. Pour into mold. Chill until firm. Yield: 6-8 servings.

May Lohmann, Miami, Okla.

Red Beet Salad

1 pkg. lemon gelatin
1 ¼ c. hot water
¾ c. beet juice
2 tbsp. vinegar
½ tsp. salt
1 ½ c. diced beets
½ c. diced celery
1 tsp. horseradish
1 tsp. Worcestershire sauce
1 tbsp. grated onion
4 drops of Tabasco sauce

Dissolve gelatin in water; cool and add remaining ingredients. Chill until firm. Yield: 8 servings.

Mrs. Carolyn Palmer, Archbold, Ohio, Favorite Recipes Food Fair

Broccoli Salad Mold

3 pkg. frozen broccoli
1 envelope unflavored gelatin
1 can beef consomme
6 hard-cooked eggs, chopped
¾ c. mayonnaise
2 tbsp. Worcestershire sauce
¼ tsp. salt
Dash of Tabasco sauce

Cook broccoli for 3 to 5 minutes. Soften gelatin in ¼ cup cold consomme. Heat remaining consomme to a boil; add gelatin and seasonings. Cool; add remaining ingredients. Grease mold with mayonnaise; fill with salad mixture. Chill. Yield: 8-10 servings.

Mrs. Howard Thomason, Cairo, Ga.

Gelatin Slaw

1 pkg. orange or lime gelatin
1 c. shredded cabbage
1 med. onion, finely chopped
2 carrots, shredded
8 to 10 radishes, finely sliced
⅓ cucumber, finely sliced
⅛ tsp. salt
⅛ tsp. garlic salt
⅛ tsp. celery salt or seed
Dash of pepper

(Continued on next page)

Mix gelatin according to package directions; refrigerate. Mix all vegetables; add seasonings. Stir vegetable mixture into gelatin; chill until firm. Yield: 8 servings.

Mrs. Lillian J. Thompson, Moody AFB, Ga.

Gelatin-Vegetable Salad

6 tbsp. sugar
1 tsp. salt
2 pkg. lemon gelatin
3 ¼ c. hot water
4 tbsp. vinegar
2 c. shredded cabbage
½ c. finely chopped celery
½ c. finely chopped green pepper
4 tbsp. chopped sweet pickle

Add sugar and salt to gelatin. Dissolve gelatin in hot water; stir in vinegar. When partially set, add vegetables. Yield: 12 servings.

Mrs. Irena Fossell, Holstein, Iowa

Slaw

8 c. shredded cabbage
2 med. carrots, shredded
1 green pepper, sliced
½ c. chopped onion
Diced celery
1 ¼ c. cold water
1 envelope unflavored gelatin
⅔ c. sugar
⅔ c. vinegar
⅔ c. oil
1 ½ tsp. salt
¼ tsp. pepper
2 tsp. celery seed

Mix cabbage with remaining vegetables. Add 1 cup cold water. Refrigerate for 4 to 5 hours. Soften gelatin in remaining cold water. Mix sugar with vinegar, oil, salt, pepper and celery seed. Bring to a boil. Add gelatin; mix. Chill until thickened. Beat well; add oil, beating well. Drain vegetables well on paper towel. Pour gelatin mixture over vegetables; mix lightly until vegetables are coated.

Mrs. Dorothy George, Rensselaer, Ind., Favorite Recipes Food Fair

Molded Carrot Salad

1 pkg. lime gelatin
2 tbsp. lemon juice
1 ½ c. carrot, grated
Salad greens
Salad dressing

Dissolve gelatin according to package directions. Add lemon juice; blend. Chill until partially set. Add carrot. Let stand until partially set. Pour into a ring mold; chill until firm. Garnish with salad greens. Serve with desired salad dressing. Yield: 8-10 servings.

Mrs. Joyce Miller, Home Economics Teacher, Berlin, Ohio

 ### One Cup Celery-Nut Salad

1 pkg. lime gelatin
1 c. hot water
1 c. cold water
1 c. celery, diced
1 c. pecan halves

Dissolve gelatin in hot water; add cold water. Refrigerate until thickened. Fold in celery and pecans. Let set for several hours or overnight. Yield: 4-6 servings.

Mrs. Janet Killian, Home Economics Teacher, Thebes, Ill.

 ### Jellied Cucumber Ring With Cottage Cheese

2 pkg. lemon gelatin
1 ½ c. boiling water
¼ c. vinegar
½ tsp. salt
2 tbsp. grated onion
2 ½ c. grated cucumber
4 c. cottage cheese
1 ½ tsp. chopped chives

Dissolve gelatin in boiling water; add vinegar and salt. Cool; add onion and cucumber. Pour into oiled ring mold; chill until firm. Fill center with cottage cheese seasoned with chopped chives. Garnish with sliced cucumbers and lettuce. Yield: 10-12 servings.

Mrs. H. A. Hoover, Roanoke, Va.

Creme D'Cucumber Salad

2 c. boiling water
1 lge. pkg. lime gelatin
1 tbsp. vinegar
1 c. mayonnaise
1 c. grated cucumbers
1 tbsp. grated onion
1 tbsp. horseradish

Pour boiling water over gelatin. Add vinegar and a small portion of mayonnaise. Add remaining ingredients. Chill in mold. If desired, cooled gelatin may be whipped before remaining ingredients are added.

Mrs. Renwick W. Speer, DeKalb, Ill.

 ### Cucumber Salad

1 pkg. lime gelatin
1 c. boiling water
1 c. cold water
1 tsp. salt
2 tbsp. vinegar
1 c. cucumber, grated
1 tsp. onion, diced

Dissolve gelatin in boiling water. Add cold water, salt and vinegar. Stir until salt is dissolved. Chill until partially thickened. Add cucumber and onion; mix well. Chill until firm. Yield: 8 servings.

Carolyn Gilmer, Home Economics Teacher, Kinnear, Wyo.

 ### Green Onion Salad

1 pkg. lemon gelatin
1 c. hot water
1 c. cottage cheese
1 c. chopped celery
4 sm. whole green onions, chopped
⅔ c. salad dressing

Dissolve gelatin in hot water; set aside to cool. Combine all ingredients; pour in 9 x 9-inch dish. Chill until firm. Cut in squares; serve on lettuce leaves. Yield: 6 servings.

Ozada Graham, Dodson, Tex., Favorite Recipes Food Fair

Jellied Potato Salad

4 to 5 med. potatoes, cooked and diced
6 tbsp. vinegar
1 sm. onion, grated
2 tbsp. salad oil
1 ¾ tsp. salt
Dash of pepper
1 pkg. lemon gelatin
1 ¼ c. hot water
½ med. cucumber, thinly sliced
5 to 6 radishes, sliced
5 tbsp. mayonnaise
2 stalks celery, sliced
¼ med. green pepper, sliced
2 hard-cooked eggs, diced

Combine potatoes, 3 tablespoons vinegar, onion, oil, salt and pepper; mix gently and set aside for 30 minutes. Dissolve gelatin in water; add remaining vinegar and pour 2/3 cup mixture in ring mold. Decorate with cucumber and radish slices; chill until firm. Chill remaining gelatin until slightly thick; beat well. Add mayonnaise, remaining vegetables, potatoes and eggs. Spoon potato-vegetable mixture over decorated gelatin; chill until firm. Yield: 6 servings.

Mrs. Fred T. Grossardt, Pratt, Kan.

 ### Cassel's Spinach Salad

1 pkg. lemon gelatin
1 c. hot water
1 ½ tbsp. vinegar
½ c. mayonnaise
½ tsp. salt
Dash of pepper
1 c. raw spinach, cooked
¾ c. small curd cottage cheese
⅓ c. diced celery
1 tsp. chopped onion

Dissolve gelatin in hot water; add vinegar, mayonnaise, salt and pepper. Blend with beater. Chill until semi-firm; whip until fluffy. Fold in spinach, cottage cheese, celery and onion. Pour into mold. Refrigerate until set. Yield: 8 servings.

Carole McCall, Pres. Officers' Wives' Club, Seattle, Wash.

Barbecue Tomato Aspic

1 pkg. lemon gelatin
1 ¼ c. hot water
1 8-oz. can tomato sauce
1 tsp. onion juice or ½ tsp. Worcestershire sauce (opt.)
1 ½ tbsp. white vinegar
½ tsp. salt
Dash of pepper
½ c. sharp cheddar cheese, cut in ¼-inch cubes

Dissolve gelatin in hot water. Add all remaining ingredients except cheese. Chill until partially thickened. Place 6 or 8 cheese cubes in mold. Pour gelatin mixture over them. Add more cheese cubes and gelatin. Chill until firm. Yield: 8 servings.

Mrs. Eleanor L. Miller, Home Economics Teacher, Mason, W. Va.

Easy Tomato Aspic

2 pkgs. lemon gelatin
2 c. tomato juice
2 tbsp. vinegar
½ tsp. salt
½ tsp. seasoned salt

Prepare gelatin according to package directions; add remaining ingredients. Chill until firm. Yield: 8 servings.

Mrs. Florence D. Sorrell, Home Economics Teacher, Benson, N. C.

 ## Jellied Tomato Salad

1 1-lb. can tomatoes
1 pkg. lemon gelatin
½ tsp. salt
½ tsp. dried onion flakes
½ tsp. dried parsley
Salad greens
Mayonnaise

Bring tomatoes to a boil; break larger pieces while heating. Add gelatin and seasonings, stirring constantly. Pour into large mold or six individual molds. Chill until firm; unmold. Serve on salad greens; garnish with mayonnaise. Yield: 6 servings.

Mrs. Eleanor J. Hayes, Alton, N. H., Favorite Recipes Food Fair

Jellied Tomato-Vegetable Salad

1 envelope lemon gelatin
½ c. boiling water
1 No. 303 can stewed tomatoes
1 sm. onion, chopped
½ c. diced green pepper
2 tbsp. vinegar
½ tsp. salt

Dissolve gelatin in boiling water; add tomatoes. Chill until partially thickened. Fold in remaining ingredients; pour into 8 x 8 x 2-inch pan. Chill until firm. Yield: 6 servings.

Nancy Jo Kent, Dodge City, Kan.

Tomato Aspic Crown

2 envelopes unflavored gelatin
3 ¼ c. tomato juice
½ tsp. salt
1 tsp. sugar
1 tsp. Worcestershire sauce
¼ tsp. Tabasco sauce
¼ c. lemon or lime juice

Sprinkle gelatin over 1 cup tomato juice in a 2-quart saucepan to soften. Place over moderate heat for 3 minutes or until gelatin is dissolved, stirring constantly. Remove from heat; stir in remaining ingredients. Pour into 1-quart ring mold; chill until firm. Unmold; fill center with coleslaw. Yield: 6 servings.

Annette Ray, Falls Church, Va.

 ## Asheville Salad

1 tbsp. unflavored gelatin
½ c. water
1 can tomato soup, heated
1 small pkg. cream cheese
1 c. celery, chopped
1 lge. green pepper, chopped
½ c. mayonnaise

Dissolve gelatin in water; pour into hot soup. Mash cheese into soup; dissolve. Add celery, green pepper, and mayonnaise. Chill until firm. Yield: 6 servings.

Jean Palmer, Home Economics Teacher, Channelview, Tex.

Beet-Cabbage Souffle

1 pkg. lemon gelatin
1 ¼ c. hot water
¼ c. beet juice
1 tbsp. vinegar
½ c. mayonnaise
¼ tsp. salt
Dash of pepper
1 c. beets, drained and diced
1 c. cabbage, shredded
1 tbsp. onion, finely chopped

Dissolve gelatin in hot water. Add beet juice, vinegar, mayonnaise, salt and pepper. Blend well with rotary beater. Pour into refrigerator freezing tray. Quick chill in freezing unit for 15 to 20 minutes or until firm about 1 inch from edge but soft in center. Whip with rotary beater until fluffy. Fold in beets, cabbage and onion. Chill for 30 to 60 minutes. Yield: 4-6 servings.

Jean Penrose, Home Economics Teacher, Loveland, Colo.

Cornflower Salad

2 No. 2 cans cream corn
1 tsp. onion, grated
1 tsp. salt
Pepper to taste
2 tbsp. sugar
3 envelopes unflavored gelatin
½ c. water
6 cooked carrots
6 medium green peppers, hollowed

Blend corn, onion, salt, pepper and sugar. Soften gelatin in water; dissolve over hot water. Add to corn mixture. Put a piece of carrot in each hollowed out pepper and fill with corn mixture. Set peppers in muffin pan to steady them while chilling. Slice and serve on salad greens with dressing.

Opal Pruitt, Buda, Ill.

Celery-Pepper Congealed Salad

   1 pkg. lemon gelatin
   1 c. hot water
   1 c. mayonnaise
   1 c. cottage cheese
   Pinch of salt
   1 c. chopped celery
   2 tbsp. finely chopped onion
   ¼ c. chopped green pepper
   Green food coloring (opt.)
   Chopped pimento (opt.)

Dissolve gelatin in hot water. Let cool. Stir in mayonnaise, cottage cheese and salt. Add remaining ingredients. Let set for several hours. Yield: 6-8 servings.

Virginia L. Langston, Baton Rouge, La.

 ### Congealed Onion Salad

   1 c. hot water
   1 pkg. lemon-lime gelatin
   1 c. ground celery
   1 c. ground onions
   1 c. sieved cottage cheese
   1 c. mayonnaise

Add hot water to gelatin; cool. Add remaining ingredients; chill.

Mrs. Wiley Breeding, Whitesburg, Tenn.

Carrot And Celery Salad

   1 envelope unflavored gelatin
   ¼ c. sugar
   ½ tsp. salt
   1 ½ c. water
   ¼ c. lemon juice
   1 ½ c. carrot, grated
   ¼ c. celery, finely diced
   ¼ c. green pepper, diced

Thoroughly mix gelatin, sugar and salt. Add ½ cup of water. Stir constantly over low heat until gelatin is dissolved. Remove from heat and stir in remaining 1 cup water and lemon juice. Chill mixture to unbeaten egg white consistency. Fold in mixed vegetables. Turn into a 3-cup mold or individual molds. Chill until firm. Unmold. Garnish with salad greens, scallions and radishes. Yield: 6 servings.

Mattie Mary Green, Home Economics Teacher, Neely, Miss.

Jellied Tomato And Cheese Salad

1 ½ tbsp. unflavored gelatin
½ c. cold water
1 c. tomato sauce
1 c. cottage cheese
2 tbsp. lemon juice
¼ c. finely chopped celery
2 tbsp. minced onion
¼ c. chopped green pepper
¼ c. diced cucumber
½ c. mayonnaise

Soften gelatin in cold water; set aside for 5 minutes. Heat tomato sauce to boiling; dissolve gelatin in hot sauce. Add cottage cheese and lemon juice; stir until well blended. Cool; add remaining ingredients. Chill until firm. Serve on lettuce leaves. Yield: 6 servings.

Dorothea McDermott, Great Falls, Mont., Favorite Recipes Food Fair

Lime Gelatin-Vegetable Salad

1 family-size pkg. lime gelatin
½ c. onion, finely chopped
¼ c. green pepper, chopped
1 or 2 cucumbers, thinly sliced

Mix gelatin according to directions on package. Let set until slightly thickened. Fold in vegetables. Let set until firm. Yield: 10 servings.

Jane L. Burnham, Home Economics Teacher, Ashland, Maine

Molded Cauliflower Salad

2 pkgs. lemon gelatin
2 tbsp. lemon juice
½ c. green onions, finely sliced
¾ c. cucumbers, diced
½ c. radishes, thinly sliced
½ c. celery, thinly sliced
½ c. raw cauliflowerets
1 tsp. salt

Prepare gelatin according to package directions. Chill until partially set. Add remaining ingredients. Chill until firm. Yield: 4-6 servings.

Anne Cole, Home Economics Teacher, Livingston, Ky.

Lime Cream Salad

1 6-oz. pkg. lime gelatin
2 tsp. salt
2 c. boiling water
2 tbsp. vinegar
2 tsp. grated onion
⅛ tsp. pepper
2 c. sour cream
½ c. mayonnaise
2 c. shredded cucumbers, well drained
Lettuce
3 tomatoes, thinly sliced

Combine gelatin and salt in large bowl. Add boiling water, stirring until gelatin is dissolved. Add vinegar, onion and pepper. Chill until mixture is the consistency of an unbeaten egg white. Fold in sour cream and mayonnaise; blend thoroughly. Fold in cucumbers. Pour into a 2-quart mold. Chill until firm. Unmold on lettuce. Arrange tomato slices around edge of mold. May be served with additional sour cream or mayonnaise, if desired. Yield: 8-10 servings.

Geneva Bateman, Memphis, Tenn.

 ### Molded Garden Salad

4 envelopes unflavored gelatin
½ c. cold water
1 c. boiling water
½ c. sugar
1 ¼ c. cold water
1 ¼ c. vinegar
2 tsp. salt
1 ½ c. radishes, sliced
1 ¾ c. cucumbers, peeled and sliced
1 ¼ c. green onions, chopped
1 tsp. dill seed
1 ½ c. sour cream
½ c. mayonnaise
½ tsp. salt
2 tsp. vinegar

Soften gelatin in cold water; add boiling water and sugar. Blend remaining cold water, 1¼ cups vinegar, and 2 teaspoons salt; add to gelatin mixture. Add radishes, cucumbers, onion and dill seed. Let set until firm. Combine sour cream, mayonnaise, ½ teaspoon salt and 2 teaspoons vinegar. Serve sour cream mixture with gelatin mixture. Yield: 12 servings.

Mrs. Mary Irey, Red Bluff, Cal.

Neopolitan Vegetable Salad

2 pkgs. lemon gelatin
4 c. hot water
3 tbsp. vinegar
3 tsp. salt
1 ½ c. raw carrots, finely chopped
1 ¾ c. cabbage, finely chopped
1 tsp. onion, minced
1 ½ c. raw spinach, finely chopped

Dissolve gelatin in hot water; add vinegar and salt. Divide gelatin into 3 parts. Chill each part until partially thickened. Add carrots to one layer of gelatin. Chill until firm. Combine cabbage and another gelatin layer. Pour over first layer. Chill until firm. Add onion and spinach to remaining gelatin layer. Pour over firmly chilled mixture. Chill until firm. Yield: 12 servings.

Ann Guth, Home Economics Teacher, Palisade, Colo.

 ## Tomato Aspic With Sauerkraut

½ No. 303 can sauerkraut, finely chopped
3 tbsp. gelatin
3 c. tomato juice
½ tsp. thyme
Salt and pepper
1 tsp. onion salt
¼ c. vinegar
1 tsp. sugar
⅛ c. finely chopped green pepper
Stuffed olives (opt.)

Drain sauerkraut, reserving ¾ cup liquid; soften gelatin in sauerkraut liquid. Heat tomato juice; add gelatin, seasonings, vinegar and sugar. Chill until partially thickened; fold in green pepper, sauerkraut and olives. Chill until set. Yield: 6-8 servings.

Mrs. Albert H. Roos, Naval Officers' Wives' Club, Seattle, Wash.

Summertime Salad

1 3-oz. pkg. lemon or lemon-lime gelatin
1 c. water
¾ tsp. onion salt
2 tbsp. vinegar
2 c. chopped mixed tomatoes, cucumbers, celery, onions, radishes and green peppers

(Continued on next page)

Dissolve gelatin in boiling water; add onion salt and vinegar. Chill until slightly thickened. Fold in salad ingredients. Pour into mold; chill until firm. Unmold on lettuce. Serve with mayonnaise, if desired. Yield: 6 servings.

Mrs. George Marschalk, Officers' Wives' Club, Savannah, Ga.

   ### Perfection Salad

   1 envelope unflavored gelatin
   ¼ c. sugar
   ¼ tsp. salt
   1 ¼ c. cold water
   ¼ c. vinegar or lemon juice
   ¾ c. finely shredded cabbage
   1 c. diced celery
   ¼ c. diced green pepper or pimento

Mix gelatin, sugar and salt together in a saucepan. Stir in ½ cup of cold water. Place over medium heat, stirring constantly, until gelatin and sugar are dissolved. Remove from heat; stir in remaining water and vinegar. Chill until mixture is the consistency of unbeaten egg white. Fold in cabbage, celery and green pepper. Turn into a 6-cup mold or individual molds. Chill until firm. If desired, unmold on salad greens; serve with mayonnaise. Yield: 6 servings. Shredded carrot may be substituted for cabbage. Diced cucumber may be substituted for all or half the celery.

Photograph for this recipe below.

Tomato Aspic

    1 pkg. lemon gelatin
    2 c. boiling tomato juice
    1 c. celery, chopped
    ¼ c. onion, chopped

Dissolve gelatin in hot tomato juice. Cool until syrupy. Add celery and onion. Chill until firm. Yield: 6 servings.

Mrs. Helen Campbell, Home Economics Teacher, Watertown, S. D.

Tomato Aspic Salad

    ½ tsp. whole cloves
    ½ tsp. whole allspice
    1 2-inch strip of cinnamon bark
    Dash of cayenne pepper
    3 tbsp. onion, chopped
    2 ¼ c. tomato juice
    1 pkg. lemon gelatin
    1 c. celery, chopped
    1 c. pecans, chopped

Simmer spices and onion in tomato juice for 10 minutes. Strain over gelatin; stir until dissolved. Chill until mixture begins to set. Add celery and pecans. Pour into a large mold or individual molds. Chill until firm. Yield: 6 servings.

Mrs. Louise J. McDonald, Home Economics Teacher, Bernice, La.

 ## Tomato Soup Salad

    2 pkg. unflavored gelatin
    ½ c. cold water
    1 can cream of tomato soup
    1 c. cottage cheese, beaten
    ½ c. mayonnaise
    1 c. chopped celery
    ½ c. chopped bell pepper
    ¼ c. sliced olives
    1 tbsp. minced onion

Sprinkle gelatin on water; set aside for 5 minutes. Heat soup; add gelatin and stir until dissolved. Remove from heat. Combine cottage cheese and mayonnaise; beat until smooth. Add to cooled mixture. Fold in celery, bell pepper, olives and onion. Chill until firm. Yield: 6 servings.

Mildred M. Gilbert, Oneonta, Ala., Favorite Recipes Food Fair

Sunset Delight Salad

1 pkg. lemon-lime gelatin
½ c. hot water
1 ½ c. cold water
½ c. small cocktail onions
½ c. small stuffed olives
½ c. cucumbers, sliced or diced

Dissolve gelatin in hot water; add cold water. Chill until partially set. Add remaining ingredients. Chill until firm. Yield: 6 servings.

Maurine Sullivan Frederick, Home Economics Teacher, Copperas Cove, Tex.

Tomato-Vegetable Aspic

1 envelope unflavored gelatin
¼ c. cold tomato juice
1 ¾ c. boiling tomato juice
1 tbsp. onion, grated
1 tsp. salt
¾ c. cabbage, finely shredded
¼ c. celery, chopped

Soften gelatin in cold tomato juice. Add gelatin, onion and salt to boiling tomato juice; stir. Chill until slightly thickened. Fold in cabbage and celery. Chill until firm. Yield: 5-6 servings.

Mrs. Frances Chappell, Home Economics Teacher, Apel, N. C.

Vegetable Mold

1 pkg. frozen or 1 16-oz. can asparagus
1 pkg. frozen or 1 16-oz. can mixed vegetables
1 pkg. lemon gelatin
1 12-oz. can vegetable juice cocktail
3 tbsp. vinegar
¼ tsp. salt
Pepper to taste
¼ c. chopped pimento

Cook frozen asparagus and mixed vegetables according to package directions; drain. Dissolve gelatin in 1 cup hot vegetable juice cocktail; add remaining cold vegetable juice, vinegar, salt, pepper, pimento and drained vegetables. Pour into 1½-quart mold. Chill until firm. Unmold and serve on salad greens with mayonnaise or salad dressing, if desired. Yield: 4-6 servings.

Mrs. W. J. Scott, Commanding Officers' Wife, Minneapolis, Minn.

Mixed Fruit and Vegetable Salads

Apple, Coconut And Celery Salad

1 ½ c. mixed diced tart apples and celery
½ c. shredded coconut
1 tbsp. lemon juice
1 tbsp. sugar
4 tbsp. salad oil
4 tbsp. orange juice
Salt to taste
Paprika to taste
Currant or plum jelly

Mix apples, celery and coconut. Sprinkle lemon juice and sugar over mixture. Mix oil, juice, salt and paprika; pour over salad. Line salad bowl with lettuce leaves; pile chilled salad in center. Dot with currant or plum jelly. Yield: 3-4 servings.

Mrs. Alvin G. Kouts, Pres. Officers' Wives' Club, Montgomery, Ala.

Apple-Sour Cream Slaw

1 c. sour cream
2 tbsp. lemon juice
2 tbsp. vinegar
2 tbsp. sugar
1 tsp. salt
¼ tsp. pepper
1 tbsp. dry mustard
1 c. sliced celery
2 c. shredded cabbage
1 c. shredded carrots
2 lge, apples, chopped
⅓ c. raisins

Combine sour cream, lemon juice, vinegar, sugar, salt, pepper and dry mustard; beat until smooth. Mix celery, cabbage, carrots, apples and raisins; toss with sour cream mixture. Yield: 8 servings.

Mrs. William T. Griffiths, Dallas, Tex.

Bab's Salad

Torn lettuce
1 can Mandarin oranges
French dressing to taste
Crisp crumbled bacon
Toasted slivered almonds

(Continued on next page)

Toss lettuce, oranges and dressing well; sprinkle bacon on top. Sprinkle with almonds. Serve immediately.

Mrs. John N. Myers, Commanding Officer's Wife, Key West, Fla.

 ## Beet And Pineapple Salad Supreme

1 pkg. strawberry gelatin
1 pkg. raspberry gelatin
1 pkg. cherry gelatin
4 c. boiling water
1 No. 303 can julienne beets
1 No. 2 can crushed pineapple
½ c. sweet pickle juice

Dissolve all gelatin in boiling water. Drain beets and pineapple, reserving liquid. Add drained liquid and pickle juice to gelatin; chill until syrupy. Stir in beets and pineapple. Pour into a 3-quart mold; chill until firm. Yield: 16-18 servings.

Mrs. Robert Byrne, Pres. Officers' Wives' Club, Fort Gordon, Ga.

Cabbage-Banana Salad

5 tbsp. salad dressing
¼ tsp. salt
2 tbsp. pineapple juice
2 ½ c. finely shredded cabbage
½ c. diced banana
¼ c. cut up salted peanuts

Combine salad dressing, salt and pineapple juice. Pour over combined remaining ingredients. Toss lightly to mix.

Terri Reasor, Huntington, Va.

 ## Cabbage Slaw

2 c. shredded cabbage
¼ c. minced onion
½ c. pineapple chunks
⅛ c. chopped pimento
¼ c. sliced stuffed olives
½ c. shredded cheddar cheese
¼ c. mayonnaise
1 tbsp. lemon juice
Dash of salt and pepper
¼ c. heavy cream, whipped

(Continued on next page)

Toss cabbage, onion, pineapple, pimento, olives and cheese. Refrigerate for 30 minutes. In large bowl, mix mayonnaise, lemon juice, salt and pepper until smooth. Fold cream into mayonnaise mixture. Pour over salad; toss well. Yield: 4 servings.

Mrs. Edward A. Rusek, Officers' Wives' Club, Washington, D. C.

 Carrot-Pineapple Salad

    1 pkg. orange gelatin
    2 c. hot water
    1 c. carrots, grated
    1 c. crushed pineapple, drained

Dissolve gelatin in hot water; chill until partially set. Add carrots and pineapple. Chill until firm. Yield: 6-8 servings.

Elizabeth M. Vail, Uriah, Ala.

 Carrot And Raisin Salad

    ½ c. raisins
    ½ c. mayonnaise
    1 tbsp. orange juice
    1 tsp. lemon juice
    1 tsp. grated orange peel
    3 c. grated carrots

Soak raisins in warm water until plump. Drain. Mix mayonnaise with fruit juices and orange peel. Add to carrots; toss lightly with fork. Serve on salad greens. Yield: 6 servings.

Mrs. John W. Bogan, Officers' Wives' Club, Milden Hall, England

Cauliflower And Apple Salad

    1 sm. cauliflower, thinly sliced
    3 apples, diced
    1 c. sliced celery
    4 sm. green onions, sliced
    ½ c. chopped parsley
    ¼ c. red wine vinegar
    ¼ c. olive or salad oil
    ½ tsp. salt
    Dash of white pepper
    1 bunch watercress

(Continued on next page)

Chill cauliflower, apples, celery, onions and parsley. Shake vinegar, oil, salt and pepper in a tightly covered jar. Pour over salad; toss lightly. Garnish with watercress. Yield: 6 servings.

Mrs. Chris Jacobs, Topeka, Kan.

 ## Citrus-Apple Salad With Lemon Honey Dressing

> Salad greens
> ½ c. diced celery
> 2 apples, unpeeled, cored and cut into thin wedges
> 1 cucumber, peeled and thinly sliced
> 4 California oranges, sliced crosswise
> 1 grapefruit, peeled and sectioned
> ½ c. salad oil
> ⅓ c. fresh lemon juice
> 1 tbsp. honey
> 1 tsp. dry mustard
> ¼ tsp. salt
> Dash of pepper
> ½ tsp. paprika
> 1 tsp. Worcestershire sauce
> ¼ c. fresh or frozen chopped chives
> ½ c. croutons
> ⅓ c. crumbled bleu cheese

Line salad bowl with greens; arrange celery, apples, cucumber, oranges and grapefruit in bowl. Combine salad oil, lemon juice, honey. mustard, salt, pepper, paprika, Worcestershire sauce and chives. Just before serving, pour enough dressing over salad to moisten, Add croutons and bleu cheese. Toss lightly. Yield: 6-8 servings.

Photograph for this recipe on page 137.

Coleslaw

> ½ med. cabbage
> ½ c. mayonnaise
> 1 c. drained crushed pineapple
> ¼ c. cut-up marshmallows (opt.)
> Salt and pepper to taste

Chill cabbage thoroughly; finely shred. Measure 4 cups cabbage. Combine remaining ingredients; pour over cabbage. Mix lightly. Yield: 6 servings.

Mrs. Robert C. Edmiston, Officers' Wives' Club, Eleuthera, Bahama Islands

Coleslaw With Grapefruit

1 c. sour cream
1 ½ tbsp. lemon juice
1 tsp. salt
1 tsp. dry mustard
½ cabbage, shredded
1 8-oz. can grapefruit sections, drained and chilled

Combine sour cream, lemon juice, salt and mustard; toss mixture with cabbage. Add grapefruit sections; toss gently. Yield: 4 servings.

Mrs. Priscilla Long, Lincoln, Neb., Favorite Recipes Food Fair

Cottage Cheese-Vegetable Salad

1 pkg. lime gelatin
1 ½ c. boiling water
⅓ c. carrots, shredded
¼ c. pepper, chopped
1 tbsp. onion, minced
½ c. celery, cut
1 c. dry cottage cheese
½ c. crushed pineapple
½ tsp. salt
¼ c. whipping cream
½ c. salad dressing

Dissolve gelatin in boiling water; chill until partially set. Add vegetables, cottage cheese, pineapple and salt. Blend cream and salad dressing together; add to gelatin mixture. Chill. Yield: 6 servings.

Shirley Nasset, Home Economics Teacher, Regent, N. D.

Cucumber Salad

1 pkg. lime gelatin
1 c. boiling water
1 No. 2 can crushed pineapple
½ c. pineapple juice
1 tsp. salt
1 tsp. grated onion
½ c. cucumbers, chopped fine
½ c. mayonnaise
2 tbsp. vinegar

(Continued on next page)

Dissolve gelatin in boiling water. When cool add remaining ingredients. Pour in molds until firm. Yield: 8 servings.

Mrs. Robert E. McNair, Wive of Governor of South Carolina, Columbia

Grapefruit Salad

> 1 1-lb. can Florida grapefruit sections
> Mixed salad greens
> 1 purple onion, thinly sliced
> ½ c. sliced radishes
> ½ cucumber, sliced

Drain grapefruit sections. Wash and dry greens; tear into bite-size pieces. Add grapefruit sections, sliced onion, radish and cucumber slices. Add French Dressing just before serving and toss lightly. Yield: 6 servings.

FRENCH DRESSING:

> 1 6-oz. can frozen Florida grapefruit juice concentrate
> ½ c. catsup
> ¼ c. salad oil

Combine undiluted grapefruit juice and catsup; blend well. Add salad oil; beat with rotary beater until blended. Cover and store in refrigerator; shake before using. Yield: 1½ cups.

Photograph for this recipe below.

Green Goddess Salad

Romaine lettuce
Head lettuce
Spinach leaves
Avocado wedges
Grapefruit sections
Whole white seedless grapes

Toss crisp greens and fruits.

DRESSING:

1 c. salad dressing
½ c. sour cream
1 clove of garlic, crushed
4 anchovies, chopped
4 tbsp. parsley, chopped
3 tbsp. chives or green onions, chopped
1 tbsp. lemon juice
1 tbsp. tarragon vinegar
½ tsp. salt
Dash of pepper

Combine all ingredients; pour over salad. Toss gently. Yield: 8 servings.

Mrs. Carleton V. Hansen, Officers' Wives' Club, Andersen AFB, Guam

Hearts Of Palm Salad A La De Vera

1 c. finely diced pineapple
4 c. sliced raw hearts of palm
¼ c. chopped dates
¼ c. chopped candied or preserved ginger
4 tbsp. vanilla ice cream
2 tbsp. crunchy peanut butter
2 tbsp. mayonnaise
Few drops of green food coloring
1 to 2 tbsp. pineapple juice

Combine pineapple, hearts of palm, dates and ginger in salad bowl. Combine ice cream, peanut butter, mayonnaise and green food coloring to tint a pale green; blend well. Add pineapple juice to thin to desired consistency; pour dressing over salad.

Mrs. Vernon P. O'Neil, Hon. Pres. Naval Officers' Wives' Club, Dallas, Tex.

Key West Sun-Ray Salad

4 king oranges
2 Bermuda onions

(Continued on next page)

Cream cheese balls
Paprika
Lettuce
½ c. French dressing

Peel oranges carefully to preserve wedges. Slice onions and cut into halves. Roll cream cheese balls in paprika; place on lettuce. Arrange oranges and onions in alternate petals around cream cheese balls. Add French dressing. Yield: 4 servings.

Mrs. Harry Anderson, Daytona, Fla.

 ## Lettuce-Avocado Delight

3 to 4 heads Bibb lettuce, torn into bite-sized pieces
½ head iceberg lettuce, torn into bite-sized pieces
2 sm. ripe avocados, sliced
3 hard-cooked eggs, sliced
½ lb. bacon, crisply fried and crumbled
1 can Mandarin oranges, drained
½ c. slivered almonds
1 envelope bleu cheese dressing mix

Combine greens, avocado, eggs, bacon, oranges and almonds. Chill. Just before serving, toss thoroughly with bleu cheese dressing prepared according to package directions. Yield: 6-8 servings.

Mrs. Charles E. Siegman, Pres. Coast Guard Officers' Wives' Club,
Sault Ste. Marie, Mich.

 ## Lettuce And Banana Salad

Lemon juice
1 lge. banana, sliced
¼ c. finely diced onion
1 sm. head lettuce, shredded
⅛ tsp. garlic powder
Salt and pepper to taste
⅓ c. mayonnaise

Sprinkle lemon juice on banana. Mix all ingredients except mayonnaise. Add mayonnaise, just before serving. Yield: 6 servings.

Mrs. H. W. Moore, Officers' Wives' Club, Ft. Stewart, Ga.

Lime Gelatin Salad

1 pkg. cream cheese
Pineapple juice plus water to make 2 c. liquid
1 pkg. lime gelatin
1 tsp. unflavored gelatin
6 lge. marshmallows
1 c. heavy cream, whipped and sweetened
1 c. drained crushed pineapple
½ c. finely chopped pecans
½ c. finely chopped celery

Bring cream cheese to room temperature. Bring juice mixture to a boil; dissolve lime gelatin in mixture. Dissolve unflavored gelatin in small amount cold water; add to lime gelatin. Add cream cheese and marshmallows; stir until dissolved. Chill until mixture begins to thicken; blend in whipped cream. Add remaining ingredients; pour into molds. Chill until firm. Green food coloring may be used. Yield: 14 servings.

Mrs. Mary P. Grubbs, Winston-Salem, N. C.

 ### Lime Velvet Salad

1 pkg. lime gelatin
1 pkg. cream cheese
1 No. 1 can crushed pineapple, drained
1 c. celery, diced
1 c. whipped cream (opt.)
Juice from pineapple

Heat pineapple juice; add gelatin. Stir in cheese; stir until gelatin and cheese have dissolved. Mix pineapple and celery with whippd cream; add to gelatin. Chill until firm. Yield: 10 servings.

Mrs. Emily Watts Norriss, Home Economics Teacher, Maurice, La.

 ### Millionaire's Salad

1 No. 2 can hearts of palm
1 No. 2 can pineapple chunks, drained
1 ripe avocado, cut up
1 c. salad dressing
1 tsp. sugar

Cut hearts of palm into bite-sized pieces. Combine al ingredients. Serve on lettuce cups. Yield: 8 servings.

Mrs. Diane Searcy, Tifton, Ga.

Molded Spiced Apple Salad

    1 14-oz. jar spiced apple rings, drained
    2 pkg. lemon gelatin
    1 c. thick applesauce
    2 3-oz. pkg. cream cheese
    ½ c. mayonnaise
    ½ c. sour cream
    1 c. chopped celery
    ½ c. chopped pecans
    ⅛ tsp. salt

Place apple rings in 11 x 7-inch dish. Add enough water to juice from apples to make 1½ cups liquid. Bring to a boil; dissolve gelatin in hot liquid. Pour half of gelatin mixture over apple rings; chill until firm. Combine remaining ingredients except reserved gelatin; spread over chilled gelatin. Cover with remaining gelatin; chill until firm. Yield: 12 servings.

Virginia Meierhoffer, Dunkirk, N. Y., Favorite Recipes Food Fair

Molded Waldorf Salad

    1 envelope unflavored gelatin
    ⅓ c. sugar
    ½ tsp. salt
    1 ½ c. water
    ¼ c. vinegar or lemon juice
    2 c. tart apples, diced
    ½ c. celery, diced
    ¼ c. pecans, chopped

Mix gelatin, sugar and salt thoroughly in a small saucepan. Add ½ cup of the water. Stir over low heat, until gelatin is dissolved. Remove from heat; stir in remaining water, vinegar or lemon juice. Chill mixture until thickened. Fold in apples, celery and nuts. Chill until firm. Yield: 6 servings.

Mrs. Jane Ann Courtney, Home Economics Teacher, Pascagoula, Miss.

One, Two Three Salad

    1 sm. onion, diced
    2 sweet pickles, chopped
    3 apples, diced
    Mayonnaise

Combine all ingredients. Yield: 4 servings.

Mrs. Jan Laney, Jacksonville, Fla.

Orange Delight

1 pkg. orange gelatin
1 c. hot water
1 c. shredded carrots
1 c. crushed pineapple

Mix gelatin and water; add remaining ingredients. Pour into 8 x 4-inch pan; chill for at least 2 hours. Cut into squares and serve. Yield: 6-8 servings.

Geneva Mitchell, Harrisburg, Ill.

 Orange-Olive Salad Plate

Crisp salad greens
6 chilled oranges, peeled and cut into thin crosswise slices
⅔ c. chopped ripe olives
⅓ c. finely chopped leeks
White ripe olives
½ c. olive oil
2 tbsp. red wine vinegar
1 tsp. ground coriander
¼ tsp. salt
¼ tsp. pepper
¼ tsp. sugar
¼ tsp. dry mustard

Line chilled salad platter with greens. Arrange orange slices on greens. Sprinkle with chopped olives and leeks. Garnish with whole olives. Shake olive oil, vinegar, coriander, salt, pepper, sugar and mustard in covered jar. Pour over oranges. Yield: 6 servings.

Mrs. Donald Wilkins, Officers' Wives' Club, Requa, Cal.

 Orange And Tomato Tossed Salad

½ head iceberg lettuce
1 head romaine
2 tomatoes
1 sm. can Mandarin oranges, drained
½ Bermuda onion, thinly sliced

Break lettuce and romaine into large salad bowl. Slice tomatoes lengthwise into eight sections. Add tomatoes and oranges to lettuce. Arrange onion slices on top. Serve with choice of dressing. Yield: 6 servings.

Mrs. George L. Nolen, Chattanooga, Tenn.

Pedro's Salad

2 avocados
2 lge. tomatoes
2 Spanish onions, cut into rings
6 leaves lettuce
French or Russian dressing
1 c. corn chips

Remove seed from avocados; cut into halves. Lay each half on cutting board, cut side down; slice crosswise, straight through to cutting board. Slice tomatoes from top to stem. Alternate slices of avocados, tomato and onion on lettuce leaves. Serve with French or Russian dressing; garnish with corn chips. Yield: 6 servings.

Mrs. John S. Tyler, Officers' Wives' Club, Honolulu, Hawaii

 ### Pineapple And Cucumber Salad

1 No. 2 can chunk pineapple, drained
1 lge. cucumber, finely sliced
4 tbsp. sour cream
Salt to taste
Pepper to taste
Dill weed to taste

Combine pineapple, cucumber and sour cream; sprinkle with seasonings. Toss lightly; chill for 1 hour. Yield: 4 servings.

Mrs. Robert Lacey, Ft. Worth, Tex.

 ### Pineapple Slaw With Roquefort Dressing

4 c. shredded cabbage
1 carrot, shredded
½ c. radishes
½ c. slivered green pepper
1 c. drained pineapple chunks
¾ c. buttermilk
¾ c. mayonnaise
⅓ c. crumbled bleu or Roquefort cheese
½ tsp. celery seed

Toss cabbage, carrot, radishes and green pepper; add pineapple. Beat remaining ingredients together; add to cabbage mixture and toss. Yield: 6-8 servings.

Mrs. R. O. Bennett, Officers' Wives' Club, Fort Greely, Alaska

 ### Red Cabbage-Orange Salad

    1 sm. red cabbage, shredded
    3 med. oranges, peeled and sectioned
    ¼ c. chopped chives
    ¼ med. green pepper, slivered
    Dash of salt
    ¾ c. farm-style cottage cheese
    Juice of 1 orange

Combine cabbage, oranges, chives, green pepper and salt. Mix in cottage cheese, adding orange juice as needed for proper consistency. Serve on lettuce garnished with alternate slivers of green pepper and orange peel, if desired. This is an ideal salad for weight watchers.

    Mrs. Edward K. Hensch, Pres. Officers' Wives' Club, Middletown, Pa.

 ### Salad Of The Islands

    Lettuce
    4 c. cubed fresh pineapple
    2 c. cubed tomatoes
    1 tbsp. grated onion
    3 tbsp. lemon juice
    3 tbsp. catsup
    ½ c. light cream
    Salt and pepper to taste

Line salad bowl with lettuce. Add pineapple and tomatoes. Sprinkle with grated onion. Combine remaining ingredients. Mix well. Pour over salad. Yield: 6 servings.

    Mrs. James R. Payne, Moultrie, Ga., Favorite Recipes Food Fair

Spinach-Avocado Salad

1 10-oz. pkg. frozen spinach
2 med. onions, chopped
2 tbsp. butter·
1 hard-cooked egg, chopped
1 ripe avocado, chopped
Salt and pepper to taste
Vinaigrette or French dressing
Crumbled bacon
Croutons

Cook spinach according to package directions; drain well. Saute onions in butter until golden. Add onions to spinach; chop well. Add egg and avocado. Season to taste; serve with vinaigrette or French dressing. Crisp crumbled bacon or croutons may be sprinkled on top. Yield: 4-6 servings.

Mrs. C. D. Lang, Des Moines, Iowa

 Tomato-Grape Salad

1 tomato or 1 c. cherry tomatoes
Dash of salt
1 c. green seedless grapes
2 tbsp. mayonnaise

Cut tomato into wedges. Add salt, grapes and enough mayonnaise to barely coat tomato; mix gently and serve on lettuce. Yield: 2-3 servings.

Mrs. Alvin R. Theiss, Pres. Officers' Wives' Club, Myrtle Beach AFB, S. C.

 Tossed Mandarin Orange-Avocado Salad

2 heads Boston lettuce
2 green onions
1 can Mandarin oranges, drained
1 ripe avocado, sliced
½ c. red wine vinegar
1 c. oil
1 onion or 2 tbsp. dry onion
½ tsp. celery seed
1 tsp. dry mustard
1 tsp. salt
½ c. sugar

Break lettuce into bite-sized pieces. Chop onions, using the green part. Add oranges and avocado. Combine remaining ingredients. Pour over salad. Dressing is better if made a day ahead. Yield: 6 servings.

Mrs. Richard O. Gordon, Birmingham, Ala., Favorite Recipes Food Fair

Watercress-Orange Salad

    2 bunches watercress
    3 heads Belgian endive, cut into ¼-in. slices
    2 oranges, peeled and sectioned
    2 shallots, finely chopped
    ⅓ c. olive oil
    2 tbsp. lemon juice
    Salt and pepper to taste

Wash, trim and cut watercress into small pieces. Place in a large bowl. Add endive and orange sections. Combine remaining ingredients; pour over salad. Toss gently. Yield: 6-8 servings.

Mrs. W. J. L. Parker, Pres. Coast Guard Officers' Wives' Club, Boston, Mass.

Waldorf Salad

    1 tbsp. sugar
    ½ tsp. lemon juice
    Dash of salt
    2 c. chopped apples
    1 c. diced celery
    ½ c. pecans, chopped
    ¼ c. salad dressing
    ½ c. heavy cream, whipped

Sprinkle sugar, lemon juice and salt over apples. Add celery and pecans. Fold salad dressing into whipped cream. Gradually fold into apple mixture; chill. Yield: 6 servings.

Mrs. Kenneth R. Moore, St. Paul, Minn.

West Indian Salad

    2 avocados, halved and pared
    Shredded lettuce
    1 cucumber, coarsely grated
    Juice of 1 lemon
    Salt and pepper to taste
    1 tbsp. olive oil

Place avocados on shredded lettuce. Season cucumber with lemon juice, salt, pepper and olive oil. Fill avocados with cucumber mixture. Yield: 4 servings.

Mrs. James K. Hess, Officers' Wives' Club, New Orleans, La.

Meat and Poultry Salads

Beef Salad

      2 c. chopped beef
    ¼ c. chopped onion
    ½ c. chopped sweet pickles
      2 boiled eggs, chopped
    ½ c. salad dressing

Mix ingredients together with salad dressing. Olives may be substituted for pickles, if desired.

Mrs. R. C. Shoffner, Maynardville, Tenn.

Beef Salad

    ½ c. French dressing
    · 2 c. diced cooked beef
    ½ c. coarsely grated carrots
    ½ c. diced cooked potatoes
    ½ c. cooked green beans
    ¼ c. chopped sweet pickles
      2 hard-cooked eggs, diced
    ½ c. mayonnaise
      4 to 6 lettuce cups

Pour French dressing over beef; chill 1 hour or longer. Chill remaining ingredients. Combine beef, carrots, potatoes, beans, pickles and eggs. Add mayonnaise; mix lightly. Serve salad in lettuce cups. Yield: 4-6 servings.

Mrs. Glenn Moore, Forbes, N. D., Favorite Recipes Food Fair

Jellied Beef Salad

      1 envelope unflavored gelatin
      1 ¾ c. water
      2 bouillon cubes
      1 ½ tbsp. lemon juice
      1 tsp. grated onion
      1 c. finely diced cooked beef
    ½ c. diced celery
    ½ c. cooked or canned peas, drained

Sprinkle gelatin on ½ cup water to soften. Add bouillon cubes. Place over low heat and stir until gelatin is dissolved. Remove from heat; add remaining water, lemon juice and onion. Chill to unbeaten egg white consistency. Fold in meat, celery and peas. Turn into a 3 cup mold; chill until firm. Cut into slices and serve on crisp lettuce. Yield: 4 servings.

Guadalupe Gonzalez, Alice, Tex.

Roast Beef Salad

3 c. ground leftover pot roast
4 hard-cooked eggs
¾ c. chopped pickles or pickle relish
1 sm. onion, chopped (opt.)
1 c. salad dressing

Combine all ingredients; chill. Serve on lettuce leaves, if desired. Yield: 6-8 servings.

Mrs. Joe Ramsey, Whitesburg, Ky.

 ## Salcom

3 lb. round steak or stew beef
1 lge. bell pepper
1 lge. onion (opt.)
1 can tomatoes, drained
Ground red pepper
4 stalks celery, ground (opt.)
½ c. beef stock
Mayonnaise

Cook meat in salty water until done; cool. Grind meat fine. Grind and add bell pepper, onion and tomatoes. Mix all together well; add a little red pepper, celery and beef stock. Add enough mayonnaise to moisten as desired. Place salad on platter; garnish with sliced fresh tomatoes, deviled eggs, pepper rings or onion rings.

Mrs. Edgar J. Maxwell, Lexington, Ga.

 ## Soup Meat Salad

2 c. cooked soup meat
2 onions, sliced
1 clove garlic, finely chopped
1 c. chopped celery
1 c. chopped green pepper
½ c. French dressing

Cut cold meat from bones which were used to make soup. Combine meat, onions, garlic, celery and green pepper. Marinate in French dressing. Place on lettuce. Yield: 4 servings.

Mrs. Lucille R. Boyter, Home Economics Teacher, St. Bernard, La.

Beefburger Loaf

2 envelopes unflavored gelatin
½ c. cold water
2 beef bouillon cubes
1 ½ c. boiling water
¾ c. salad dressing
2 lb. ground beef
½ c. finely chopped onions
¼ c. sliced stuffed olives

Soften gelatin in cold water; stir over low heat until dissolved. Add bouillon cubes dissolved in boiling water. Cool; gradually add to salad dressing, mixing until well blended. Chill until slightly thickened. Brown meat; add onion and cook until tender. Drain and cool. Fold meat and olives into gelatin mixture; pour into 8 x 4 x 2-inch pan. Chill until firm. Unmold. May be kept in refrigerator two to three days. Yield: 8 servings.

Mrs. Edward McVickar, Sumner, Ill.

 ### Mexican Salad

1 lb. ground beef
¼ c. chopped onion
2 c. drained kidney beans
½ c. bottled French dressing
½ c. water
1 tbsp. chili powder
4 c. shredded lettuce
½ c. sliced green onions
8 oz. sharp cheddar cheese, shredded

Brown meat; add onion and cook until tender. Stir in beans, French dressing, water and chili powder. Simmer for 15 minutes. Combine lettuce and green onions. Add meat sauce and 1½ cups cheese; toss lightly. Sprinkle with remaining cheese. Serve with crisp tortillas. Yield: 4-6 servings.

Mrs. Russell A. Berg, Officers' Wives' Club, Los Angeles, Cal.

Congealed Corned Beef Salad

1 can beef consomme
1 pkg. lemon gelatin
1 can corned beef, chopped
1 c. salad dressing or mayonnaise
1 c. chopped celery
1 sm. onion, chopped
2 tbsp. chopped pimento (opt.)
3 hard-cooked eggs, chopped

Add enough water to consomme to make 2 cups liquid; pour into saucepan. Bring to a boil; stir in gelatin until dissolved. Chill until thickened. Fold in corned beef, salad dressing, celery, onion, pimento and eggs. Pour into mold; chill until firm. Yield: 8 servings.

Mrs. T. C. Grubbs, Officers' Wives' Club, Heidelberg, Germany

Corned Beef-Gelatin Salad

2 sm. pkg. lemon gelatin
3 c. boiling water
1 sm. green pepper, thinly sliced
1 sm. onion, diced
1 c. diced celery
1 tbsp. vinegar
1 pt. salad dressing
1 can corned beef, separated into small pieces

Dissolve gelatin in boiling water. Chill slightly. Mix remaining ingredients; add to gelatin mixture. Pour into square or oblong pan; store in refrigerator for 12 hours. To serve, cut into squares; serve on salad greens with additional salad dressing, if desired. Yield: 12 servings.

Mrs. Roy F. Creech, San Diego, Cal.

Corned Beef Molded Salad

2 pkg. lemon gelatin
3 ½ c. hot water
2 cans corned beef
3 hard-cooked eggs, chopped
3 c. chopped celery
½ c. chopped cucumber
½ c. chopped onion
½ tsp. salt
2 tbsp. horseradish
1 c. sour cream

(Continued on next page)

Dissolve gelatin in water. Chill until slightly thickened. Mix remaining ingredients; pour into 10 x 13-inch pan. Pour gelatin over mixture. Refrigerate until set. Yield: 12-16 servings.

Mrs. Sidney M. Hay, Coast Guard Officers' Wives' Club, Cleveland, Ohio

 ### Corned Beef Salad

  1 ½ c. V-8 juice
½ c. water
  1 pkg. lemon gelatin
  1 can corned beef, shredded
  2 hard-cooked eggs, chopped
  1 ½ c. chopped celery
  2 tbsp. chopped green pepper
½ sm. onion, finely minced
  1 c. salad dressing

Heat V-8 juice and water; dissolve gelatin. Cool. Add remaining ingredients. Pour into 8 x 8-inch pan; refrigerate overnight. Cut into squares for serving. Yield: 6-8 servings.

Mrs. Donald Hawks, Sioux Falls, S. D., Favorite Recipes Food Fair

 ### Guess What Salad

  1 box lemon gelatin
  1 8-oz. can corned beef
½ c. mayonnaise
Dash of salt
  1 c. finely chopped celery
  2 finely chopped slices onion
½ c. chopped olives
  4 chopped hard-cooked eggs
¼ c. chopped green pepper

Make gelatin as package directs, using only 1½ cups liquid. Let set until gelatin has begun to set; mix in remaining ingredients. Chill until firm. Yield: 12 servings.

Mrs. Stewart Rowles, Newman, Ill.

 ### Molded Corned Beef Salad

  1 box lemon gelatin
  1 c. boiling water

(Continued on next page)

1 c. corned beef
2 c. chopped celery
½ onion, diced
¾ c. chopped green pepper
1 c. mayonnaise

Dissolve gelatin in boiling water. Cool. Add corned beef, celery, onion and green pepper. Stir in mayonnaise; mix well. Pour into a large mold or individual molds. When set, serve on lettuce leaves. Yield: 4-6 servings.

Barbara Gaylor, Lansing, Mich.

 ## Pressed Beef

1 can corned beef
3 hard-boiled eggs
1 c. (about) mayonnaise
3 tsp. unflavored gelatin
⅓ c. lemon juice
Mustard and pickle to taste (opt.)
Red pepper to taste
Salt to taste

Put meat and eggs through food chopper; mix with mayonnaise. Soften gelatin in small amount of cold water; dissolve in small amount of hot water and lemon juice. Add gelatin mixture to meat mixture; add remaining ingredients. Mix well; put into mold. Refrigerate until set.

Mrs. John Hugh Boulware, Winnsboro, S. C.

 ## Frankfurter-Potato Salad

8 skinless frankfurters
6 lge. potatoes
½ c. heavy cream, whipped
1 c. mayonnaise
2 tsp. prepared mustard
Snipped scallions
Bottled capers
1 ½ tsp. salt
⅛ tsp. pepper
12 to 16 hard, thin, skinless salami slices
Parsley sprigs

Simmer frankfurters for 5 minutes; drain. Cover and refrigerate overnight. Cook potatoes; cool and dice. Cover; refrigerate overnight. Slice frankfurters into ¾-inch slices. Combine whipped cream, mayonnaise, mustard, 1/3 cup

(Continued on next page)

snipped scallions, 1½ tablespoons capers, salt and pepper. Fold in potatoes and all but ten frankfurter slices. Mound into 1-quart salad bowl. Decorate with ten frankfurter slices, scallions and capers. Make salami roses from salami and parsley. Tuck around edges. Yield: 8 servings.

Nancy Barnes, Officers' Wives' Club, Virginia Beach, Va.

 ## Frankfurter Salad Bake

3 tbsp. butter
3 tbsp. flour
1 ½ tsp. salt
¾ tsp. dry mustard
¼ tsp. pepper
1 ¼ c. milk
¾ c. mayonnaise
6 med. potatoes, cooked and cubed
1 box frozen cut green beans, cooked
1 onion, chopped
8 or 9 frankfurters, cut in 1 in. pieces
Bread crumbs

Melt butter; remove from heat. Add flour, salt, mustard and pepper. Slowly add milk; cook over low heat until mixture thickens. Remove from heat; add mayonnaise. Fold in potatoes, green beans, onion and wieners. Put in casserole; cover top with bread crumbs. Dot with butter. Bake at 350 degrees for 45 minutes. Yield: 8-10 servings.

Mrs. A. G. Nordgren, Caldwell, N. J.

 ## Colorado Lamb Salad

3 c. slivered cold roast lamb
1 c. bottled Italian salad dressing
Cucumber slices
Cherry tomatoes
Slivered Swiss cheese
Green pepper rings (opt.)
Crisp salad greens

Marinate lamb in salad dressing for several hours in refrigerator. Combine lamb and dressing with remaining ingredients; toss well or arrange as desired. Yield: 4 servings.

Photograph for this recipe on page 153.

Meat-Potato Salad

    8 to 10 medium cooked potatoes, diced
    3 hard-cooked eggs, diced
    ½ c. diced cheese
    ¼ c. diced onions
    3 tbsp. diced green pepper
    ¼ c. diced pickles
    1 tbsp. celery seed
    1 can luncheon meat, diced
    ½ to ¾ c. salad dressing
    Salt and pepper to taste

Mix all ingredients with salad dressing. Sprinkle with paprika; serve on lettuce. Yield: 10-12 servings.

Mrs. Tommy Long, Home Economics Teacher, Scottsville, Ky.

 ### Meat Salad

    1 can luncheon meat
    2 hard-cooked eggs
    1 lge. dill pickle
    2 tbsp. finely chopped olives
    1 sour apple, finely chopped
    ½ c. chopped celery
    1 tbsp. chopped pimento
    Salt and pepper to taste
    3 tbsp. salad dressing

Combine all ingredients; chill for 2 hours. Yield: 6-8 servings.

Lynda Freeman, Mesquite, Tex.

Pepperoni And Onion Salad

    1 head iceberg lettuce, torn
    1 long link pepperoni, chopped
    1 med. onion, chopped
    2 sm. tomatoes, chopped
    1 cucumber, chopped
    Salt to taste
    Vinegar and oil dressing
    Parmesan cheese
    Toast

Place lettuce, pepperoni, onion, tomatoes and cucumber in salad bowl. Salt to taste; toss. Pour vinegar and oil dressing over salad; toss again. Sprinkle with Parmesan cheese. Serve with crisp dry toast. Yield: 4 servings.

Mrs. Gary Davis, Dallas, Tex.

Maurice Salad

½ c. mayonnaise
2 tbsp. sweet pickle liquid
¼ c. salad or apple cider vinegar
1 tbsp. Worcestershire sauce
3 hard-cooked eggs, minced
1 tbsp. minced onion
¼ c. minced sweet pickle
1 lge. head lettuce, torn into bite-sized pieces
1 c. cooked chicken, diced
1 c. cooked ham, diced
1 med. tomato, diced

Blend first four ingredients. Stir in eggs, onion and pickle. Refrigerate dressing at least 1 hour. Toss lettuce with dressing. Serve lettuce on individual plates. Top with chicken, ham and tomato. Yield: 6 servings.

Mrs. Floyd Buse, Lennox, S. D.

Chicken Mousse

3 egg yolks
1 ½ c. milk
1 ½ tbsp. gelatin
¼ c. cold water
½ c. hot chicken stock
1 can mushrooms, chopped fine
½ c. mushroom stock
2 pimentos, mashed
2 c. cooked chicken, minced
Salt and pepper
Lemon juice
1 pt. whipped cream

Mix egg yolks and milk; cook till custard consistency. Soak gelatin in water; dissolve in hot chicken broth. Stir into custard; add mushrooms, stock, pimentos, minced chicken and seasonings. When cool, fold in whipped cream and mold.

PIQUANT SAUCE:

1 c. mayonnaise
½ c. whipped cream
Juice of ½ lemon
¼ grated onion
½ c. slivered almonds

Combine all ingredients. Serve with mousse.

Mrs. Enoch B. Benson, Auburn, Ala.

Curried Chicken And Grape Salad

3 c. diced cooked chicken
1 ½ c. thinly sliced celery
1 c. green seedless grapes
2 tbsp. lemon juice
1 ¼ tsp. salt
¼ tsp. black pepper, freshly ground
1 ½ tsp. curry powder
6 tbsp. mayonnaise
3 tbsp. slivered toasted almonds

Combine all ingredients; toss lightly. Chill. Serve on lettuce; garnish with almonds. Yield: 6 servings.

Lois Pullen, Baton Rouge, La.

Chicken Salad With Fruit

5 to 6 cups diced cooked chicken
1 ½ cups chopped celery
Fresh or canned fruits
Salad greens

Combine chicken with celery and mound in center of large platter. Arrange fruits with salad greens around chicken salad. Serve with creamy orange dressing and curry-honey mayonnaise. Yield: 8 servings.

Photograph for this recipe below.

Ginger-Cream Chicken Salad

6 c. diced cooked chicken
3 c. diced celery
3 tsp. salt
½ tsp. pepper
6 tbsp. finely chopped candied ginger
3 tsp. honey
3 c. sour cream
Paprika
Lettuce

Combine chicken, celery, salt and pepper. Chill for 2 hours. Just before serving combine honey, ginger and sour cream. Stir half of ginger mixture into chicken mixture. Spoon onto a bed of lettuce. Top with remaining ginger mixture. Sprinkle with paprika. Yield: 12 servings.

Mrs. Ruby Thompson King, Hahira, Ga.

Gourmet Chicken Salad

2 c. cubed chicken breast
2 c. white grapes, halved and seeded
½ c. almonds, slivered
½ c. fruit salad dressing
6 lettuce leaves

Chill all ingredients. Just before serving combine chicken, grapes, almonds and salad dressing. Serve on lettuce. Yield: 6 servings.

Zelma Cromer, Home Economics Teacher, Lexington, Okla.

Mayonnaised Chicken

2 pkg. unflavored gelatin
1 c. chicken stock
1 pt. mayonnaise
1 hen, cooked and diced
1 sm. can tiny peas
2 c. diced celery
4 hard-cooked eggs, chopped
1 tbsp. chowchow
2 c. chopped almonds

Dissolve gelatin in chicken stock; add gradually to mayonnaise, stirring constantly. Fold in remaining ingredients. Chill until firm. Yield: 12 servings.

Mrs. G. B. Greene, Officers' Wives' Club, Randolph AFB, Tex.

Jellied Chicken Almond

1 tbsp. unflavored gelatin
¼ c. cold water
1 c. cold chicken broth
½ c. mayonnaise
½ tsp. salt
½ c. heavy cream, whipped
1 ½ c. diced cooked chicken
¾ c. halved, green seedless grapes
¾ c. slivered almonds
Lettuce
Stuffed olives, sliced

Soften gelatin in cold water; dissolve over hot water. Add chicken broth; remove from heat and cool. Combine with mayonnaise, salt and whipped cream. Fold in chicken, grapes and almonds. Spoon into individual molds and chill until firm. Unmold on lettuce and garnish with stuffed olive slices. Yield: 8 servings.

Mrs. Paul L. Dick, Roswell, N. M.

Pressed Chicken Salad

2 c. cooked chopped chicken
4 hard-cooked eggs, finely chopped
3 sm. pimentos, finely chopped
½ c. finely chopped stuffed olives
1 sm. dry or 4 green onions, finely chopped
1 stalk celery, finely chopped
1 tbsp. unflavored gelatin
4 tbsp. olive oil or salad oil
3 tbsp. tarragon vinegar
3 tbsp. water
1 tsp. Worcestershire sauce
½ tsp. salt
¼ tsp. pepper
¼ tsp. paprika

Combine chicken, eggs, pimentos, olives, onion and celery. Combine remaining ingredients in saucepan. Cook over medium heat, stirring constantly, until gelatin is dissolved, about 5 to 8 minutes. Add chicken mixture; blend well. Press into a 6-cup mold or six to eight individual molds. Chill for several hours or overnight. Unmold onto lettuce and garnish with tomatoes, cucumbers, olives and radishes, if desired. Yield: 6-8 servings.

Mrs. Larry Jones, Miami, Fla.

Mrs. Eisenhower's Chicken Jewel Ring Salad

2 envelopes unflavored gelatin
1 c. cranberry juice cocktail
1 1-lb. can whole cranberry sauce
2 tbsp. lemon juice
¾ c. cold water
1 tbsp. soy sauce
1 c. mayonnaise
1 ½ c. diced cooked chicken
½ c. diced celery
¼ c. coarsely chopped toasted almonds

Sprinkle 1 envelope unflavored gelatin on cranberry juice cocktail in saucepan to soften. Dissolve gelatin over low heat, stirring constantly. Break up cranberry sauce; stir into gelatin mixture with lemon juice. Pour into 6-cup ring mold; chill until almost firm. Sprinkle remaining gelatin on cold water in saucepan to soften. Dissolve over low heat, stirring constantly. Remove from heat; stir in soy sauce. Cool. Gradually stir gelatin mixture into mayonnaise until blended. Mix in remaining ingredients. Spoon over chilled cranberry layer. Chill until firm. Unmold onto salad greens. Yield: 8 servings.

Mrs. Dwight D. Eisenhower, Gettysburg, Pa.

Baked Turkey Salad

2 c. diced cooked turkey
2 c. diced celery
½ tsp. salt
1 tbsp. minced onion
½ c. chopped nuts
1 c. mayonnaise
2 tbsp. lemon juice
½ c. sliced stuffed olives
½ c. grated cheddar cheese
1 c. finely crushed potato chips

Combine all ingredients except cheese and potato chips. Spoon into buttered 1½-quart casserole. Combine cheese and potato chips; sprinkle over turkey mixture. Bake at 375 degrees for 20 minutes. Serve hot. Yield: 10 servings.

Mary Ella Ingram, Home Economics Teacher, Wagram, N. C.

Exotic Turkey Salad

4 c. cooked coarsely cut turkey
2 5-oz. cans water chestnuts

(Continued on next page)

1 lb. seedless green grapes or 2 sm. cans green grapes
1 c. sliced celery
1 to 1½ c. toasted slivered almonds
1 ½ c. mayonnaise
1 tbsp. lemon juice
2 tsp. curry powder
1 tbsp. soy sauce
1 sm. can litchi nuts
2 c. fresh or canned pineapple chunks

Combine turkey, chestnuts, grapes, celery and almonds. Blend mayonnaise with lemon juice, curry powder and soy sauce; toss with turkey mixture. Serve litchi nuts and pineapple chunks separately to be added, as desired. Yield: 6 servings.

Mrs. Royce K. Skow, Bethesda, Md.

Salad Supper

1 c. hot chicken broth
2 pkg. lemon flavored gelatin
1 c. mayonnaise
2 7-oz. bottles Seven-Up
3 c. grated cabbage
3 tbsp. prepared horseradish
2 8-oz. cans smoked turkey
2 1-lb. cans jellied cranberry sauce
Bibb lettuce

Add broth to gelatin; cool. Beat in the mayonnaise. Add Seven-Up. Partly congeal. Stir in cabbage and horseradish. Chill till firm in 8-cup mold. Serve with smoked turkey and cranberry sauce on crisp lettuce. Yield: 7-10 servings.

Mrs. Joe C. Parrish, Kenbridge, Va.

Turkey-Almond Salad

2 c. cubed cooked turkey
1 c. chopped red grapes, seeded
⅓ c. diced celery
½ c. almonds, toasted
Salad dressing

Combine turkey, grapes, celery and almonds. Add enough salad dressing to moisten. Serve on lettuce. Yield: 6-8 servings.

Ila Rea, Home Economics Teacher, Dayton, Pa.

Turkey-Cranberry Salad

TURKEY LAYER:

> 2 envelopes unflavored gelatin
> ½ c. cold water
> 1 ½ c. turkey broth
> 1 tbsp. lemon juice
> ½ tsp. salt
> ¾ c. mayonnaise
> 1 ½ c. finely diced turkey
> ½ c. finely diced celery

Heat 1 cup broth. Soften gelatin in cold water; add to hot broth and stir until dissolved. Add remaining broth, lemon juice and salt. Cool. Blend a little of the gelatin mixture into the mayonnaise until smooth. Add remaining gelatin; chill until syrupy. Fold in turkey and celery. Pour into oiled oblong baking dish and chill until firm.

CRANBERRY LAYER:

> 1 1-lb. can jellied cranberry sauce
> 1 tbsp. lemon juice
> ¼ tsp. salt
> 1 envelope unflavored gelatin
> ¼ c. cold water
> ½ c. boiling water

Mash cranberry jelly with fork; add lemon juice and salt. Soften gelatin in cold water; dissolve in hot water. Add cranberry sauce; blend well. Pour over firm turkey layer. Chill until firm. Yield: 10 servings.

Mrs. Kelley Storey, Home Economics Teacher, Paris, Tex.

Turkey-Pineapple-Almond Salad

> 1 c. sugar
> 2 eggs
> ¾ c. vinegar
> ½ tsp. dry mustard
> 4 c. pineapple chunks
> 1 ¼ c. evaporated milk
> 1 c. salad dressing
> 8 c. cooked diced turkey
> 2 c. slivered almonds

Make a dressing by combining sugar, eggs, vinegar and mustard. Cook until mixture begins to thicken. Remove from heat; cool. Drain pineapple; reserve ¼ cup juice. Blend in evaporated milk, pineapple juice and salad dressing. Toss turkey and pineapple with dressing; chill thoroughly. Just before serving add almonds and toss gently. Yield: 25-30 servings.

Barbara Gillogly, Champaign, Ill.

Party Pork Crown

1 3-oz. pks. celery flavored gelatin
1 c. hot water
½ c. cold water
1 tbsp. cider vinegar
½ c. mayonnaise or salad dressing
½ tsp. prepared mustard
¼ tsp. salt
1 12-oz. can pork luncheon meat, diced
1 8-oz. can peas, drained
Romaine leaves

Dissolve gelatin in hot water; stir in cold water and vinegar. Beat in mayonnaise, mustard and salt; pour into a shallow pan. Freeze for 20 minutes. Spoon into medium bowl; beat until light. Fold in meat and peas; spoon into 4-cup ring mold. Chill until firm. Unmold onto serving plate; garnish with romaine leaves. Yield: 4-6 servings.

Mrs. Allie C. Woodcock, New Orleans, La., Favorite Recipes Food Fair

Pork And Apple Salad

2 c. diced cooked pork
2 c. diced unpeeled red apples
1 c. diced celery
¼ c. India or sweet relish
1 tbsp. lemon juice
¼ tsp. onion juice
Dash of salt
⅓ c. mayonnaise

Combine all ingredients; chill. Serve on lettuce. Yield: 4 servings.

Mrs. Charles DeKeyser, Aiea, Hawaii

Russian Salad

4 lb. pork, cooked, cooled and diced
½ pkg. spaghetti, cooked
3 tomatoes, chopped
4 hard-cooked eggs, chopped
1 lge. can peas
1 can pimento
1 sm. onion, diced
3 celery hearts, diced
1 sm. head lettuce, shredded
1 pt. mayonnaise

(Continued on next page)

Stuffed olives
Sliced avocados

Combine all ingredients except olives and avocados; toss lightly. Serve garnished with olives and sliced avocados. Potatoes may be substituted for spaghetti.

Mrs. William M. Momyer, Officers' Wives' Club, Randolph AFB, Tex.

 ## Buffet Ham Ring

   1 can tomato soup
  ¾ c. water
   2 tbsp. gelatin, softened in ½ c. cold water
   1 3-oz. pkg. cream cheese
   2 tbsp. lemon juice
   1 tbsp. grated onion
  ½ c. mayonnaise
   2 tbsp. prepared mustard
   2 c. cooked ground ham

Combine soup and water; heat thoroughly. Remove from heat; add softened gelatin and cream cheese. Beat smooth with rotary beater; cool. Add lemon juice, onion, mayonnaise, mustard and ham. Rinse ring mold with cold water. Pour in mixture; chill 3 to 4 hours. Unmold on salad leaves. Garnish with hard-cooked eggs and stuffed olives. Yield: 8-10 servings.

Mrs. Jean Emerson, Bowbells, N. D.

 ## Ham And Cucumber

   2 3-oz. pkg. lemon-lime gelatin
   1 tsp. salt
   2 c. boiling water
   1 ½ c. cold water
  ¼ c. vinegar
   1 c. slivered cooked ham
   1 c. sliced celery
   1 9-oz. can drained pineapple chunks
  ½ c. thinly sliced quartered cucumber
  ¾ tsp. grated onion
   3 tbsp. prepared horseradish

Dissolve gelatin and salt in boiling water. Add cold water and vinegar. Chill until thick. Fold in remaining ingredients. Pour into 1-quart ring mold. Chill until firm. Yield: 8 servings.

Mrs. H. M. Callaway, Home Economics Teacher, Lexington, Ga.

Ham Aspic Salad

1 ½ tbsp. unflavored gelatin
½ c. cold water
3 c. tomato juice
Dash of salt
1 tsp. sugar
½ bay leaf
1 tbsp. chopped onion
3 c. minced baked ham

Soften gelatin in cold water for 5 minutes. Heat tomato juice, salt, sugar, bay leaf and onion; simmer for 10 minutes. Strain; add gelatin. Stir and cool. Add ham; pour into mold. Chill until firm. Yield: 6-8 servings.

Mrs. William H. Chitty, Jr., Officers' Wives' Club, Tucson, Ariz.

 ## Ham Salad Bowl

2 c. diced cooked ham
1 c. diced celery
2 hard-cooked eggs, chopped
¼ c. mayonnaise
1 tbsp. chopped sweet pickles
1 tbsp. catsup

Combine ham, celery and eggs. Add mayonnaise, pickles and catsup; toss well. Place in lettuce cups; chill. Serve with crackers. Yield: 4 servings.

Georgia Matthews, Home Economics Teacher, Oliver Springs, Tenn.

 ## Hot Baked Ham Salad

3 c. diced cooked ham
1 c. diced celery
½ c. chopped stuffed olives
2 hard-cooked eggs, diced
2 tsp. diced onion
1 tbsp. lemon juice
2 tbsp. prepared mustard
⅛ tsp. pepper
¾ c. margarine
1 c. crushed potato chips

Combine all ingredients except potato chips; place in greased 8 x 8-inch square pan. Sprinkle with potato chips. Bake at 400 degrees for 20 minutes. Yield: 6 servings.

Mrs. Pershing Kettelson, Albion, Neb.

Ham Mold

1 c. hot water
1 pkg. lemon gelatin
¾ c. cold water
3 tbsp. vinegar
1 tbsp. grated onion
½ tsp. Worcestershire sauce
⅓ c. chopped sweet pickles
½ c. diced celery
½ c. diced canned pimento
⅓ c. mayonnaise
1 c. (firmly packed) ground cooked ham

Pour hot water over gelatin; stir until dissolved. Add cold water and vinegar; let set until slightly thickened. Beat with rotary beater until the consistency of whipped cream; add remaining ingredients. Chill until firm. Garnish with lettuce; serve with olives, potato chips and crackers.

Ima Willes, Babbitt, Nev.

 ## Imperial Ham Salad

2 c. chopped cooked ham
½ c. sliced pitted ripe olives
½ c. chopped unpeeled cucumber
⅓ c. sliced green onions
2 tbsp. chopped pimento
Sandwich spread
Pineapple slice
Chopped parsley

Combine ham, olives, cucumber, onions, pimento and enough sandwich spread to moisten; toss lightly. Garnish with pineapple and parsley. Chill. Yield: 4 servings.

June M. Sippy, Meadville, Pa.

 ## Kidney Bean Salad

1 can kidney beans, drained
½ c. chopped celery
½ c. diced green pepper
1 onion, cut in circles
½ c. chopped pickles
½ lb. chopped cheese

(Continued on next page)

1 lb. ham, cut in strips
2 hard-cooked eggs, sliced
Mayonnaise

Combine and toss all ingredients except mayonnaise. Chill. Just before serving, add mayonnaise and mix carefully. Place in lettuce cups.

Mrs. Mary Ann Lea, Vilonia, Ark.

 ## Make-A-Meal Salad Bowl

1 clove of garlic (opt.)
½ c. oil
2 tbsp. vinegar
¾ tsp. salt
⅛ tsp. pepper
½ tsp. dry mustard
¼ tsp. paprika
½ head lettuce, broken into 1½-inch pieces
2 tbsp. chopped green pepper
½ c. diced celery
½ c. thinly sliced cauliflower
½ c. cooked or canned asparagus tips
½ lb. baked ham, diced

Chill all ingredients. Rub inside of salad bowl with garlic. Combine oil and vinegar; add seasonings. Beat with fork until well mixed. Add remaining ingredients in order given; toss lightly until each piece of salad is coated with dressing. Serve immediately. Yield: 6-8 servings.

Mrs. James L. Stanley, Officers' Wives' Club, Griffiss AFB, N. Y.

 ## Rabbit Salad

1 rabbit
1 c. chopped celery
2 boiled eggs, chopped
Salt and pepper
Salad dressing

Boil the rabbit until tender in water containing salt and a little chopped onion. Remove from bones and dice. Combine the rabbit with celery and chopped eggs; season. Add salad dressing to make consistency for salad. Chill. To vary the recipe, add nuts or olives or substitute chopped apple for the celery.

Mrs. Lawrence Brady, Franklin, Tex.

Chicken Liver Salad

½ lge. onion, chopped
2 tbsp. chicken fat or cooking oil
1 lb. fresh chicken livers
4 hard-cooked eggs
Salt and pepper

Saute one-fourth of onion in fat; add chicken livers. Cook thoroughly over medium-low heat. Do not let livers get a crust coating. Cool livers and eggs; put through meat grinder. Add remaining onion and mix thoroughly; season to taste. Yield: 4-6 servings.

Mrs. Richard D. Conn, Officers' Wives' Club, Texarkana, Ark.

 ### Medley Supper Salad

½ lb. chicken livers, diced
2 tbsp. butter
Salt
1 clove of garlic
4 c. torn salad greens
1 red onion, thinly sliced
3 hard-cooked eggs, cubed
½ c. crumbled Bleu cheese
½ c. French dressing

Cook chicken livers in butter until lightly browned; sprinkle lightly with salt. Cool. Rub salad bowl with cut garlic. Combine livers with remaining ingredients; toss lightly. Yield: 4-6 servings.

Mrs. Dwight E. Beach, Hon. Pres., Officers' Wives' Club, Seoul, Korea

Tongue Salad A La Peterson

6 slivered slices tongue
¼ lb. slivered Swiss cheese
2 hard-cooked eggs
1 cucumber, chopped
1 green pepper, chopped
1 carrot, chopped
2 tomatoes, chopped
1 tsp. minced onion
1 tsp. vinegar
4 tbsp. mayonnaise

(Continued on next page)

3 tbsp. milk or cream
Sharp cream dressing

Combine all ingredients except cream dressing. Serve with sharp cream dressing. Yield: 6 servings.

Pearle Peterson, Home Economics Teacher, Perth Amboy, N. J.

 ## Veal Salad Mold

1 small shank or other bone pieces
Water to cover meat and bones
2 lbs. cubed veal meat
1 tsp. salt
White pepper to taste
6 to 8 peppercorns
1 medium bay leaf
½ c. diced celery

Cook until meat is tender. Lift meat and bones from broth. Remove any meat on bones; discard bones. Coarsely grind meat. Strain broth. Add cubed meat; season with salt, white pepper, peppercorns, bay leaf, and celery. Simmer until broth just covers meat. Pour into pyrex loaf pan or any desired mold. Chill. When congealed, ease sides loose and remove to serving plate. Garnish with parsley, olives, carrot curls, etc. Serve with vinegar or other meat seasoning sauces. Yield: 8 servings.

Edith M. Anderson, Home Economics Teacher, Austin, Tex.

 ## Jellied Veal Or Chicken

2 tbsp. unflavored gelatin
2 c. beef consomme or meat juice
3 c. diced veal or chicken
1 ½ tsp. salt
½ c. finely diced carrots
1 c. diced celery
Tomato slices
Peas

Dissolve gelatin in heated consomme. Add remaining ingredients except tomatoes and peas. Arrange tomatoes and peas in bottom of individual dishes. Add gelatin mixture. Chill until firm. Serve on lettuce leaf and garnish.

Mrs. Nannie Giese, Walburg, Saskatchewan, Canada

Jellied Veal With Sauce

4 lb. veal and knuckle, cut into pieces
1 lge. onion
1 bunch celery tops
1 tbsp. salt
1 tbsp. gelatin
¼ c. water
3 tsp. Worcestershire sauce

Combine veal, onion, celery tops and salt. Cover with water; cook until tender. Remove veal; strain broth. Grind meat. Dissolve gelatin in cold water; add to hot broth. Add meat and Worcestershire sauce; chill until set.

SAUCE:

1 c. mayonnaise
2 hard-cooked eggs, chopped
½ c. English walnuts
12 stuffed olives, sliced
1 tsp. grated onion
½ pt. heavy cream, whipped
2 c. diced celery

Combine all ingredients; serve with jellied veal. Yield: 12 servings.

Mrs. David L. Schneider, Chillicothe, Ohio, Favorite Recipes Food Fair

Tangy Meat Salad

1 lb. veal, cubed
½ lb. pork, cubed
1 No. 2 can peas, drained
2 c. cut celery
⅓ sm. can chopped pimento
Minced green pepper, parsley and onion to taste
Juice of 1 lemon
Salad dressing
4 hard-boiled eggs, chopped
1 sm. bottle stuffed olives, sliced

Cook meat until tender, using most of the water in the cooking. Cool. Add peas, celery, pimento, green pepper, parsley and onion; mix together. Sprinkle lemon juice over all; add desired amount of salad dressing. Mix well by tossing. Add chopped egg and olive slices. Garnish with parsley or egg slices. Yield: 12 servings.

Mrs. H. L. Angst, Abilene, Kan.

Seafood Salads

Frozen Tomato-Caviar Salad

6 med. tomatoes, peeled
1 tsp. salt
Dash of pepper
1 3½-oz. jar black caviar
¼ c. mayonnaise
Lettuce

Hollow out tomatoes slightly at stem end. Sprinkle with salt and pepper; invert and chill. Drain. Chill in freezer tray for 1 hour. Blend caviar with mayonnaise. Serve tomatoes on lettuce; top with caviar-mayonnaise mixture. Yield: 6 servings.

Mrs. Irving Lee Kanof, Officers' Wives' Club, Rome, Italy

Clam Salad

1 cucumber, peeled and sliced
3 stalks celery, sliced
2 carrots, sliced
1 root lotus, sliced (opt.)
2 doz. medium uncooked clams, chopped into lge. pieces
1 c. vinegar
⅔ c. sugar
2 tbsp. lemon juice
½ tsp. monosodium glutamate

Combine cucumber, celery, carrots, lotus and clams. Combine remaining ingredients for dressing; toss with clam mixture. Chill; serve in lettuce cups if desired. Yield: 6 servings.

Mrs. Henry Matt, Birmingham, Ala., Favorite Recipes Food Fair

Frozen Fish Salad

1 1-lb. pkg. frozen cod fish
½ tsp. salt
4 tbsp. chopped pickle
4 tbsp. chopped onion
4 tbsp. chopped pimento
Salad dressing

Place frozen fish in salted water. Cook until well done, about 15-20 minutes. Combine pickles, onion, pimento and fish. Add salad dressing to moisten. May be used as sandwich filling, cream cheese dip, or as spread for crackers. Yield: 8 servings.

Billie Lue Bosher, Home Economics Teacher, Amherst, Tex.

Barbecue Salad

> 1 pkg. lemon gelatin
> 1 c. hot water
> 1 8-oz. can tomato sauce
> 1 ½ tbsp. vinegar
> 1 tsp. Worcestershire sauce
> Dash of pepper
> ½ tsp. salt
> 1 tsp. grated onion
> 1 6½-oz. can crab meat
> 1 c. diced celery

Dissolve gelatin in hot water. Add tomato sauce, vinegar, Worcestershire sauce, pepper and salt. Chill until mixture starts to thicken. Add onion, crab meat and celery. Pour into a 1-quart ring mold or individual molds; chill until firm.

Mrs. John Bailey, San Antonio, Tex.

 ## Bayley's West Indies Salad

> 1 lb. fresh lump crab meat
> 1 medium onion, finely chopped
> 4 oz. salad oil
> 3 oz. cider vinegar
> 4 oz. ice water
> Salt and pepper

Place half of the chopped onion in bottom of bowl. Separate crab meat lumps; place on top of onion. Spread remaining onion over crab meat. Salt and pepper to taste. Pour oil, then vinegar and lastly ice water over crab-onion. Cover and refrigerate from 2-12 hours. Toss lightly just before serving. Yield: 6 servings.

Grace Lunsford, Home Economics Teacher, Foley, Ala.

Chesapeake Bay Crab Salad

> 1 lb. fresh crab meat
> 1 c. chopped celery
> ½ c. chopped sweet pickles
> ¼ c. mayonnaise
> 2 tbsp. sweet pickle juice
> Salt and pepper to taste

Combine crab with celery and pickles. Blend mayonnaise with pickle juice; add to crab mixture. Sprinkle with salt and pepper; toss lightly. Garnish with paprika; chill. Yield: 4 servings.

Mrs. Ray I. Etheridge, Officers' Wives' Club, Key West, Fla.

Crab Aspic

    2 envelopes unflavored gelatin
    ½ c. cold water
    1 can tomato soup
    3 3-oz. pkg. cream cheese
    1 c. chopped celery
    1 sm. onion, chopped
    ¼ c. chopped green pepper
    1 c. Thousand Island dressing
    1 7½-oz. can crab meat

Soften gelatin in water. Heat soup in double boiler; add cheese and gelatin. Stir until cheese melts; add celery, onion, green pepper, dressing and crab meat. Place in mold; refrigerate for 3 hours before serving. Yield: 8 servings.

Mrs. A. B. Scott, Oakland, Cal.

 ## Crab Louis Salad

    3 cans crab meat
    6 c. shredded lettuce
    2 hard-cooked eggs, diced
    2 tbsp. chopped chives
    2 med. tomatoes, peeled and quartered
    1 ⅓ c. mayonnaise
    ⅓ c. heavy cream
    ½ c. chili sauce
    2 tbsp. horseradish
    4 tsp. lemon juice
    1 tsp. salt
    ¼ tsp. freshly ground black pepper
    ⅓ c. chopped scallions
    2 tbsp. chopped capers
    ¾ tsp. Worcestershire sauce

Flake crab meat into a large salad bowl. Add lettuce; mix well. Sprinkle with eggs and chives. Garnish with tomato wedges. Combine remaining ingredients for dressing; mix well. Pour dressing over salad; toss lightly. Yield: 5 servings.

Mrs. Albert S. Borchik, Jr., Rome, N. Y.

Crab Mousse

> 2 pkg. cream cheese
> 1 can cream of mushroom soup
> 1 c. mayonnaise
> 1 pkg. unflavored gelatin
> ¼ c. cold water
> 1 c. crab meat
> 1 c. chopped celery
> ½ sm. onion, grated
> 1 tbsp. Worcestershire sauce
> 1 can cranberry sauce

Heat cream cheese, soup and mayonnaise in a double boiler until smooth. Dissolve gelatin in cold water; add with crab meat, celery, onion and Worcestershire sauce to cheese mixture. Mix well. Pour into individual molds; refrigerate until set. Slice cranberry sauce ½-inch thick; unmold crab mixture onto cranberry slices. Yield: 8 servings.

Mrs. Clarence Jackson, Officers' Wives' Club, Columbus, Ohio

 ### Crab-Pear Salad With Hot Vinaigrette Dressing

> 1 7½-oz. can Alaskan King crab, drained and sliced
> 1 c. chopped celery
> 2 hard-cooked eggs, chopped
> ¼ tsp. powdered mustard
> 1 tsp. salt
> ⅛ tsp. pepper
> ¼ tsp. garlic powder
> 1 tbsp. chopped chives
> ½ c. salad oil
> 2 tbsp. vinegar
> 2 tbsp. fresh lemon juice
> 1 1-lb. 13-oz. can Bartlett pear halves, drained

Toss crab with celery and eggs. Blend mustard, salt, pepper, garlic powder, chopped chives, salad oil, vinegar and lemon juice; heat to boiling. Add pear halves; simmer for 5 minutes. Remove pears to platter. Pour hot sauce over crab mixture, tossing lightly. Heap crab in center of pear platter. Garnish with crisp celery greens, if desired. Yield: 4 servings.

Mrs. William R. Swift, Officers' Wives' Club, Fort Lewis, Wash.

 ### Crab-Stuffed Avocado

> 2 cans King crab
> 1 hard-cooked egg, minced

(Continued on next page)

1 dill pickle, finely chopped
1 sm. onion, minced
6 sm. celery stalks, chopped
30 to 40 capers
3 tbsp. mayonnaise
3 cloves of garlic, pressed
1 tbsp. tarragon vinegar
3 ripe avocados

Combine all ingredients except avocados; add salt and pepper to taste. Split avocados; remove seed. Stuff with crab filling. Serve on lettuce leaves, if desired. Yield: 6 servings.

Mrs. John Hanlin, Albuquerque, N. M.

 ## Grapefruit-Crab Cocktail

1 c. frozen crab meat, thawed
1 tbsp. lemon juice
1 1-lb. can grapefruit sections, chilled and drained
1 c. mayonnaise or salad dressing
2 tbsp. catsup
1 tbsp. lemon juice
Few drops of Tabasco sauce

Flake crab meat; sprinkle with lemon juice. Alternate grapefruit sections and crab meat in salad bowls. Combine remaining ingredients; pour over grapefruit and crab meat. Yield: 6-8 servings.

Mrs. James Osborn, Officers' Wives' Club, El Paso, Tex.

 ## King Crab Salad

1 6-oz. can King crab, drained
2 c. diced celery
½ sm. onion, grated
½ c. chili sauce
1 ½ c. mayonnaise
4 tbsp. fresh lemon juice
Salt to taste
1 c. slivered toasted almonds
4 avocados, pared and cut into wedges
2 hard-cooked eggs, sliced

Combine crab meat, celery and onion. Mix chili sauce, mayonnaise, lemon juice and salt. Toss with crab meat mixture; add almonds. Garnish with avocados and eggs. Yield: 12 servings.

Mrs. Gordon H. Austin, Newburgh, N. Y.

Pacific Crab Salad

½ c. sour cream
¼ c. minced celery
2 tbsp. chopped olives
1 tbsp. grated onion
1 tbsp. chopped parsley
2 tbsp. chili sauce
¼ tsp. salt
Shredded lettuce
2 lge. tomatoes, peeled and halved crosswise
1 6½-oz. can crab meat, drained, flaked and chilled
1 hard-cooked egg, sliced

Combine sour cream, celery, olives, onion, parsley, chili sauce and salt; chill to blend flavors. Arrange beds of lettuce on four salad plates; place a tomato half on each. Pile crab meat on each tomato; spoon sour cream dressing over top. Cover with egg slices. Yield: 4 servings.

Mrs. Don W. Bailey, Fort Worth, Tex.

Bouillabaisse Salad

1 c. cooked crab meat
1 c. cooked lobster
½ lb. cooked shrimp
1 c. cooked whitefish
2 tomatoes, sliced
Mixed salad greens
6 ripe olives, halved
French dressing
Salad dressing

Arrange crab, lobster, shrimp, whitefish and tomatoes on a bed of mixed greens; garnish with olives. Toss with French or hot spice dressing. Yield: 6 servings.

Mrs. Stephen W. Downey, Killeen, Tex.

Molded Shrimp And Crab Salad

2 pkg. Italian or lemon salad gelatin
1 c. boiling water
1 c. cold water
1 can frozen shrimp soup, thawed
1 8-oz. pkg. cream cheese
1 c. mayonnaise
1 ½ c. diced celery

(Continued on next page)

1 tsp. minced onion
1 9-oz. can crab meat

Dissolve gelatin in boiling water. Add cold water. Allow to thicken slightly. Add remaining ingredients; pour into mold. Refrigerate until firm. Yield: 6-8 servings.

Mrs. John Knight, Miami, Fla., Favorite Recipes Food Fair

 ## Fresh Seafood Salad

1 c. cooked flaked halibut
1 c. cooked flaked fresh crab meat
¾ c. finely diced celery
¼ c. drained and finely chopped sweet pickles
1 tbsp. lemon juice
½ tsp. dry mustard
¼ c. mayonnaise
Salt and pepper to taste

Combine ingredients and mix well. Chill. Garnish with watercress, tomatoes and cucumbers. Yield: 4 servings.

Mrs. Lillian Wise, Home Economics Teacher, Rabun Gap, Ga.

 ## Lobster Aspic Parisienne

3 envelopes unflavored gelatin
1 ⅓ c. cold water
2 cans bouillon, heated
2 tbsp. lemon juice
2 tsp. Worcestershire sauce
1 ½ lb. lobster, cooked
1 ½ c. cooked peas
1 c. diced cooked carrots
1 ½ c. diced cooked potatoes
2 tsp. salt
⅔ c. mayonnaise

Soften gelatin in water; dissolve in bouillon. Add lemon juice and Worcestershire sauce. Chill until thick. Pour 1 cup gelatin mixture into 4-cup mold. Arrange pieces of lobster, red-side down, in gelatin mixture. Chill until almost set. Dice remaining lobster; add peas, carrots, potatoes, salt and mayonnaise. Add to remaining gelatin mixture. Carefully pour over firm gelatin. Chill until firm. Unmold onto lettuce; garnish with wedges of tomato, hard-cooked eggs, ripe olives and lemon wedges if desired. Yield: 8-10 servings.

Mrs. James B. Miller, Officers' Wives' Club, Argentia, Newfoundland

Mock Lobster Salad

1 lge. slice halibut
1 onion, sliced
1 c. water
1 tsp. salt
1 can tomato soup
Chopped celery
Mayonnaise
Garlic salt
Pepper

Place halibut, onion, water and salt in saucepan; cook for 15 to 20 minutes or until fish is white. Drain, reserving stock; cool. Flake fish; add soup and enough reserved stock to cover fish. Refrigerate overnight. Drain fish through a sieve, allowing fish to drain for 1 hour. Mash fish; add celery, mayonnaise, garlic salt and pepper to taste. Yield: 4-5 servings.

Mrs. Sidney Weinberg, Def. Constru. Supply Center, Columbus, Ohio

Lobster-Melon Salad With Puffs

½ c. mayonnaise
¼ c. sour cream
2 tbsp. chopped green onion
2 tbsp. finely chopped parsley
1 tbsp. tarragon vinegar
1 tbsp. lemon juice
1 sm. clove of garlic, crushed
¼ tsp. salt
Pepper
2 5½-oz. cans lobster, drained
2 c. canataloupe or honeydew melon balls
¾ c. self-rising corn meal
¾ c. self-rising flour
1 c. water
½ c. butter
4 eggs

Blend mayonnaise, sour cream, onion, parsley, vinegar, lemon juice, garlic, salt and pepper. Stir in lobster; refrigerate. Just before serving, fold in melon balls. Mix corn meal and flour. In saucepan, bring water and butter to a boil, stirring until butter melts. Add dry ingredients all at once. Reduce heat; cook and stir until mixture is smooth and forms a ball. Remove from heat; cool slightly. Add eggs, one at a time, beating well after each addition. Drop batter by rounded tablespoonfuls onto baking sheet to make 10 shells. Bake at 350 degrees for 30 to 35 minutes or until firm to touch. Cool on wire rack. Cut tops off shells; remove soft interiors. Divide lobster salad among the shells. Refrigerate until ready to serve.

Mrs. George McPherson, Mobile, Ala.

185

Lobster-Egg Salad

  2 c. flaked lobster
  1 c. diced celery
  3 hard-cooked eggs, chopped
  ¼ tsp. salt
  ⅛ tsp. pepper
  Mayonnaise

Combine all ingredients with enough mayonnaise to moisten; chill. Serve on lettuce leaves if desired.

Mrs. Edward Sole, San Francisco, Cal.

 ### Lobster Mousse

  3 3-oz. pkg. cream cheese
  1 can tomato soup
  2 tbsp. gelatin
  1 c. cold water
  ½ to ¾ c. chopped celery
  2 tbsp. chopped green onion
  ¼ to ½ c. chopped green pepper
  1 ½ c. cooked or canned lobster
  1 c. mayonnaise
  Salt and pepper to taste
  Tabasco sauce to taste
  Worcestershire sauce

Blend cheese and soup; heat until smooth. Soak gelatin in cold water; add to hot mixture. Chill until mixture begins to congeal; add celery, onion, green pepper and lobster. Add mayonnaise and seasonings to taste. Pour into 2-quart fish mold; chill until firm.

Mrs. Everett W. Holstrom, Officers' Wives' Club, Davis Monthan AFB, Ariz.

Lobster-Potato Salad

  ½ tsp. powdered mustard
  2 tbsp. instant minced onion
  2 tbsp. water
  2 c. cooked chopped lobster
  1 c. cold diced cooked potatoes
  2 tbsp. fresh lemon juice
  1 ½ tsp. salt
  ¼ tsp. garlic powder
  ⅛ tsp. pepper

(Continued on next page)

⅓ c. mayonnaise
1 head lettuce
Paprika

Soak mustard and onion in water for 10 minutes; add lobster, potatoes, lemon juice, salt, garlic, pepper and mayonnaise. Mix lightly. Serve on lettuce. Garnish with paprika. Yield: 6 servings.

Mrs. Charles E. Bartels, Officers' Wives' Club, Prestwick AFB, Scotland

 ## Lobster Salad In Pineapple Shells

1 ripe pineapple
2 c. sour cream
2 tbsp. lemon juice
1 tsp. salt
1 tbsp. curry powder
½ c. chopped green mango chutney
4 c. chopped cooked lobster
1 c. sliced pimento-stuffed olives
½ c. toasted almonds

Halve pineapple and crown lengthwise, leaving crown on pineapple. Carefully cut out fruit in wedges, leaving ½-inch shell. Remove core; cut fruit into 1½-inch wedges. Blend sour cream, lemon juice, salt, curry powder and chutney; toss lightly with lobster, sliced olives and pineapple wedges. Heap into pineapple shells; sprinkle with almonds. Yield: 6 servings.

Mrs. Al Hood, Atlanta, Ga.

Lobster Salad

5 med. lobster tails
1 ½ c. diced celery
1 tsp. minced onion
1 tsp. lemon juice
1 tsp. paprika
½ c. mayonnaise
½ c. sour cream
2 lge. tomatoes, chopped
6 lettuce leaves

Place lobster in 5 quarts boiling water; cook for 40 minutes or until lobster tails are light pink. Cool; clean lobster. Cut into small pieces. Blend in remaining ingredients. Serve on lettuce leaves and garnish with paprika, if desired. Yield: 6 servings.

Mrs. Charlie R. Baker, Officers' Wives' Club, Key West, Fla.

South African Rock Lobster Curry Salad

    1 6-oz. pkg. curry rice mix
    4 4-oz. frozen South African rock lobster tails
    1 9-oz. pkg. frozen Italian green beans, cooked, drained and
       chilled
    1 1-lb. can chick peas, drained
    2 c. sliced celery
    ½ c. chopped chutney
    ¾ c. French dressing
    1 head Western iceburg lettuce

Prepare curry rice mix according to package directions following instructions for drier rice. Cool rice; chill. Drop lobster tails into boiling salted water. When water reboils, cook tails for 7 minutes. Drain and drench with cold water. Cut away underside membrane with scissors. Pull meat from shell; cut into ½-inch crosswise slices. Mix lobster with rice, green beans, chick peas and celery. Add chutney and French dressing; toss lightly. Serve in a bowl edged with wedges of iceburg lettuce. Yield: 6 servings.

Photograph for this recipe on page 177.

 ## Avocado Salad

    1 c. diced cooked or canned lobster
    2 c. cooked or canned crab meat
    2 tbsp. chopped chives
    1 tbsp. salt
    ⅓ c. mayonnaise or salad dressing
    1 tbsp. Worcestershire sauce
    2 tbsp. chili sauce
    2 avocados
    Lemon juice
    Pimento strips
    Watercress or lettuce

Combine lobster, crab meat, chives, salt, mayonnaise, Worcestershire sauce and chili sauce. Cut avocados into halves; remove seed. Sprinkle with lemon juice. Pack with lobster-crab meat mixture. Garnish tops with pimento strips; serve on bed of watercress or lettuce. Yield: 4 servings.

Mrs. Eugene Parish, Pensacola, Fla., Favorite Recipes Food Fair

 ## Mackerel Salad

    1 can mackerel
    3 mashed potatoes
    2 c. crushed crackers

(Continued on next page)

½ c. vinegar
1 onion, cut fine
Sugar
3 boiled eggs

Mix mackerel with potatoes. Add cracker crumbs. Add vinegar and onion.
Sweeten to taste. Add boiled eggs. Stir to smooth in bowl. Refrigerate 1 to 2
hours before serving.

Mrs. E. V. Hill, Corbin, Ky.

 ## Real Cool Fish

2 1-lb. cans mackerel
1 to 3 c. chopped hard-cooked eggs
1 8-oz. pkg. cream cheese
½ c. butter
2 tbsp. lemon juice
Few drops Tabasco sauce
1 c. chopped celery
1 c. chopped green pepper
2 tbsp. grated onion
Pimento
Olives

Combine all ingredients except pimento and olives; blend well. Pack mixture into a 6-cup fish mold. Chill for 2 or 3 hours. To unmold, loosen edges with a
sharp knife. Invert mold on a serving platter; hold hot compresses to mold.
until mixture falls on platter. Decorate fish with thin strips of pimento for
scales and tail stripes; use olive sections for eyes. Cut smiling mouth from green
pepper. Yield: 6 servings.

Sally Marnen, Home Economics Teacher, Coraopolis, Pa.

Oyster Salad

2 No. 1 cans oysters, undrained
1 med. can pimentos
8 hard-cooked eggs
4 sour pickles
4 tbsp. margarine, melted
30 soda crackers
Salt and vinegar to taste

Grind all ingredients together; mix well. Add salt and vinegar to taste. Yield:
12 servings.

Mrs. Joyzelle Sauls, Home Economics Teacher, Brownsville, Tex.

Oyster Salad

2 eggs, well beaten
¼ c. vinegar
4 tbsp. sugar
½ tsp. salt
1 tsp. prepared mustard
2 tbsp. water
3 cans cove oysters
12 soda crackers, crumbled
8 hard-cooked eggs, diced
1 c. finely chopped sweet pickles
¼ tsp. black pepper
1 c. finely cut celery

Mix the first 6 ingredients. Cook over hot water or low heat until mixture is consistency of soft custard. Cool. Mash oysters in their liquid. Add remaining ingredients; toss well. Add dressing. Chill several hours before serving. Yield: 8 servings.

Kathryn Davis, Home Economics Teacher, Pinckeyville, Ill.

Oyster Salad

⅓ c. finely chopped celery
¼ c. minced parsley
2 tbsp. finely chopped pimento
¼ tsp. pepper
¼ tsp. salt
⅓ c. French dressing
4 c. chopped poached oysters, chilled

Combine celery, parsley, pimento, pepper, salt and French dressing. Add oysters; mix lightly. Serve in mounds on bed of greens and garnish with tomato wedges if desired. Yield: 4 servings.

Mrs. L. D. Reneau, Officers' Wives' Club, Grafenwohr, Germany

Cold Salmon With Cucumber Dressing

2 med. cucumbers
½ c. heavy cream
¼ c. mayonnaise
1 tsp. salt
2 tbsp. vinegar
Dash of Tabasco sauce
1 can salmon

(Continued on next page)

Grate cucumbers; drain for 15 minutes. Whip cream; fold in mayonnaise, salt, vinegar, Tabasco sauce and cucumbers. Chill salmon overnight; drain and remove skin and bones. Arrange on lettuce beds and garnish with lemon, if desired. Serve with cucumber dressing. Yield: 6 servings.

Mrs. Milton R. Moore, Officers' Wives' Club, Sheppard AFB, Tex.

 ## Luncheon Salmon Salad

> 1 1-lb. can pink salmon, drained
> 2 hard-cooked eggs, finely chopped
> 2 tbsp. slivered onion
> ½ tsp. celery seed
> ½ c. mayonnaise
> Salt and pepper to taste
> Sprinkle of parsley flakes
> ½ c. sour cream
> 2 tbsp. dry onion soup mix

Combine all ingredients except sour cream and dry onion soup mix; arrange on lettuce leaf. Top with sour cream; sprinkle with onion soup mix. To serve hot, place salmon mixture on eight bread slices; place under broiler until heated. Top with sour cream and onion soup mixture. Yield: 4 servings.

Mrs. Edward May, Des Moines, Iowa

 ## Salmon Mold

> 1 envelope gelatin
> 1 c. tomato juice
> ½ c. mayonnaise
> 1 tbsp. vinegar
> 1 tbsp. grated onion
> 2 tsp. Worcestershire sauce
> ½ tsp. salt
> ½ c. heavy cream, whipped
> 1 can salmon, flaked
> 2 hard-cooked eggs, quartered

Sprinkle gelatin over ¼ cup tomato juice. Bring remaining tomato juice to a boil; add to gelatin. Stir until dissolved. Blend mayonnaise, vinegar, onion, Worcestershire sauce and salt into gelatin mixture. Chill until thickened. Fold in whipped cream and salmon. Arrange eggs in oiled 1-quart mold or individual molds. Spoon mixture over eggs. Chill. Serve on greens garnished with tomato wedges, if desired.

Mrs. Elliott Bloxom, Officers' Wives' Club, Honolulu, Hawaii

Salmon Mousse

4 3¾-oz. cans dietetic pack salmon
2 envelopes unflavored gelatin
⅓ c. cold water
1 c. boiling water
3 tbsp. vinegar
1 tsp. onion juice
½ c. low-calorie mayonnaise dressing
2 egg whites, stiffly beaten

Drain salmon; remove skin and bones. Mash very fine or whirl in blender. Soften gelatin in cold water; add boiling water. Stir well to dissolve; cool. Add salmon, vinegar, onion juice and dressing; chill until thick. Fold in beaten egg whites; spoon into 5-cup mold. Chill for 3 to 4 hours or until set. Unmold; garnish with green pepper. Yield: 6 servings.

Mrs. Peter Coffield, Jacksonville, Ark.

 ### Salmon-Pepper Salad

2 lge. green peppers
1 8-oz. pkg. cream cheese
1 ½-lb. can red salmon
¼ tsp. salt
¼ tsp. paprika
1 tbsp. minced parsley
1 tsp. minced onion
Tomatoes, sliced

Remove seed from end of peppers. Combine cheese and salmon; add salt, paprika, parsley and onion. Mix thoroughly; stuff peppers with mixture. Wrap in waxed paper; chill for 6 to 8 hours. Slice peppers crosswise with sharp knife. Serve in overlapping slices, alternating with slices of fresh tomatoes. Yield: 6-8 servings.

Mrs. Louis P. Testa, Officers' Wives' Club, Athens, Greece

Summer Salmon

2 tbsp. gelatin
⅓ c. boiling water
1 lb. salmon, cooked, drained and flaked
1 med. cucumber, chopped
1 c. finely chopped celery
1 tsp. horseradish
1 tsp. minced onion
1 tsp. lemon juice

(Continued on next page)

Tuna goes Hawaiian in a blend of fruits nested in pineapple shells. Tuna also goes cool when heaped in a lime-sour cream ring mold.

HAWAIIAN TUNA SALAD

1 med. pineapple
2 7-oz. cans tuna, drained
¾ c. sliced peaches
1 med. banana, sliced
½ c. flaked coconut
1 med. apple, cored and diced
½ c. mayonnaise
¼ c. orange juice
1 tsp. aromatic bitters
¼ tsp. salt
Stemmed red Maraschino cherries
Parsley

Cut pineapple in half; remove fruit, leaving ½-inch shell. Reserve shells; dice pineapple. Combine pineapple, tuna, peaches, banana, coconut and apple; mix lightly. Chill. Blend mayonnaise, orange juice, bitters and salt. Chill. Add dressing to tuna salad; toss lightly but well. Fill shells with salad. Garnish with cherries and parsley. Yield: 4 servings.

TUNA-LIME RING

2 3-oz. pkg. lime gelatin
2 c. boiling water
2 c. cold water
1 c. dairy sour cream
2 7-oz. cans tuna, drained
½ c. chopped celery
¼ c. chopped canned pimento
1 tbsp. dehydrated minced onion
3 tbsp. vinegar
Cucumber slices
Parsley

Dissolve gelatin in boiling water. Add cold water; chill until slightly thickened. Beat in sour cream until smooth. Turn into an 8-inch ring mold. Chill until firm. Combine tuna, celery, pimento, onion and vinegar; mix well. Unmold lime ring onto serving platter. Fill center with tuna mixture. Garnish with cucumber and parsley. Yield: 6 servings.

See photograph on reverse page.

1 tsp. salt
¼ tsp. pepper
1 ½ c. sour cream

Soak gelatin in a small amount of cold water; dissolve in boiling water. Mix remaining ingredients in a bowl; add gelatin. Mix thoroughly. Pour into mold; chill until set. Serve garnished with lettuce, hard-cooked eggs and tomato wedges. Yield: 8 servings.

Mrs. Bill Jones, Chattanooga, Tenn.

 Pecan-Sardine Salad

4 tomatoes
¼ c. chopped pecans
2 cans sardines, broken
2 tsp. lemon juice
½ tsp. prepared mustard
3 tbsp. mayonnaise
½ c. diced celery
1 tbsp. chopped olives
4 hard-cooked eggs, cubed
Salt and pepper

Peel and halve tomatoes. Dice top of each and add to pecans, sardines, celery, eggs and other ingredients. Place salad on remaining tomato halves. Chill. Serve on endive or Romaine lettuce.

Mrs. R. C. Bouse, Jr., Port Bolivar, Tex.

 Avocado-Shrimp Salad

1 med. can deveined shrimp
1 sm. box macaroni, cooked
1 avocado, cut into sm. pieces
1 stalk celery, chopped
1 onion, chopped
½ green pepper, diced
4 hard-cooked eggs, sliced
1 c. salad dressing
2 tsp. evaporated milk
½ tsp. white vinegar
½ tsp. sugar
Paprika

Mix shrimp, macaroni, avocado, celery, onion, green pepper and eggs in large glass bowl. Using wooden spoon, mix salad dressing, milk, vinegar and sugar;

(Continued on next page)

beat thoroughly. Add to salad. Cover and refrigerate for 4 hours. Sprinkle with paprika. Yield: 8 servings.

Mrs. William Koll, Naval Officers' Wives' Club, Sigonella, Sicily

 ## Curried Shrimp And Melon Salad

    1 ½ tbsp. mild curry powder
    6 tbsp. sour cream
    4 c. cooked cleaned shrimp
    1 c. mayonnaise
    1 ½ tbsp. grated onion
    2 tbsp. lemon juice
    1 ½ c. chopped celery
    1 ½ tsp. salt
    1 lge. honeydew melon
    1 c. chopped nuts
    1 c. grated coconut
    1 c. chutney

Blend curry powder into sour cream; mix with shrimp, mayonnaise, onion, lemon juice, celery and salt; chill for several hours. Scoop balls out of melon. Remove remaining melon from shell; fill shell with salad. Garnish with melon balls. Serve with chopped nuts, grated coconut and chutney as condiments. Yield: 8 servings.

Mrs. James L. Jarnagin, Cascade, Md.

Curried Shrimp Salad

    4 lb. cooked shrimp
    2 tbsp. lemon juice
    ½ tbsp. grated onion
    1 ½ tbsp. salt
    1 ½ tbsp. curry powder
    6 tbsp. sour cream
    1 c. mayonnaise
    1 c. melon balls
    ½ c. chopped celery
    ½ c. pineapple chunks
    French dressing

Combine shrimp, lemon juice, onion and salt; chill overnight. Mix curry powder, sour cream and mayonnaise; let stand for several hours. Marinate melon balls, celery and pineapple chunks in French dressing for several hours. One hour before serving, combine all ingredients; chill until serving time. Yield: 8 servings.

Mrs. Thomas B. Whitehouse, Officers' Wives' Club, Bangkok, Thailand

Fresh Shrimp Salad

2 lb. cleaned cooked shrimp
4 hard-cooked eggs, chopped
2 c. cooked elbow macaroni
½ c. minced celery
2 tbsp. minced onion
2 tsp. minced parsley
1 c. tiny peas
2 tbsp. capers (opt.)
Mayonnaise to taste
Salt and pepper to taste

Slice shrimp into halves lengthwise. Combine all ingredients. Chill well. Garnish with lettuce, tomato wedges and egg slices. Yield: 8 servings.

Mrs. Robert Allen, Nashville, Tenn.

 ### Hawaiian Shrimp Salads

1 ½ c. cooked cleaned shrimp
1 c. sliced celery
1 c. fresh, frozen or canned pineapple chunks
½ c. broken pecans
½ tsp. minced onion
½ c. mayonnaise
¼ c. French dressing
Salt
Lemon juice to taste
¼ c. sliced stuffed olives (opt.)
Lettuce
2 papayas or 2 avocados (opt.)

Combine all ingredients except lettuce and papayas. Refrigerate until well chilled. Serve in lettuce cups or place in halves of chilled, seeded and pared papayas arranged on lettuce. Yield: 4 servings.

Mrs. Bill Riddle, Jacksonville, Fla.

 ### Louisiana Shrimp Salad

1 c. cooked shrimp
½ c. mayonnaise
1 c. chopped celery
3 hard-cooked eggs, sliced
Salt and pepper to taste
Tabasco sauce to taste

(Continued on next page)

2 tbsp. chopped pickle
2 lge. avocados, diced
Juice of ½ lemon

Combine all ingredients; serve on lettuce leaves if desired. Yield 4-5 servings.

Mrs. Dracos D. Burke, Officers' Wives' Club, Bellevue, Neb.

Mandarin-Shrimp Salad

⅓ c. heavy cream, whipped
½ c. mayonnaise
2 lb. shrimp, boiled and cleaned
1 5¼-oz. can water chestnuts, drained and thinly sliced
1 11-oz. can Mandarin oranges, drained
2 dashes of Tabasco sauce
Salt
White pepper
Lettuce leaves
1 bunch watercress
1 2-oz. jar pimento strips, drained

Fold whipped cream into mayonnaise. Combine shrimp, mayonnaise mixture, water chestnuts, orange segments and Tabasco sauce; add salt and white pepper to taste. Marinate for 30 minutes in refrigerator. Line cold serving plates with lettuce leaves; spoon salad onto lettuce. Place two large sprigs of watercress on each salad at opposite sides of serving plates. Place pimento strips on top of salad just before serving. Yield: 4 servings.

Mrs. Carl Raines, Galveston, Tex.

Mock Crab Salad

1 4-oz. can pimento, diced
1 5-oz. can shrimp, diced
3 hard-cooked eggs, diced
8 oz. vermicelli, cooked
3 tbsp. vinegar
½ tsp. onion salt
1 tsp. salt
¼ tsp. pepper
5 to 6 tbsp. mayonnaise

Combine pimento, shrimp and eggs; add cut up vermicelli. Add vinegar, onion salt, salt, pepper and enough mayonnaise to moisten. Refrigerate for at least 1 hour. Yield: 8 servings.

Mrs. William Luther, Officers' Wives' Club, Middletown, Pa.

Oriental Salad

1 c. shredded lettuce
2 c. cleaned cooked shrimp
4 slices boiled ham, cut into thin strips
1 c. celery strips
½ c. green pepper strips
½ c. toasted blanched slivered almonds or macadamia nuts
1 can crisp chow mein noodles

Combine lettuce, shrimp, ham and vegetables; chill. Just before serving, add nuts, noodles and desired dressing. Yield: 4 servings.

Mrs. Norman Ching, Officers' Wives' Club, Duluth, Minn.

 ### Quick Shrimp Salad

2 8-oz. pkg. frozen shrimp, cleaned
2 c. chopped celery
1 c. radish slices
2 tbsp. minced onion
2 tbsp. minced dill pickle
1 tsp. salt
¼ tsp. pepper
4 tbsp. salad oil
2 tbsp. lemon juice

Boil shrimp; chill well. Combine with remaining ingredients; chill for several hours. May be served with sliced tomato and hard-cooked egg slices and topped with sour cream. Yield: 6-8 servings.

Mrs. Oliver C. Harvey, Philadelphia, Pa., Favorite Recipes Food Fair

Shrimp Hawaiian

1 14-oz. can pineapple chunks
6 c. broken salad greens
2 5-oz. cans deveined shrimp, drained
1 5-oz. can water chestnuts, drained and coarsely chopped
½ c. mayonnaise or salad dressing
¼ c. crumbled Roquefort cheese

Drain pineapple, reserving 2 tablespoons syrup. Place salad greens in a large bowl; pile shrimp, pineapple chunks and water chestnuts in rows on top. Blend reserved pineapple syrup into mayonnaise and cheese. Drizzle over salad mixture; toss lightly to mix. Yield: 6 servings.

Mrs. J. R. Pennington, Myrtle Beach, S. C.

197

Shrimp Salad With Peas

Mayonnaise
Cream
2 c. fresh cooked shrimp
1 c. diced celery
4 hard-cooked eggs, diced
1 c. cooked peas
Salt and pepper to taste
Lettuce

Thin mayonnaise with cream. Combine shrimp, celery, eggs and peas. Season; moisten with mayonnaise. Serve on lettuce. Yield: 8 servings.

Mrs. R. F. Christian, Officers' Wives' Club, Eleuthera, Bahamas

 ### California Tuna Salad

2 6½ or 7-oz. cans tuna in vegetable oil
2 c. orange sections
1 avocado, halved lengthwise and seeded
1 tbsp. lemon juice
1 c. chopped celery
½ c. toasted blanched slivered almonds
1 ½ tsp. curry powder (opt.)
½ c. mayonnaise or salad dressing
Salad greens

Drain tuna. Break into large pieces. Reserve 12 orange sections for garnish. Cut remaining sections into halves. Peel and slice avocado; sprinkle with lemon juice to prevent discoloration. Reserve 6 slices avocado for garnish; cut remaining slices into fourths. Combine orange, avocado, celery, almonds and tuna. Combine curry powder and mayonnaise. Pour over tuna mixture; blend lightly. Chill. Serve on salad greens. Garnish with orange sections and avocado slices. Yield: 6 servings.

Mrs. Buddy Goldberg, New York, N. Y.

 ### Congealed Tuna Salad

1 envelope gelatin
¼ c. cold water
¼ c. hot water
⅔ c. mayonnaise
2 tsp. prepared mustard
2 tsp. lemon juice
1 sm. can tuna
1 hard-cooked egg, chopped

(Continued on next page)

½ c. peas
2 tbsp. grated onion
2 tbsp. chopped pimento (opt.)

Soften gelatin in cold water; dissolve in hot water. Add remaining ingredients in order given. Chill until set.

Mrs. J. L. Carson, Officers' Wives' Club, Ft. McPherson, Ga.

Fifteen Minute Salad

1 7-oz. can tuna, drained
1 c. mayonnaise
1 No. 303 can small peas, drained
2 or 3 dill pickles, chopped
2 or 3 sweet pickles, chopped
1 sm. onion, chopped or packaged minced onion
¾ tsp. salt
½ tsp. pepper
1 1-lb. pkg. egg noodles, cooked and rinsed
3 hard-cooked eggs, chopped

Combine tuna, mayonnaise, peas, pickles, onion, salt and pepper in salad bowl. Add noodles and 2 eggs; toss lightly. Garnish with remaining egg. Yield: 6-8 servings.

Mrs. Peter Kelligrew, Officers' Wives' Club, Fort Devens, Mass.

Kidney Bean-Tuna Salad

1 1-lb. can red kidney beans, drained
1 7-oz. can chunk tuna, drained
6 anchovy fillets, quartered
1 c. sliced celery
2 tbsp. instant minced onion
¼ tsp. instant minced garlic
¼ tsp. pepper
1 ½ tsp. salt
1 ½ tsp. basil leaves
1 tsp. vinegar
¼ c. mayonnaise
Lettuce
Tomato wedges

Combine all ingredients except tomato and lettuce; mix lightly. Chill for at least 1 hour; serve on lettuce. Garnish with tomato wedges. Yield: 6 servings.

Mrs. Allan Gunter, Panama City, Fla.

Molded Tuna-Egg Salad

2 sm. pkg. lemon gelatin
2 c. boiling water
1 c. mayonnaise
1 c. heavy cream, whipped
3 cans tuna, flaked
2 c. chopped celery
2 tsp. salt
1 green pepper, diced
2 tbsp. grated onion
6 hard-cooked eggs, chopped
1 c. pecans

Dissolve gelatin in boiling water; chill. Whip. Add mayonnaise to whipped cream; fold into gelatin mixture. Add remaining ingredients; place in 9 x 13-inch pan or mold. Yield: 12-16 servings.

Mrs. B. D. Johnson, Memphis, Tenn.

Tropical Tuna Salad

1 tbsp. mayonnaise
1 tsp. salt
1 tbsp. prepared mustard
1 ½ c. flaked tuna
½ c. diced celery
½ c. diced pineapple
1 c. sliced bananas
2 tbsp. chopped sweet pickles
1 head crisp lettuce, shredded or cups

Mix mayonnaise, salt and mustard; add remaining ingredients. Blend lightly. Serve on beds of shredded lettuce or in lettuce cups. Yield: 4-6 servings.

Mrs. Craig Owens, Atlanta, Ga.

Tuna-Apple Salad

1 9-oz. can tuna, flaked
3 hard-cooked eggs, chopped
2 sweet pickles, chopped
1 Delicious apple, chopped
½ c. salad dressing or mayonnaise
Lettuce

Combine all of the ingredients except lettuce in mixing bowl; arrange on lettuce bed on platter or individual plates.

Mrs. Jose Enriquez, Naval Officers' Wives' Club, Naha AB, Okinawa

Tuna-Bean Bowl

1 med. can white tuna
1 No. 303 can pork and beans
½ c. chopped sweet pickles
1 head lettuce, chopped
1 c. mayonnaise

Break tuna into lima bean-sized chunks; combine all ingredients in a large bowl. Mix gently. Yield: 6 servings.

Mrs. James Lindberg Hughes, Officers' Wives' Club, Griffiss AFB, N. Y.

 ### Tuna-Cabbage Hong Kong

1 can (6½ or 7 oz.) tuna in vegetable oil
½ c. sliced onion
½ c. sliced celery
4 c. shredded cabbage
1 can (8 oz.) seasoned stewed tomatoes
2 tbsp. soy sauce

Drain vegetable oil into large skillet and heat. Add onion and celery; saute a few minutes, toss in cabbage and saute about 5 minutes, stirring occasionally. Stir in tuna, tomatoes, and soy sauce. Cover; continue to cook 5 minutes longer. Serve immediately. Yield: 2-3 servings.

Photograph for this recipe below.

Tuna-Corn Chip Salad

    1 7-oz. can tuna, drained
    ½ c. mayonnaise
    1 c. diced celery
    2 hard-cooked eggs, coarsely chopped
    ½ c. diced sweet pickles
    Salt and white pepper to taste
    1 c. crushed corn chips

Combine all ingredients except corn chips; chill. Add corn chips just before serving. Yield: 4 servings.

Mrs. Jerry Hamner, Mobile, Ala.

 ### Tuna-Egg Salad

    1 clove of garlic, crushed
    ¾ tsp. salt
    ½ c. salad dressing
    1 tbsp. wine vinegar
    ¼ tsp. Worcestershire sauce
    1 qt. salad greens
    2 to 4 tomatoes, quartered
    6 to 8 radishes, sliced
    3 hard-cooked eggs, sliced
    1 can tuna

Combine garlic, salt, salad dressing, vinegar and Worcestershire sauce. Wash and drain salad greens; chill. Combine salad greens, tomatoes, radishes, eggs and tuna in a salad bowl. Toss with dressing. Yield: 4 servings.

Mrs. Marvin L. Kramer, Officers' Wives' Club, Dreux AFB, France

Tuna-Orange Cups

    6 oranges
    1 7-oz. can tuna, drained and flaked
    ½ c. sliced celery
    ½ c. cooked peas
    2 tbsp. chopped pimento
    ⅔ c. French dressing
    1 tbsp. Worcestershire sauce

Slice tops off oranges; scallop edges. Remove pulp; cut into cubes. Toss cubes with remaining ingredients; fill orange shells. Yield: 6 servings.

Mrs. Brendan Dixon, Officers' Wives' Club, Charleston, S. C.

Cereal and
Pasta Salads

Easy Macaroni Salad

> 1 c. uncooked shell macaroni
> ¼ c. finely chopped onion
> ½ clove of garlic, minced
> 1 tbsp. salad oil
> 1 tbsp. vinegar
> 1 tbsp. salt
> ½ c. chopped celery
> ¼ c. chopped dill pickles
> 6 radishes, thinly sliced
> ¼ c. mayonnaise

Cook macaroni according to package directions; drain well. Combine ingredients; chill. May be garnished with radishes. Yield: 6-8 servings.

Mrs. William E. Fox, Officers' Wives' Club, Goeppingen, Germany

Hot Or Cold Macaroni Salad

> 4 oz. elbow macaroni
> 4 strips bacon, cut in ½-inch pieces
> ½ c. celery, diced
> ¼ c. green pepper, chopped
> ¾ c. cucumber pickles, chopped
> ¼ c. onion, chopped
> 2 tbsp. chili sauce
> ½ tsp. Worcestershire sauce
> 1 tsp. salt
> ⅛ tsp. pepper
> 1 tsp. sugar
> ¼ c. mayonnaise

Cook macaroni in boiling salted water about 12 minutes. Drain and rinse. Cook bacon bits until crisp. Fold all ingredients into the macaroni. Heat in top of double boiler. Serve hot or chill overnight before serving. Yield: 8 servings.

Mrs. Mary C. Williamson, Home Economics Teacher, Hallsboro, N. C.

My Mother's Macaroni Salad

DRESSING:

> 2 tbsp. salad dressing or mayonnaise
> 1 to 3 tbsp. vinegar
> ½ tsp. prepared mustard
> 2 tsp. sugar
> Salt to taste

(Continued on next page)

Combine all ingredients.

    1 ½ c. macaroni
    2 stalks celery, chopped or ½ tsp. celery seed
    1 green pepper, chopped
    1 cucumber, chopped
    ½ medium onion, chopped
    2 medium tomatoes, cut in pieces
    1 carrot, chopped

Cook macaroni in salted water until almost dry. Mix all ingredients with warm macaroni. Garnish as desired. Pour dressing over macaroni mixture and marinate for at least an hour before serving. Yield: 10 servings.

Mrs. Eileen Skaggs, Home Economics Teacher, Alderson, W. Va.

Salad Supreme

    1 c. uncooked macaroni
    1 c. celery, chopped
    6 tbsp. sweet pickle, chopped
    3 tbsp. pimento, chopped
    6 tbsp. green pepper, chopped
    1 c. sharp cheese, diced
    ½ c. green peas, cooked
    ½ c. salad dressing

Cook macaroni according to package directions. Drain and chill for 2 hours. Add celery, pickles and pimento. Toss lightly. Add remaining ingredients; toss. Chill. Yield: 6 servings.

Mary Nan Fitch, Home Economics Teacher, Electra, Tex.

Sweet Macaroni Salad

    2 c. cooked macaroni
    2 c. miniature marshmallows
    ½ c. Maraschino cherries, quartered
    ⅓ c. mayonnaise
    Light cream
    1 or 2 bananas, sliced

Combine macaroni, marshmallows and cherries. Thin mayonnaise with cream; combine with macaroni mixture. Chill thoroughly. Add bananas; mix lightly. Yield: 6-8 servings.

Mrs. Maurice W. Dunn, Officers' Wives' Club, Fort Riley, Kan.

Summer Salad

2 c. elbow macaroni, cooked and rinsed
1 med. apple, cut into wedges
1 med. orange, sliced
1 13-oz. can frozen grapefruit sections, thawed and drained
⅓ c. chopped salted peanuts
½ c. French dressing

Combine macaroni, apple, orange, grapefruit, peanuts and dressing. Toss lightly. Yield: 4-6 servings.

Mrs. Anne Black, Ogden, Utah

California Sprout, Beef And Macaroni Salad

1 tbsp. salt
3 qt. boiling water
2 c. uncooked elbow macaroni
1 10-oz. pkg. frozen California Brussels sprouts
1 c. cooked corned beef strips
1 med. onion, chopped
¼ c. sliced canned pimento
½ c. mayonnaise
1 tbsp. prepared horseradish
1 tbsp. sugar
3 tbsp. vinegar

Add salt to rapidly boiling water. Gradually add macaroni so that water continues to boil. Cook, uncovered, stirring occasionally, until tender. Drain in colander. Rinse with cold water; drain. Cook Brussels sprouts according to package directions; drain if necessary. Combine macaroni, Brussels sprouts, corned beef, onion and pimento; toss lightly but thoroughly. Chill. Combine remaining ingredients; mix well. Arrange macaroni mixture on bed of crisp lettuce, if desired. Top with mayonnaise mixture. Yield: 4-6 servings.

Mrs. Ralph W. Cooke, Greenville, S. C.

German Macaroni Salad

¾ c. raw elbow macaroni, cooked and rinsed
¼ lb. liverwurst, cubed
½ c. chopped sweet pickles
½ c. sliced celery
⅓ c. mayonnaise
2 tbsp. chili sauce
¾ tsp. salt

(Continued on next page)

Combine macaroni, liverwurst, pickles and celery; blend remaining ingredients. Toss with macaroni mixture. Garnish with tomato wedges, green pepper rings or egg slices, if desired. Chill. Yield: 4-6 servings.

Mrs. Ernest C. Fusan, Hon. Pres. Officers' Wives' Club, Jacksonville, N. C.

Corned Beef With Macaroni Salad

1 pkg. lemon gelatin
1 ½ c. hot water
1 ½ c. celery, finely diced
1 c. salad dressing
1 tbsp. onion, chopped
½ green pepper, finely chopped
3 hard-cooked eggs, chopped
1 can corned beef, shredded
2 tbsp. vinegar
4 oz. ring macaroni

Cook macaroni according to package directions. Dissolve gelatin in hot water. Chill until slightly congealed. Gently fold in remaining ingredients. Refrigerate until firm. Yield: 8 servings.

Mrs. Bonnie Shaw, Clarkfield, Minn., Favorite Recipes Food Fair

Macaroni Salad With Frankfurters

1 8-oz. pkg. elbow macaroni, cooked and drained
1 tsp. salt
¼ tsp. pepper
1 c. chopped celery
¾ c. pared sliced cucumbers
⅓ c. minced green pepper
¼ c. minced onion
½ c. sliced stuffed olives
4 hard-cooked eggs, chopped
2 tsp. prepared mustard
1 c. cooked salad dressing
1 lb. cooked frankfurters, chopped

Combine all ingredients; toss gently until blended. Chill thoroughly. Yield: 8 servings.

Mrs. George L. Oakley, Pres. Coast Guard Officers' Wives' Club,
New Orleans, La.

Vienna-Macaroni Salad

1 8-oz. pkg. macaroni, cooked and drained
1 c. chopped celery
1 c. chopped sweet pickles, drained
2 tbsp. grated onion
2 small cans Vienna sausage
½ c. mayonnaise
1 tsp. salt
2 tbsp. juice from pickles

Combine macaroni with celery, pickles, onion and 1 can sausage, cut into thin slices. Blend mayonnaise, salt, and pickle juice into macaroni mixture. Arrange on lettuce and spoke remaining sausage around top of salad.

Pat Haney, Denver, N. C.

Main Dish Salad

4 oz. elbow macaroni
1 c. cooked chicken, turkey, or tuna, chopped
2 hard-cooked eggs, diced
½ c. crushed pineapple, drained
¼ c. radishes, sliced
¼ c. nuts, chopped
1 tbsp. onion, chopped
⅓ c. mayonnaise
1 ½ tbsp. pineapple juice
¼ tsp. celery seed
¼ tsp. salt
Dash of pepper

Cook macaroni as directed on package. Combine poultry or tuna, eggs, pineapple, radishes, nuts and onion. Add macaroni; toss lightly. Combine mayonnaise and pineapple juice; mix until smooth. Stir in celery seed, salt and pepper. Pour over macaroni mixture. Toss until well blended. Chill. Serve on salad greens. Yield: 4 servings.

Mrs. Ruth A. Blomgren, Silver Spring, Md.

Macaroni-Chicken Salad Bowl

1 8-oz. pkg. elbow macaroni
4 c. water
½ tsp. salt
1 c. celery, sliced
1 ½ c. cooked chicken, diced
⅓ c. sweet pickle, chopped
1 tbsp. onion, scraped
¼ c. French dressing
Mayonnaise or salad dressing

Cook macaroni in water in a 2-quart saucepan. Add salt; bring to a rapid boil. Stir; cover and boil until tender. Drain and cool. Mix celery, chicken, pickles, onion and French dressing; blend with mayonnaise or salad dressing. Mix with Macaroni. Chill. Garnish with sliced sweet pickles. Yield: 8 servings.

Mrs. Sarah Musgrave, Home Economics Teacher, Rattan, Okla.

 ### Best Tuna-Macaroni Salad

1 ½ tbsp. lemon juice
1 tbsp. vegetable oil
1 c. raw macaroni, cooked
1 can tuna, flaked
2 hard-cooked eggs, chopped
1 tbsp. chopped onion
½ c. chopped celery
¼ c. grated carrots
½ c. mayonnaise
½ tbsp. salt
Dash of pepper
Salad greens

Mix lemon juice with vegetable oil; combine with macaroni. Fold in tuna, eggs, onion, celery and carrots. Fold in mayonnaise; add salt and pepper. Mix well. Arrange on greens. Yield: 4-6 servings.

Mrs. James G. Dyer, Officers' Wives' Club, Goeppingen, Germany

Crab-Macaroni Salad

1 8-oz. pkg. elbow or shell macaroni
1 can crab meat
½ c. shredded cabbage or 1 c. diced carrots
1 c. diced cucumber
1 c. diced celery
¼ c. chopped or thinly-sliced onion

(Continued on next page)

½ c. chopped or thinly-sliced green pepper
1 sm. jar pimento, cut in strips
3 hard-cooked eggs, sliced
Salt and pepper to taste
Mayonnaise or dressing

Boil macaroni according to package directions; drain well and chill. Flake crab; combine with macaroni, cabbage, cucumber, celery, onion, green pepper, pimento and eggs. Season with salt and pepper. Mix with mayonnaise or boiled dressing. Garnish with thin slices of tomatoes and radishes. Chill at least 30 minutes. Yield: 6 servings.

Mrs. Sally D. Pickering, Rumford Center, Maine

 Favorite Tuna-Macaroni Salad

1 6-oz. can tuna
1 c. macaroni rings
3 hard-cooked eggs, chopped
½ c. celery, chopped
1 tbsp. onion, chopped
1 tbsp. pickle, chopped or relish
½ c. salad dressing
2 tbsp. evaporated milk
2 tbsp. lemon juice or pickle juice
1 tbsp. mayonnaise

Cook macaroni rings according to directions on package. Combine tuna, eggs, celery, onion and pickle. Add macaroni. Combine salad dressing, evaporated milk and lemon or pickle juice. Fold dressing carefully into salad mixture and chill for several hours. Just before serving add mayonnaise. Garnish with egg slices, olives and paprika. Yield: 8 servings.

Mrs. Esther E. Smith, Home Economics Teacher, Westfield, Pa.

 Macaroni-Salmon Salad

2 c. cooked macaroni, cooled
1 c. cucumber, diced
1 8-oz. can salmon, flaked
1 tbsp. onion, grated
1 tbsp. parsley, minced
¾ c. mayonnaise
½ tsp. salt
¼ tsp. pepper

Combine all ingredients; toss together until blended. Yield: 4-6 servings.

Mrs. Linda J. McCraw, Home Economics Teacher, Gaffney, S. C.

Maca-Salmon Salad

    2 c. uncooked macaroni
    1 c. cheese, diced
    1 c. sweet pickle, diced
    1 c. celery, diced
    ¼ c. pimento, diced
    ¼ c. green pepper, minced
    ¼ c. onion, minced
    4 c. canned salmon, drained and flaked
    2 c. mayonnaise
    2 tbsp. prepared mustard
    6 tbsp. vinegar
    2 heads lettuce

Cook macaroni according to directions on package. Drain. Add cheese; toss until well mixed. Cool. Add pickles, celery, pimento, green pepper and onion. Add salmon. Blend mayonnaise, mustard and vinegar. Pour over salad; chill thoroughly. At serving time, use crisp outer leaves of lettuce to line big bowls or chop plates. Cut remaining lettuce; add to salad and toss lightly. Yield: 14-18 servings.

Mrs. Ellen D. Feagan, Home Economics Teacher, Las Cruces, N. M.

Macaroni-Shrimp Salad

    1 7 or 8-oz. pkg. shell macaroni
    1 4-6 oz. shrimp
    1 c. pineapple, diced
    1 c. celery, diced
    ½ c. sweet pickle, diced
    2 tbsp. onion, minced
    ½ c. mayonnaise
    1 tbsp. prepared mustard
    1 tsp. salt
    Dash of pepper
    1 tbsp. pimento, diced
    2 tbsp. lemon juice

Cook macaroni in boiling salted water for 10 minutes, or until tender. Drain and blanch with cold water; drain again. Combine all ingredients and toss thoroughly. Refrigerate until ready to serve. Garnish with greens or radish roses. Yield: 4-6 servings.

Mrs. Marguerite S. Drechsel Darnall, Campo, Cal.

Salad Supper

> 1 7-oz. pkg. shell or lge. elbow macaroni
> 1 7-oz. can tuna, drained
> 1 small onion, finely chopped
> 2 hard-cooked eggs, sliced
> 1 c. celery, diced
> ½ c. ripe olives, sliced and pitted
> 2 tomatoes, quartered
> Mayonnaise
> Salt to taste

Cook macaroni in small amount of water. Cool. Mix all ingredients except eggs and tomatoes, adding enough mayonnaise to moisten. Garnish with eggs and tomatoes. Chill before serving. Yield: 4 servings.

Mrs. Joe D. Gamble, Home Economics Teacher, Friendswood, Tex.

 ### Salmon-Macaroni Salad

> 1 c. cooked macaroni
> 1 c. salmon, shredded
> 2 tbsp. lemon juice
> ½ c. pickle, chopped
> 2 tbsp. onion, finely chopped
> Salt
> Pepper
> Paprika
> Mayonnaise
> Shredded cabbage

Cook macaroni according to package directions; rinse in cold water and drain. Combine macaroni, salmon, lemon juice, onion and pickle. Moisten with mayonnaise. Season to taste and mix lightly with 2 forks. Chill. Serve on a bed of crisp, shredded cabbage. Yield: 3-4 servings.

Lois Gruneberg, Home Economics Teacher, Williamsport, Pa.

 ### Salmon Salad

> 2 c. cooked shell macaroni
> 2 c. salmon, flaked
> 4 hard-cooked eggs, diced
> ½ c. celery, diced
> ½ c. process cheese, diced
> ½ tsp. salt
> 2 medium tomatoes, diced
> ½ c. salad dressing

(Continued on next page)

Mix macaroni, salmon, eggs, celery and cheese. Add salt, tomatoes and salad dressing; mix lightly. Chill. Yield: 6 servings.

Frances Watson, Millbury, Ohio

Sharon's Shrimp Salad

2 c. macaroni
1 c. celery, finely chopped
1 can shrimp
2 hard-cooked eggs, finely chopped
¼ c. pimento
¼ tsp. paprika
½ tsp. salt
1 c. mayonnaise
¼ c. French dressing

Cook macaroni according to package directions; cool. Add celery, shrimp, eggs, pimento, paprika and salt. Mix mayonnaise and French dressing and add to macaroni mixture.

Mrs. Sharon Nelson, Home Economics Teacher, Karlstad, Minn.

Shrimp And Macaroni Salad

1 ½ tbsp. lemon juice
1 tbsp. vegetable oil
1 c. elbow macaroni, cooked
1 ½ c. diced cooked shrimp
2 hard-cooked eggs
2 tbsp. chopped green pepper
1 tsp. chopped onion
½ c. chopped celery
½ c. diced fresh tomato
¼ c. chopped stuffed olives
2 tbsp. sour cream
½ tsp. salt
¼ c. mayonnaise or salad dressing
Salad greens

Mix lemon juice and vegetable oil; combine with macaroni. Chill for several hours, stirring occasionally. Fold in shrimp, eggs, green pepper, onion, celery, tomato and olives. Blend sour cream, salt and mayonnaise; fold into macaroni mixture. Arrange on crisp salad greens. Yield: 4-6 servings.

Mrs. Robert M. Kridle, Pres. Officers' Wives' Club, Baguio City, Philippines

Shrimp-Macaroni Surprise

1 c. uncooked macaroni
1 c. chopped celery
¼ c. chopped green onions
½ c. chopped green pepper
¼ c. chopped pimento
2 hard-cooked eggs, sliced
½ tsp. salt
¼ tsp. paprika
1 7-oz. can shrimp
1 c. mayonnaise
¼ c. Italian dressing

Cook macaroni in boiling, salted water until tender. Drain. Chill. Add remaining ingredients except mayonnaise and dressing. Mix. Moisten with mayonnaise and Italian dressing. Serve on lettuce. Garnish with tomato slices, if desired. Yield: 6 servings.

Mrs. John Malcolm Beaton, Fallon, Nev.

Tuna-Cheese Macaroni Salad

1 7 or 8-oz. pkg. macaroni, boiled
1 6½-oz. can tuna
1 c. cheddar cheese, cubed
½ c. sweet pickle, chopped
¼ c. onion, minced
½ c. mayonnaise
2 tbsp. prepared mustard
1 tbsp. sugar
1 No. 303 can peas, drained

Drain cooked macaroni; rinse in cold water. Add tuna, cheese, pickles and onion. Mix mayonnaise, mustard and sugar. Combine the 2 mixtures. Add peas and salt to taste; mix well. Yield: 6 servings.

Mrs. Robert Berkner, Home Economics Teacher, Lamberton, Minn.

Tuna-Roni Salad

½ c. shell macaroni
1 can tuna, flaked
1 No. 303 can English peas, drained
½ c. celery, diced
1 c. cheese, cubed
⅓ c. sweet pickles, chopped

(Continued on next page)

3 pimentos, chopped
¾ to 1 c. salad dressing
Salt and pepper to taste

Cook macaroni in boiling water until tender; drain. Rinse with cold water. Combine all ingredients. Mix well. Garnish with pimento strips, paprika or egg wedges. Salad may be made the day before serving if desired. Yield: 8-10 servings.

Mrs. Thelma Cravy, Home Economics Teacher, Jacksonville, Tex.

 Yularda Salad

1 12-oz. pkg. yularda twist macaroni
2 cans crab meat
1 med. onion, grated
2 tbsp. chopped pimento
½ green pepper, chopped
Mayonnaise
Salt and pepper

Boil macaroni until tender; drain. Add crab, onion, pimento and green pepper; toss. Add mayonnaise, salt and pepper to taste. Chill. Yield: 6 servings.

Mrs. Ben L. Openshaw, Hon. Pres. Officers' Wives' Club, Pt. Arena AFS, Cal.

 Cabbage-Macaroni Salad

1 c. uncooked elbow or shell macaroni
2 finely shredded cabbage
½ c. grated carrots
¼ c. thinly sliced green pepper
2 tbsp. minced onion
1 7-oz. can tuna, drained and flaked
½ c. mayonnaise
2 tbsp. prepared mustard
1 tsp. salt
2 tsp. vinegar

Cook macaroni in boiling salted water until tender; drain and rinse. Combine macaroni with cabbage, carrots, green pepper, onion and tuna. Blend mayonnaise with mustard, salt and vinegar; pour over macaroni-tuna mixture and toss. Serve hot or cold on salad greens. Yield: 6 servings.

Mrs. Albert Adams, Seattle, Wash.

Cucumber Canoes

3 medium cucumbers
1 c. cooked elbow macaroni
1 12-oz. can luncheon meat, cubed
½ c. carrots, grated
¼ c. green pepper, chopped
½ c. mayonnaise
2 tbsp. vinegar
2 tbsp. horseradish
Salt and pepper

Cut cucumbers in half lengthwise. Scoop out pulp from each half, leaving a shell ¼ inch thick. Chop pulp and combine with macaroni, luncheon meat, carrots and green pepper. Blend mayonnaise, vinegar and horseradish. Add to meat mixture; toss lightly. Season to taste with salt and pepper. Pile salad into cucumber shells. Yield: 6 servings.

Mrs. Ruth Voigt, Home Economics Teacher, Monroeville, Pa.

Easter Egg Salad

1 tbsp. salt
3 qt. boiling water
½ lb. elbow macaroni
½ c. salad dressing
2 tbsp. French dressing
1 tsp. salt
3 drops Tabasco sauce
1 c. cooked kidney beans, drained
3 hard-cooked eggs, diced
¼ c. sweet pickles, chopped
Watercress

Combine 1 tablespoon salt, boiling water and macaroni. Cook for 8 minutes or until macaroni is tender; drain and rinse. Combine salad dressing, French dressing, 1 teaspoon salt and Tabasco sauce. Fold in kidney beans, eggs, pickles and macaroni. Serve on nests of watercress. Yield: 4 servings.

Mrs. Rhonda Chunn, Detroit, Mich., Favorite Recipes Food Fair

Hearty Macaroni Salad

½ c. uncooked macaroni
¼ lb. luncheon meat, cubed
½ c. canned green peas, chilled
½ c. celery, chopped
¼ lb. cheddar cheese, cubed
1 tbsp. onion, chopped

(Continued on next page)

1 tbsp. parsley, minced
1/4 c. green pepper, chopped
Salt and pepper to taste
1/3 c. salad dressing
1 hard-cooked egg, sliced

Cook macaroni according to package directions. Toss all ingredients together except egg. Chill. Garnish with egg slices. Yield: 6 servings.

Mrs. Stewart Knight, Home Economics Teacher, Hale Center, Tex.

 Sweet And Sour Macaroni Salad

4 to 5 tbsp. mayonnaise or salad dressing
4 tbsp. vinegar
2 to 3 tbsp. sugar
1 to 2 tbsp. water
1/2 c. chopped green pepper
1/2 c. chopped onion
1/2 c. shredded carrots
3/4 lb. macaroni, cooked and drained

Combine mayonnaise, vinegar, sugar and water in bowl. Add green pepper, onion, carrots and macaroni; mix thoroughly. Chill for 2 to 3 hours. Yield: 10-12 servings.

Mrs. John R. Zeman, Officers' Wives' Club, Yuma, Ariz.

Talk Of The Town Salad

1 small head lettuce, torn
2 tomatoes, cut as desired
1/4 c. celery, diced
1 4-oz. can mushrooms
1/8 c. Velveeta cheese, diced
2 tbsp. Bleu cheese, diced
2/3 c. canned peas or French-cut beans
8 stuffed olives, sliced
1/2 tsp. onion salt
Dash of garlic salt
1 1/2 c. chicken, crab, lobster, shrimp or combination
1 tsp. lemon juice
French dressing
Salt and pepper to taste
1 c. cooked macaroni (opt.)

Toss all ingredients together in a large salad bowl. Yield: 4 servings.

Annabelle Wikkerink, Home Economics Teacher, Amery, Wis.

Macaroni-Vegetable Salad

1 tbsp. salt
3 qt. boiling water
2 c. elbow macaroni
½ c. diced celery
½ c. diced green pepper
½ c. shredded carrot
¼ c. finely chopped onion
⅔ c. mayonnaise
1 tbsp. lemon juice
½ tsp. salt
¼ tsp. pepper
¼ tsp. dry mustard
Salad greens

Add salt to rapidly boiling water. Gradually add macaroni so that water continues to boil. Cook, uncovered, stirring occasionally, until tender. Drain in colander. Rinse with cold water; drain again. Combine macaroni with remaining ingredients; toss lightly and chill. For a picnic, turn into chilled wide-mouth vacuum jug. At home, serve on crisp salad greens garnished with additional shredded carrot. Yield: 4-6 servings.

Photograph for this recipe below.

Curried Rice Salad

1 ½ c. cooked rice
¼ c. minced onion
1 tbsp. vinegar
2 tbsp. salad oil
1 tsp. curry powder
2 tsp. salt
1 c. chopped celery
1 c. cooked green peas
½ c. salad dressing or mayonnaise

Combine rice, onion, vinegar, salad oil, curry powder and salt; chill for several hours. Add remaining ingredients just before serving. Yield: 4-6 servings.

Mrs. John R. Snow, Officers' Wives' Club, Fort Monroe, Va.

 Rice Salad

1 c. raw rice
Paprika
4 hard-cooked eggs, chopped
½ c. celery, chopped
¼ c. onion, chopped (opt.)
½ c. sweet pickles, chopped
¼ c. green pepper, chopped
1 small can pimento, chopped (opt.)
½ c. salad dressing
Salt to taste

Cook rice according to package directions. Cool; sprinkle with paprika. Add eggs, celery, pickles, pepper, pimento, salad dressing and onion if desired. Toss lightly to mix. Salt to taste. Yield: 8-12 servings.

Mrs. Christine Weems, Hazen, Ark.

Gelatin-Rice Salad

1 pkg. raspberry or lime gelatin
1 c. boiling water
1 c. whipped cream
1 small can crushed pineapple, drained
2 c. cooked rice, drained and sweetened

Dissolve gelatin in boiling water. Add rice. Chill 2 to 3 hours so rice will take up flavor of the gelatin. Blend pineapple and whipped cream into gelatin mixture. Serve on crisp lettuce. Yield: 6-8 servings.

Mrs. Patsy Stemple, Home Economics Teacher, Gillham, Ark.

Salade De Rie (France)

1 c. instant rice
1 c. water
1 tomato, chopped
1 green pepper, diced
1 sm. cucumber, diced
1 sm. onion, diced
2 tbsp. mayonnaise
1 tsp. lemon juice
Salt and pepper to taste

Cook rice according to package directions. Place in refrigerator to cool. Combine all ingredients; chill before serving. Serve on lettuce leaf. Yield: 4 servings.

Mrs. Stanley Lopes, Pres. Officers' Wives' Club, Morocco

Aladdin's Rice Ring

1 ½ c. water
2 c. milk
½ tsp. salt
½ c. uncooked rice
½ c. sugar
2 envelopes unflavored gelatin
½ tsp. grated lemon peel
2 tbsp. lemon juice
1 c. dry instant non-dairy coffee creamer
Honeyed bananas
Coarsely chopped pecans

Heat water, 1½ cups milk and salt in top of double boiler. Add rice; cover and cook over simmering water, stirring occasionally, for 45 minutes or until rice is tender. Mix ¼ cup sugar with gelatin; stir into rice until gelatin dissolves. Remove from heat; cool. Mix in lemon peel and juice. Chill until mixture mounds slightly when dropped from a spoon. Chill bowl, beaters and remaining milk for 15 minutes. Blend coffee creamer, chilled milk and remaining sugar in chilled bowl. Whip at high speed with electric mixer for 3 to 5 minutes or until soft peaks form. Fold whipped topping into rice mixture. Turn into 5½-cup ring mold; chill until firm. Unmold onto plate; fill center with honeyed bananas. Sprinkle nuts on top. To make honeyed bananas, heat ½ cup honey and ¼ cup water to boiling. Blend 2 teaspoons cornstarch with 1 tablespoon lemon juice. Stir into boiling mixture with 1 tablespoon butter. Cook and stir until mixture boils for 1 minute. Chill. Before serving, add 4 medium yellow bananas, sliced. Yield: 8 servings.

Photograph for this recipe on page 203.

Strawberry-Rice Salad

2 pkg. strawberry gelatin
3 c. hot water
2 c. cooked rice
1 c. miniature marshmallows
1 c. crushed pineapple
1 c. whipped cream

Dissolve gelatin in hot water; cool. Add rice, marshmallows and pineapple. When mixture begins to congeal, add whipped cream. Chill. Yield: 12-15 servings.

Elaine Crane, Home Economics Teacher, Mallard, Iowa

 ### Rice And Meat Salad

1 ½ c. cooked rice, chilled
1 ½ c. chicken, tuna or turkey, diced
1 c. English peas
1 c. raw carrots, shredded
4 tbsp. chili sauce (opt.)
¼ tsp. curry powder
½ tsp. salt
½ c. French dressing

Mix rice with meat and vegetables; toss lightly. Mix chili sauce, curry powder, salt and French dressing. Pour over salad and toss lightly. Yield: 6 servings.

Mrs. Harriet Krause, Home Economics Teacher, Pasadena, Tex.

 ### Delicious Chicken Salad

1 tbsp. lemon juice
¾ c. mayonnaise or salad dressing
½ c. sliced stuffed green olives
2 c. cooked long-grain rice
2 c. diced cooked chicken
1 c. diced celery
2 tbsp. thinly sliced green onion
¼ c. sliced almonds, toasted
Dash of pepper
6 lettuce cups

Add lemon to mayonnaise; blend well. Combine with remaining ingredients except lettuce cups; mix lightly and chill. Serve in individual lettuce cups; garnish with additional sliced olives. Yield: 6 servings.

Mary E. Parker, Biloxi, Miss.

Crab-Wild Rice Salad

1 c. King crab meat
1 c. cooked wild rice
½ c. mayonnaise
¼ tsp. dry mustard
2 tbsp. vinegar
Salad greens
2 avocados, sliced or halved

Remove any cartilage from crab, leaving crab in fairly large pieces. Toss crab with rice. Blend mayonnaise, mustard and vinegar; mix with crab and rice. Chill. Serve on lettuce; garnish with avocado slices. Yield: 4 servings.

Mrs. David B. Savage,, Officers' Wives' Club, Fort Richardson, Alaska

Rice-Shrimp Salad Deluxe

3 c. cold cooked rice
1 c. boiled shrimp
6 hard-cooked eggs
1 c. sweet or sour pickles, diced
Salt and pepper to taste
1 c. celery, diced
1 c. stuffed olives, finely chopped
Salad dressing

Combine all ingredients. Garnish with additional hard-cooked eggs. Yield: 6-8 servings.

June Wright Curtis, Home Economics Teacher, Hamshire, Tex.

Tomato And Spaghetti Salad

1 c. elbow spaghetti
1 can chicken, turkey or tuna
1 c. celery, diced
2 tsp. onion, grated
¼ tsp. salt
Cracked black pepper to taste
½ c. mayonnaise or undiluted cheddar cheese soup
5 tomatoes, peeled
Lettuce

Cook spaghetti according to package directions. Add meat, celery, onion, salt, pepper and mayonnaise or soup to cooked spaghetti. Cut tomatoes from flower end down to the stem end into four or eight sections. Place tomato on lettuce and fill with salad. Yield: 5 servings.

Mrs. Gloria Hixson, Home Economics Teacher, Scranton, Ark.

Egg and Cheese
Salads

American Cheese Ring

1 lb. medium-sharp American cheese
1 c. mayonnaise
1 c. finely chopped nuts
Dash of onion juice
Strawberry preserves

Grate cheese; add mayonnaise, nuts and onion juice. Press into ring mold; let stand until congealed. Unmold; serve with strawberry preserves in center.

Mrs. Robert McNeill, Perry, Ga.

Cheese-Pineapple Salad

¾ c. pineapple juice
1 tsp. vinegar
1 tbsp. cornstarch
1 egg, beaten
1 c. whipped cream
½ lb. American cheese, grated
¾ lb. miniature marshmallows
1 No. 2½ can crushed pineapple

Combine pineapple juice, vinegar, cornstarch and egg in double boiler; cook until thick. Cool. Add cream, cheese, marshmallows and pineapple; mix. Chill overnight. Yield: 4 servings.

Sarah Henry, Home Economics Teacher,
Redwater, Tex., Favorite Recipes Food Fair

Pineapple Cream

1 tbsp. unflavored gelatin
¼ c. cold water
¾ c. sugar
½ c. pineapple syrup
1 c. crushed pineapple, drained
1 c. grated American cheese
1 c. heavy cream, whipped

Soften gelatin in cold water. Dissolve sugar in pineapple syrup over low heat; add gelatin, stir until dissolved. Chill until partially set; add pineapple and cheese; fold in whipped cream. Turn into 1-quart mold. Chill until firm. Yield: 6-8 servings.

Mrs. Maxie Lee Dixon, Home Economics Teacher, Walker, La.

Golden Salad

2 pkg. lemon gelatin
2 c. hot pineapple juice-water
1 can pimento, ground
1 lge. can sliced pineapple, drained and ground
1 c. whipped cream
½ lb. American cheese, ground

Dissolve gelatin in pineapple juice-water mixture. Add pimento, pineapple, cheese and whipped cream. Pour into a large mold or individual molds; congeal. Yield: 6-8 servings.

Mrs. Mabel Williamson, Home Economics Teacher, Lexington, Ky.

 ## Camembert Mousse

¼ c. cold water
1 envelope unflavored gelatin
2 1½-oz. wedges Camembert cheese
3 1¼-oz. wedges Roquefort cheese
1 tsp. Worcestershire sauce
1 egg, separated
½ c. heavy cream, whipped

Pour cold water into measuring cup; add gelatin. Set cup in pan of hot water until gelatin dissolves. Blend cheeses together until smooth. Beat in Worcestershire sauce, egg yolk and gelatin. Beat egg white until stiff; fold egg white and cream into cheese mixture. Pour into 4 individual molds or one 2 or 3-cup mold. Refrigerate overnight. Unmold onto lettuce leaves or watercress. Yield: 4 servings.

Mrs. Harry S. Dennis, Jr., West Palm Beach, Fla.

 ## Cheese Mold

1 12-oz. carton cream-style cottage cheese
2 3-oz. pkg. softened cream cheese
½ c. finely chopped celery
2 tbsp. finely chopped onion
¼ tsp. salt
2 dashes of garlic salt
1 tbsp. unflavored gelatin
¼ c. cold water
1 c. mayonnaise

Beat together cottage cheese and cream cheese till fluffy. Stir in celery, onion and salts. Soften gelatin in cold water; dissolve over hot water. Stir into cheese

(Continued on next page)

mixture. Stir in mayonnaise; pour into round 1-quart mold. Chill till firm. This salad, cut in wedges, can be served with alternating wedges of tomato aspic. Garnish with parsley.

Mrs. Harold Finley, Knoxville, Tenn., Favorite Recipes Food Fair

 ## Cheese-Olive Salad

8 oz. cream cheese
1 tsp. salt
½ c. sugar
1 envelope unflavored gelatin
½ c. cold water
½ c. cream or milk
½ c. chopped nuts
2 tbsp. grated onion
1 red or green pepper, chopped
1 sm. bottle olives
2 lb. cottage cheese

Cream the cream cheese, salt and sugar. Add gelatin to cold water; heat. Add to creamed mixture. Add cream, nuts, onion, pepper, olives and cottage cheese. Pour into mold which has been greased with oil. When set, invert on serving dish. Garnish with lettuce, radishes and olives.

Mrs. Sara Dale Casey, Shelbyville, Ky.

 ## Continental Salad

2 3-oz. pkg. cream cheese
1 2-oz. pkg. Roquefort or Bleu cheese
1 pkg. Italian or celery gelatin
2 c. boiling water
1 green pepper, finely chopped
1 med. onion, minced
1 c. mayonnaise
½ tsp. salt

Beat cheeses together until smooth. Dissolve gelatin in boiling water. Mix thoroughly with cheeses. Chill until partly set. Blend in remaining ingredients; turn into 6-cup ring mold or individual molds. Chill until firm. Yield: 8 servings.

Mrs. Donald I. Willis, Officers' Wives' Club, Savanna Army Dep., Ill.

Cottage Cheese Fruit Salad

1 3-oz. pkg. lemon gelatin
1 c. hot water
1 No. 303 can crushed pineapple, drained
½ pt. heavy cream, whipped
¼ tsp. salt
¼ c. chopped walnuts
1 pt. cottage cheese

Dissolve gelatin in water; cool until it begins to set. Combine pineapple, cream, salt, nuts and cottage cheese; add to gelatin. Place in 8-inch square pan; chill until firm. Yield: 6-8 servings.

Anna M. Westesen, Esparto, Cal.

Cottage Cheese Tossed Salad

1 pkg. cottage cheese
1 med. tomato, chopped
1 med. green pepper, chopped
2 stalks celery, chopped
4 radishes, sliced
1 sm. onion, diced
1 carrot, diced
2 tbsp. salad dressing
Salt and pepper to taste

Combine all ingredients; toss lightly. Chill; serve on lettuce, if desired. Yield: 6 servings.

Mrs. Robert D. Naylor, Pres. Officers' Wives' Club, Eglin AFB, Fla.

Date Treat

2 c. cottage cheese
1 c. chopped dates
1 c. chopped tart red apples
Mayonnaise dressing
Whipped cream

Combine cheese, dates and apples; moisten with mayonnaise. Mix lightly with 2 forks. Serve on crisp lettuce. Top each serving with 1 teaspoonful whipped cream. Yield: 6 servings.

Mrs. Goldie Hall, Olive Hill, Ky., Favorite Recipes Food Fair

Fruit Fluff

1 sm. can pineapple
1 pkg. lime gelatin
1 c. whipping cream
1 ½ c. cottage cheese
¼ lb. marshmallows, cut up
½ c. nuts, chopped

Drain pineapple; reserve fruit. Heat juice; add gelatin and boil 2 minutes. Cool. Whip cream; add cooled gelatin. Add reserved pineapple and remaining ingredients. Chill until firm. Yield: 4-6 servings.

Mrs. Agnes Husonko, Home Economics Teacher, Longview, Wash.

Harlequin Salad

2 c. cottage cheese
Salt and pepper
2 tbsp. sliced radish
2 tbsp. chopped sweet onion
2 tbsp. chopped green pepper
2 tbsp. thinly sliced celery
2 tbsp. cubed cucumber

Season cottage cheese with salt and pepper; add remaining ingredients. Chill for several hours until flavors blend. Serve very cold. Yield: 6 servings.

Mrs. E. C. McKenna, Officers' Wives' Club, Ansbach, Germany

Lime Delight

1 pkg. lime gelatin
1 pkg. lemon gelatin
1 c. hot water
1 c. cold water
1 c. cottage cheese
1 c. mayonnaise
1 tsp. almond extract

Dissolve gelatins in hot water; add cold water. Cool; add remaining ingredients. Chill until partially set; mix. Chill until firm. Yield: 6 servings.

Mrs. Rosalie Turner, Tacoma, Wash., Favorite Recipes Food Fair

Mary Minnick's Salad

1 pkg. lime gelatin
1 c. hot water
1 c. ginger ale
1 16-oz. carton creamed cottage cheese
1 small can crushed pineapple, drained
½ c. celery, finely diced
½ c. nuts, chopped

Dissolve gelatin in hot water. Let cool. Add ginger ale, cottage cheese, pineapple, celery and nuts. Chill until firm. Yield: 9 servings.

Nancy Kimbrell, Home Economics Teacher, Tallahassee, Fla.

Summer Salad

1 12-oz. pkg. cottage cheese
½ c. carrots, grated
½ c. celery, finely chopped
2 tsp. onion, minced
¼ c. salad dressing
Salt and pepper to taste

Combine cottage cheese, carrots, celery and onion. Add salad dressing, salt and pepper; mix well. Chill before serving. Yield: 6 servings.

Mrs. Lois Brichacek, Home Economics Teacher, Great Bend, Kan.

Tangy Cottage Cheese Salad

1 3-oz. pkg. lemon gelatin
1 3-oz. pkg. lime gelatin
1 c. boiling water
1 No. 2 can crushed pineapple
1 1-lb. carton cottage cheese
1 c. salad dressing
1 c. milk
2 tbsp. horseradish

Dissolve lemon and lime gelatins in boiling water. Drain pineapple, reserving 1 cup juice. Add pineapple juice to dissolved gelatin; stir in pineapple. Chill until almost congealed. Combine cottage cheese, salad dressing, milk and horse-

(Continued on next page)

radish. Fold into gelatin-pineapple mixture. Turn into 6½ x 10 x 2-inch loaf pan. Chill until firm. Yield: 8 servings.

Mrs. Malcolm L. Blessing, Officers' Wives' Club, Middletown, Pa.

Whipped Velvet Fruit Ring

1 3-oz. pkg. lime gelatin
¾ c. hot limeade
1 c. evaporated milk
2 tbsp. lemon juice
¾ c. chopped celery
1 c. cottage cheese
Canned or fresh fruit

Dissolve gelatin in limeade. Chill until consistency of unbeaten egg white. Chill evaporated milk in refrigerator tray for 15 to 20 minutes or until soft crystals form around edges. Whip for 1 minute or until stiff. Add lemon juice and whip for 2 minutes or until very stiff. Add celery and cottage cheese to gelatin. Fold in whipped evaporated milk. Turn into 6-cup ring mold. Chill. Unmold; fill center with fruit. Yield: 4-6 servings.

Photograph for this recipe below.

Orange Coke Salad

> 2 3-oz. pkg. cream cheese
> 2 pkg. orange gelatin
> 4 small Coca-Colas
> 1 c. nuts, chopped

Cream together the cheese, gelatin and ½ bottle Coca-Cola, using a blender or beater. Heat remaining Coca-Cola to boiling. Combine with cheese and gelatin mixture. Add nuts. Pour into greased mold. Chill until firm. Yield: 8-10 servings.

> *Marjorie W. Browning, Home Economics Teacher, Pensacola, Fla.*

 ## Pineapple-Nut Salad

> 1 No. 2½ can crushed pineapple
> 1 pkg. lemon gelatin
> 2 sm. pkg. cream cheese
> ½ pt. whipped cream
> 1 sm. bottle Maraschino cherries, sliced
> 2 c. pecans, chopped

Drain pineapple; reserve fruit. Heat pineapple juice; add gelatin. Stir until dissolved; chill until thickened. Mash cream cheese; add whipped cream. Fold into thickened gelatin. Add reserved pineapple, cherries and pecans. Pour into mold; chill until firm. Yield: 10-12 servings.

> *Rachel Brewster, Home Economics Teacher, Petrolia, Tex.*

Spring Salad

> 3 c. boiling water
> 1 pkg. lemon gelatin
> 1 pkg. lime gelatin
> 24 lge. marshmallows
> 2 sm. pkg. cream cheese
> 2 tbsp. vinegar
> 1 sm. can pineapple
> 1 c. pecans, finely chopped

Pour boiling water over gelatins and marshmallows; stir until dissolved. Chill until mixture begins to thicken. Mix cream cheese with vinegar; blend until smooth. Drain pineapple; add juice to cheese-vinegar mixture. Blend thoroughly; add pecans and pineapple. Chill. Combine cheese and gelatin mixtures. Chill until firm. Yield: 8-10 servings.

> *Hilda Harman, Home Economics Teacher, Smithville, Miss.*

Green Cheese Ring

> 2 c. cottage cheese
> 1 3-oz. pkg. cream cheese, softened
> 1 tbsp. unflavored gelatin
> ¼ c. cold water
> ½ tbsp. grated onion
> ½ c. mayonnaise
> ½ tbsp. lemon juice
> Cayenne pepper
> Salt
> 2 tbsp. chopped green pepper (opt.)
> Few drops of green coloring

Beat cottage cheese smooth with electric beater; beat in cream cheese. Dissolve gelatin in cold water; melt over hot water. Add remaining ingredients, tinting pale green with food coloring.

PUERTO RICAN DRESSING:

> ¼ c. powdered sugar
> 1 tbsp. steak sauce
> ¼ c. tarragon wine vinegar
> ½ tsp. grated onion
> Paprika
> 1 tbsp. lemon juice
> 1 tsp. Worcestershire sauce
> ⅓ c. catsup
> 1 tsp. salt
> ½ c. salad oil

Place all ingredients except oil in jar; blend thoroughly. Add oil; shake well. Yield: 4 servings.

Mrs. Howard Persons, Colorado Springs, Colo.

Mrs. Truman's Cheese Ring

> 1 c. milk
> 2 tbsp. gelatin
> 2 pkg. cream cheese
> 1 c. grated yellow American cheese
> Dash of salt
> 1 c. heavy cream, whipped

Heat milk. Dissolve gelatin in cold water; add to hot milk. Mash cream cheese; blend in grated cheese and salt. Fold into gelatin mixture; chill until thickened. Fold in whipped cream; chill until firm. Salad may be used as a base for fruit gelatin salad or served plain with fresh fruit.

Mrs. Harry S. Truman, Wife of former President of the United States

Olympian Cream

1 pt. whipping cream, whipped
3 3-oz. jars pimento cheese
2 sm. cans crushed pineapple, drained
1 can grapes, drained
1 c. miniature marshmallows

Combine whipped cream and cheese; mix thoroughly. Fold in remaining ingredients; chill. Yield: 8-12 servings.

Mrs. Noah McFodden, Paris, Tex., Favorite Recipes Food Fair

Pimento Creme Ring

1 ½ c. milk
3 3-oz. pkg. pimento cream cheese, cut into sm. squares
½ tsp. salt
2 envelopes unflavored gelatin
¼ c. cold water
2 c. heavy cream, whipped
Mixed fresh fruit
Mayonnaise

Scald milk in top of double boiler over boiling water; add cheese squares and salt. Stir until cheese is melted. Soften gelatin in cold water; add to hot cheese mixture. Stir until dissolved. Chill mixture until consistency of unbeaten egg white. Fold in whipped cream. Spoon into 2-quart ring mold. Chill until set. Turn onto serving plate. Fill center of ring with fresh fruit; serve with mayonnaise. Yield: 12-16 servings.

Mrs. Charles E. Pond, Officers' Wives' Club, Carlisle Barracks, Pa.

Pimento Fruit Salad

2 glasses pimento cheese
1 sm. can crushed pineapple, drained
1 8-oz. pkg. miniature marshmallows
½ c. salad dressing
1 c. heavy cream, whipped

Mix cheese and pineapple thoroughly; add marshmallows and salad dressing. Fold in whipped cream. Let stand overnight. Serve on lettuce. Yield: 8-10 servings.

Mrs. A. B. Joyner, Jr., Southport, N. C.

Saucy Salad

½ lb. cheese, grated
1 can pimentos, finely chopped
3 apples, finely chopped
3 hard-boiled eggs, finely chopped
3 pickles, finely chopped
1 egg
1 tsp. salt
1 tsp. sugar
½ c. cream or milk
½ tsp. black pepper
2 tbsp. flour

Set aside small amount cheese. Combine remaining cheese, pimentos, apples, hard-boiled eggs and pickles. Combine remaining ingredients; heat in double boiler to custard consistency. Cool. Combine dressing with salad mixture; sprinkle with grated cheese.

Mrs. L. D. Grimes, Maud, Tex.

 ### Royal Frosted Fruit Mold

1 c. milk
2 envelopes unflavored gelatin
2 12-oz. cartons cream-style cottage cheese
½ c. crumbled bleu cheese
1 6-oz. can frozen limeade concentrate, thawed
½ c. broken pecans, toasted and salted
6 drops green food coloring
1 c. whipped cream

Pour milk into large saucepan. Sprinkle gelatin over milk to soften. Place over low heat and stir until gelatin is dissolved. Remove from heat. Beat cottage cheese and bleu cheese together until well blended. Stir in gelatin mixture; add limeade concentrate, pecans and food coloring. Fold in whipped cream. Turn into 6-cup ring mold; chill until firm, about 4 to 6 hours. Unmold on serving plate and garnish with frosted grapes and mint leaves. Yield: 10 servings.

Mrs. F. L. Love, Miami, Fla.

St. Patrick Salad

2 pkg. lemon gelatin
1 c. boiling water
1 No. 2½ can crushed pineapple

(Continued on next page)

1 pt. cottage cheese
1 4-oz. pkg. cream cheese
½ c. salad dressing
Few drops green food coloring
1 c. cucumbers, diced

Dissolve gelatin in boiling water; cool. Drain pineapple; reserve fruit. Add water to pineapple juice to make 1 cup liquid; blend with cottage cheese. Blend in cream cheese and salad dressing. Stir cheese mixture into gelatin. Add food coloring. Fold in reserved pineapple and cucumber. Chill for 4 hours. Yield: 10 servings.

Estelle Delgado, Home Economics Teacher, Banning, Cal.

Stuffed Lettuce Salad

1 sm. firm head lettuce
1 4-oz. pkg. Roquefort or bleu cheese
1 3-oz. pkg. cream cheese
1 3-oz. pkg. pimento cream cheese
1 tbsp. chopped chives
1 tbsp. milk

Wash lettuce; drain well. Hollow out center from stem end, leaving 1 to 1½-inch shell. Blend softened cheeses with other ingredients; pack into center of lettuce. Wrap tightly in foil, waxed paper or plastic bag; chill well. Cut into wedges; serve with French dressing. Yield: 4-6 servings.

Mrs. Charles W. Evans, Tuscaloosa, Ala., Favorite Recipes Food Fair

Swiss Salad Supreme

¼ c. French dressing
¼ c. mayonnaise
1 tsp. horseradish
⅛ tsp. pepper
½ tsp. salt
1 sm. onion, thinly sliced
½ lb. Swiss cheese, cubed
2 hard-cooked eggs, sliced
1 c. sliced celery

Combine French dressing, mayonnaise, horseradish, pepper and salt. Pour over remaining ingredients; toss lightly. Yield: 6 servings.

Mrs. Elton M. Nelson, Pres. Officers' Wives' Club,
Soesterberg AB, The Netherlands

Swiss Cheese Salad

½ lb. Swiss cheese
6 hard-cooked eggs
¾ c. sour cream
1 ½ tsp. mustard
1 tsp. horseradish
1 tsp. salt
1 tsp. caraway seed

Cut cheese into ½-inch cubes; chop eggs coarsely. Combine and toss with sour cream and seasonings. Arrange on bed of greens. Yield: 4 servings.

Mrs. J. W. Hallum, Nashville, Tenn.

 ## Bacon-Egg Salad

1 head lettuce, torn into sm. pieces
1 sm. onion, chopped
2 hard-cooked eggs, chopped
Salt and pepper to taste
Mayonnaise to taste
4 slices bacon, fried and crumbled

Combine lettuce, onion, eggs, salt and pepper with mayonnaise. Top with bacon. Serve immediately. Yield: 6 servings.

Beth White, Home Economics Teacher, Goliad, Tex.

 ## Chinese Eggs

12 hard-cooked eggs
1 qt. boiling water
3 tbsp. orange pekoe tea
1 tsp. anise seed
4 tbsp. soy sauce
1 ½ tbsp. salt

Shell eggs carefully so whites are not broken. Pour boiling water over tea; let steep for 5 minutes. Strain; combine with anise seed, soy sauce and salt. Add whole eggs; simmer for 1 hour. Store, covered, in refrigerator. Yield: 12 servings.

Lucile B. McGehee, South Decatur, Ga.

Crunchy Egg Salad

6 hard-cooked eggs, chopped
½ c. diced celery
¼ c. diced green pepper
1 tbsp. chopped pimento
½ c. mayonnaise
½ tsp. salt
¼ tsp. pepper

Combine all ingredients. Serve on lettuce. Garnish with additional pimento. Yield: 4 servings.

Winifred Blackwood, Home Economics Teacher, Hominy, Okla.

 ## Egg And Cheese Salad

6 hard-cooked eggs, mashed
¼ c. chopped chives
¾ c. small curd cottage cheese
½ c. salad dressing
3 tbsp. vinegar
1 tbsp. white sugar
Salt and pepper to taste

Combine eggs, chives and cottage cheese. Blend salad dressing, vinegar, sugar, salt and pepper. Combine the 2 mixtures. Serve on lettuce as salad or use as sandwich spread. Yield: 8 servings.

Dorothy Tenniswood, Home Economics Teacher, New Troy, Mich.

 ## Egg And Lettuce Salad

1 ½ c. chopped lettuce
3 hard-cooked eggs
1 tbsp. vinegar
3 tbsp. salad oil
¼ tsp. salt
¼ tsp. pepper

Place lettuce in bowl; add chopped egg whites. Mash egg yolks; add vinegar, salad oil and seasonings. Mix well; pour over lettuce. Toss and serve. Yield: 2 servings.

Mrs. Max Rose, Liberal, Mo.

Eggs And Peas On Lettuce

6 hard-cooked eggs, chopped
½ med. onion, chopped
1 pkg. frozen green peas, cooked and drained
¾ c. mayonnaise
Lettuce

Combine all ingredients except lettuce; chill for several hours. Serve on lettuce leaves. Yield: 6-8 servings.

Mrs. Stuart F. Wilder, Pres. Officers' Wives' Club, Anchorage, Alaska

 ### Egg Salad

6 hard-cooked eggs, diced
½ c. diced sour pickles
½ c. finely diced celery
¼ tsp. salt
⅓ c. mayonnaise
1 sm. head lettuce

Combine eggs, pickles, celery, salt and mayonnaise; toss gently. Cover; chill in refrigerator. Serve in lettuce cups. Yield: 5 servings.

Mrs. William E. McCaleb, Cheyenne, Wyo.

 ### Egg Salad With Tomato

8 hard-cooked eggs, coarsely chopped
1 c. finely diced celery
¼ c. salad dressing
1 tsp. Worcestershire sauce
1 tbsp. lemon juice
1 tsp. scraped onion
Salt and pepper to taste
6 thick tomato slices
Salad greens
Paprika
Celery curls

Combine eggs, celery, dressing and all seasonings except paprika. Press into molds and chill. Unmold on tomato slices placed in a bed of salad greens. Sprinkle with paprika; garnish with celery curls and additional seasoning. Yield: 6 servings.

Helen Marks, Macon, Ga.

Costain's Egg Ring

1 envelope unflavored gelatin
¼ c. cold water
½ c. boiling water
6 hard-cooked eggs, chopped
1 c. mayonnaise
1 tbsp. catsup
Juice of ½ lemon
½ c. chopped watercress or parsley
Salt to taste
¼ onion, chopped
½ clove of garlic, chopped
½ tsp. Worcestershire sauce

Soak gelatin in cold water; dissolve in boiling water. Combine with all remaining ingredients. Pour into mold; chill until firm. Yield: 8 servings.

Mrs. William T. Page, Stony Brook, N. Y., Favorite Recipes Food Fair

Egg Crowned Supper Mold

4 hard-cooked eggs
1 tbsp. plain gelatin
1 ¾ c. chicken broth
3 tbsp. prepared mustard
3 tbsp. sweet pickle relish
3 tbsp. diced green pepper
2 tbsp. instant minced onion
1 tsp. sugar
½ tsp. celery salt
2 ½ c. finely diced cooked potatoes
2 cups diced baked ham
½ c. mayonnaise

Shell hard-cooked eggs; cut in half, crosswise. Cut each piece in half; reserve. Soften gelatin in ¼ cup chicken broth. Heat remaining liquid. When hot, add gelatin; stir to dissolve. Float a 6-cup ring mold in a pan of ice and water. Using ½ cup broth, pour 2 or 3 tablespoons into bottom of mold; rotate to coat bottom of pan. Stand egg pieces on end in a circle on congealed gelatin. Spoon remaining ½ cup gelatin around egg pieces. Let stand long enough to set. Combine mustard, pickle relish, green pepper, onion, sugar and celery salt. Add remaining broth. Add potatoes, ham and any remaining pieces of egg. Season with freshly ground black pepper. Place pan in ice and water; when liquid starts to thicken fold in mayonnaise. Spoon mixture over eggs in mold. Chill several hours or until firm. Unmold on tray. Fill center and around mold with crisp garden lettuce. Garnish with stuffed olives. Yield: 6 servings.

Photograph for this recipe on page 223.

Deviled Egg Mold

1 envelope unflavored gelatin
½ c. water
1 tsp. salt
1 to 2 tbsp. lemon juice or vinegar
¼ tsp. Worcestershire sauce
 Cayenne pepper to taste (opt.)
¾ c. mayonnaise or salad dressing
1 ½ tsp. onion, grated
¼ to ½ c. green pepper, finely diced
¼ c. pimento, chopped
4 hard-cooked eggs, chopped
½ c. celery, finely chopped

Soften gelatin in cold water; place over hot water to melt. Remove from heat and add salt, lemon juice, Worcestershire sauce and cayenne pepper. Cool. Stir in mayonnaise; fold in remaining ingredients. Turn into a 3-cup mold or individual molds. Chill until firm. Yield: 6 servings.

Sister Mary Louise, Home Economics Teacher, Clarksburg, W. Va.

Egg-Seafood Mold

12 hard-cooked eggs
2 envelopes unflavored gelatin
½ c. cold water
1 c. boiling water
2 c. mayonnaise
1 c. pickle relish
½ c. chili sauce
 Juice of 1 lemon, plus 1 tsp.
1 c. catsup
1 tsp. Worcestershire sauce
¼ tsp. salt
¼ tsp. paprika
¼ tsp. Tabasco sauce
⅔ lb. shrimp or crab
¼ pt. heavy cream, whipped

Put eggs through sieve or ricer. Soften gelatin in cold water; dissolve in boiling water. Add mayonnaise, pickle relish, chili sauce, juice of 1 lemon and gelatin to eggs. Pour into 10 to 12-cup ring mold or individual molds; chill until firm. Combine catsup, Worcestershire sauce, salt, paprika, Tabasco sauce and 1 teaspoon lemon juice. Unmold salad ring; fill center with shrimp or crab. Fold whipped cream into sauce; pour over seafood. Yield: 12 servings.

Mrs. William C. Meyer, Naval Officers' Wives' Club, San Diego, Cal.

Egg And Shrimp Salad

1 envelope unflavored gelatin
¼ c. cold water
1 bouillon cube
1 c. hot water
1 c. salad dressing
6 hard-cooked eggs, sliced
1 can small cocktail shrimp
1 c. diced celery
2 tbsp. chopped green pepper
2 tbsp. chopped pimento
2 tbsp. pickle relish
Salt and pepper

Soften gelatin in cold water; dissolve with bouillon cube in hot water. Cool; blend with salad dressing. Oil a ring mold; place slices of 2 eggs on bottom. Add all remaining ingredients to gelatin-bouillon mixture; pour into mold. Chill until firm. Unmold; garnish with tomato wedges and watercress. Yield: 10-12 servings.

Mrs. H. W. Christensen, Salt Lake City, Utah, Favorite Recipes Food Fair

Glenna's Egg Salad

1 pkg. lemon gelatin
1 c. hot water
6 hard-cooked eggs, riced
1 tsp. mustard
1 tsp. celery salt
½ tsp. paprika
½ tsp. salt
⅓ c. vinegar
⅓ c. mayonnaise

Dissolve gelatin in hot water. Add all remaining ingredients; beat. Cool; serve on lettuce with additional mayonnaise.

Glenna A. Starbird, Home Economics Teacher, Norway, Maine.

Molded Egg Salad

1 tbsp. unflavored gelatin
½ c. cold water
1 tbsp. lemon juice
Salt
1 c. mayonnaise
4 hard-cooked eggs, diced
½ c. diced celery
2 tbsp. chopped pickle or sweet relish
2 tbsp. chopped pimento
2 tbsp. chopped green pepper

Soak gelatin in cold water; dissolve over hot water. Add lemon juice and salt; blend with mayonnaise. Stir in all remaining ingredients. Pour into buttered mold; chill. Top with additional mayonnaise.

Mrs. William T. Bates, Steubenville, Ohio

 ## Pennsylvania Dutch Red Beet Eggs

5 med. beets
1 c. vinegar
1 c. water
½ c. sugar
1 tsp. salt
8 hard-cooked eggs

Boil beets until tender; remove skins and slice ½ inch thick. Blend vinegar, water, sugar and salt. Pour mixture over beets; refrigerate overnight. Next day remove half the beet slices; add whole shelled eggs. Refrigerate another day until eggs become rosy-red in color. Use sliced eggs as salad garnish or serve with beets as salad. Yield: 8 servings.

Lucy M. Bamberger, Home Economics Teacher, Myerstown, Pa.

Smoked Eggs

6 hard-cooked eggs
¼ c. vinegar
1 ¾ c. cold water
2 tsp. liquid smoke

Place hot eggs in jar; add all remaining ingredients. Cover and refrigerate for several hours. Eggs may be kept in liquid smoke as long as desired. Yield: 6 servings.

Doris H. Schlumpf, Home Economics Teacher, Durand, Wis.

Deviled Eggs

> 6 hard-cooked eggs
> 2 tbsp. mayonnaise
> 1 tsp. mustard
> ½ tsp. salt
> ¼ tsp. paprika
>   Dash of pepper
> 1 tbsp. chopped sweet pickle
> 1 tbsp. chopped stuffed olives

Halve eggs lengthwise with a wet knife. Remove yolks; mash with fork. Add all remaining ingredients; blend well. Stuff whites with yolk mixture. Garnish with a dash of paprika, additional olives or a sprig of parsley. Chill before serving.

Mrs. D. J. Dear, Bay Springs, Miss.

 Deviled Eggs With Wine

> 4 hard-cooked eggs
> 1 tbsp. melted butter
> 1 tbsp. grated onion
> Salt and pepper to taste
> 2 tbsp. deviled ham
> 1 tbsp. gelatin
> 1 c. chicken stock
> Tarragon sprigs
> ½ c. dry white wine
>   Mayonnaise

Cut eggs into halves lengthwise; remove yolks. Add butter, onion, salt and pepper to yolks; beat until smooth. Blend in deviled ham. Fill egg whites; press together, forming whole eggs. Chill. Soften gelatin in ¼ cup chicken stock. Bring remaining stock to boil with a sprig of tarragon; simmer for 2 to 3 minutes. Remove tarragon; dissolve gelatin in hot liquid. Cool; add wine. Pour a ½-inch layer of gelatin mixture into 4 custard cups; chill until set. Place 1 egg in each cup; fill with gelatin mixture. Chill until set. Unmold onto salad greens; place a tarragon sprig on each. Serve mayonnaise separately. Yield: 4 servings.

Mrs. Vincent Davis, Wives' Club, Goose AB, Labrador

Shrimp-Stuffed Deviled Eggs

> 1 doz. hard-cooked eggs, halved
> 1 c. finely chopped cooked shrimp
> 1 tsp. mustard

(Continued on next page)

3 tbsp. mayonnaise
Lemon juice
Salt and pepper
Russian or French dressing

Scoop out egg yolks; blend with all ingredients except whites. Fill egg whites. Serve on lettuce leaves with dressing.

Marion R. Eckert, Schwenksville, Pa., Favorite Recipes Food Fair

Stuffed Eggs

6 hard-cooked eggs, halved lengthwise
Cubed ham, olives or pimento
3 tbsp. butter, softened
1 tsp. Worcestershire sauce
2 tbsp. mayonnaise
Salt and pepper to taste

Remove egg yolks; force through a fine sieve. Place 1 cube of ham in each egg white. Combine yolks with all remaining ingredients; beat until smooth. Force egg yolk mixture through a pastry tube onto egg whites. Yield: 6 servings.

Mrs. Bethel Schmidt, Home Economics Teacher, Vicksburg, Mich.

Stuffed Eggs Curry

12 hard-cooked eggs
1 c. mayonnaise
1 tsp. chicken seasoned stock base
¼ tsp. instant onion powder
¼ tsp. white pepper
1 tsp. curry powder
½ tsp. salt
1 c. finely minced cooked chicken (opt.)
Anchovies
Olive slices
Capers

Cut eggs into halves, crosswise; slice a small cap off ends. Remove yolks; mash or force through sieve. Add mayonnaise, stock base, onion powder, pepper, curry powder, salt and chicken; mix thoroughly. Refill egg whites, piling yolk mixture high. Cap each with smaller sliced-off portion of white; top with rolled anchovies, sliced olives and capers. Yield: 24 servings.

Charlotte Blount, Des Moines, Iowa

Frozen Salads

Alaskan Sunset

   1 sm. can crushed pineapple, drained
   2 tbsp. powdered sugar
   1 sm. jar Maraschino cherries, chopped
   1/3 lb. yellow cheese, grated
   1 tbsp. mayonnaise
   1/2 pt. heavy cream, whipped

Combine all ingredients; pour into an 8-inch square pan. Freeze. Serve on bed of lettuce, if desired. Yield: 8 servings.

Mrs. Jack M. Shortridge, Officers' Wives' Club, Ft. Richardson, Alaska

 ### Apple-Orange Frost

   1 No. 2 can applesauce
   1 small can orange juice
   2 to 3 tbsp. lemon juice
   3 egg whites, stiffly beaten
   Artificial sweetener equivalent to 3 tbsp. sugar

Combine applesauce, orange juice, lemon juice and sweetener. Fold in egg whites. Freeze until firm. Salad will keep from 2 to 4 weeks in freezer. Yield: 12 servings.

Mrs. Janet Krumme, Home Economics Teacher, Seymour, Ind.

Arctic Fantasy

   1 c. pineapple juice
   2 tbsp. flour
   2 tbsp. sugar
   1/2 c. butter
   1 egg
   Pineapple
   60 miniature marshmallows
   8 Maraschino cherries, cut in eighths
   Fresh or canned peaches
   Fresh grapes
   1 pt. whipped cream

Combine pineapple juice, flour, sugar, butter and egg; cook until thick. Add fruit and marshmallows. Cool; fold in whipped cream. Freeze. Yield: 20 servings.

Mrs. Less Feichtinger, Excelsior, Minn., Favorite Recipes Food Fair

Banana Salad Tantalizer

    1 tbsp. lemon juice
½ to 1 tsp. salt
    2 tbsp. mayonnaise
    2 3-oz. pkg. cream cheese, softened
    2 tbsp. crushed pineapple
½ c. Maraschino cherries, quartered
½ c. nuts, chopped
½ c. whipped cream
    3 ripe bananas, cubed

Blend lemon juice, salt and mayonnaise; stir into cheese. Add pineapple, cherries and nuts. Fold in whipped cream. Add bananas. Freeze. Yield: 10 servings.

Mrs. Betty Hastings, Home Economics Teacher, Lodi, Ohio

 Banana-Sour Cream Jubilee

    2 c. sour cream
¾ c. sugar
    2 tbsp. lemon juice
    1 small can crushed pineapple
Salt to taste (opt.)
    2 to 4 tbsp. Maraschino cherries, chopped
½ c. miniature marshmallows (opt.)
    1 to 2 bananas, crushed
¼ to ½ c. nuts, chopped

Combine all ingredients in order; mix. Pour into paper baking cups; freeze. Serve on lettuce. Garnish with additional Maraschino cherries or nuts, lemon twists, mint leaves or orange slices. Yield: 12 servings.

Mrs. Dorothy West, Littlefield, Tex.

 Bridge Luncheon Salad

    1 3-oz. pkg. cream cheese, softened
½ c. mayonnaise
¼ c. sugar
    3 tbsp. lemon juice
⅓ c. nuts, chopped
⅓ c. coconut
¼ c. Maraschino cherries, chopped
    2 c. bananas, sliced
⅔ c. evaporated milk, chilled

(Continued on next page)

Blend cheese, mayonnaise, sugar and 2 tablespoons lemon juice. Stir in nuts, coconut and cherries. Add bananas. Whip milk until it holds a peak. Add remaining lemon juice; blend. Fold milk into cheese mixture; freeze. Serve immediately after removing from freezer. Yield: 8 servings.

Charlotte Carter, Carpinteria, Cal.

 ## Charlene's Banana-Apricot Delight

> 2 ⅔ c. sugar
> 1 c. water
> 1 12-oz. pkg. frozen strawberries
> 1 c. crushed pineapple
> 4 bananas, sliced
> 4 c. apricot nectar
> 1 egg
> Juice of 1 orange
> Juice of 1 lemon
> 1 c. whipped cream

Boil 2 cups sugar and water until syrupy; add strawberries. Cool. Add bananas, pineapple and apricot nectar. Freeze. Combine 2/3 cup sugar, egg, orange and lemon juice. Cook until thick. Cool. Fold in whipped cream. Spread on top of frozen mixture. Freeze. Yield: 8-10 servings.

Charlene Swanson, Home Economics Teacher, Elwood, Neb.

 ## Molded Cottage Cheese Salad

> 1 envelope unflavored gelatin
> ¼ c. cold water
> ½ tsp. salt
> 2 c. creamed cottage cheese
> ¼ c. bleu or Roquefort cheese, crumbled
> 2 tbsp. chopped chives
> ½ c. whipping cream, whipped
>
> Mandarin oranges, avocado, bananas, unpeeled apples, and/or strawberries

Soften gelatin in water; set in pan of boiling water and allow gelatin to dissolve. Add salt. Blend cheeses together; add liquid gelatin. Mix well. Fold in chives and whipped cream. Fill buttered individual molds; freeze until firm. Unmold and serve with desired fruits. Yield: 6 servings.

Photograph for this recipe on page 245.

 ### Creamy Strawberry Salad

2 c. sour cream
¾ c. sugar
1 tbsp. lemon juice
1 c. crushed fresh strawberries, lightly sweetened or 1 pkg.
frozen sliced strawberries

Combine all ingredients. Place in freezer tray; freeze until firm. Cut into servings. Yield: 4 servings.

Mrs. Daniel A. Nolan, Jr., Hon. Pres. Officers' Wives' Club,
Ft. Brooke, Puerto Rico

 ### Creamy Tomato Freeze

1 tbsp. unflavored gelatin
¼ c. cold water
2 c. tomato juice
1 sm. can crushed pineapple, drained
½ c. mayonnaise
1 ½ tsp. salt
1 carton sour cream
⅛ tsp. dry mustard
¼ tsp. dry ginger
Dash of red pepper
1 tsp. onion juice
Tabasco sauce to taste

Soak gelatin in cold water; dissolve in a little hot tomato juice. Add remaining ingredients, mixing well. Freeze in ice cream freezer or an ice tray. Stir 3 times at 30 minute intervals to prevent flaking. Yield: 8 servings.

Mrs. James White, Memphis, Tenn.

Crunchy Apple-Pineapple Salad

 2 eggs, beaten
 ½ c. sugar
 ¼ tsp. salt
 3 tbsp. lemon juice
 ½ c. mixed pineapple syrup and water
 1 9-oz. can crushed pineapple, drained
 2 c. unpeeled apples, finely diced
 ½ c. celery, finely diced
 1 c. whipped cream

Combine eggs, sugar, salt, lemon juice and syrup-water mixture. Cook over low heat, stirring constantly until thick. Chill. Fold in pineapple, apples, celery and whipped cream. Pour into a 2-quart refrigerator tray or salad mold; freeze. Yield: 12 servings.

Mrs. Barbara Deane, Home Economics Teacher, Hoxie, Kan.

Date-Cheese Salad

 1 small can evaporated milk, chilled
 ¼ c. lemon juice
 2 pkg. cream cheese, softened
 ½ c. mayonnaise
 ½ c. pecans, chopped
 ½ c. almonds, slivered
 1 c. dates, chopped
 1 8½-oz. can crushed pineapple

Whip the milk; gradually add lemon juice as it begins to thicken. Blend cheese and mayonnaise together; blend into milk mixture. Fold in remaining ingredients. Freeze. Yield: 8-10 servings.

Carolyn Lutkemeier, Frankfort, Ky.

Delectable Fruit Freeze

 1 tsp. unflavored gelatin
 2 tbsp. lemon juice
 1 3-oz. pkg. cream cheese
 Pinch of salt
 1 pkg. dessert topping mix
 ½ c. sugar
 1 No. 2½ can fruit cocktail, drained
 ½ c. nuts
 ½ tsp. red food coloring (opt.)

(Continued on next page)

Soften gelatin in lemon juice; dissolve over hot water. Cream the cheese; add salt and gelatin mixture. Prepare dessert topping mix according to package directions; gradually add sugar. Fold in fruit cocktail, cheese-gelatin mixture, nuts and food coloring, if desired. Pour into trays lined with waxed paper. Freeze. Yield: 10-12 servings.

Inez Dykstra, Home Economics Teacher, Lovington, N. M.

"Duncan And Hinds" Frozen Fruit Salad

12 tsp. unflavored gelatin
½ c. cold fruit juice
2 c. hot fruit juice
6 tbsp. sugar
1 tsp. salt
1 c. mayonnaise
2 c. cream or evaporated milk, whipped
6 c. fresh or canned fruit, drained and diced

Soften gelatin in cold fruit juice; dissolve in hot fruit juice. Add sugar and salt; stir until dissolved. Chill until mixture begins to thicken. Beat mayonnaise gradually into whipped cream or milk. Fold in gelatin and fruit. Fill quart containers to within ½ inch of top; seal. Freeze; shaking vigorously twice during the first hour. May be stored for several months in freezer. Yield: 50 servings.

Mrs. Myrtle Duncan Brookshire, Home Economics Teacher,
Mountain City, Tenn.

French Fruit Salad

1 tbsp. lemon juice
2 bananas, diced
¾ c. pineapple, diced
12 red Maraschino cherries, chopped
⅓ c. French dressing
1 c. whipped cream
½ c. mayonnaise
⅛ tsp. salt
2 tbsp. confectioner's sugar

Pour lemon juice over bananas; add pineapple, cherries and French dressing. Chill for 2 hours. Drain. Fold whipped cream into mayonnaise; add salt and sugar. Fold in fruit mixture. Freeze—do not stir. Yield: 6 servings.

Mrs. Ray Sartor, Home Economics Teacher, Ripley, Miss.

Freda's Frozen Salad

1 sm. pkg. cream cheese
Few grains of salt
1 sm. can crushed pineapple
18 to 20 miniature marshmallows, halved
½ pt. heavy cream, whipped

Blend cheese and salt; mix in crushed pineapple. Add marshmallows; fold in whipped cream. Freeze. May be served on lettuce and topped with mayonnaise. Garnish with celery or nuts, if desired. Yield: 6 servings.

Mrs. B. N. Gockel, Officers' Wives' Club, Naha, Okinawa

 ### Frosty Cranberry Salad

1 lb. fresh cranberries, ground
2 c. miniature marshmallows
1 c. granulated sugar
2 c. apples, ground
1 pt. whipped cream

Combine cranberries, marshmallows, sugar and apples; let stand for 30 minutes. Add whipped cream. Freeze. Yield: 15 servings.

Mrs. Frank Clark, Home Economics Teacher, Elmwood, Ill.

Frosty Cranberry Tip-Tops

1 1-lb. can cranberry sauce
2 to 3 tbsp. lemon juice
1 c. whipped cream
1 3-oz. pkg. cream cheese, whipped
¼ c. mayonnaise
¼ c. sifted confectioners' sugar
1 c. nuts, chopped (opt.)

Crush cranberry sauce with a fork; add lemon juice and blend well. Pour into small paper cup. Combine remaining ingredients; spread over cranberry mixture. Freeze. Yield: 6-8 servings.

Mrs. Julian A. Raburn, McRae, Ga.

Frosty Mint Cubes

Juice drained from pineapple
2 tsp. unflavored gelatin
½ c. mint jelly
Dash of salt
1 No. 2 can crushed pineapple, drained
1 c. whipped cream
Green food coloring

Soften gelatin in pineapple juice; add jelly and salt. Heat, stirring constantly, until gelatin dissolves and jelly melts. If necessary, beat to blend in jelly. Add pineapple. Chill until mixture is thick and syrupy. Fold in whipped cream; tint with few drops of food coloring. Freeze until firm. Cut into cubes or slices to serve. Yield: 8-10 servings.

JoAnn L. Bedore, Home Economics Teacher, Grand Blanc, Mich.

Frozen Cranberry-Pineapple Cream

1 1-lb. can cranberry jelly or sauce
1 9-oz. can crushed pineapple, drained
1 c. sour cream

Combine ingredients; freeze in tray. Cut in squares before serving. Yield: 8 servings.

Catherine E. Strom, Prosser, Wash., Favorite Recipes Food Fair

Frozen Peppermint Dessert-Salad

1 No. 2 can crushed pineapple
1 pkg. strawberry gelatin
¼ c. cinnamon candies
1 10½-oz. pkg. miniature marshmallows
2 c. heavy cream
¼ lb. soft butter mints, crushed

Combine pineapple, gelatin powder, cinnamon candies and marshmallows; mix well. Chill overnight. The next day set refrigerator control at lowest temperature. Beat the cream, one cup at a time, in a chilled bowl with chilled beaters until cream piles softly. Pour cream and mints into chilled pineapple mixture. Fold together thoroughly and pour into refrigerator trays. Freeze 2 to 3 hours or until firm. Yield: 20 servings.

Ada Newell, Home Economics Teacher, Garden City, Kan.

Frozen Fruit Salad Deluxe

   1 No. 2 can crushed pineapple, drained
   2 eggs, beaten
   1 c. sugar
  ½ c. lemon juice
   1 tbsp. butter
   1 tbsp. cornstarch
  ½ tsp. salt
  ½ pt. heavy cream, whipped
   1 11-oz. can Mandarin oranges, drained and cut into small
      pieces
 12 Maraschino cherries, drained and chopped
   1 ½ c. miniature marshmallows

Drain pineapple, reserving ½ cup juice. Combine eggs, sugar, lemon juice, pineapple juice, butter, cornstarch and salt; cook until thick. Cool. Fold in whipped cream, fruits and marshmallows; pour into 11 x 7 x 1½-inch pan. Freeze. Cut into squares; serve on lettuce, if desired. Yield: 8-10 servings.

Mrs. David Cook, Wives' Club, Anniston, Ala.

 ### Frozen Salad In Orange Shells

  4 oranges
  2 3-oz. pkg. cream cheese, softened
¼ c. mayonnaise
  1 tbsp. vinegar
¼ tsp. mustard
  1 ½ c. diced fresh fruit
¼ c. slivered almonds
½ c. heavy cream, whipped

Cut oranges into halves; scoop out centers, reserving half of the orange pulp. Dice reserved orange pulp. Blend cheese with mayonnaise, vinegar and mustard; combine with orange pulp, diced fruit and nuts. Gently fold in whipped cream. Heap into orange shells; freeze until firm. Let shells stand at room temperature 10 minutes before serving. Yield: 8 servings.

Mrs. J. T. Poindexter, Officers' Wives' Club, Corvallis, Ore.

Frozen Waldorf Salad

  3 eggs
½ c. sugar
½ c. pineapple juice
¼ c. lemon juice
 Pinch of salt

(Continued on next page)

½ c. chopped celery
½ c. crushed pineapple
½ c. chopped nuts
½ c. fresh red grapes (opt.)
2 apples, cored and chopped
1 c. heavy cream, whipped

Beat eggs; add sugar, juices and salt. Cook until thick; cool. Add remaining ingredients. Turn into 9 x 9-inch pan. Freeze. Yield: 12 servings.

Mrs. W. S. Harrell, Greenville, Ala.

Fruit And Cheese Coupe

1 lg. pkg. cream cheese
1 c. heavy sour cream
2 tbsp. lemon juice
⅛ tsp. salt
1 c. canned pineapple, diced
1 c. grapes, seeded
1 c. cherries, pitted
1 banana, sliced
1 c. whipped cream
¾ c. mayonnaise
½ c. marshmallows, quartered

Cream the cheese, sour cream, lemon juice and salt. Add fruits and whipped cream. Fold in mayonnaise and marshmallows; freeze. Yield: 8 servings.

Mrs. Lenore W. Shearer, Home Economics Teacher, Port Royal, Pa.

Fruit Cooler

1 tall can evaporated milk, chilled
2 tbsp. lemon juice
1 can fruit cocktail, drained
1 can peaches or 2 c. fresh peaches, sliced
¾ c. sugar
1 can pineapple chunks, drained
1 small bottle Maraschino cherries, drained
3 tbsp. cherry juice
1 c. miniature marshmallows
½ c. pecans, chopped

Beat chilled milk until stiff with electric mixer set at high speed. Add lemon juice. Fold in remaining ingredients. Freeze. Yield: 20 servings.

Mrs. Sudie Mitchell Bell, Isola, Miss.

Fruit-Mallow Fizz

1 9-oz. can crushed pineapple
1 3-oz. pkg. cream cheese, softened
1 7-oz. bottle 7-Up or lemon-lime carbonated beverage
2 to 2½ c. frozen peaches, thawed, drained and diced
1 c. seedless grapes, halved
1 c. whipped cream
1 ½ c. miniature marshmallows

Blend pineapple into cheese. Stir in 7-Up or carbonated beverage. Mix fruit into the mixture. Freeze until partially thickened. Fold whipped cream and marshmallows into the cheese mixture. Freeze until firm. Let stand at room temperature for a few minutes before serving. Yield: 8-10 servings.

Charline Webb, Home Economics Teacher, Gaylesville, Ala.

Fruit Salad Piquant

2 lge. ripe bananas
1 sm. can crushed pineapple, well drained
2 tbsp. chopped Maraschino cherries
¾ c. sugar
2 c. sour cream
2 tbsp. lemon juice
½ c. chopped pecans

Mash bananas gently with fork; blend in remaining ingredients. Stir well; pour into ice tray or mold. Place in freezing compartment of refrigerator; freeze until firm. Cut into slices; serve on lettuce, if desired. Yield: 6 servings.

Mrs. Henry J. Yaeckle, Officers' Wives' Club, Bayreuth, Germany

Fruit Salad Swirl

1 small can crushed pineapple, drained
3 tbsp. (rounded) flour
½ c. sugar
1 egg, beaten
1 lg. pkg. cream cheese
1 lg. can fruit cocktail, drained
½ pt. whipped cream

Combine juice drained from pineapple with flour, sugar and egg; cook until thick, stirring constantly. Add cream cheese to hot mixture. Mix until smooth. Cool. Add pineapple and fruit cocktail; fold in whipped cream. Freeze. Yield: 10 servings.

Mrs. Virginia Smith, Home Economics Teacher, Evansville, Ind.

Ginger Ale Jumble

1 ½ tsp. unflavored gelatin
2 tbsp. orange juice
1 tbsp. lemon juice
2 tbsp. sugar
½ c. pale dry ginger ale
¼ c. drained canned crushed pineapple
⅓ c. diced canned pears
¼ c. halved strawberries
⅓ c. chopped nuts (opt.)
⅓ c. mayonnaise or salad dressing
½ c. heavy cream, whipped

Soak gelatin in orange juice for 5 minutes; add lemon juice. Place over boiling water; stir until gelatin is dissolved. Add sugar and ginger ale; stir until sugar is dissolved. Add fruits and nuts. Mix thoroughly. Fold in mayonnaise and whipped cream. Pour mixture into small freezing tray. Freeze until mixture is firm. Yield: 6 servings.

Mrs. David R. Hamlin, Wives' Club, Norfolk, Va.

 ## Golden Fruit For The Gods

GOLDEN FRUIT DRESSING:
1 tbsp. butter
¼ c. orange juice
¼ c. pineapple juice
1 tsp. lemon juice
¼ c. sugar
3 egg yolks
½ c. whipped cream

Combine all ingredients, folding in whipped cream last.

GOLDEN FRUIT SALAD:
½ c. oranges, drained and diced
⅓ c. pineapple, drained and diced
¾ c. Royal Anne cherries, pitted
¼ c. Maraschino cherries, drained
¾ c. bananas, diced
1 c. Golden Fruit Dressing

Combine all ingredients; mix thoroughly. Freeze. May be kept in freezer for as long as 2 months. Yield: 6 servings.

Laura E. Sumner, Home Economics Teacher, Bayard, N. M.

Grapefruit-Avocado Salad

1 8-oz. pkg. cream cheese, softened
1 c. sour cream
¼ tsp. salt
½ c. sugar
1 grapefruit, sectioned
1 avocado, diced
1 c. halved seedless white grapes
½ c. broken pecans

Blend cream cheese and sour cream; add salt and sugar. Stir until well blended. Add grapefruit sections, avocado, grapes and pecans. Pour into 9 x 5-inch loaf pan; freeze until firm. Slice and serve on salad greens with French dressing, if desired. Yield: 6-8 servings.

Mrs. Darwin Brendlinger, Officers' Wives' Club, Montgomery, Ala.

Grape-Pineapple Treat

2 3-oz. pkg. cream cheese, softened
2 tbsp. mayonnaise
2 tbsp. pineapple syrup
24 marshmallows, quartered
1 No. 2 can pineapple bits, drained
1 c. whipped cream
2 c. Tokay grapes, halved and seeded

Blend cream cheese with mayonnaise. Beat in pineapple syrup. Add marshmallows and pineapple. Fold in whipped cream and grapes. Pour into 1-quart tray. Freeze until firm. Yield: 6-8 servings.

Mrs. Beverly Soden, Home Economics Teacher, Wisner, Neb.

Helen's Fruit Salad

1 No. 2 can crushed pineapple, drained
1 No. 2 or 2½ can fruit cocktail, drained
1 can Mandarin oranges
1 10-oz. pkg. miniature marshmallows
½ c. mayonnaise
1 pt. small curd cottage cheese
1 pkg. dessert topping mix

Blend fruit and marshmallows together. Add mayonnaise and cheese. Beat dessert topping mix; add to fruit mixture. Freeze. Yield: 15-20 servings.

Mrs. Helen E. Stanford, Home Economics Teacher, Union, Ore.

Heavenly Hash

1 can crushed pineapple
½ lb. marshmallows, cut into quarters
½ lb. almonds, blanched and slivered
4 egg yolks
4 tbsp. sugar
2 tbsp. vinegar
½ pt. heavy cream

Combine pineapple, marshmallows and almonds; chill overnight. Combine all remaining ingredients, except cream, in top of double boiler; cook until thick and smooth. Combine dressing and fruit mixture; fold in cream. Turn into mold; freeze for 4 hours. Yield: 6 servings.

Mrs. Ruth Hughes, Nashville, Tenn., Favorite Recipes Food Fair

Iced Fruit

2 3-oz. pkg. cream cheese
½ to 1 tsp. salt
2 tbsp. salad dressing or mayonnaise
1 to 3 tbsp. lemon juice
½ c. crushed pineapple, drained
½ c. Maraschino cherries, coarsely chopped
½ c. pecans or walnuts, coarsely chopped
2 c. ripe bananas, diced
½ c. marshmallows, diced (opt.)
1 c. whipped cream

Mash cheese; blend with salt, salad dressing and lemon juice. Mix well. Fold in pineapple, cherries, nuts, bananas and marshmallows if desired. Fold in whipped cream. Freeze until firm with refrigerator freezer control set at coldest setting. Yield: 8-10 servings.

Mrs. Alice E. Blackburn, Montevallo, Ala.

Icy Fruit Salad

2 3-oz. pkg. cream cheese
1 c. mayonnaise
1 lge. can crushed pineapple, drained
½ c. Maraschino cherries, diced
2 bananas, mashed
1 No. 2 can fruit cocktail, drained
¾ c. sugar
½ tsp. salt

(Continued on next page)

24 lge. marshmallows, finely chopped
1 c. heavy cream, whipped
Red food coloring
½ c. slivered almonds

Blend cream cheese and mayonnaise. Add fruits, sugar, salt and marshmallows. Color whipped cream with food coloring; fold into fruit mixture. Mix well; add almonds. Pour into two loaf pans and freeze overnight. Yield: 12 servings.

Mary Lucille Simmons, Gilmon, Iowa

 ## Idaho Cherry Salad

2 tbsp. sugar
1 tbsp. flour
½ c. honey
1 egg
⅓ c. lemon juice
2 c. fruit cocktail, drained
1 c. bananas, sliced
⅓ c. orange slices, diced
¼ c. Maraschino or Bing cherries, pitted and quartered
1 c. whipped cream

Combine sugar, flour and honey. Bring to a boil; cook 1 minute, stirring constantly. Beat egg while gradually adding lemon juice. Add a small amount of the honey mixture to the egg; mix well. Return mixture to heat and bring to a boil, stirring constantly. Remove from heat; cool. Combine fruits; add to honey mixture. Fold in whipped cream. Freeze. Yield: 6-8 servings.

Mrs. Georgia Balls, Home Economics Teacher, Pocatello, Idaho

 ## Kansas City Salad

2 eggs, beaten
½ c. sugar
¼ tsp. salt
3 tbsp. lemon juice
½ c. mixed pineapple syrup and water
1 9-oz. can crushed pineapple, drained
2 c. unpeeled apples, finely diced
½ c. celery, finely diced
1 c. whipped cream

Combine eggs, sugar, salt, lemon juice and syrup-water mixture. Cook over low heat, stirring constantly until thick. Chill. Fold in pineapple, apples, celery and whipped cream. Pour into a 2-quart refrigerator tray or salad mold; freeze. Yield: 12 servings.

Mrs. Barbara Deane, Home Economics Teacher, Hoxie, Kan.

Luscious Cranberry Salad

    1 No. 2 can crushed pineapple
    1 lb. marshmallows, cut
    1 lb. cranberries, ground
    2 c. sugar
    1 c. whipped cream

Combine pineapple and marshmallows; let stand overnight. Combine cranberries and sugar; let stand overnight. Combine mixtures; fold in whipped cream. Freeze. Yield: 6 servings.

June Stultz, Renton, Wash.

 ### Mint-Pineapple Salad

    1 No. 2 can crushed pineapple, drained
    1 c. miniature marshmallows
    1 c. white cherries, drained and pitted
  ½ c. mayonnaise
    2 tbsp. lemon juice
  ⅛ tsp. peppermint extract
    1 c. whipped cream
    Few drops green food coloring
  ¼ c. green Maraschino cherries, chopped

Combine pineapple, marshmallows and white cherries. Beat mayonnaise, lemon juice and peppermint extract into whipped cream. Tint light green with food coloring. Fold in fruit mixture. Arrange Maraschino cherries in bottom of an oiled loaf pan. Carefully pour in salad. Freeze until firm. Yield: 10-12 servings.

Barbara Barker, Home Economics Teacher, Arlington Heights, Ill.

Mint Salad Freeze

  12 lge. marshmallows
    1 tbsp. pineapple juice
  ⅛ tsp. green food coloring
  ⅛ tsp. peppermint extract
    1 c. crushed pineapple
  ¼ c. salad dressing
  ¼ c. whipped cream

Melt marshmallows in pineapple juice over low heat. Add food coloring and peppermint extract; cool. Add pineapple, salad dressing and whipped cream. Freeze until firm. Yield: 4 servings.

Mrs. Carolyn Arthur, Home Economics Teacher, Mayville, Wis.

Mother's Salad Quickie

1 6-oz. pkg. cream cheese
⅓ c. mayonnaise
1 c. crushed pineapple, drained
1 sm. pkg. miniature marshmallows
1 sm. bottle Maraschino cherries, chopped
½ pt. heavy cream or canned milk, whipped

Blend cream cheese and mayonnaise; add remaining ingredients. Mix well; pour into ice trays. Freeze several hours before serving.

Adelaine Sather, Astoria, Ore.

 ### Pear And Cream Cheese Salad

1 1-lb. can pears
2 3-oz. pkg. cream cheese
6 tbsp. French dressing
Salad greens
Mayonnaise

Drain juice from pears, reserving juice. Cut pears into thin lengthwise slices. Mash the cream cheese; add pear juice and 6 tablespoons French dressing. Beat with a hand or electric beater until smooth. Arrange pear slices in refrigerator tray. Pour cheese mixture over pears. Freeze until firm enough to slice into squares. Arrange on salad greens; serve with mayonnaise or additional French dressing. Yield: 8-10 servings.

Mrs. Franklin A. Nichols, Officers' Wives' Club, Goldsboro, N. C.

 ### Pear Salad Freeze

1 pkg. lime or cherry gelatin
1 ¾ c. pear juice
Juice of ½ lemon
2 3-oz. pkg. cream cheese
1 No. 3 can pears, drained and diced
½ pt. whipped cream
½ c. almonds, slivered (opt.)

Heat pear juice. Add gelatin and dissolve. Add lemon juice and cream cheese; mix well. Chill. Add pears, nuts and whipped cream. Pour into 9 x 9-inch pan. Freeze; stirring once or twice. Yield: 10-12 servings.

Mrs. Ruth DeFriese, Home Economics Teacher, Knoxville, Tenn.

Pineapple Blizzard

    1 3-oz. pkg. cream cheese
    ¼ c. mayonnaise
    2 tbsp. lemon juice
    15 marshmallows, quartered
    1 c. pineapple, drained and diced
    ¼ c. dates, diced
    1 c. whipped cream

Combine cheese and mayonnaise; mix until smooth. Add lemon juice, marshmallows, pineapple and dates. Fold in whipped cream. Freeze.

A. Dorothea Nevramon, Steele, N. D.

 ### Pink Raspberry Whip

    1 No. 2 can crushed pineapple
    2 3-oz. pkg. raspberry gelatin
    1 lge. can condensed milk, chilled and whipped
    Nuts, chopped

Heat pineapple; add gelatin and stir until dissolved. Chill. Add whipped cream. Sprinkle with nuts. Freeze. Yield: 12 servings.

Mrs. Eleanor Finley, Home Economics Teacher, Belle Vernon, Pa.

 ### Pink Snow Salad

    2 3-oz. pkg. cream cheese
    ½ to 1 c. mayonnaise or salad dressing
    1 No. 2½ can fruit cocktail, drained
    ½ c. Maraschino cherries, drained and quartered
    2 ½ c. miniature marshmallows
    1 c. nuts (opt.)
    1 c. whipped cream
    Red food coloring or cherry juice (opt.)

Soften cream cheese; blend with mayonnaise. Stir in fruit, marshmallows and nuts, if desired. Fold in whipped cream. Tint with few drops red food coloring or cherry juice, if desired. Freeze until firm. Yield: 9-12 servings.

Charlotte Chafin, Home Economics Teacher, Killeen, Tex.

Pink Salad Loaf

1 1-lb. 1-oz. can fruit cocktail, drained
2 c. sour cream
3 c. miniature marshmallows
2 tbsp. fresh lemon juice
¼ tsp. salt
1 or 2 drops of red food coloring

Place ½ cup fruit cocktail in bottom of 5-cup mold. Combine sour cream, marshmallows, lemon juice, salt and enough food coloring to tint very light pink. Add remaining fruit cocktail; mix lightly. Spoon into mold over fruit. Freeze until firm. Unmold; cut into slices to serve. Yield: 8 servings.

Mrs. Charles Franz, Atlanta, Ga.

Quick Frozen Fruit Salad

1 c. fruit cocktail, drained
¼ c. cherries, chopped
½ c. miniature marshmallows
½ c. fruit cocktail juice
1 tbsp. lemon juice
1 tsp. confectioner's sugar
¼ c. nuts, chopped
1 c. dessert topping mix

Combine fruit cocktail, cherries and marshmallows. Stir in juices and sugar. Add nuts; mix well. Fold in dessert topping mix prepared according to package directions. Freeze until firm. Yield: 6-8 servings.

Dianne Warnock, Home Economics Teacher, Oregon, Ohio

Rainbow Salad

½ tbsp. unflavored gelatin
¼ c. cold water
1 c. salad dressing
1 c. whipped cream
¾ c. Royal Anne cherries, drained and halved
2 slices pineapple, drained and diced
½ c. Maraschino cherries, drained and sliced
1 11-oz. can Mandarin oranges, drained and diced
1 banana, diced

Soften gelatin in cold water; dissolve over hot water. Cool. Add salad dressing. Fold in whipped cream and fruit. Freeze until firm. Yield: 8 servings.

Cecelia Butler, Clayton, N. M., Favorite Recipes Food Fair

Raisin Carnival Snow

1 c. dark or golden raisins
1 11-oz. can Mandarin oranges, drained
1 9-oz. can pineapple tidbits, drained
1 8-oz. pkg. cream cheese
½ tsp. salt
2 tsp. vanilla
½ tsp. almond extract
1 tbsp. lemon juice
½ tsp. lemon rind, grated
2 c. miniature marshmallows
½ c. Maraschino cherries, halved
1 c. whipped cream
Red food coloring (opt.)

Combine raisins and juice from oranges and pineapple; heat to simmering. Remove from heat; cover and cool. Blend cream cheese until soft; beat in salt, vanilla, almond extract, lemon juice and rind. Blend in raisin mixture. Stir in fruits and marshmallows. Fold in whipped cream. Add food coloring if desired. Freeze. Yield: 8-10 servings.

Madelyn Thames Everett, Home Economics Teacher, Magee, Miss.

Rare Delight

½ cantaloupe, diced
4 ripe red plums, diced
1 c. halved fresh red cherries
1 c. halved white grapes
1 can frozen orange juice, slightly thawed

Lightly mix fruits. Place in ice cube tray or similar tin. Pour orange juice over all; freeze only until ice chips begin to form or freeze completely until needed, but serve in ice chip state. Yield: 4 servings.

Mrs. John M. Danielsen, Pres. Wives' Club, Norfolk, Va.

Raves Salad

¾ c. mayonnaise
1 8-oz. pkg. cream cheese, softened
1 No. 2½ can apricots, drained and cut
1 No. 2 can pineapple tidbits, drained
6 green Maraschino cherries, chopped
6 red Maraschino cherries, chopped

(Continued on next page)

Gradually add mayonnaise to cream cheese; beat until creamy. Add apricots. Stir in pineapple and cherries. Freeze. Yield: 10-12 servings.

Mrs. Marjorie P. Kibelbek, Home Economics Teacher, Brownsville, Pa.

Ruth's Pineapple-Orange Salad

   2 tbsp. flour
   1 c. pineapple juice
   ¼ to ½ c. butter
   ⅛ c. sugar
   Pinch of salt
   1 egg, slightly beaten
   2 tbsp. lemon juice
   4 slices pineapple, finely cut
   2 oranges, finely cut
   ¼ c. nuts, chopped
  10 marshmallows
   8 Maraschino cherries
   1 pt. whipped cream

Make a paste of flour and some of the pineapple juice. Gradually add remaining juice. Add butter, sugar and salt. Cook in top of double boiler for about 10 minutes. Add egg and continue cooking for a few minutes longer, stirring constantly. Cool. Add lemon juice, pineapple, oranges, nuts, marshmallows and cherries; fold in whipped cream. Pour in refrigerator tray; freeze. Yield: 8 servings.

Mrs. Ruth Johnson, Dallas, Tex.

Seafood Salad Supreme

   2 tsp. unflavored gelatin
   ⅓ c. cold water
   2 c. flaked crab meat, shrimp or lobster
   ⅔ c. catsup
   2 tbsp. lemon juice
   3 tbsp. vinegar
   1 tsp. prepared horseradish
   ¼ tsp. salt
   ½ c. mayonnaise
   Tomato slices
   Lettuce

Soften gelatin in cold water; dissolve over hot water. Combine with seafood, catsup, lemon juice, vinegar, horseradish and salt; fold in mayonnaise. Freeze

(Continued on next page)

in refrigerator tray until firm. Cut into cubes; arrange on tomato slices on lettuce. Yield: 6 servings.

Mrs. Jack L. Thedford, Officers' Wives' Club, Albuquerque, N. M.

Spiced Peach Salad

1 1-lb. 14-oz. jar spiced peaches
1 3-oz. pkg. cream cheese
¼ c. sugar
⅓ c. evaporated milk
1 c. miniature marshmallows
½ c. chopped pecans
⅔ c. evaporated milk, partially frozen
1 tbsp. lemon juice

Drain peaches, reserving ½ cup liquid. Discard peach stones; chop peaches coarsely. Blend cheese and sugar until smooth. Slowly beat in 1/3 cup evaporated milk and spiced peach syrup. Stir in peaches, marshmallows and pecans. Whip partially frozen evaporated milk until very stiff. Beat in lemon juice to blend thoroughly. Fold into cheese mixture. Turn into two 1-quart ice cube trays. Freeze until firm. Yield: 10-12 servings.

Photograph for this recipe below.

Strawberry-Cheese Salad

1 pt. strawberries
2 tbsp. sugar
2 tsp. lemon juice
2 3-oz. pkg. cream cheese
½ c. whipped cream

Crush strawberries with sugar. Mix with cream cheese and lemon juice. Fold in whipped cream. Freeze. Yield: 6-8 servings.

Rony E. Bolton, Home Economics Teacher, Seaman, Ohio

Strawberry-Pineapple Delight

CRUST:

¼ c. sugar
⅓ c. butter or margarine, melted
1 ½ c. graham cracker crumbs

Combine sugar, melted butter and crumbs; mix well. Firmly press mixture into a greased 9 x 9-inch pan. Chill.

SALAD:

1 envelope unflavored gelatin
2 tbsp. cold pineapple syrup
¼ c. hot pineapple syrup
1 c. sweetened strawberries, drained and sliced
1 9-oz. can pineapple tidbits, drained
8 marshmallows, chopped
¼ c. pecans, broken
¼ c. mayonnaise or salad dressing
1 c. whipped cream
½ c. coconut

Soften gelatin in cold pineapple syrup; dissolve in hot pineapple syrup. Combine fruit, marshmallows and pecans. Add gelatin. Fold mayonnaise into whipped cream; add to fruit mixture. Fold in coconut or sprinkle over the top of fruit mixture. Spread in chilled crust or if desired, omit the crust and pour mixture into paper cups set in a muffin pan. Freeze. Yield: 12 servings.

Mrs. Merlin R. Miller, Home Economics Teacher, Hettinger, N. D.

Strawberry Salad Elegante

2 pkg. strawberry gelatin
1 c. hot water
1 c. cold water

(Continued on next page)

2 10-oz. pkg. frozen strawberries, thawed
1 envelope dessert topping mix, whipped
2 tbsp. sugar
1 3-oz. pkg. cream cheese, softened

Dissolve gelatin in hot water; stir in cold water. Add 2 ice cubes; chill. Add strawberries. Pour half of mixture in oblong glass baking dish. Freeze. Chill remaining half of mixture until nearly set. Combine dessert topping mix, sugar and cream cheese. Beat until smooth. Spread dessert topping mixture on top of frozen layer; top with chilled gelatin. Chill for several hours. Yield: 8 servings.

Mrs. Fayma Drummond, Petersburg, Tex., Favorite Recipes Food Fair

 Strawberry Salad Superb

1 6-oz. pkg. cream cheese
2 tbsp. honey
1 c. sweetened strawberries, crushed
½ c. canned pineapple, diced
¼ c. lemon juice

Blend cheese with honey; add strawberries, pineapple and lemon juice. Freeze. Yield: 6 servings.

Sister Del Rey, Home Economics Teacher, Dell Rapids, S. D.

Sunnyside Salad

½ tsp. salt
1 ½ to 2 tbsp. vinegar
1 ½ tbsp. flour
¼ c. sugar
¾ c. pineapple juice
1 egg (opt.)
3 bananas, crushed
1 c. pineapple, diced
12 Maraschino cherries, chopped
1 c. pears, diced
1 c. whipped cream
Nuts, chopped

Combine salt, vinegar, flour, sugar, pineapple juice and egg, if desired. Cook in double boiler until thick; cool. Add bananas, pineapple, cherries and pears. Fold in whipped cream. Pour into 2 trays; freeze. Garnish with nuts and additional whipped cream, if desired. Yield: 12 servings.

Leona Ferch Smith, Sunnyside, Wash.

Tangy Salad Treat

    1 1-lb. can cranberry sauce
    1 8¾-oz. can crushed pineapple
    1 c. miniature marshmallows
    1 tbsp. lemon juice
    ¼ c. whipped cream
    ¼ c. mayonnaise
    ¼ c. confectioner's sugar

Combine cranberry sauce, pineapple, marshmallows and lemon juice. Combine whipped cream, mayonnaise and sugar; spread over cranberry mixture. Freeze. Yield: 6 servings.

Mrs. Mary Campbell, Home Economics Teacher, Canton, Pa.

Whipped Wonder

    1 lge. pkg. cream cheese
    1 c. heavy sour cream
    2 tbsp. lemon juice
    ⅛ tsp. salt
    1 c. canned pineapple, diced
    1 c. grapes, seeded
    1 c. cherries, pitted
    1 banana, sliced
    1 c. whipped cream
    ¾ c. mayonnaise
    ½ c. marshmallows, quartered

Cream the cheese, sour cream, lemon juice and salt. Add fruits and whipped cream. Fold in mayonnaise and marshmallows; freeze. Yield: 8 servings.

Mrs. Lenore W. Shearer, Home Economics Teacher, Port Royal, Pa.

Zippy Tomato-Cheese Salad

    1 c. tomato sauce
    1 c. cottage cheese, drained
    ½ tsp. salt
    ½ tsp. horseradish
    1 2¼-oz. can deviled ham
    ¼ to ½ tsp. onion juice
    ½ c. stuffed olives, sliced
    2 tbsp. catsup

Combine all ingredients except olives and catsup. Beat until well blended. Pour into 9-inch pie plate. Spread catsup on top; garnish with olive slices. Cover securely with aluminum foil. Freeze. Yield: 6 servings.

Mrs. Fred Beers, Jr., McDonough, Ga., Favorite Recipes Food Fair

Party and Dessert Salads

Almond-Peach Cream

    1 c. heavy cream
    2 tbsp. sugar
    ¼ tsp. almond flavoring
    2 ½ c. sliced peaches
    ½ c. shredded coconut

Whip cream; add sugar and flavoring. Fold in peaches and coconut. Chill.

Mrs. O. Waterman, Cambridge, Mass., Favorite Recipes Food Fair

Ambrosia In Orange Cups

    6 oranges
    2 tbsp. grated orange rind
    ½ c. whipping cream
    2 tbsp. lemon juice
    3 tbsp. sugar
    1 lb. seedless grapes
    1 sm. can grated coconut
    Nutmeg
    6 Maraschino cherries

Remove a ½-inch slice from top of each orange. Remove pulp from oranges. Refrigerate orange cups. Remove seed and membranes from orange pulp. Add grated orange rind to whipping cream; chill. Whip cream until it forms soft mounds; add lemon juice and sugar. Fold in orange pulp, grapes and coconut. Spoon into orange cups. Garnish each with nutmeg and a cherry. Yield: 6 servings.

Mrs. Ernestine A. McLeod, Home Economics Teacher, Wickes, Ark.

Angel Hash

    2 tbsp. cornstarch
    ¼ c. sugar
    1 c. mixed pineapple syrup and water
    2 egg yolks
    1 c. whipped cream
    1 No. 2 can pineapple tidbits, drained
    ¼ c. walnuts, chopped
    15 marshmallows, quartered
    6 bananas, sliced

Combine cornstarch and sugar. Gradually add pineapple syrup, stirring to blend. Cook, stirring constantly, until thickened. Add part of mixture to egg yolks: blend well and return to hot mixture. Cook, stirring constantly, for 2

(Continued on next page)

minutes. Cool. Fold in whipped cream. Fold in pineapple, walnuts and marsh-mallows. Chill overnight. Add bananas just before serving. Garnish with maraschino cherries and serve in lettuce lined salad bowl. Yield: 10-12 servings.

Mrs. Marjorie Neilson, Arlington, S. D.

Apricot-Pineapple Ring Mold

4 tbsp. gelatin
¾ c. cold water
2 c. apricot nectar
Dash of salt
3 tbsp. lemon juice
1 c. crushed pineapple
½ c. salad dressing
2 3-oz. pkg. cream cheese
1 c. chopped celery
1 c. chopped walnuts

Soften 2 tablespoons gelatin in ½ cup cold water; add apricot nectar, salt and lemon juice. Chill until mixture begins to thicken; fold in pineapple. Pour half of mixture into oiled ring mold; chill until almost firm. Blend salad dressing with cream cheese; add celery and walnuts. Soften remaining gelatin in remaining cold water; dissolve over hot water. Add cheese mixture; spread over firm layer of apricot gelatin. Chill; pour remaining apricot gelatin over cheese layer. Chill until firm.

Mrs. John A. Beall, Officers' Wives' Club, Fort McPherson, Ga.

Blushing Pears

1 sm. can pecan pieces, finely chopped
1 8-oz. pkg. cream cheese, softened
1 No. 2 can Bartlett pears, drained
1 bottle red food coloring
Lettuce leaves

Add chopped pecans to cheese; roll into balls the size of the hollow of the pears. Press one ball gently between 2 pear halves, filling the cavity. Put remaining cheese into a decorating tube. Cover edges of pear halves with cheese, starting at the bottom of the pear, going up the side, around the top and down the other side. Place a small amount of red coloring on a paint brush; in one stroke, paint a red line on the center of each pear half down to the base of the pear. The color will blend outward to the edges hidden under the cheese and give a blushing appearance to the pear. Serve on lettuce leaves. Yield: 4-6 servings.

Mrs. Lynn Coleman, Biloxi, Miss.

273

Candlestick Salad

8 pineapple rings, drained
8 lettuce leaves
4 bananas, cut in halves crosswise
8 strawberries, maraschino cherries or candied cherries
Shredded coconut
½ c. whipped cream or fruit salad dressing

Arrange a slice of pineapple on lettuce for the candle base or holder. Dip bananas in pineapple juice to prevent discoloration. Place half of banana in pineapple ring to make candle. Add cherry or strawberry for flame. Put coconut in cherry for wick. Dribble whipped cream down banana to make it look as if candle is melting. For a colorful Christmas salad, red or green candied apple rings may be used instead of pineapple, and lemon juice used on banana. Yield: 8 servings.

Mrs. Lawrence A. Boyd, Home Economics Teacher, Vernon, Tex.

Cantaloupe Party Mold

1 tbsp. unflavored gelatin
¾ c. grapefruit juice
⅓ c. sugar
⅛ tsp. salt
½ c. cold water
⅓ c. lemon juice
2 c. cantaloupe balls
Cream cheese

Soften gelatin in ¼ cup grapefruit juice; melt over hot water. Add remaining grapefruit juice, sugar, salt, water and lemon juice. Chill until mixture begins to thicken. Fold in cantaloupe balls. Oil a 2½-cup mold and a 1½-cup mold; fill each with cantaloupe mixture. Refrigerate until firm. Just before serving, unmold large salad onto serving plate. Center small salad on top of larger one. Garnish with cream cheese and serve with mayonnaise or fruit salad dressing. Yield: 4 servings.

Mrs. Gladys Evans, Camp Point, Ill.

Cherries In Cream

2 1-lb. cans red water-packed cherries, drained
1 13-oz. can pineapple tidbits, drained
1 3½-oz. can flaked coconut
1 c. miniature marshmallows
¾ c. confectioner's sugar
¼ tsp. salt
2 c. sour cream

(Continued on next page)

Combine cherries, pineapple, coconut, marshmallows, sugar and salt. Carefully fold sour cream into cherry mixture. Turn into a bowl. Cover and refrigerate overnight. Yield: 6-8 servings.

Mrs. Truman Thornton, Biloxi, Miss.

 ## Cherry-Lime Crunch

> *1 6-oz. pkg. cherry gelatin*
> *1 6.-oz. pkg. lime gelatin*
> *1 8-oz. pkg. cream cheese*
> *½ c. milk*
> *½ c. maraschino cherries, chopped and drained*
> *½ c. nuts, chopped*
> *½ c. celery, chopped*
> *Parsley flakes*

Dissolve cherry gelatin according to package directions. Chill until firm. Mix lime gelatin according to package directions, using ½ cup less water than called for. Chill to egg white consistency. Combine cream cheese and milk. Beat chilled lime gelatin until foamy. Add cream cheese-milk mixture and continue beating until cheese and gelatin are blended and mixture is green and foamy. Add nuts, cherries and celery. Pour over firm cherry gelatin. Sprinkle with parsley flakes. Chill. Yield: 12 servings.

Mrs. Dorothy Burford, Home Economics Teacher, Atlanta, Ga.

 ## Chicken In Cheese Shell

> *½ c. American cheese, shredded*
> *½ c. shortening*
> *½ tsp. salt*
> *1 ½ c. sifted flour*
> *4 to 5 tbsp. cold water*
> *1 ½ c. cooked or canned chicken, diced*
> *1 9-oz. can pineapple tidbits, drained*
> *1 c. walnuts, chopped*
> *½ c. celery, chopped*
> *1 c. sour cream*
> *⅔ c. salad dressing*

Combine 1/3 cup cheese and shortening. Add salt, flour and water. Bake in 8-inch pie pan at 450 degrees for 12 minutes. Cool. Combine chicken, pineapple, nuts and celery. Blend sour cream and salad dressing; add 2/3 cup to chicken mixture. Spoon into pie shell; top with remaining sour cream mixture. Sprinkle with remaining cheese. Chill. Yield: 6 servings.

Mrs. Blanche Ivanish, Malta, Mont.

Christmas Cheer

    1 pkg. cherry gelatin
    3 c. boiling water
    1 can whole cranberry sauce
  ½ c. pecan halves
    1 pkg. lemon gelatin
    1 3-oz. pkg. cream cheese
    1 c. crushed pineapple
    1 pkg. lime gelatin
    1 c. grapefruit juice
    1 c. grapefruit sections

Dissolve cherry gelatin in 1 cup boiling water, stirring until dissolved. Add cranberry sauce. Chill until mixture begins to congeal. Add nuts; pour into 8¾ x 4½ x 2¾-inch pan. Chill until firm. Add 1 cup boiling water to lemon gelatin; stir until dissolved. Add cream cheese to hot mixture; beat until smooth. Add pineapple; chill until partially congealed. Pour over firm cherry layer; chill until congealed. Add remaining water to lime gelatin; stir until dissolved. Add grapefruit juice; chill until mixture congeals. Arrange grapefruit sections over chilled cheese layer. Pour syrupy lime gelatin over grapefruit. Chill until firm. Unmold onto platter; garnish with endive and cranberries if desired. Yield: 8 servings.

Mrs. Charles D. Knight, Pres. Officers' Wives' Club, March AFB, Cal.

Chicken Salad Ring

    1 envelope unflavored gelatin
    2 c. hot chicken broth
    5 c. diced, cooked chicken
  ¾ c. finely chopped celery
    1 whole pimento
    2 tbsp. chopped sweet pickles
    1 tsp. French's minced green onion
  ½ tsp. French's rosemary, crushed
    2 tsp. lemon juice
  ⅓ c. mayonnaise or salad dressing

Soften gelatin in ¼ cup water; add to hot broth. Stir to dissolve. Pour ¼ cup into bottom of 6-cup mold; chill. Cut part of pimento into thin strips; place in a pattern on top of congealed layer. Spoon over a little cooled broth; chill again. Add remaining ingredients, except mayonnaise, to remaining broth; add salt and pepper to taste. When mixture starts to thicken, fold in mayonnaise; fill mold. Chill. Unmold on serving platter; garnish with radish roses and parsley. Serve with crisp greens and mayonnaise. Yield: 10 servings.

Photograph for this recipe on page 271.

Coeur A La Creme

1 lb. cottage cheese
1 lb. cream cheese
2 c. heavy cream
Salt
Mint
Strawberries or raspberries

Beat cottage cheese and cream cheese until smooth; gradually add cream. Season with salt. Line a heart-shaped basket with cheesecloth; fill with cheese. Place basket on a plate; refrigerate overnight. Unmold onto glass platter; remove cheesecloth. Garnish with mint and strawberries or raspberries. Yield: 6 servings.

Mrs. James B. Saum, Saint Joseph, La.

 ## Creamy Fruit Salad

1 lge. can pineapple chunks, drained
3 lge. bananas, sliced
½ c. chopped nuts
2 oranges, peeled and diced
1 lge. can pitted black cherries, drained
1 c. miniature marshmallows
½ c. shredded coconut
2 apples, peeled and diced
1 ½ c. evaporated milk, whipped and sweetened

Combine all ingredients, folding in whipped milk last. Chill for several hours. Yield: 8 servings.

Mrs. Donovan E. Boyd, Officers' Wives' Club, Harrogate, England

 ## Cucumber Mousse

1 lge. unpeeled cucumber, grated
¾ c. evaporated milk
2 pkgs. low-calorie lime gelatin
½ c. boiling water
1 tsp. onion, grated
¼ tsp. salt

Chill a small mixing bowl and beaters. Chill evaporated milk in freezing compartment until ice crystals form around edge. Dissolve gelatin in boiling water. Add onion, salt and undrained cucumber. Chill until slightly thickened. Whip

(Continued on next page)

evaporated milk in chilled bowl until stiff. Fold gelatin mixture into whipped milk. Pour into mold and chill until firm. Unmold on bed of greens; garnish with mayonnaise. Yield: 6-8 servings.

Mrs. Eileen Roberts, Home Economics Teacher, Westfield, Wis.

 ## Dessert Salad For Twelve

1 can pineapple
1 envelope unflavored gelatin
1 ½ c. chopped pecans or walnuts
1 stalk celery, diced
1 lge. green pepper, diced (opt.)
1 pt. cottage cheese
¾ c. mayonnaise
1 pt. heavy cream, whipped
¼ c. sugar
1 head lettuce

Drain pineapple, reserving juice. Soak gelatin in one-fourth of the cold pineapple juice. Heat remaining juice; pour over gelatin and stir until dissolved. Cool. Mix finely chopped pineapple, nuts, celery, pepper, cottage cheese and mayonnaise thoroughly. Add gelatin mixture. Sweeten whipped cream with sugar; fold into gelatin mixture. Turn into individual molds. Chill until firm. Serve on lettuce with additional mayonnaise and dash of paprika, if desired. Yield: 12 servings.

Mrs. Harlan D. Foster, Officers' Wives' Club, St. Albans, N. Y.

Double-Decker Cherry Salad

1 No. 2 can sliced pineapple, drained
1 3-oz. pkg. cherry gelatin
1 3-oz. pkg. cream cheese
2 to 3 tbsp. light cream or top milk
Pineapple juice plus water to make 1¾ c. liquid
1 No. 2 can Bing cherries, pitted and drained
⅓ c. lemon juice
1 pkg. orange gelatin
½ c. stuffed olives, sliced

Heat mixed pineapple juice and water to boiling. Add cherry gelatin; stir to dissolve. Chill until partially set. Cut pineapple slices in ⅛-inch pieces; add to cherry gelatin mixture. Pour into an oiled 8-inch square pan. Chill until firm. Soften cheese with cream; spread over firm gelatin. Combine cherry juice and

(Continued on next page)

lemon juice; add water to make 1¾ cups liquid. Heat liquid to boiling; add orange gelatin and dissolve. Chill until partially set. Add cherries and olives. Spread over cheese. Chill until firm. Yield: 9 servings.

Virginia B. Dotson, Home Economics Teacher, Buffalo, W. Va.

Eggnog Christmas Salad

2 8¾-oz. cans crushed pineapple with juice
1 tbsp. unflavored gelatin
3 tbsp. fresh lime juice
1 ½ c. eggnog
¾ c. chopped celery
1 3-oz. pkg. raspberry gelatin
1 ½ c. boiling water
1 10-oz. pkg. frozen cranberry-orange relish
Salad greens

Drain pineapple juice into saucepan; heat to boiling. Soften gelatin in lime juice; dissolve in boiling pineapple juice. Cool. Add eggnog; chill until partially set. Fold in drained pineapple and celery. Pour into mold; chill until firm. Dissolve raspberry gelatin in boiling water; add cranberry-orange relish, stirring the mixture until relish is thawed. Chill until mixture begins to thicken. When eggnog mixture is almost firm, pour raspberry gelatin mixture on top. Chill until set. Unmold on salad greens.

Photograph for this recipe below.

Filled Tomato Cups

6 lge. firm tomatoes
½ c. chopped ham
2 tbsp. finely chopped onion
3 tbsp. finely chopped olives
2 tbsp. finely chopped pimento
1 c. diced celery
1 c. diced hard-cooked eggs
¼ tsp. salt
1 c. mayonnaise thinned with whipped cream

Wash and peel tomatoes; scoop out centers. Chill. Combine remaining ingredients. Fill tomatoes with mixture. Chill before serving.

Mrs. Victor H. Weipert, Monroe, Mich.

Flaming Christmas Candle Salad

1 4-oz. pkg. cream cheese
4 tbsp. pineapple juice
4 bananas
Lettuce
1 8½-oz. can sliced pineapple
4 cubes sugar
1 tbsp. lemon flavoring

Soften cream cheese at room temperature; whip until fluffy. Gradually add pineapple juice, continuing to beat until well blended. Cut ends from bananas so that bananas will be straight. Arrange lettuce leaves on four salad plates; place 1 slice pineapple on each lettuce leaf. Stand bananas in center of pineapple rings using cream cheese as support. Top bananas with 1 teaspoon cream cheese. Dip sugar cube into lemon flavoring; place on top cream cheese. Light sugar cube; serve flaming. Cherries may be substituted for flaming sugar cubes. Yield: 4 servings.

Mrs. Robert P. Hunt, Williamsburg, Va., Favorite Recipes Food Fair

Frozen Berry-Ice Cream Salad

1 qt. vanilla ice cream
½ c. mayonnaise
1 c. canned pineapple, drained
1 c. blueberries, drained
2 c. raspberries or strawberries

Soften ice cream; quickly blend in mayonnaise. Add fruit; mix. Freeze 2 to 3 hours or until firm.

Mrs. Violet Moseley, Home Economics Teacher, Avon Park, Fla.

Fruit Cocktail Marshmallow Whip

1 No. 303 can fruit cocktail
¼ lb. marshmallows, cut up
1 tsp. lemon juice
1 tbsp. grated lemon rind
1 c. heavy cream, whipped

Combine fruit cocktail and marshmallows, reserving ¼ cup fruit. Refrigerate 1 hour; drain. Add lemon juice and rind. Fold in whipped cream. Garnish each serving with reserved fruit. Yield: 6 servings.

Mrs. Cecil Richards, Portland, Maine

 ### Fruit-Cheese Loaf Salad

1 pkg. cherry gelatin
1 pt. hot water
1 No. 303 can fruit cocktail, drained
¾ c. hot fruit cocktail juice
½ to 1 c. mayonnaise
1 3-oz. pkg. cream cheese
1 envelope unflavored gelatin
¼ c. cold water

Dissolve cherry gelatin in hot water; cool. Add fruit cocktail. Pour half of mixture into a tray. Chill until firm. Dissolve unflavored gelatin in cold water and hot fruit juice. Cream mayonnaise, cheese and fruit juice. Place cheese mixture on firm gelatin. Chill until partially set. Add remaining gelatin. Chill until firm. Two different flavored and colored gelatins may be used for interest leaving one without fruit and adjusting amount of hot fruit juice and water. Yield: 12 servings.

Mrs. Irene J. Hodgen, Callawhee, N. C.

Fruit Salad In Avocado Boats

　　3 med. ripe avocados
　　3 tsp. fresh lime juice
　　1 c. fresh grapefruit sections
　　1 c. fresh pineapple wedges
　¼ c. olive or salad oil
　　1 tbsp. vinegar
　½ tsp. salt
　　Dash of pepper
　½ tsp. ground cumin seed

Wash avocados; cut into halves. Remove seed. Brush with about 2 teaspoonfuls lime juice to prevent discoloration. Fill cavities with grapefruit sections and pineapple wedges. Combine remaining ingredients; beat with rotary beater. Serve over salad. Yield: 6 servings.

Mrs. Charlotte Clark, Minneapolis, Minn.

 ### Grapefruit Boats

　　5 grapefruit
　　3 pkg. lemon gelatin
　¾ c. boiling water
　　1 tsp. unflavored gelatin
　½ c. cold water

Cut grapefruit from stem to tip; remove all pulp and juice. Dissolve lemon gelatin in boiling water. Soften unflavored gelatin in cold water. Stir gelatin mixtures into grapefruit pulp. Fill grapefruit halves; let congeal in refrigerator.

DRESSING:

　⅓ c. sugar
　　2 tbsp. flour
　　2 egg yolks, well beaten
　　8 marshmallows, diced
　　Juice of 2 lemons
　½ c. heavy cream
　⅔ c. chopped pecans

Combine sugar, flour, egg yolks and marshmallows in double boiler; cook until thick, stirring constantly. Cool; add lemon juice. Whip cream; add pecans. Fold in cooked mixture. Serve with grapefruit boats.

Mrs. Edward L. Uher, Officers' Wives' Club, Myrtle Beach, S. C.

Green Goddess Seafood Mold

LEMON LAYER:

>   1 pkg. lemon gelatin
>   1 ½ tsp. garlic salt
>   ½ tsp. salt
>   Dash of pepper
>   1 c. hot water
>   1 c. cold water
>   2 tbsp. wine vinegar
>   1 tsp. chopped parsley
>   ½ c. diced celery
>   1 c. flaked crab
>   1 ⅓ c. boiled diced lobster tail

Comibne lemon gelatin, garlic salt, salt and pepper. Dissolve in hot water. Add cold water, vinegar and parsley. Chill until slightly thickened; fold in celery, crab and lobster. Pour into oiled 2-quart mold; chill until almost firm.

LIME LAYER:

>   1 pkg. lime gelatin
>   1 ½ tsp. garlic salt
>   Dash of pepper
>   1 c. hot pepper
>   ¾ c. sour cream
>   ¼ c. mayonnaise
>   1 tbsp. wine vinegar
>   1 2-oz. can anchovies, finely chopped

Combine lime gelatin, garlic salt and pepper. Dissolve in hot water. Add sour cream, mayonnaise, vinegar and anchovies. Whip until well blended. Spoon mixture over lemon gelatin. Chill until firm. Garnish with watercress, if desired. Yield: 6-8 servings.

Mrs. Nancy Arnold, Toledo, Ohio

Gum Drop Salad

>   1 c. syrup drained from pineapple
>   30 marshmallows, cut in pieces
>   1 No. 2 can pineapple, drained
>   ½ lb. grapes, cut in pieces
>   1 pt. whipped cream
>   ½ lb. small gum drops, cut in pieces

Heat pineapple syrup and marshmallows until melted. Cool. Add pineapple and grapes; chill. Fold in whipped cream and gum drops. Refrigerate for 24 hours. Yield: 8 servings.

Mrs. Ruth Thompson, Home Economics Teacher, El Paso, Tex.

Layered Pineapple Salad

    1 pkg. lime gelatin
    2 c. hot water
    ¾ c. canned pineapple juice
    1 c. crushed pineapple, drained
    1 pkg. lemon gelatin
    ¾ c. cold water
    ½ c. whipped cream
    1 3-oz. pkg. cream cheese

Dissolve lime gelatin in 1 cup hot water. Add pineapple juice and pineapple. Chill until firm. Dissolve lemon gelatin in remaining cup of hot water; add cold water and chill until slightly thickened. Place the bowl of lemon gelatin in a larger bowl of ice and water. Be sure it rests firmly. Whip gelatin until fluffy and thick. Gradually add whipped cream to cream cheese; whip until thick and smooth. Fold cheese mixture into the whipped gelatin mixture; pour over the firm lime-pineapple layer. Chill until firm. Yield: 9 servings.

Ruth Skidmore, Gassaway, W. Va., Favorite Recipes Food Fair

Million Dollar Salad

    2 egg yolks
    2 tbsp. flour
    1 c. top milk
    Juice of 2 lemons
    1 pt. whipping cream
    1 lb. marshmallows, cut up
    1 lge. can sliced pineapple, drained
    1 lge. can white cherries, drained

Mix egg yolks and flour; add milk. Stir in lemon juice very slowly. Cook until consistency of boiled custard. Whip cream; stir dressing into cream. Add marshmallows, drained pineapple and drained cherries. Let stand for 24 hours.

Lurleen B. Wallace, Governor of Alabama, Montgomery

Orange Sherbet Salad

    2 3-oz. pkgs. orange or pineapple gelatin
    2 cans Mandarin oranges, drained
    1 lge. can pineapple chunks, drained
    1 pt. orange sherbet
    2 c. mixed orange and pineapple juice, heated
    ½ tbsp. unflavored gelatin

(Continued on next page)

Dissolve unflavored gelatin in small amount of cold water. Dissolve orange gelatin in hot juice. Add unflavored gelatin; cool. Add sherbet. Pour over mixed fruit in mold. Chill. Yield: 10 servings.

Mrs. Dera Dossey, Nacogdoches, Tex.

 ## Pineapple-Coconut Fluff

1 pkg. orange gelatin
1 ⅓ c. hot water
1 4-oz. pkg. cream cheese, softened
1 flat can crushed pineapple
¾ c. coconut, flaked

Dissolve gelatin in hot water. Add cream cheese. Whip until blended and bubbly. Stir in pineapple and coconut. Mold and chill until firm. Yield: 4-6 servings.

Mrs. Jessie Gilliland, Home Economics Teacher, Muleshoe, Tex.

 ## Pineapple Parfait

1 20-oz. can pineapple chunks
1 3-oz. pkg. lemon gelatin
1 c. evaporated milk
2 tbsp. lemon juice
1 c. chopped celery
½ c. chopped nuts
⅓ c. mayonnaise

Drain pineapple; reserve syrup. Heat 1 cup pineapple syrup to boiling; pour over gelatin. Stir to dissolve. Chill until thickened. Chill milk in freezer until crystals form; whip until stiff. Add lemon juice; whip very stiff. Add remaining ingredients to gelatin; fold into whipped milk mixture with pineapple chunks. Place in tall glasses; chill until firm. Yield: 6 servings.

Mrs. Robert Sieck, Officers' Wives' Club, Baltimore, Md.

 ## Pineapple-Ice Cream Delight

1 pkg. lime or other flavored gelatin
1 c. boiling water
1 pt. vanilla ice cream
1 c. crushed pineapple
½ to 1 c. nuts, finely cut (opt.)

(Continued on next page)

Dissolve gelatin in boiling water; add ice cream and stir until melted. Mix in pineapple and nuts if desired. Chill until firm. Do not freeze. Yield: 8 servings.

Pearl Oliver, Cadillac, Mich.

 ### Pineapple Surprise

> 6 eggs, beaten
> 3 tbsp. cold water
> 3 tbsp. vinegar
> 1 tbsp. sugar
> 1 tsp. salt
> 1 tsp. mustard
> 1 pt. heavy cream, whipped
> 2 lge. cans crushed pineapple, drained
> 1 lb. marshmallows

Combine eggs with water, vinegar, sugar, salt and mustard in double boiler. Cook until thick, stirring constantly. Cool slightly. Fold in whipped cream, pineapple and marshmallows. Chill for several hours or overnight. Yield: 14 servings.

Mrs. Jack Harrison, Dothan, Ala.

 ### Pineapple-Wine Supreme

> 1 No. 2 can pineapple chunks, drained
> 1 ¼ c. juice plus water
> 2 tbsp. gelatin
> ½ c. cold water
> ½ c. sugar
> ¼ c. lemon juice
> ¾ c. pecans, broken
> 1 ¼ c. sherry wine

Soften gelatin in cold water. Heat syrup to boiling point; add softened gelatin. Stir until dissolved. Add pineapple chunks, sugar, lemon juice, nuts and sherry. Arrange some of pineapple and nuts in bottom of mold. Pour enough gelatin over them to hold in place. Chill until firm. Pour in remaining mixture. Chill. Yield: 6-8 servings.

Mrs. Joni Vermette, Sarasota, Fla.

Pretty Party Salad

12 grape leaves
1 8-oz. pkg. cream cheese
2 tbsp. mayonnaise
Halved white seedless grapes

Arrange 3 grape leaves on each salad plate. Place 1 pear half on leaves. Soften cream cheese; add mayonnaise. Cover pear half with frosting. Press grape halves into frosting to resemble bunch of grapes. Yield: 4 servings.

Mrs. R. R. Miller, Charleston, S. C.

Quick Christmas Cranberry Candles

1 3-oz. pkg. raspberry gelatin
1 No. 101 can whole cranberry sauce
Salad dressing or whipped cream
Lettuce leaves

Prepare gelatin according to package directions. Chill until mixture is consistency of egg whites. Add cranberry sauce; blend well. Pour in small frozen juice cans or small paper cups. Let set several hours or overnight. Unmold on lettuce leaves and garnish with salad dressing or whipped cream. Yield: 4 servings.

Mrs. Martha F. Jenkins, Home Economics Teacher, Hildebran, N. C.

Red Apple Salad

6 med. tart apples
¾ c. red cinnamon candies
2 c. water
1 3-oz. pkg. cream cheese
2 tbsp. cream
1 tsp. lemon juice
⅓ c. chopped dates
1 c. chopped pineapple, drained
2 tbsp. pecans
6 lettuce cups

Pare and core apples. Cook candies in water until dissolved. Add apples; cook slowly, uncovered, for 15 to 20 minutes or until just tender. Turn once during cooking. Chill in syrup for several hours, turning once. Blend cheese, cream and lemon juice; add dates, pineapple and nuts. Drain apples; place on lettuce cups. Stuff center with cream cheese mixture. Yield: 6 servings.

Mrs. Harold Leifeste, Officers' Wives' Club, Brindisi, Italy

Rainbow Salad

1 pkg. lime gelatin
1 pkg. lemon gelatin
1 pkg. cherry gelatin
4 ½ c. hot water
1 small can crushed pineapple
1 pkg. cream cheese
1 c. whipping cream
½ c. cold water

Dissolve lime gelatin in 1 cup hot water; add cold water. Cool. When slightly thickened, fold in pineapple. Chill. Dissolve lemon gelatin in 1½ cups hot water. Cool until slightly thickened. Whip cream and cheese. Add to the cool lemon gelatin. Pour mixture over firm lime gelatin. Let set. Dissolve cherry gelatin in remaining 2 cups of hot water. When it begins to set, pour over firm lemon layer. Chill until firm. Yield: 9 servings.

Mrs. Martha Waltner, Freeman, S. D.

Rosy Fruit Cocktail Slices

2 3-oz. pkg. cream cheese, softened
1 c. mayonnaise
1 c. heavy cream, whipped
1 No. 2½ can fruit cocktail, drained
½ c. Maraschino cherries, drained and quartered
2 ½ c. chopped or miniature marshmallows
Few drops of red food coloring or cherry juice

Blend cream cheese with mayonnaise; fold in remaining ingredients. Pour into two 1-quart round ice cream or freezer containers. Freeze until firm. Remove from freezer; let stand for a few minutes. Remove from container; slice. May be served on salad greens and garnished with cherries. Yield: 10-12 servings.

Alice Cunningham, Hart, Mich., Favorite Recipes Food Fair

Ribbon Salad

1 to 2 3-oz. pkgs. lime gelatin
5 c. hot water
4 c. cold water
1 3-oz. pkg. lemon gelatin
½ c. or more miniature marshmallows
1 c. pineapple juice
1 8-oz. pkg. cream cheese
1 1-lb. 4-oz. can crushed pineapple, drained
1 c. whipped cream

(Continued on next page)

A profusion of seafood, dewy vegetables and a delectable sauce are the ingredients for this hearty main dish salad that's easy to prepare and a delight to behold. For an adventure in good eating, try this unusual salad.

FISHERMAN'S FEAST

2 10-oz. pkg. frozen California Brussels sprouts
1½ lb. shrimp, cooked, shelled and deveined
1½ c. cooked lobster pieces
1 c. small whole white onions, cooked
2 c. cooked, sliced potatoes
1 c. cherry tomatoes or tomato wedges

Cook Brussels sprouts according to package directions; drain. Combine sprouts with all remaining ingredients in large, shallow bowl.

GREEN SAUCE:

¾ c. olive or salad oil
⅓ c. wine vinegar
⅓ c. finely chopped parsley
1 clove garlic, crushed
2 tbsp. anchovy paste
1 tbsp. sugar
1 tsp. salt
¼ tsp. black or cracked pepper

Combine all sauce ingredients. Pour over Brussels sprout mixture. Chill for 2 hours, stirring occasionally.

See photograph on reverse page.

1 c. mayonnaise (opt.)
1 to 2 3-oz. pkgs. cherry, raspberry or strawberry gelatin
½ c. pecans, chopped (opt.)

Dissolve lime gelatin in 2 cups hot water; add 2 cups cold water. Chill until partially set. Dissolve lemon gelatin in 1 cup hot water in top of double boiler. Add marshmallows; stir to melt. Remove from heat. Add pineapple juice and cream cheese; beat until well blended. Stir in pineapple. Cool slightly. Fold in whipped cream, mayonnaise and nuts if desired. Chill until thickened but not completely set. Pour over lime gelatin. Chill until almost set. Dissolve cherry gelatin in 2 cups hot water; add 2 cups cold water. Chill until syrupy. Pour over pineapple layer. Chill until firm. Yield: 24 servings.

Mrs. Winifred Robinson, Home Economics Teacher, Homedale, Idaho

Salad Of The Angels

1 pkg. miniature marshmallows
1 lge. can crushed pineapple, drained
12 Maraschino cherries, chopped
1 3-oz. pkg. cream cheese
2 tbsp. sugar
2 tbsp. mayonnaise
½ pt. whipped cream
½ c. pecans, chopped (opt.)

Combine marshmallows and pineapple. Mix cherries, cream cheese, sugar and mayonnaise together. Add to pineapple mixture. Whip cream and fold in pineapple mixture. Add pecans if desired. Chill. Yield: 8 servings.

Mrs. Maury Watkins, Home Economics Teacher, New Edinburg, Ark.

Salad Divine

1 No. 2 can pineapple
1 egg, well beaten
¼ tsp. salt
1 tbsp. flour
½ lb. marshmallows, quartered
1 lb. grapes, cut and seeded
¼ lb. blanched almonds, chopped
½ pt. heavy cream, whipped

Drain pineapple, reserving juice. Heat pineapple juice with egg, salt and flour in double boiler until thickened; pour over marshmallows. Cool. Add chopped pineapple, grapes and almonds; blend well. Fold in whipped cream. Chill for 12 to 24 hours before serving. Yield: 8 servings.

Mrs. Dale Faler, Officers' Wives' Club, Los Alamitos, Cal.

St. Nick Salad

1 pkg. raspberry gelatin
1 c. hot water
½ c. cold water
1 sm. orange, peeled and cut into chunks
1 lge. can jellied or whole cranberry sauce
¼ c. chopped walnuts

Dissolve gelatin in hot water; add cold water. Chill until partially thickened. Fold in orange, cranberry sauce and nuts. Pour into mold; chill until firm. Yield: 8 servings.

Mrs. Tom Searcy, Baton Rouge, La.

 ### St. Patrick's Day Salad

1 pkg. lime gelatin
1 c. red sweet cherries, pitted
1 c. white sweet cherries, pitted
Lettuce
Salad dressing
1 to 2 c. cottage cheese

Prepare gelatin according to package directions. Arrange cherries in mold; pour part of gelatin over cherries. Chill until firm. Add remaining gelatin. Chill until firm. Unmold onto bed of lettuce. Serve with salad dressing and cottage cheese. Yield: 8 servings.

Mrs. John R. Turner, Officers' Wives' Club, Bayonne, N. J.

Strawberry Cream Squares

2 pkgs. strawberry gelatin
2 c. boiling water
2 10-oz. pkgs. frozen strawberries
1 c. sour cream or ½ c. sour cream and ½ c. cream cheese
1 ½ to 2 c. crushed pineapple
2 to 3 lge. firm ripe bananas, finely diced (opt.)
1 c. nuts, coarsely chopped (opt.)

Dissolve gelatin in boiling water. Add berries, stirring occasionally until thawed. Add pineapple, bananas and nuts if desired. Pour half of mixture into 8 x 8 x 2-inch pan; chill until firm. Spoon an even layer of sour cream over firm gelatin. Stir and gently pour remaining gelatin over sour cream; chill until firm. If desired, nuts may be combined with sour cream instead of with fruit and gelatin. Yield: 9 servings.

Elaine L. Smith, Home Economics Teacher, Union City, Ind.

Strawberry Glace

  2 pkgs. strawberry gelatin
  1 8-oz. pkg. cream cheese, softened
  ½ c. nuts, finely chopped
  1 pt. whole strawberries, lightly sugared or 1 lge. pkg. frozen
    strawberries
  2 c. boiling water
  2 c. cold water

Dissolve gelatin in hot water; add cold water. Chill until slightly thickened. Shape cream cheese balls; roll in nuts. Alternate cheese balls and strawberries in 9-inch ring mold. Cover with a layer of gelatin. Continue making layers. Chill until firm. Fill center with pineapple sherbet. Yield: 6-8 servings.

Frances Hallett, Southington, Conn.

Stuffed Apple

  6 apples, pared and cored
  ½ c. red cinnamon candies
  ¼ c. sugar
  2 c. water
  2 tbsp. pecans, broken
  10 dates, pitted and chopped
  ½ c. crushed pineapple, drained
  ¼ c. mayonnaise
  Grated cheese (opt.)

Dissolve candies and sugar in water over low heat. Add whole apples and cook slowly until transparent but not soft. Chill. Combine remaining ingredients; stuff apples. Serve on lettuce. Garnish with a small amount of grated cheese if desired. Yield: 6 servings.

Mrs. Freddie E. Taylor, Dierks, Ark.

Stuffed Pear Salad

  1 ¾ c. pear or raspberry and pear juice
  1 pkg. raspberry gelatin
  6 pear halves
  1 c. fresh or frozen red raspberries, partially thawed
  Lettuce
  ⅓ c. mayonnaise
  Cream

Heat juice; add gelatin. Stir until gelatin is completely dissolved. Pour 1/3-inch layer into a glass baking dish that has been rinsed with cold water. Chill until

(Continued on next page)

gelatin layer is firm. Place pears, with hollow side up on gelatin; fill hollows with raspberries. Carefully pour remaining gelatin over berries. Chill until firm. Cut in squares with stuffed pears in the center. Serve on lettuce with mayonnaise and whipped cream. Yield: 6 servings.

Mrs. Helen L. Ware, Home Economics Teacher, Salem, N. J.

 ## Summer Luncheon Cooler

> 1 lge. cantaloupe, peeled and sliced in 10 crosswise slices
> Head lettuce leaves, rinsed and chilled
> Bibb lettuce, rinsed and chilled
> 5 nectarines or peaches, unpeeled
> 2 bananas, slivered and soaked in lemon juice
> 5 red or blue plums, unpeeled
> 10 small bunches white, blue or red grapes
> 30 fresh pineapple spears
> Watermelon balls
> Honeydew melon wedges
> Pineapple sherbet
> Orange sherbet
> Lime sherbet

Place a cantaloupe slice on alternated Bibb and head lettuce leaves for color. Prop the cantaloupe slice on end with a piece of lettuce heart. Surround front and sides with ½ nectarine or peach, a sliver of banana, ½ plum, one bunch grapes, 3 pineapples spears, watermelon balls and honeydew melon wedges. Top with a scoop of each flavor of sherbet. Add a sprig of fresh mint in center of each sherbet for color and delightful aroma. Serve with cheese straws or grilled cheese sandwiches. Yield: 10 servings.

Mary L. Adams, Danville, Ky., Favorite Recipes Food Fair

Thanksgiving Cranberry Salad

> 1 orange
> 1 qt. cranberries
> 2 pkg. lemon gelatin
> 2 c. hot water
> 2 c. sugar
> ½ c. chopped nuts

Peel orange, reserving peel; section and chop pulp. Grind cranberries and orange rind in food chopper. Dissolve gelatin in hot water; add sugar. Stir until dissolved. Chill gelatin mixture until thickened. Add cranberries, orange rind, nuts and orange. Place in 9 x 11-inch pan; chill until firm.

Mrs. Robert Blickenstaff, Officers' Wives' Club, Athens, Greece

Tiered Salad Deluxe

½ pt. heavy cream
1 c. cottage cheese
1 pkg. lemon gelatin
2 pkg. cherry gelatin
1 c. pineapple chunks
1 c. pecans, chopped
1 can Royal Anne cherries, drained

Whip cream; add cottage cheese. Dissolve lemon gelatin in 1½ cups hot water; cool. Combine cooled lemon gelatin with cream and cottage cheese; turn into 7 x 12 x 2-inch glass dish. Chill until firm. Dissolve cherry gelatin in 2 cups hot water. Drain pineapple; reserve juice. Add juice to gelatin; chill until thickened. Fold in pineapple, nuts and cherries. Turn mixture over firm lemon-cottage cheese mixture. Chill until firm. Cut into squares; serve. Yield: 12-14 servings.

Mrs. Susan Lee, Chattanooga, Tenn.

 ### Valentine Salad

¼ c. red-hot cinnamon candies
1 c. boiling water
1 pkg. lemon gelatin
1 c. unsweetened applesauce
1 3-oz. pkg. cream cheese
2 tbsp. cream
2 tbsp. mayonnaise

Dissolve red-hot candies in boiling water. Pour over lemon gelatin. Dissolve; allow to cool. Add applesauce. Put half of mixture in heart-shaped mold. Chill until set. Combine cheese, cream and mayonnaise. Spread on set gelatin mixture. Pour remaining gelatin on top of cheese. Chill until firm. Yield: 6 servings.

Mrs. Helen M. Godwin, Home Economics Teacher, Greensboro, N. C.

Vanilla Dream

1 3-oz. pkg. lime gelatin
1 c. hot water
1 pt. vanilla ice cream
1 med. can fruit cocktail, drained

Dissolve gelatin in hot water; add vanilla ice cream, stirring until ice cream melts. Add fruit cocktail. Pour into molds. Place in refrigerator until firm. May be garnished with whipped topping and cherry.

Mrs. Virginia Rutledge, Officers' Wives' Club, Rainstein AFB, Germany

Vermillion Cream Delight

1 8-oz. pkg. hot red cinnamon candies
2 ½ c. water
2 pkgs. cherry gelatin
1 No. 303 can applesauce
1 6-oz. pkg. cream cheese, softened
1 c. nuts, chopped

Boil candies in water until dissolved. Remove from heat; add cherry gelatin. Cool. Add applesauce. Refrigerate until firm. Thin cream cheese with cream until spreading consistency is reached. Spread over firm gelatin mixture. Top with nuts. Refrigerate until serving time. Yield: 12 servings.

Mrs. Jack H. Topping, Home Economics Teacher, Vinita, Okla.

Waffles A La Fruit Salad

1 to 2 apples
1 to 2 oranges
1 to 2 bananas
1 medium can pineapple chunks
6 to 8 Maraschino cherries
4 to 5 marshmallows, cut up
Waffles
½ pt. whipped cream
3 tbsp. powdered sugar
1 tsp. vanilla

Combine fruits and marshmallows. Mix whipped cream, sugar and vanilla; add to fruit mixture. Top waffles with salad. Yield: 4-6 servings.

Mrs. Carol Arnold, Home Economics Teacher, Cascade, Idaho

Whipped Cream Swirl

1 No. 2½ can fruit cocktail
1 6½-oz. can crushed pineapple
1 c. miniature marshmallows
3 oz. cream cheese
½ pt. heavy cream
Sugar
½ c. chopped nuts

Drain fruits in colander, reserving juice. Add marshmallows to fruits. Chill for 3 hours. Whip cream cheese; add about 1/3 cup of mixed fruit juices. Fold into fruit mixture. Whip cream; add a small amount of sugar. Fold into fruits; add nuts. Chill overnight. Yield: 8 servings.

Mrs. George P. Antonio, Officers' Wives' Club, Hawthorne, Nev.

Foreign Salads

Fruit Salad (Antigua)

½ c. water
1 c. sugar
2 tbsp. lime juice
2 oranges, peeled and diced
2 mangoes, peeled and diced
2 bananas, diced
1 ripe papaya, diced
Crushed ice

Combine water, sugar and lime juice. Combine fruits, mixing lightly; pour sugar syrup over fruits. Serve in fruit cups with crushed ice.

Mrs. Harold L. Beaver, Officers' Wives' Club, Antigua, West Indies

 ### Spinach Salad (Armenia)

1 pkg. fresh spinach
Olive oil
Lemon juice
2 eggs, beaten
1 tbsp. sugar
1 tsp. salt
½ tsp. paprika
½ tsp. dry mustard
1 tsp. Worcestershire sauce
Garlic salt to taste
½ c. catsup
1 pt. salad oil
½ c. vinegar
⅔ c. warm water

Cut spinach into strips; sprinkle with olive oil and lemon juice. Chill. Combine eggs, sugar, salt, paprika, dry mustard, Worcestershire sauce, garlic salt and catsup. Mix for 10 seconds in blender or rotary beater; gradually add salad oil alternately with vinegar. Blend or beat until thickened; gradually add warm water. Place spinach in salad bowl; pour dressing over salad. Toss lightly. Garnish with tomato wedges, asparagus spears and hard-cooked egg slices, if-desired.

Mrs. William W. Gray, Ft. Carson, Colo., Favorite Recipes Food Fair

 ### Assyrian Salad

1 c. Assyrian wheat or wheat germ
1 head lettuce, broken in bite-size pieces
1 lb. tomatoes, finely diced

(Continued on next page)

1 small bunch parsley, finely diced
1 onion, finely diced
1 cucumber, finely diced
Juice of 2 lemons
3 tbsp. olive oil
Salt to taste
Sugar (opt.)
Carrots (opt.)
Celery (opt.)

Cover wheat with warm water; let stand for 30 minutes. Combine vegetables; add soaked wheat. Combine remaining ingredients; pour over salad. Serve immediately. Yield: 6 servings.

Mrs. Alma L. Graven, Home Economics Teacher, Blackwell, Okla.

 ## Hapsburg Cucumbers (Austria)

3 med. cucumbers
1 lge. mild onion, very thinly sliced
Salt
½ c. salad oil
½ c. vinegar
1 c. sour cream
⅛ tsp. pepper
1 tsp. chopped parsley
¼ tsp. paprika

Peel cucumbers; score with a fork. Cut into paper-thin slices. Layer cucumbers and onion in bowl, sprinkling each layer heavily with salt. Cover with ice water; chill for several hours. Drain; wash quickly in running water. Drain again. Cover with oil and vinegar; marinate for several hours. Drain; add sour cream and pepper. Garnish with parsley and paprika. Yield: 6-8 servings.

Mrs. Harold V. Ellingson, San Antonio, Tex.

 ## Palmito Salad (Brazil)

1 lge. can palmito
3 tbsp. olive oil
6 tbsp. lemon juice or vinegar
1 tsp. salt
½ tsp. pepper
Minced garlic (opt.)
2 med. tomatoes, sliced
1 med. onion, sliced

(Continued on next page)

Drain palmito; slice into ½ to 1-inch slices. Combine oil, lemon juice, salt, pepper and garlic in jar; shake vigorously. Combine with sliced palmito, tomatoes and onion. Cover and chill for at least 1 hour. Drain and serve on lettuce. Yield: 4 servings.

Mrs. John R. Moore, Key West, Fla.

 ### Crisp Wun Tun (China)

½ lb. lean pork, chicken or shrimp
8 water chestnuts, finely chopped
2 green onions, finely chopped
2 tsp. soy sauce
3 slices fresh ginger root
1 tsp. salt
Dash of pepper
½ tsp. monosodium glutamate
36 Wun Tun Pee wrappers

Finely chop meat or put through food chopper. Mix with remaining ingredients except Wun Tun Pee wrappers. Place a wrapper with a point toward you. Put a teaspoonful of filling on lower half of wrapper; fold top half over, making a triangle. Moisten edges and press together; do not leave a pocket of air inside. Now cross the right and left points by bringing them together on the opposite side of the fold from the point toward you. Moisten and press together. Fry in hot deep oil at 375 degrees until brown. Serve as an appetizer. Yield: 36 servings.

Mrs. Nuiko Jordon, Officers' Wives' Club, Jusmag, Philippines

 ### Salata Bedingan—Eggplant Salad (Egypt)

1 eggplant, peeled and cut in ½-inch slices
Butter
2 tomatoes, sliced

Fry eggplant in butter until soft. Drain on absorbent paper. Alternate rows of eggplant and tomatoes on a platter. Serve with oil and vinegar dressing seasoned to taste. Yield: 4 servings.

Ruth Metaweh, Home Economics Teacher, Villard, Minn.

Dawson's Pepper Salad (England)

> 2 c. green peppers, cut into julienne strips
> 1 ¼ c. chopped celery
> 1 c. sliced pimento
> ½ c. sliced onion
> 6 tbsp. olive oil
> 3 tbsp. wine vinegar
> Juice of 1 lge. clove of garlic
> Pinch monosodium glutamate
> 1 tbsp. dark prepared mustard
> 1 tsp. Worcestershire sauce
> Salt to taste

Combine green pepper, celery, pimento and onion in salad bowl. Combine remaining ingredients. Pour over salad; marinate for 1 hour before serving. Yield: 4 servings.

Mrs. Spiro S. Babalis, Officers' Wives' Club, Mobile, Ala.

 Beet Salad (Finland)

> 1 c. cooked beets, diced
> 2 c. cooked potatoes, diced
> ¾ c. cooked carrots, diced
> 2 tbsp. onion, diced
> ¾ c. herring or anchovies
> ¼ c. vinegar
> Salt to taste
> Lettuce
> Hard-cooked egg slices

Combine all ingredients except lettuce and egg slices. Chill for 2 to 4 hours. Serve in lettuce cups; garnish with egg slices. Yield: 6 servings.

Mrs. Eric Thomson, Kalamazoo, Mich.

 Asparagus And Shrimp Salad (France)

> 1 lb. asparagus
> ¾ lb. fresh shrimp
> Mayonnaise
> Lemon juice
> 6 cooked artichoke hearts
> French dressing
> 1 hard-cooked egg
> Parsley

(Continued on next page)

Cook asparagus; reserve 6 of the best stalks. Cut remaining asparagus into 1-inch pieces. Cook and clean shrimp; reserve 6. Dice remainder. Combine cut asparagus and diced shrimp gently with thin mayonnaise and lemon juice; chill. Marinate artichoke hearts in French dressing. Place salad in bowl; sprinkle with sieved egg. Arrange reserved asparagus on top to resemble spokes of wheel. Drain artichoke hearts; garnish each with mayonnaise, 1 whole shrimp and sprig of parsley. Place around salad; serve immediately. Yield: 6 servings.

Mrs. Vance Dunkelberger, Pres. Officers' Wives' Club, Canal Zone

 ## Salade Nicoise (France)

> 5 tomatoes, quartered
> ½ onion, finely sliced
> 1 green pepper, sliced
> 1 handful radishes
> 4 stalks celery, chopped
> 8 anchovy fillets
> 2 hard-cooked eggs, quartered
> 10 black olives
> 1 clove of garlic, crushed
> 1 family-sized can chunk tuna

Chill all ingredients well. Place in large salad bowl in order listed.

DRESSING:

> 2 tbsp. wine vinegar
> 6 tbsp. oil
> Pinch of fresh basil

Combine all ingredients in jar; shake well. Pour over salad; mix gently.

Mrs. Coleman Smith, Naval Officers' Wives' Club, London, England

Salade D' Endives (France)

> 4 heads endive
> 2 apples
> ½ c. walnuts, broken
> 4 tbsp. French dressing

Wash and drain endive; thoroughly dry it. Break into small pieces. Peel apples: slice into thin pieces. Place in salad bowl with endive and walnuts. Pour French dressing over salad and toss. Yield: 4 servings.

Mrs. Robert L. Burnett, Vandenberg AFB, Cal., Favorite Recipes Food Fair

Bouillabaisse Salad (France)

1 c. cooked crab meat
1 c. cooked lobster
½ lb. cooked cleaned shrimp
1 c. cooked whitefish
2 tomatoes, sliced
¾ c. cooked small green peas
Mixed salad greens
8 ripe olives, cut into halves
Classic French dressing
1 tsp. chopped capers

Arrange crab, lobster, shrimp, whitefish, tomatoes and green peas on bed of mixed greens; garnish with olives. Toss with French dressing and capers; serve very cold.

Mrs. Sam Rorex, Jr., New York, N. Y.

 ### Potato Salad (Germany)

6 med. potatoes
1 tbsp. oil
3 tbsp. wine vinegar
2 tbsp. lemon juice
3 tbsp. chopped onion
2 slices bacon, cooked and crumbled
4 tbsp. hot stock
Salt and pepper to taste

Boil potatoes in their skins; peel while warm. Slice into a large bowl. Blend oil, wine vinegar, lemon juice, onion, bacon, hot stock, salt and pepper in a pan. Bring to the boil; pour over potatoes immediately. Mixed dried or fresh herbs, diced cucumber or anchovies may be added. Yield: 6 servings.

Mrs. Robert C. Furrer, Officers' Wives' Club, Mannheim, Germany

Fleisch Salat—Meatsalad (Germany)

½ lb. boiled veal
½ lb. apples
2 hard-cooked eggs
1 or 2 dill pickles
1 tsp. capers
2 egg yolks
2 tsp. mustard
2 tsp. sugar
¼ tsp. salt
2 tbsp. vinegar or lemon juice
1 c. salad oil
2 tbsp. (heaping) cornstarch
1 tsp. chopped parsley

Cut meat, apples, eggs and pickles into small strips; place in a dish with capers. Place egg yolks, mustard, sugar, salt and vinegar or lemon juice in a mixing bowl; beat until creamy. Add 1 to 2 tablespoons oil at a time; beat well. Blend 1 cup water with cornstarch; bring to a boil, stirring constantly. Add immediately to mayonnaise; beat well. Pour mayonnaise and parsley over salad; toss lightly. Yield: 6 servings.

Mrs. Robert Tolar, Arlington, Va.

 ### Red Cabbage Slaw (Germany)

6 strips bacon, diced
1 2-lb. head red cabbage, shredded
1 apple, diced
4 tbsp. water
4 tbsp. sugar
2 tsp. salt
Pepper to taste
6 to 8 tbsp. vinegar or red wine

Brown bacon in a heavy saucepan. Add cabbage, apple and water. Cover tightly; steam slowly about 1 hour. Stir often to prevent burning. Add sugar, salt, pepper and vinegar; stir. Serve warm. Will keep in refrigerator for several days. Yield: 8 servings.

Margaret S. Yoder, Home Economics Teacher, East Greenville, Pa.

Heart Of Palm Salad (Greece)

3 heads Bibb or romaine lettuce, torn into bite-sized pieces
3 lge. avocados, diced
3 14-oz. cans hearts of palm, sliced ¼-in. thick
¼ c. vinegar

(Continued on next page)

¾ c. olive oil
1 tsp. salt
1 tsp. cayenne pepper

Place lettuce in large salad bowl. Add avocados and hearts of palm. Combine remaining ingredients in small jar; shake well. Pour over salad. Yield: 15 servings.

Mrs. Andy A. Lippcomb, Fort Polk, La., Favorite Recipes Food Fair

 ### Chicken Salad (Hawaii)

2 ½ c. chopped cooked chicken
1 14-oz. can pineapple, drained
1 c. celery, chopped into ½-in. pieces
3 tbsp. salad oil
2 tbsp. lemon juice
¼ tsp. salt
5 tbsp. mayonnaise
¼ c. shredded almonds

Combine chicken, pineapple and celery. Blend oil, lemon juice and salt; pour over chicken mixture. Marinate salad for 1 hour. Add mayonnaise; mix well. Serve on crisp lettuce; sprinkle with almonds. Yield: 6 servings.

Mrs. Larry G. Jones, Officers' Wives' Club, American Embassy, Israel

Erwten Sla—Dutch Pea Salad (Holland)

4 c. diced pared potatoes
2 10-oz. pkg. frozen peas
1 lb. frankfurters, cut into ¼-in. slices
1 sm. onion, diced
1 tbsp. butter or margarine
2 tbsp. brown sugar
2 tbsp. cider vinegar
2 tbsp. water
1 tsp. salt
¼ tsp. pepper
Lettuce

Cook potatoes in boiling salted water just until tender; drain. Place in large bowl. Cook peas following label directions; drain. Add to potatoes. Saute frankfurter slices and onion in butter, stirring frequently just until heated through. Stir in brown sugar, vinegar, water, salt and pepper; heat slowly, stirring constantly, to boiling. Pour over potato mixture; toss lightly to mix. Spoon into lettuce-lined deep bowl; may be garnished with a few onion rings. Serve warm. Yield: 6 servings.

Mrs. E. C. Oldfield, Norfolk, Va.

Peaches With Curried Chicken Salad (India)

1 1-lb. 13-oz. can cling peach halves
¼ c. mayonnaise
¼ c. sour cream
½ tsp. curry powder
½ c. drained finely chopped chutney
2 ½ c. diced cooked chicken
1 c. chopped celery
½ c. toasted coconut chips or flakes
Salt to taste
Crisp salad greens

Chill peaches thoroughly. Blend mayonnaise, sour cream, curry powder and chutney; add chicken, celery and coconut. Toss lightly; add salt to taste. Drain peaches thoroughly; arrange cup-side up on salad greens. Top each peach half with a mound of chicken salad. Yield: 6 servings.

Mrs. William Kingery, Officers' Wives' Club, Robins AFB, Ga.

Tomato Sambal (India)

6 ripe tomatoes, sliced
4 green onions, chopped
2 green chilies, peeled and chopped
¼ c. salad oil
2 tbsp. lemon juice
½ tsp. salt
Grated coconut

Arrange tomato slices on serving platter. Combine remaining ingredients except coconut; pour over tomato slices. Sprinkle with grated coconut. This goes well with curried dishes. Yield: 12 servings.

Mrs. Connie McCall, Albany, N. Y.

Gado-Gado (Indonesia)

1 lb. bean sprouts
½ lb. cabbage, chopped
½ lb. green beans, chopped
1 tsp. salt
2 tsp. brown sugar
1 tsp. lemon juice
1 tsp. soy sauce
1 onion, sliced and fried
1 or 2 cloves of garlic, chopped and fried

(Continued on next page)

½ tsp. ground red pepper
¼ to ½ lb. peanut butter
1 cucumber, sliced
1 bunch radishes, sliced
2 hard-cooked eggs, sliced

Parboil bean sprouts, cabbage and green beans in small amount of water for a few minutes; drain and reserve stock. Blend salt, brown sugar, lemon juice, soy sauce, onion, garlic, red pepper and peanut butter into hot stock. Arrange layers of cabbage, beans, bean sprouts, cucumber and radishes in salad bowl; garnish with eggs. Serve with peanut butter dressing. Yield: 8 servings.

Mrs. Mort B. Brigadier, Officers' Wives' Club, Canal Zone, Rep. of Panama

 ## Ensalada Italiana (Italy)

3 med. ripe tomatoes
3 green peppers
2 cloves of garlic, crushed
Salt and pepper to taste
¼ tsp. oregano
¼ tsp. dried basil
⅓ c. salad oil
2 tbsp. vinegar

Place tomatoes and green peppers directly on burner of stove; set for low heat. Turn often; the skins will blacken and blister and the peppers should become quite soft. Remove skins; core and remove seed from peppers. Core tomatoes. Cut peppers into long strips; cut tomatoes into eighths. Place tomatoes and green peppers in flat container; sprinkle with garlic, salt, pepper, oregano and basil. Pour oil and vinegar over tomatoes and peppers. Lift lightly with fork to coat. Let stand in refrigerator for 1 hour. Yield: 6 servings.

Mrs. W. J. Carrington, Offutt AFB, Neb.

 ## Finocchio Salad (Italy)

Large finocchio (fennel)
Oil and vinegar dressing

Cut finocchio into 1-inch pieces, using only the bulbous white part as the stalks are hollow and tough. Toss with favorite oil and vinegar dressing. Yield: 4 servings.

Mrs. Richard A. Billings, Officers' Wives' Club, Sigonella, Sicily

Almond-Sesame-Lettuce Salad (Japan)

DRESSING:

>   4 tbsp. sugar
>   3 tsp. salt
>   2 tsp. monosodium glutamate
>   1 tsp. pepper
>   ½ c. salad oil
>   6 tbsp. white vinegar

Combine all ingredients.

SALAD:

>   3 boiled chicken breasts
>   ⅓ pkg. saifun, cut into 3-in. pieces or ½ c. fried noodles
>   1 head crisp lettuce, diced
>   4 green onions, cut into thin strips
>   3 oz. sliced almonds, roasted
>   4 tbsp. sesame seed, roasted

Shred chicken into thin pieces; fry a small amount at a time in hot oil until crisp. Drop pieces of saifun into hot oil; cook until white and crisp. Toss dressing with lettuce, onions and chicken; top with roasted almonds, sesame seed and saifun. Yield: 8 servings.

Mrs. John L. Martin, Los Angeles, Cal.

Eggplant With Yogurt Salad (Jordan)

>   1 eggplant, peeled and cubed
>   1 clove garlic
>   Salt and pepper to taste
>   1 box yogurt
>   3 tbsp. olive oil

Boil eggplant until tender; drain and mash. Mash garlic with salt and pepper; mix with yogurt. Pour yogurt mixture over eggplant; mix. Sprinkle olive oil over salad just before serving.

Mrs. Creasia Stone, Home Economics Teacher, Red Rock, Okla.

Bean Sprout Salad (Korea)

>   2 green onions, finely chopped
>   1 clove garlic, crushed
>   2 tsp. prepared sesame seed
>   1 sm. red sweet pepper or 1 canned pimento, chopped
>   2 tbsp. soy sauce
>   2 c. canned bean sprouts, drained

(Continued on next page)

1 tbsp. vinegar
2 tbsp. corn oil
½ tsp. salt
¼ tsp. pepper
1 hard-cooked egg, thinly sliced

Combine onions, garlic, sesame seed, sweet pepper and soy sauce; pour over bean sprouts. Combine vinegar, oil, salt and pepper; add to bean sprout mixture and toss lightly. Chill. Garnish with egg slices. Yield: 6 servings.

Mrs. Avis E. Colgrove, Home Economics Teacher, Fort Lupton, Colo.

Tabbuli (Lebanon)

½ lb. bulghour wheat (cracked wheat)
4 fresh tomatoes, cubed, or canned tomatoes
Minced garlic (opt.)
1 sm. bunch scallions, coarsely chopped
6 parsley sprigs, finely chopped
4 mint leaves, fresh or diced
3 tbsp. olive oil
¼ c. lemon juice
½ tsp. salt
Lettuce leaves

Soak cracked wheat for 15 minutes; drain thoroughly. Combine tomatoes, garlic, scallions, parsley, mint, olive oil, lemon juice and salt. Toss lightly. Add cracked wheat; toss lightly. Arrange on lettuce leaves on individual salad plates. Sprinkle additional olive oil over each portion. Yield: 8 servings.

Mrs. Annie R. Gonzales, Home Economics Teacher, Baton Rouge, La.

Ensalada De Frijole—Bean Salad (Mexico)

2 c. cooked pinto beans
½ c. celery, diced
3 green hot chili peppers, fresh or canned
2 med. cucumber pickles, chopped
½ sm. onion, chopped
Salt and pepper to taste
2 tbsp. prepared mustard
6 tbsp. cream or evaporated milk
Lettuce
Red chili powder

Combine all ingredients except mustard, cream, lettuce and chili powder; mix thoroughly. Beat mustard and cream; add to bean mixture. Serve on lettuce; sprinkle with red chili powder. Yield: 6-8 servings.

Lelia Cook Greenwald, Home Economics Teacher, Socorro, N. M.

Stuffed Green Chilies (Mexico)

2 ripe avocados, peeled and mashed
1 tbsp. lemon or lime juice
¼ tsp. salt
¼ tsp. pepper
¼ tsp. chili powder
1 tbsp. grated onion
2 6-oz. cans peeled and roasted green chilies, drained
Lettuce
Tomato wedges
Sour cream
Paprika

Combine avocados, juice, salt, pepper, chili powder and onion. Mix well. Stuff each chili with avocado mixture. Serve 1 or 2 stuffed chilies on shredded lettuce with tomato wedges; garnish with sour cream. Sprinkle cream with paprika. Yield: 6-8 servings.

Mrs. Robert J. McBrinn, El Paso, Tex., Favorite Recipes Food Fair

 ### Hummer Smat—Lobster Salad (Norway)

½ tsp. salt
¼ tsp. pepper
¼ tsp. dry mustard
¼ c. white wine
2 egg yolks
4 tbsp. tomato puree
1 c. olive oil
1 head lettuce
1 ½ c. cooked or canned lobster
1 ½ c. cooked codfish
½ c. macaroni, cooked
Toast
Caviar

Combine salt, pepper and mustard in bowl; add wine. Mix well; add egg yolks and tomato puree. Do not beat. Add 1/3 of the oil; beat with rotary beater until mixture begins to thicken. Add ½ remaining oil; beat for 1 minute. Set aside. Wash lettuce; separate leaves. Drain and chill until crisp. At serving time, line salad bowl with lettuce; pile lobster, cod and macaroni in center. Pour dressing over all; mix lightly with fork. Garnish bowl with small rounds of toast covered with Caviar. Yield: 6 servings.

Mrs. Wm. Peterson, Officers' Wives' Club, Phalsbourg AFB, France

Panamanian Salad (Panama)

Grapefruit halves
Avocado, peeled and diced
Orange sections, diced
Grapefruit sections, diced
Canton ginger, finely chopped
Green pepper, minced
Mayonnaise
Cognac

Scoop meat from grapefruit halves. Scallop the edges. Pile diced fruits into grapefruit cups. Sprinkle with ginger and green pepper. Serve with mayonnaise flavored with minced ginger and cognac. Chill before serving. Garnish with watercress.

Mrs. Blanche Gavin Sims, Home Economics Teacher, Waynesboro, Miss.

 ## Pineapple-Tuna Salad (Philippines)

2 12½-oz. cans chunk-style tuna
1 c. chopped sweet mixed pickles
½ c. lime juice
½ c. sour cream
2 med. fresh pineapples

Combine tuna, pickles, lime juice and sour cream. Cut pineapples into halves lengthwise; remove fruit, leaving ½-inch shells. Reserve shells. Dice pineapple; combine with tuna mixture. Chill. Fill pineapple shells with tuna salad; serve with additional sour cream, if desired. Yield: 4 servings.

Mrs. S. P. Himic, Officers' Wives' Club, Jusmag, Philippines

 ## Beet Salad (Poland)

4 medium beets, cooked and thinly sliced
¼ c. walnuts, ground
Juice of ½ lemon
½ tsp. salt
1 tbsp. sugar
1 tbsp. parsley, minced
1 green onion, chopped

Combine all ingredients. Toss lightly with a fork.

Alice Zanolini, Home Economics Teacher, Shinglehouse, Pa.

Baked Pepper Salad (Puerto Rico)

    10 green peppers
    ¼ c. vinegar
    1 tsp. salt
    ½ c. olive oil
    ¼ tsp. pepper

Bake peppers until tender; place in cold water. Remove skin and seed; cut into strips. Mix vinegar, salt, oil and pepper. Arrange peppers in bowl; pour dressing over peppers. Let stand for 2 hours. Yield: 8-10 servings.

Mrs. Richard Africano, Officers' Wives' Club, Mt. Laguna Air Sta., Cal.

 Summer Salad A La Russe (Russia)

    2 c. pickled beets
    2 or 3 cucumbers
    1 pt. sour cream
    2 tbsp. chopped chives
    Salt and pepper
    2 tbsp. snipped fresh dill

Drain beets; dry thoroughly on paper toweling. Cut into strips. Peel and slice cucumbers. Combine sour cream, chives, salt and pepper to taste; pour over beets and cucumbers, tossing lightly. Chill thoroughly. Toss again just before serving. Sprinkle generously with dill. Yield: 6-8 servings.

Mrs. Philip Russell, Ft. Worth, Tex., Favorite Recipes Food Fair

 Ensalada Rusa (Spain)

    6 med. potatoes
    1 lge. bass
    ½ lb. shrimp, cooked
    1 1-lb. can green peas
    1 8½-oz. can pitted black olives
    Mayonnaise
    1 sm. can pimento

Cook potatoes until tender; peel and cut into cubes. Boil fish until tender; remove meat from bones. Cook shrimp until done. Combine potatoes, fish, shrimp, peas and half the olives. Toss well; garnish with mayonnaise, pimento and remaining olives. Yield: 12 servings.

Elena Brannon, Ames, Iowa

Combination De Aceitunas Y Cake Pones— Olive-Shrimp Mold (Spain)

4 envelopes unflavored gelatin
1 1-qt. 14-oz. can tomato juice
¼ tsp. Tabasco
½ tsp. chili powder
½ tsp. paprika
½ c. lemon juice
1 8-oz. pkg. cream cheese, softened
⅓ c. mayonnaise
1 ½ lb. shrimp, cooked, shelled, deveined and finely chopped
1 c. finely chopped pimento-stuffed olives
1 c. finely chopped celery
Sliced pimento-stuffed olives

Sprinkle gelatin over 2 cups tomato juice. Add remaining tomato juice, Tabasco, chili powder and paprika; mix well. Cook over boiling water, stirring constantly, until gelatin dissolves. Add lemon juice; cool. Beat cream cheese and mayonnaise together until smooth. Gradually add tomato mixture, blending well. Chill until slightly thickened. Fold shrimp, 1 cup chopped olives and celery into tomato mixture. Turn into 2½-quart mold. Chill until set. Unmold. Garnish with sliced pimento-stuffed olives. Yield: 6-8 servings.

Photograph for this recipe on page 295.

Herring Salad (Sweden)

2 lge. salt herring
2 c. canned beets, cubed
2 c. cold boiled potatoes, diced
½ c. onions, finely chopped
1 c. tart apples, peeled, cored and cubed
½ c. dill pickles, diced
½ c. English walnuts, chopped
1 c. mayonnaise
1 tsp. prepared mustard
Salt to taste
½ tsp. ground black pepper
5 tbsp. vinegar
½ tsp. sugar
½ c. sour cream
Red food coloring

Soak herring in cold water for at least 5 hours; change water every hour. Skin fillets; cut into small pieces. Combine herring, beets, potatoes, onions, apples, pickles and walnuts. Toss thoroughly. Combine remaining ingredients; add to herring mixture and toss. Let stand overnight. When ready to serve, add a

(Continued on next page)

mixture of additional mayonnaise and sour cream to moisten if necessary. Salad will keep for 3 or 4 days if refrigerated. Yield: 6 servings.

Mrs. Inez K. Waechter, Home Economics Teacher, Anna, Ill.

 ### Fruit Salad (Syria)

> 2 pt. yogurt
> ½ lb. miniature marshmallows
> 1 sm. can Mandarin oranges
> 1 No. 2 can pineapple chunks
> 3 tart apples, unpeeled
> 4 firm ripe bananas
> 2 c. seedless grapes
> 1 c. pine nuts
> ¾ c. shredded coconut

Combine yogurt and marshmallows; refrigerate overnight. Next day, drain oranges and pineapple; reserve pineapple juice. Cut apples and bananas into bite-sized pieces; dip into pineapple juice to prevent discoloring. Combine oranges, pineapple, apples and bananas with grapes, pine nuts and coconut. Add yogurt mixture; toss lightly. Turn into four trays; place in refrigerator freezing section for 2 to 3 hours before serving to chill firmly; do not freeze solid. Cut into squares; serve on crisp greens. Yield: 10-12 servings.

Mrs. Donald F. Brandt, Officers' Wives' Club, Essex, England

 ### Yalandgi Dolmas—Stuffed Grape Leaves (Turkey)

> 1 c. rice
> 3 medium onions, chopped
> 1 tsp. mint leaves, chopped
> ½ tsp. salt
> ¼ tsp. pepper
> 3 tbsp. olive oil
> 3 doz. grape, cabbage or lettuce leaves
> Juice of 1 lemon

Cook rice, onions, mint, salt, pepper and olive oil in frying pan for 15 minutes. Stir often. Wash leaves and remove midrib sections. Cover leaves with boiling water; cook until slightly tender. Drain. Put 1 teaspoonful of rice mixture on each leaf. Roll leaf tightly, tucking in the ends. Place in layers in large pan; cover with water. Add lemon juice; cover pan. Simmer until water is absorbed. If rice is not sufficiently cooked, add a little boiling water and continue cooking until it is tender. Yield: 18 servings.

Theresa M. Lunden, Home Economics Teacher, Puyallup, Wash.

Appetizers

Hors d'oeuvres are intended to excite the taste buds, but never, never to satisfy the appetite. You must approach your hors d'oeuvre or appetizer as though you were "setting the stage" for things to come.

The essential difference between the appetizer that accompanies a cocktail and the one that is served as a first course is a matter of convenience. The guest who must balance a glass in one hand appreciates the convenience of appetizers he can hold in the other hand and dispose of in one or two bites.

Appetizers provide a very simple way to balance and vary a menu, to say nothing of giving the hostess a chance to be artistic and decorative. Follow the rule of opposites when planning your hors d'oeuvres. Bland or substantial main courses require crisp and tart appetizers. Vegetable or salad hors d'oeuvres complement a meal rich in protein or carbohydrates.

Appetizers may be hot or cold—take your choice. You only have to be sure that those to be served cold are indeed crisp and cold, not lukewarm and wilted. Hot appetizers should be piping hot.

Canapés Or Hors D'oeuvres

In American food talk the terms hors d'oeuvre, appetizer and canapé are often used interchangeably. It is true that both hors d'oeuvres and canapés are appetizers; however, there is a difference.

Canapés—Morsels of food with a base of bread, pastry or crackers. Finger food.

Hors d'oeuvre—Can be served hot or cold but is always eaten at the table, with a knife and fork.

Appetizer—Any finger food that does not have a base, and is eaten before the meal.

Cold fish and shellfish piquantly spiced are admittedly the most effective of all spurs to appetite and thirst.

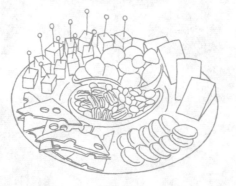

Hot Cranberry Punch Cocktail

¾ c. brown sugar
1 c. water
¼ tsp. salt
½ tsp. cinnamon
½ tsp. allspice
¾ tsp. cloves
2 1-lb. cans cranberry jelly, crushed with fork
3 c. water
1 qt. pineapple juice
3 c. strong tea

Boil first 6 ingredients together for 1 minute. Add next 3 ingredients to hot syrup. Stir until jelly dissolves. Add tea. Punch is better if prepared day before serving and reheated. Use a cinnamon stick in each glass for stirring.

Ruth Bergee, Home Economics Teacher, Circle Pines, Minn.

 ## Hot Cranberry Tea

1 lb. cranberries
3 qt. water
Juice of 3 lemons
Juice of 3 oranges
2 ½ c. sugar
1 c. red hots
8 to 10 whole cloves

Cook cranberries in 1 quart water until tender; strain and press. Add 2 quarts water and remaining ingredients. Heat and serve hot. Yield: 15-20 servings.

Alice Hogwood, Center, Colo.

Spizarinctum

2 eggs
½ c. sugar
⅛ tsp. salt
Juice of 1 lemon
Juice of 3 oranges
2 c. cranberry juice

Beat eggs, sugar and salt until thick and lemon colored. Add juices and blend. Pour over cracked ice. Yield: 6 glasses.

Mrs. Shirley M. Seavey, Groveland, Mass., Favorite Recipes Food Fair

Mock Pink Champagne

½ c. sugar
1 ½ c. water
2 c. cranberry juice
1 c. pineapple juice
½ c. orange juice
2 7-oz. bottles lemon-lime carbonated beverage

Boil sugar and water until sugar dissolves; cool. Stir in cranberry, pineapple, and orange juice. Chill. Just before serving add carbonated beverage. Yield: 14 servings.

Mrs. Deanna House, Home Economics Teacher, Monroe, Wis.

 ## Pineapple-Lemon Foam Cocktail

1 No. 2 can pineapple juice
⅔ c. fresh, canned frozen lemon juice
⅓ c. sugar
½ c. water
2 egg whites
1 c. finely crushed ice

Combine all ingredients in jar or shaker. Stir well. Cover; shake until frothy. Pour into cocktail glasses. Yield: 6 servings.

Mrs. John M. Abbott, Pres. Officers' Wives' Club, Winnemucca, Nev.

 ## Slush

2 bananas, mashed
Juice and pulp of 2 oranges
Juice and pulp of 2 lemons
1 sm. can crushed pineapple
1 tsp. grated lemon and orange rind
1 c. sugar
1 pt. ginger ale

Mix all ingredients, adding ginger ale last; stir well. Freeze to slush stage. Keeps well; may be used as appetizer or in place of beverage. Yield: 15 servings.

Mrs. Ruth Paulsen, Winside, Neb.

Tomato Cocktail With Zing

1 peck ripe tomatoes, chopped
1 red pepper, chopped
1 green pepper, chopped
1 bunch celery, chopped
6 lge. onions, chopped
6 whole cloves
2 tbsp. salt
1 c. sugar
½ c. vinegar

Combine all ingredients; boil for 1 hour. Strain; reheat juice to boiling. Seal in sterilized jars.

Mrs. S. F. Frook, Sault Ste. Marie, Mich.

Vivian's Tomato Cocktail

4 c. tomato juice
1 c. water
½ c. sugar
1 c. celery, finely cut
1 tbsp. salt
Pepper to taste
2 tbsp. lemon juice
2 tbsp. Worcestershire sauce

Cook all ingredients except lemon juice and Worcestershire sauce until celery is soft enough to strain through a colander. Add Worcestershire sauce and lemon juice. Cook two minutes longer.

Mrs. Vivian Petz, Home Economics Teacher, Northumberland, Pa.

A Zippy Tomato Drink

2 c. tomato juice
1 tsp. lemon juice
½ tsp. salt
¼ tsp. pepper
1 lge. cucumber, peeled, seeded and grated
Few drops of Tabasco sauce
¾ c. cracked ice

Place all ingredients in blender; blend for 10 to 15 seconds. Serve in frosted glasses. Garnish with paper-thin lemon slices. Yield: 3-4 servings.

Mrs. John R. Erickson, Woods Hole, Mass.

Cheese Boxes

> 1 loaf white bread, unsliced
> ¼ lb. grated American cheese
> ¼ lb. butter, softened
> 1 egg white, unbeaten
> Paprika to taste
> Dry mustard to taste
> Cayenne to taste

Cut fresh white bread into 1-inch squares. Mix cheese, butter and egg white into well-blended paste. Season to taste. Spread on sides of bread squares with cheese paste. Bake at 350 degrees for 15 to 20 minutes. Serve with tea or cocktails.

Mrs. Robert A. Reade, Officers' Wives' Club, Mannheim, Germany

 ### Cheese Rounds

> ½ lb. cream cheese
> 1 tbsp. onion juice or onion salt
> ½ tsp. baking powder
> 1 egg yolk
> Salt to taste
> 24 small bread rounds
> 1 2½-oz. jar deviled ham

Blend cheese, onion juice, baking powder, egg yolk and salt. Toast bread rounds on one side. Spread deviled ham on untoasted side of bread. Cover ham with cheese mix. Place on cookie sheet; bake at 350 degrees for 10 to 15 minutes. Bread rounds are made by cutting thinly sliced bread with small biscuit cutter.

Mrs. Carl R. Willey, Victorville, Cal.

 ### Cheezy 'N' Easy

> 10 slices bread
> ¼ c. chopped onion
> ½ c. grated Parmesan cheese
> 1 ½ c. mayonnaise
> Pinch of cayenne pepper (opt.)

Cut five rounds from each slice of bread, using a 1½-inch cookie cutter. Toast both sides of rounds at 350 degrees. Mix onion, cheese, mayonnaise and pepper; spread mixture generously on toast rounds. Sprinkle top with a small amount of Parmesan cheese; broil for 2 minutes. Yield: 10 servings.

Mrs. W. R. Boehm, Pres. Officers' Wives' Club, San Diego, Cal.

Curry Canapes

> 1 ½ c. shredded Cheddar cheese
> 1 c. chopped ripe olives
> ½ c. chopped onion
> ½ c. mayonnaise
> 1 tsp. curry

Combine all ingredients; refrigerate in covered jar. Serve on buttered rounds; broil until bubbly.

Mrs. Theodore Banick, Glendale, Ariz.

 Nachos

> Fried tortilla chips or king-sized corn chips
> Salt
> Cheddar cheese
> Jalapeno peppers

Cut tortillas into pie-shaped wedges; fry until crisp. Salt lightly. Cut cheese slices to fit tortilla chips. Place 1 thin slice of jalapeno pepper on top of cheese. Bake at 400 degrees until cheese melts slightly. Serve at once.

Jenny Steadham, Valdosta, Ga.

Surprise Cheese Puffs

> 1 lb. sharp cheddar cheese, shredded
> ½ lb. butter, softened
> 1 tsp. Worcestershire sauce
> 1 tsp. fresh onion juice
> ½ tsp. hot sauce
> 1 lge. loaf unsliced sandwich bread

Allow cheese to remain at warm room temperature for at least 1 hour. Blend in softened butter thoroughly; do not melt butter or cheese. Add Worcestershire sauce, onion juice, and hot sauce. Remove all crusts from bread loaf; cut lengthwise, into 1-inch slices. Spread top and sides with cheese mixture; cut into 1-inch strips. Spread sides of strips with cheese; cut into 1-inch cubes. Cover sides of cubes, leaving bottom uncovered. Place carefully on cookie sheet so puffs do not touch; stack with wax paper between layers. Place in freezer until puffs are frozen; store in plastic bags until needed. Remove from freezer at serving time; place immediately in preheated 375-degree oven. Bake for 10 to 12 minutes or until corners are golden. Serve at once. Yield: 80-100 pieces.

Mrs. Ralph L. Hunnicutt, Boston, Mass.

Toasted Cheese Sandwich

> 1 lb. strong store cheese, grated
> 1 recipe thin white sauce
> Paprika
> Toast

Blend cheese into white sauce; cook until cheese melts and sauce is smooth. Sprinkle with paprika; serve on toast.

Mrs. Franklin D. Roosevelt

 ### Chutney And Peanut Butter Canapes

> 1 pkg. cream cheese
> ½ lb. crunchy peanut butter
> 4 oz. chutney, cut into small pieces
> ¼ tsp. Worcestershire sauce
> ¼ tsp. seasoned salt
> Dry red wine

Combine cream cheese, peanut butter, chutney, Worcestershire sauce and salt; moisten with enough dry red wine to spread easily. Spread on crackers or thin party rye bread. May be stored in covered jar in refrigerator for weeks.

Mrs. H. H. Caldwell, Hon. Pres. Officers' Wives' Club, Jacksonville, Fla.

Bacon Bits

> 20 slices bread
> 2 tbsp. melted butter
> 1 c. grated sharp cheese
> 2 egg whites
> ⅔ c. chopped green pepper
> 1 tsp. chopped parsley
> ½ tsp. salt
> Dash of pepper
> 3 slices bacon, finely chopped

With 2-inch cookie cutter, cut 20 bread rounds. Toast on one side under broiler. Brush untoasted sides with melted butter. Fold cheese into stiffly beaten egg whites; add green pepper, parsley, salt and pepper. Spoon mixture on buttered side of bread rounds. Sprinkle tops with finely chopped bacon. Broil 4 or 5 inches from heat for 10 minutes or until bacon browns and cheese melts. Yield: 20 servings.

June L. Schwar, Home Economics Teacher, Millersville, Pa.

Cocktail Pizza

1 jar chili sauce
8 oz. grated strong cheese
½ lb. uncooked bacon, finely chopped
1 onion, finely chopped
English muffins, quartered

Combine sauce, cheese, bacon and onion; spread on English muffin sections. Bake at 350 degrees for 30 minutes. Yield: 8 servings.

Mrs. Walter H. Cooper, Officers' Wives' Club, Mannheim, Germany

Dried Beef Spread

1 8-oz. pkg. cream cheese
1 jar chipped dried beef
1 tsp. horseradish
1 tsp. prepared mustard
1 tbsp. salad dressing

Cream the cheese. Shred the dried beef by hand. Combine all ingredients with cheese; mix thoroughly. Serve as an appetizer on crackers or potato chips or use as sandwich filling. Yield: 8-10 servings.

Gertrude E. Swartz, Home Economics Teacher, Auburn Heights, Mich.

 Hospitality Liver Spread

1 lb. liver sausage, mashed
¼ c. mayonnaise
2 tbsp. dill pickle juice
1 tsp. Worcestershire sauce
3 drops Tabasco sauce
¼ tsp. garlic salt
⅓ c. finely chopped dill pickle
¼ c. finely chopped onion
1 8-oz. pkg. cream cheese, softened
½ c. finely chopped salted peanuts

Combine all ingredients except half of cream cheese and nuts; mix well. Pack firmly in 2-cup mixing bowl lined with foil; chill for several hours or until firm. Remove from bowl; frost with remaining cream cheese. Refrigerate until ready to serve. Cover with peanuts. Yield: 10-20 servings.

Dora McDonald, Wellington, Kan., Favorite Recipes Food Fair

Hot Ham Bouches

2 tbsp. butter
1 med. tomato, peeled and finely sliced
2 tbsp. finely chopped green onion and tops
½ c. finely chopped ham
2 eggs, slightly beaten
30 sm. bread rounds
Parmesan cheese

Melt butter in large frying pan; saute tomato for 5 minutes. Mix in onion, ham and eggs; cook over low heat until thick. Cool. Heap mixture on bread rounds; sprinkle with Parmesan cheese. Broil before servings.

Mrs. John Schneider, Officers' Wives' Club, Kenai, Alaska

 ### Hot Ham And Cheese Rolls

½ lb. sliced boiled ham, chopped
½ lb. sharp Cheddar cheese, cut in ¼-in. cubes
⅓ c. sliced onion
2 hard-cooked eggs, sliced
½ c. sliced pimento-stuffed olives
3 tbsp. mayonnaise
½ c. chili sauce
12 hot dog buns, split

Toss all ingredients except buns with mixture of mayonnaise and chili sauce, mixing well. Spread in buns; wrap in foil, twisting ends securely. Bake at 400 degrees for 12 minutes. Yield: 12 servings.

Arline Dolge, Milwaukee, Wis.

 ### Liver Paste

1 round roll soft liverwurst
2 hard-cooked eggs
1 tsp. dried parsley
1 tsp. onion, chopped
¼ c. celery, finely chopped
2 tbsp. mayonnaise

Blend liverwurst and eggs together. Add remaining ingredients; blend well. Use as a spread on assorted crackers for appetizers. Yield: 50-75 servings.

Phyllis P. Nash, Home Economics Teacher, Berwyn, Pa.

Mexican Tostadas Tapatias

30 tortillas
½ lb. spicy sausage
1 lb. frijole beans, mashed
⅓ c. sharp cheese, grated
2 onions, chopped
6 tomatoes, cut in pieces
3 avocados, cut in pieces
Canned green chili peppers in vinegar or jalapenos

Fry tortillas in oil until crisp. Brown sausage. Add mashed beans; simmer, spread sausage-bean mixture on crisp tortillas. Spread cheese, onions, tomatoes, avocados and more cheese over the beans. Top with green pepper slivers. Yield: 30 servings.

Phyllis Christmann, Home Economics Teacher, Carrington, N. D.

 ## Anchovy Spread A La Carty

1 small pkg. cream cheese
1 can flat anchovies, cut
½ medium Bermuda onion
½ c. sour cream
Dash of Worcestershire sauce

Mix all ingredients thoroughly with a fork. Serve as a spread for crackers. If a thinner consistency is desired for use as a dip, add more sour cream. Yield: 20-25 servings.

Mrs. George D. Carty, Tamassee, S. C.

 ## Tangy Anchovy Canapes

10 anchovies
6 tbsp. chopped pecans
1 tbsp. chopped parsley
½ clove of garlic, minced
1 tbsp. anchovy oil
1 tsp. lemon juice
Toast rounds

Mash all ingredients except toast rounds. Spread on toast rounds.

Mrs. David L. McDonald, Washington, D. C.

 ### Clam Canapes

1 sm. pkg. cream cheese
1 can minced clams, drained
Salt to taste
Dash of red pepper
¾ tsp. Worcestershire sauce
1 tsp. minced green onion
Paprika

Whip cheese with a fork. Add clams; mix well. Add remaining ingredients and whip well. Cover; refrigerate. To serve, heap generously on crackers; bake at 300 degrees for 20 minutes. Sprinkle with paprika, if desired. Yield: 18 servings.

Mrs. Hugh A. Richeson, Hon. Pres. Officers' Wives' Club, Pirmasens, Germany

Crab Salad In Puff Shells

1 c. crab meat, flaked
¼ c. mayonnaise or salad dressing
½ c. finely chopped celery
1 tbsp. sweet pickle relish
1 tsp. grated onion
1 c. chopped hard-cooked eggs
Salt and pepper to taste
36 1-in. puff shells

Combine all ingredients except shells; chill. Remove tops from shells; fill with crab mixture. Replace tops and serve.

Helen Schott, Kodiak, Alaska

Crab Toastlets

Sliced bread
1 7½-oz. can Alaskan crab, drained and finely sliced
⅓ c. mayonnaise
2 tbsp. chopped green olives
1 tbsp. minced onion
1 tsp. prepared mustard
¼ tsp. salt
½ c. grated cheddar cheese
1 tbsp. lemon juice
Few drops hot pepper sauce

Cut bread into 2-inch rounds with cookie cutter. Toast on one side under broiler. Combine crab with remaining ingredients. Mound on untoasted side of bread rounds. Place on cookie sheet. Broil 5 inches from heat until hot and bubbly. Serve hot. Yield: 30 servings.

Mrs. John B. Des Portes, Hon. Pres. Officers' Wives' Club, Beale AFB, Cal.

 Toasted Parmesan Crab Canapes

3 tbsp. Parmesan cheese
1 c. mayonnaise
1 can crab meat
30 thin slices small white onions
30 small rounds of bread

Mix Parmesan cheese with mayonnaise and crab meat. Place a slice of onion on each round of bread; top with cheese mixture. Place on cookie sheet; sprinkle with additional grated Parmesan cheese. Refrigerate. Broil until tops are bubbly and brown. Yield: 12 servings.

Mrs. Lowell Fisher, Cheyenne, Wyo.

 Lobster In Biscuits

1 can prepared biscuits
¼ lb. butter, softened
Lemon juice
1 tbsp. parsley
10 to 12 pieces cooked or canned lobster

Roll out biscuits until they are flat. Mix butter, lemon juice and parsley. Put 2 bite-sized pieces of lobster and pat of prepared butter on each biscuit. Fold over edges, pressing firmly together. Bake according to directions on prepared biscuits. Yield: 6 servings.

Mrs. C. B. Brinkley, Officers' Wives' Club, Captieux, France

Lobster Rounds

Sandwich bread
1 can lobster meat
White sauce
1 egg yolk, beaten
Salt and pepper
Dry sherry
Grated cheese

Cut bread into small circles, 1½ inches in diameter. Shred lobster; mix with enough white sauce to hold meat together. Add beaten egg yolk; season with salt, pepper and sherry. Pile mixture on bread rounds; sprinkle with grated cheese. Broil until cheese is browned.

Mrs. Samuel B. Thornton, Pres. Officers' Wives' Club, Ansbach, Germany

Bajan Mystery Sandwiches

2 hard-cooked eggs
¼ lb. sharp cheddar cheese
½ sm. onion
½ sweet pepper
⅛ tsp. salt
1 tin of sardines or anchovies
Vegetable oil

Put all ingredients through food mincer, using finest cutter. Mix thoroughly. If needed, add oil until of spreading consistency. Allow to stand for several hours to blend flavors. Spread on crackers or small toast rounds for snacks. Yield: 12 servings.

Mrs. William S. Fortenberry, Officers' Wives' Club, Antiqua, T.W.I. Island

Curried Shrimp Spread

Juice of 1 lemon
2 lb. cooked shrimp, diced
½ grated onion
2 tsp. curry powder
¾ c. mayonnaise

Squeeze lemon juice over shrimp. Add onion and curry powder to mayonnaise. Let stand overnight in refrigerator. To serve, place in bowl; surround with cocktail crackers. Yield: 2½ cups.

Mrs. Victor N. Curtis, Camarillo, Cal., Favorite Recipes Food Fair

Ebi Toastu-Shrimp Toast

1 ½ lbs. raw shrimp
½ c. finely chopped onion
1 5-oz. can water chestnuts, finely chopped
½ tsp. salt
Dash of pepper
1 tbsp. sherry
2 egg whites
1 tbsp. cornstarch
Bread, cut into 1 to 1½-in. squares

Put shrimp, onion and water chestnuts through meat grinder, using coarse chop blade. Add remaining ingredients except bread; mix well. Spread on bread squares; fry in deep oil until golden brown. Serve hot with small bowls of shoyu and hot mustard for dipping, if desired. Yield: 8 servings.

Dorothy Price, Demopolis, Ala.

Shrimp Hors D' Oeuvres

1 lb. med. shrimp
1 sm. bay leaf
1 tsp. salt
½ tsp. peppercorns
1 tsp. vinegar
3 thin slices of lemon
¼ tsp. cayenne
Sliced bread
Green pepper

Boil shrimp in seasonings for 12 to 15 minutes. Peel; chill for several hours. Cut rounds 2½-inches in diameter from white bread slices. Spread with mayonnaise. Sliver green pepper to form stem and leaf. Place shrimp on bread round to give flower effect.

Mrs. Charles H. Bradley, Commanding Officers' Wife, Fallon AFS, Nev.

 ## Artichoke Appetizer

6 toast rounds
Anchovy butter
6 sm. artichoke hearts
Capers
Whipped cream cheese

Spread toast rounds with anchovy butter; top with artichokes. Decorate edge of toast rounds with capers and cream cheese. Yield: 6 servings.

Mrs. Daniel Smith, Hon. Pres. Officers' Wives' Club, Patuxeut River, Md.

Eggplant Spread

> 1 med. eggplant
> 3 tbsp. minced onion
> 2 tbsp. salad or oilve oil
> 4 tbsp. lemon juice
> 1 ½ tsp. salt
> ¼ tsp. pepper
> 1 tsp. sugar

Bake eggplant at 475 degrees until skin turns dark brown. Cool and peel. Chop eggplant until very smooth; stir in onion, oil, lemon juice, salt, pepper and sugar. Chill; serve with dark bread and tomato wedges. Yield: 4-6 servings.

Mrs. B. G. Leigh, Lexington, Ky.

 ### Hot Onion Canapes

> Slices of bread
> Mayonnaise
> Grated onion
> Grated Romano cheese

Cut bread into small rounds. Spread each with a thin layer of mayonnaise. Place ¼ teaspoon of onion in each round; cover with more mayonnaise. Top with Romano cheese. Place on cookie sheet. Broil at 450 degrees until brown. Serve immediately.

Mrs. William Gentner, Officers' Wives' Club, Taipei, Taiwan

Appetizer Cheese Mousse

> 2 tsp. unflavored gelatin
> ¼ c. cold water
> 2 c. sour cream
> 2 tsp. Italian salad dressing mix
> ¼ c. crumbled bleu cheese
> 1 c. small curd cottage cheese

Soften gelatin in cold water. Place over boiling water and stir until gelatin dissolves. Stir into sour cream. Add salad dressing mix, bleu cheese and cottage cheese. Beat with electric or rotary beater until well blended. Pour into 3½-cup ring mold or small loaf pan. Chill until firm. Unmold. Garnish with parsley and carrot curls. Arrange crisp crackers around mold.

Mrs. Frederick B. Becker, Pres. Officers' Wives' Club,
Philadelphia Naval Hospital, Pa.

Bleu Cheese Ball

½ clove garlic
1 lb. cream cheese
¼ lb. bleu cheese
1 tbsp. Worcestershire sauce
1 dash Tabasco sauce
Brazil nuts, sliced

Blend cheeses and sauces in bowl which has been rubbed with garlic. Form mixture into a ball and roll in sliced nuts. Serve with crackers or chips. Yield: 6 servings.

Mrs. Clarice J. Hubbard, Home Economics Teacher, Mitchell, S. D.

 ### Brandied Cheese Balls

1 lb. sharp cheddar cheese
3 tbsp. mayonnaise
2 oz. brandy or bourbon
2 dashes bitters
Salt to taste
1 or 2 dashes red pepper

Let cheese stand at room temperature for several hours; put through meat grinder. Cream cheese thoroughly with remaining ingredients. Chill thoroughly; roll into small balls. Sprinkle with paprika and top with a sprig of green, if desired. Store in refrigerator until ready to use.

Mrs. C. F. Broton, Officers Wives' Club, Panama City, Fla.

Cheese Ball

2 ½ lb. sharp cheddar cheese
2 3-oz. pkg. cream cheese
Red wine or sherry
¼ c. olives
¼ c. pimento
¼ c. nuts
Chili powder, paprika or nuts
Parsley

Grate cheddar cheese; let stand at room temperature to soften. Combine with cream cheese. Add enough red wine or sherry to blend cheeses well. Fold in olives, pimento and nuts. Mold into ball; chill. Roll in chili powder, paprika or nuts; garnish with parsley. Serve with crackers.

Mrs. Frederick E. Booth, Albuquerque, N. M.

Cream Cheese Balls

1 1-lb. pkg. ceram cheese
6 slices crisply fried bacon, crumbled
Dash of Tabasco sauce
Dash of Worcestershire sauce
Salt and pepper to taste

Combine all ingredients until well blended. Roll into marble-sized balls. These may then be rolled in chopped nuts or crushed crackers. Yield: 24 balls.

Mrs. Edward J. Milanowski, Yorktown, Va.

 ### Roquefort Rolls

2 3-oz. pkg. cream cheese
1/8 lb. Roquefort cheese
2 tbsp. celery, finely chopped
1 tbsp. onion, finely chopped
Dash of cayenne pepper
Salad dressing
1 1/2 c. California walnut meats, finely chopped

Blend cream and Roquefort cheeses. Add celery, onion, cayenne, and salad dressing. Form in tiny rolls (or balls if preferred). Roll in nut meats and chill. Yield: 16-20 rolls.

Mrs. Jo Frances Weimar, Home Economics Teacher, Alto, Tex.

 ### Swiss Cheese Balls

1/3 stick butter
2 (heaping) tbsp. flour
1/2 c. hot milk
1/2 lb. Swiss cheese, grated
Salt to taste
Pepper to taste
Nutmeg to taste
2 egg yolks

Melt butter in pan; stir in flour. Add milk, stirring vigorously. Add cheese, salt, pepper and nutmeg; mix well. Stir in egg yolks. Bake at 300 degrees for 10 minutes. Remove from oven; cool in refrigerator. Form into balls. Roll in additional flour. Fry in deep fat until brown. Yield: 30-40 balls.

Mrs. William D. Matthews, Albert Lea, Minn.

Cheese Cocktail Balls

> 8 oz. cream cheese
> 4 oz. cheddar cheese, grated
> 4 oz. bleu cheese
> 1 tbsp. grated onion
> Garlic salt

Cream all ingredients; form into ball. Sprinkle with paprika, if desired.

Mrs. C. M. Mason, Officers' Wives' Club, Panama City, Fla.

 ## Cheese-Nut Ball

> ¼ lb. bleu cheese
> 3 oz. cream cheese
> ¼ lb. cheddar cheese, softened
> 1 sm. onion, grated
> 1 tsp. Worcestershire sauce
> ¼ lb. coarsley chopped pecans

Mix all ingredients except nuts with electric mixer until well blended. Add half the pecans. Form into large ball; wrap in waxed paper. Refrigerate overnight. Remove cheese ball from refrigerator 1 hour before serving. Roll in remaining nuts. If necessary, add more nuts to completely cover ball. Serve with crackers surrounding the ball. Yield: 1½ cups.

Mrs. James W. Firoved, Key West, Fla., Favorite Recipes Food Fair

Chili-Cheese Log

> 2 c. shredded sharp-process American cheese
> 1 3-oz. pkg. cream cheese, softened
> 1 tbsp. lemon juice
> ¼ tsp. garlic powder
> Dash of red pepper
> ¼ c. finely chopped pecans
> 1 tsp. chili powder
> 1 tsp. paprika

Let shredded cheese stand at room temperature to soften. Combine cheeses, lemon juice, garlic powder and red pepper; beat with electric or rotary beater until light and fluffy. Stir in nuts; shape into a roll about 1½ inches across. Sprinkle with mixture of chili powder and paprika. Chill for several hours. Before serving, let stand at room temperature for 10 minutes. Yield: 12 servings.

Mrs. Richard A. Nash, Officers' Wives' Club, Pusan Base, Korea

Deluxe Cheese Ball

1 8-oz. pkg. cream cheese
1 4-oz. pkg. cream cheese
1 sm. jar Roquefort cheese spread
1 sm. jar bacon and cheese spread
1 sm. jar Old English cheese spread
2 cloves of garlic, crushed
Onion juice
Worcestershire sauce
Tabasco sauce
Celery salt
Cayenne pepper
Monosodium glutamate
1 c. chopped pecans
2 tbsp. minced parsley
Paprika

Blend cheeses well; add garlic, onion juice, Worcestershire sauce, Tabasco sauce, salt, pepper and monosodium glutamate. Mix in ½ cup chopped pecans and 1 tablespoon parsley. Roll into two small cheese balls. Roll each ball in a mixture of remaining pecans and parsley. Sprinkle paprika over top. Use as a spread for crackers. May be frozen; allow one day to thaw in refrigerator.

Mrs. Lloyd Jacobson, Tacoma, Wash.

Litpauer Cheese Roll

1 8-oz. pkg. cream cheese, softened
¼ c. butter or margarine
1 tbsp. drained capers
4 anchovy fillets, chopped
1 tbsp. chopped chives
½ tsp. Worcestershire sauce
1 dash Tabasco sauce
1 tsp. paprika
½ tsp. dry mustard
½ c. chopped nuts (opt.)
¼ c. chopped parsley (opt.)

Combine cream cheese and butter; beat until smooth. Add remaining ingredients except nuts and parsley; beat well. Chill mixture until firm enough to shape into roll. Roll in plastic wrap; refrigerate for 2 to 4 hours to mellow. Just before serving mix nuts and parsley; roll cheese roll in nut-parsley mixture. Do not store longer than 2 to 4 hours for the flavor of anchovies and chives becomes too pronounced for most tastes.

Mrs. William Provost, Commanding Officer's Wife. Guam. Midway Islands

Garlic Balls

    1 8-oz. pkg. cream cheese
    2 jars Old English cheese
    1 jar Roka cheese
    1 tsp. wine vinegar
    1 tsp. garlic powder
    ½ c. chopped pecans

Bring cheeses to room temperature; blend in vinegar and garlic powder. Form 1 large or 2 small balls; roll in pecans. Serve with small crackers. May be frozen. Yield: 24 servings.

Brenda Johnson, Springfield, Ill.

 ### Pecan-Cheese Roll

    11 oz. cream cheese
    ¼ c. rum
    1 4-oz. wedge Roquefort cheese
    1 lb. cheddar cheese
    2 ½ c. broken pecans

Mix cream cheese and rum until smooth. Grind or grate Roquefort and cheddar cheese. Add to cream cheese mixture. Mix thoroughly; pat into rolls 1½ inches in diameter. Roll in broken pecans. Chill overnight. Yield: Five 8-inch rolls.

Mrs. Bruce A. Mathews, Mountain Home, Idaho

 ### Cheddar Chips

    ½ c. butter
    ½ lb. sharp cheese, grated
    1 c. flour
    ¼ tsp. salt
    3 tbsp. dry onion soup mix

Combine all ingredients; shape into a roll. Wrap in foil; freeze. Let stand at room temperature for 10 minutes; slice. Bake at 375 degrees for 10 minutes. Serve hot.

Mrs. Logan Atterbury, Olathe, Kan.

Cheese Straws

2 oz. cheddar cheese, grated
2 oz. butter, softened
2 oz. flour
Pinch of cayenne pepper

Mix all ingredients. Refrigerate for several hours. Roll out to ¼ inch thickness; cut into ½-inch strips. Place on cookie sheet; bake at 350 degrees until lightly browned.

Mrs. John Hyland, Officers' Wives' Club, Yokosuka, Japan

Cheese Surprises

¼ c. soft butter or margarine
1 c. grated sharp cheese
¼ tsp. salt
¼ tsp. paprika
½ c. sifted flour
12 med. stuffed olives
12 pieces water chestnuts
12 pieces pepperoni or sausage

Cream butter and cheese until blended; add salt, paprika and flour. Mix well. Chill for 15 to 20 minutes. Shape a small portion of dough around each olive, chestnut and piece of meat. Bake at 400 degrees for 15 minutes. Yield: 36 servings.

Mrs. Richard B. Gilmore, Snyder, Tex.

Cocktail Biscuit

½ c. butter
1 c. grated sharp cheese
½ tsp. Worcestershire sauce
⅛ tsp. cayenne pepper
1 c. sifted flour
Mango chutney

Mix butter, cheese and Worcestershire sauce with electric mixer. Stir cayenne pepper into flour; work into cheese mixture. Form into a 1-inch roll; wrap in waxed paper. Refrigerate. Shortly before serving, cut into thin slices. Place on cookie sheet. Top each with a dash of chutney. Bake at 350 degrees for 15 minutes. Serve hot. Yield: 2 dozen.

Mrs. Bob Keys, Richmond, Va.

Hot Cheese Devils

2 c. firmly packed grated cheddar cheese
½ stick butter or margarine, softened
1 c. flour
Tabasco sauce
1 jar small olives

Using hands, mix cheese, butter and flour. Add 8 drops of Tabasco sauce. Roll into tiny balls. Make indentation with finger and stick small olive in each. Close hole and roll again. Place on ungreased cookie sheet allowing room for spreading. Bake at 350 degrees for 15 minutes.

Mrs. John T. Cooper, Pres. Officers' Wives Club,
Peshawar Air Station, West Pakistan

Pickle-Cheese Pineapple

2 8-oz. pkg. cream cheese, softened
½ c. grated process Swiss cheese
½ c. grated process cheddar cheese
½ c. peanut butter
½ c. sweet pickle relish
Sweet gherkins

Combine cheeses, peanut butter and pickle relish; blend. Chill thoroughly. Shape into oval. Garnish with sweet gherkin slices and strips to resemble a pineapple. Serve as a spread for rye bread.

Photograph for this recipe on page 313.

Anchovy Dip

1 clove of garlic, minced
½ tsp. salt
½ tsp. ground pepper
½ tsp. prepared mustard
⅓ c. chopped parsley
3 tbsp. onion or chives, chopped
3 tbsp. vinegar or red wine
1 c. mayonnaise
½ c. sour cream
1 can anchovies, finely cut

Mix all ingredients. Chill for at least 2 hours. Stir again; serve with raw vegetable sticks or chips.

Mrs. Stanley G. Kozlowski, Pres. Officers' Wives' Club, Taipei, Taiwan

Avocado Paste

    1 *lge. ripe avocado*
    ½ *c. mayonnaise*
    1 *tsp. grated onion*
    1 *tsp. Worcestershire sauce*
    Dash of red pepper
    2 *tbsp. chili sauce*

Blend peeled avocado, mayonnaise and onion in electric blender until smooth. Add remaining ingredients. Place in serving dish. Surround with potato or corn chips.

Mrs. H. E. Palmer, San Francisco, Cal.

 ### Green Goodness

    1 *soft, ripe avocado*
    1 *c. sour cream*
    ¼ *c. mayonnaise*
    ½ *tsp. salt*
    ½ *tsp. seasoning salt*
    ½ *c. parsley, finely chopped*
    ¼ *c. green onions, finely chopped*

Mash avocado well; add sour cream and mayonnaise. Mix well. Add salt and seasoning salt and mix well. Fold in chopped parsley and chopped green onions. Serve cold with chips or crackers. Yield: 2½ cups.

Mrs. Marie Lovil, Home Economics Teacher, McLeod, Tex.

Guacamole Cream

    2 *avocados, peeled, seeded and sliced*
    2 *tbsp. lemon juice*
    2 *tbsp. olive oil*
    1 *clove of garlic*
    1 *tbsp. chives or green onion tops*
    1 *tsp. salt*
    1 *tsp. dill weed*
    Dash of hot pepper sauce

Place all ingredients in blender. Cover and blend on high speed until smooth, stopping to stir down if necessary. Store in refrigerator, covered, until ready to serve. Yield: 1 pint.

Mrs. John A. Damm, Fallon, Nev., Favorite Recipes Food Fair

Black Bean Dip

> Oil
> 1 lge. onion, chopped
> 2 cans condensed black bean soup
> 1 ½ tsp. Tabasco sauce
> Garlic powder to taste
> 12 to 18 corn tortillas, quartered

Add oil to frying pan to cover bottom. Saute onion. Blend soup, Tabasco sauce and garlic powder thoroughly with electric mixer. Add to onion; mix well. Serve hot in chafing dish with fried quarters of corn tortillas, salted with garlic salt.

Mrs. Calvin Bass, Pres. Officers' Wives' Club, Topeka, Kan.

 ### Carrot Dip

> 3 med. carrots
> 3 medium dill pickles
> 1 small jar pimentos
> 2 green peppers
> 1 small onion
> 3 hard-cooked eggs, chopped
> Salt and pepper to taste
> Mayonnaise

Grind together carrots, pickles, pimentos, peppers and onion. Drain on paper towels or cheese cloth. Add eggs, salt, pepper and enough mayonnaise to hold mixture together.

Mrs. Jane Wisdom, Home Economics Teacher, Hillsboro, Ill.

 ### Avocado-Roquefort Dip

> 1 pt. sour cream
> 1 ripe avocado, mashed
> ¼ lb. Roquefort cheese, cubed
> 1 tsp. Worcestershire sauce

Fold sour cream into avocado. Add cheese and Worcestershire sauce. Serve with chips.

Mrs. Hazel C. Jacobsen, Home Economics Teacher, Ault, Colo.

Bleu Cheese Dip

> 1 c. mayonnaise
> ½ c. Bleu cheese
> 1 sm. clove of garlic, minced
> 2 hard-cooked eggs, chopped
> 2 tbsp. chopped pimento
> 4 sm. sweet pickles, chopped
> 1 tsp. capers
> 1 tsp. dry mustard
> ⅛ tsp. Tabasco sauce

Cream mayonnaise and cheese until smooth; add remaining ingredients. Mix well. Let stand in refrigerator for at least 4 hours before serving. Place in a small bowl; serve with raw vegetables.

Mrs. Wm. M. Summers, Ft. Sam Houston, Tex.

 Hot Stuff

> 2 cans chili without beans
> 1 lb. sharp cheddar cheese
> 1 lge. onion, finely chopped
> 2 or 3 hot chili peppers, finely chopped

Combine chili, grated cheese, onion and chili peppers; place in baking dish. Bake at 350 degrees until cheese melts and dip is hot and bubbly. Keep hot; serve with corn chips.

Mrs. Arthur Disher, Officers' Wives' Club, Philippine Islands

Shrimp Dip

> 2 4½-oz. cans shrimp
> 1 8½-oz. pkg. extra sharp Cheddar cheese, grated
> 2 sm. onions, grated
> 1 ½ c. mayonnaise
> Garlic salt to taste
> 1 ½ tsp. Worcestershire sauce

Mash shrimp with fork. Combine all ingredients. Cover; refrigerate for 2 hours. Serve as dip or spread on toast; place under broiler until cheese is melted. Yield: 6-8 servings.

Mrs. Ronald H. Ballard, Norfolk, Va.

Clam Dip

4 strips bacon, chopped
1 clove of garlic, minced
1 7-oz. can minced clams, drained
½ tsp. dried basil
¼ c. tomato sauce
¼ tsp. salt
⅛ tsp. pepper
2 tsp. parsley flakes
2 tbsp. grated Parmesan cheese

Saute bacon with garlic until crisp. Reserve 2 tablespoons bacon drippings in skillet; pour remainder of drippings and bacon into bowl. Add clams and basil to bacon in bowl. Add tomato sauce, salt and pepper to bacon drippings in skillet. Cook until thick and bubbly hot. Add clam and bacon mixture, parsley and cheese; cook until thick. Serve hot in chafing dish with corn chips. Yield: 1¼ cups.

Mrs. Ashton C. Miller, Jr., Naval Officers' Wives' Club, London, England

 ### Albuquerque Dip

1 qt. cottage cheese
¼ c. milk
1 pkg. onion soup mix

Mix all ingredients in blender or with electric mixer until cheese is smooth.

Mabel Moorhouse, Home Economics Teacher, Albuquerque, N. M.

 ### Shrimp Party Dip

½ lb. cooked shrimp, finely chopped
1 c. creamy cottage cheese
3 tbsp. chili sauce
½ tsp. onion juice
   Dash of lemon juice
¼ tsp. Worcestershire sauce
⅓ c. milk

Blend shrimp and cottage cheese. Stir in chili sauce, onion juice, lemon juice and Worcestershire sauce. Gradually beat in enough milk to give dipping consistency. Serve with potato chips, crackers, carrot strips or celery.

Mrs. William Senn, Coast Guard Officers' Wives' Club, San Juan, Puerto Rico

Caper Sauce For Cold Lobster

½ c. sm. curd cottage cheese
⅓ c. milk
½ c. mayonnaise
 Few grains of salt
⅛ tsp. paprika
⅛ tsp. dry mustard
3 tbsp. caper liquid
1 tbsp. anchovy paste
Whole capers

Blend cottage cheese in blender with milk until of whipped cream consistency. Add remaining ingredients except capers. Blend 2 minutes on high speed. Pile in bowl and chill. Garnish with whole capers. Cut lobster into bite-sized pieces and skewer each piece with toothpick; serve on chipped ice centered with sauce bowl.

Willie B. Barry, Home Economics Teacher, Laredo, Tex.

Curry Cheese

1 pt. cottage cheese
½ c. mayonnaise
½ tsp. salt
½ tsp. curry powder
1 tsp. grated onion

Combine all ingredients. Blend well; serve chilled. Yield: 2 cups.

Mrs. James D. McCracken, Officers' Wives' Club, Columbus AFB, Miss.

Crab Hot Dip

2 tbsp. minced onion
2 tbsp. margarine
2 tbsp. flour
1 c. warm milk
1 6-oz. can crab meat
¼ c. grated very sharp cheese
 Dash of Tabasco sauce

Saute the onion in margarine until soft. Add flour; blend well. Gradually add milk; cook until thickened, stirring constantly. Add the crab meat, cheese and Tabasco sauce. Serve hot.

Mrs. Kenneth Fish, Bucks Harbor, Maine

Aloha Dip

8 oz. cream cheese, softened
1 c. crushed pineapple, drained
1 c. grated coconut
1 ½ tsp. ground ginger
2 tsp. lemon juice
½ c. chopped pecans

Mash cream cheese well. Add remaining ingredients; stir well. Chill for several hours before serving. Serve with Ritz crackers.

Mrs. James F. Hoffman, El Paso, Tex.

 ## Always A Favorite Dip

1 8-oz. pkg. cream cheese
¼ c. canned milk
1 tbsp. lemon juice
1 tbsp. onion flakes or minced onion
Dash of paprika

Soften cream cheese. Add milk; blend. Add lemon juice and blend. Add onion and paprika. Mix well. For variation, any of the following may be added:

1 can smoked clams or oysters
1 c. pimento cheese
½ to 1 c. small shrimp
¼ c. grated carrots
¼ c. grated green pepper

Mrs. Elsie Strum Hutchinson, Home Economics Teacher,
Jacksonville Beach, Fla.

 ## Anchovy Dip

1 8-oz. pkg. cream cheese
2 tbsp. cream
2 tsp. grated onion
½ tsp. celery seed
1 tbsp. lemon juice
2 tsp. anchovy paste

Soften cream cheese until it is smooth with an electric mixer. Beat in other ingredients. Beat until fluffy.

Mrs. Flo Brame, Home Economics Teacher, Waco, Tex.

Avocado Dip

1 lge. ripe avocado
½ pkg. cream cheese, softened
Juice of ½ onion
Dash of garlic salt

Peel avocado; mash in small bowl. Add cream cheese; blend thoroughly. Add onion juice and garlic salt; mix well. Chill. Serve with corn or potato chips.

Mrs. Julia Grey, Orlando, Fla.

Green Chili Cheese

1 lge. avocado, peeled
1 8-oz. pkg. cream cheese
2 oz. peeled green chilies
½ tsp. garlic salt

Place all ingredients in blender; mix well.

Mrs. Eugene R. West, Glendale, Ariz., Favorite Recipes Food Fair

Bacon Dip

1 8-oz. pkg. cream cheese, softened
2 tbsp. mayonnaise
1 clove of garlic, pressed
1 tbsp. lemon juice
1 tbsp. Worcestershire sauce
2 to 4 green olives, chopped
4 slices bacon, cubed and fried crisp

Mix all ingredients. Add a small amount of milk or cream for proper consistency. Serve with potato or corn chips.

Mrs. Charles F. Brewer, Officers' Wives' Club, Hanau, Germany

Best Beau Dip

2 pkg. cream cheese
1 tbsp. water
2 ½ tsp. Beau Monde seasoning salt
2 tsp. fine chopped dried parsley

Mix ingredients and refrigerate several hours before serving.

Elaine M. McCoy, Cle Elum, Wash.

Chicken-Cheese Dip Or Spread

    1 8-oz. pkg. cream cheese
    ¾ c. cooked chicken, finely ground
    ¼ c. olives, ground
    2 tsp. onion, grated
    1 c. celery, grated
    1 tsp. Worcestershire sauce
    Mayonnaise

Mix ingredients in order listed; add enough mayonnaise to moisten. Yield: 2 cups.

Shirley Mae Griffiths, Home Economics Teacher, Easton, Pa.

 ### Chutney Spread

    1 8-oz. pkg. cream cheese, softened
    ⅓ c. chopped chutney
    4 tbsp. finely chopped pecans or walnuts
    2 tbsp. chopped pimento
    ½ tsp. curry powder
    1 tsp. lemon juice
    1 to 2 drops garlic juice (opt.)

Blend all ingredients; place in small bowl or mold. Chill. Serve with toast rounds or crackers.

Mrs. Homer Waller, Phoenix, Ariz.

Clam-Cheese Dip

    1 7 to 7½-oz. can minced clams
    2 3-oz. pkg. cream cheese
    ¼ tsp. salt
    2 tsp. onion, grated
    1 tsp. Worcestershire sauce
    3 drops Tabasco sauce
    1 tsp. parsley, chopped
    2 tsp. lemon juice

Drain clams; reserve liquid. Soften cheese at room temperature. Combine all ingredients except clam liquid; blend into paste. Add liquid, 1 tablespoon at a time, beating after each addition until desired consistency is reached. Chill. Yield: 1 Pint.

Mrs. Irene B. Knudsen, Home Economics Teacher, Crescent City, Cal.

Crab Dip Or Spread

1 8-oz. pkg. cream cheese, softened
2 tbsp. mayonnaise
1 tsp. instant onion powder
½ c. chili sauce
¼ tsp. Tabasco sauce
¼ tsp. Worcestershire sauce
1 7½-oz. can crab, drained and chopped

Blend cheese with mayonnaise until light and fluffy. Add remaining ingredients. Chill. Serve as dip or as spread on wheat thins.

Mrs. Stanley E. Jones, Bremerton, Wash.

 ### Hot Crab Cocktail Dip

3 8-oz. pkg. cream cheese
3 lge. cans King crab
½ tsp. garlic salt
½ c. mayonnaise
2 tsp. prepared mustard
¼ c. Sauterne
2 tsp. powdered sugar
1 tsp. onion juice
½ tsp. seasoned salt

Melt cream cheese in top of double boiler. Add remaining ingredients; mix well. Place in chafing dish; serve warm with crackers or chips. May be frozen and reheated.

Mrs. Joe King, Augusta, Ga.

Curried Cheese Dip

3 tbsp. chopped chutney
1 tbsp. crystalized ginger
3 tbsp. coconut
½ tsp. curry powder
1 c. cream cheese
Lemon juice
Toasted almonds, chopped

Mix all ingredients except almonds; sprinkle with almonds. Serve in scooped out pineapple half. Yield: 10 servings.

Mrs. Robert Brenner, St. Louis, Mo.

Curry-Chutney Dip

1 8-oz. pkg. cream cheese
1 tbsp. curry powder
¼ tsp. garlic powder
½ c. chopped chutney
½ c. sour cream
2 tbsp. milk

Blend cheese with curry and garlic powders; add chutney, sour cream and milk. May be served with corn chips, crackers or vegetable pieces.

Mrs. Charles S. Minter, Jr., New York, N. Y.

Cucumber Dip

1 8-oz. pkg. cream cheese
¼ to ½ c. unpeeled cucumber, shredded and drained
¼ tsp. Worcestershire sauce
Dash of garlic salt

Combine cream cheese and cucumber; blend until smooth. Add Worcestershire sauce and garlic salt; mix well. Serve with potato chips.

Mrs. Grace E. Kukuk, Home Economics Teacher, Negaunee, Mich.

 ### Deviled Cheese Dip

2 3-oz. pkg. cream cheese
½ tsp. prepared mustard
¼ c. mayonnaise
1 hard-cooked egg, finely chopped
1 sm. can deviled ham
Dash of salt and pepper

Cream the cheese; add mustard, mayonnaise and egg. Blend the deviled ham, salt and pepper. Serve with crackers or chips.

Mrs. Richard K. Dutton, Officers' Wives' Club, Canal Zone

Deviled Ham Dip

2 3-oz. pkg. cream cheese, softened
⅔ c. evaporated milk
1 4½-oz. can deviled ham
2 tbsp. drained sweet pickle relish
2 tbsp. drained horseradish
¼ tsp. salt

Blend cream cheese and milk; add deviled ham, relish, horseradish and salt. Mix well; chill thoroughly. Serve as dip for crackers or potato chips.

Mrs. John Yockey, Jr., Chandler, Minn., Favorite Recipes Food Fair

Green Chili Dip

1 8-oz. pkg. cream cheese
½ c. sour cream
½ c. salad dressing
4 to 5 tbsp. chopped green chilies
4 tbsp. minced onion
Dash of salt

Mix all ingredients in order given; chill overnight. Serve with corn chips or crackers. Yield: 6 servings.

Mrs. E. A. Stalzer, Officers' Wives' Club, Abilene, Tex.

Smoked Oyster Dip

1 3-oz. pkg. cream cheese, softened
2 tbsp. milk
¼ c. mayonnaise
¼ tsp. salt
½ tsp. seasoned salt
⅛ tsp. pepper
2 tsp. lemon juice
1 3¼-oz. jar smoked oysters, finely chopped

Combine cream cheese and milk. Add mayonnaise, salt, seasoned salt, pepper and lemon juice; stir in chopped oysters. Serve with potato chips, celery or cucumber slices. Yield: 1½ cups.

Mrs. William B. Robinson, Officers' Wives' Club, Pusan, Korea

Smoked Oysters Marguerite

    1 8-oz. pkg. cream cheese
    ¼ c. light cream or milk
    2 tsp. lemon juice
    1 tsp. Worcestershire sauce
    Salt and pepper
    1 tbsp. onion, grated
    1 flat can smoked oysters, drained and chopped

Beat together all ingredients except oysters. Add oysters; chill.

           Mrs. Marguerite McGinness, Danbury, Tex.

Raw Mushroom Dip

    2 3-oz. pkg. cream cheese
    1 tbsp. minced onion
    1 c. finely chopped raw mushrooms
    ½ tsp. salt
    Dash of monosodium glutamate (opt.)
    Minced parsley

Whip cream cheese and onion until light and fluffy; stir in mushrooms, salt and monosodium glutamate. Sprinkle with parsley. Serve as dip or use as spread for open-faced sandwiches.

Mrs. F. K. Mearns, Hon. Pres. Officers' Wives' Club, Darmstadt, Germany

 ### Sardine Dip

    8 oz. cream cheese
    ½ c. lemon juice
    12 oz. sardines
    ½ tsp. paprika
    2 tbsp. chopped parsley
    Salt to taste
    Pinch of cayenne pepper

Cream cheese in mixer or blender until smooth. Add lemon juice and sardines; beat until smooth. Add seasonings. Serve dip with saltines or cheese crackers.

           Mrs. Gerald Howe, Norman, Okla.

Seafood Dip

1 8-oz. pkg. cream cheese
1 c. sour cream
1 7-oz. can shrimp
1 7-oz. can clams
1 7-oz. can crab meat
1 pkg. cream of leek soup
Lemon juice to taste

Whip cream cheese and sour cream. Add remaining ingredients; mix well.

Mrs. David C. Turner, Officers' Wives' Club, Tehran, Iran

 ### Mexican Cheese Dip

½ stick melted butter or margarine
4 tbsp. flour
1 tsp. (heaping) paprika
¼ tsp. ground mustard
1 tsp. chili powder
¼ to ¾ tsp. cumin seed
1 tbsp. plain catsup
1 tsp. pepper sauce from jalapeno peppers
2 c. milk
½ pod jalapeno pepper, finely chopped
6 oz. grated process cheese
Clove of garlic, finely chopped

Cook butter and flour over low heat for 1 minute. Add paprika, mustard, chili powder, cumin seed, catsup and pepper sauce. Mix well. Add milk, pepper pod, cheese and garlic. Cook mixture over low heat until thick, stirring constantly to avoid lumping. More jalapeno pepper and sauce may be added to make a hotter dip.

Mrs. Horace L. Griffith, Officers' Wives' Club, Fort Hood, Tex.

 ### Zippy Dip

1 4-oz. pkg. dried beef, diced
1 c. sour cream
¾ tsp. caraway seed
½ tsp. dried mustard
1 3-oz. pkg. cream cheese
¼ tsp. curry powder
¼ c. minced onion

Combine all ingredients; cool in refrigerator for 3 to 4 hours. Yield: 2 cups.

Pauline Smith, Leeds, Ala.

Mock Oyster Rockefeller

1 onion, finely chopped
Margarine
1 lge. can mushrooms, drained and finely chopped
1 can cream of mushroom soup
1 pkg. broccoli, chopped and cooked
1 roll garlic cheese
Hot sauce to taste

Saute onion in margarine; add other ingredients. Serve hot on crackers.

Mrs. Lucille Gelpi, Home Economics Teacher, Hahnville, La.

 ### Prairie Fire Dip

1 can ranch-style beans, sieved
½ lb. butter
½ lb. sharp cheese, grated
2 hot chili peppers, finely chopped
1 med. onion, finely grated
1 clove of garlic, finely chopped

Mix all ingredients in top of double boiler over hot water until cheese melts. Pour into a chafing dish. Serve warm with corn or potato chips. If more liquid is needed, add juice from peppers, a small amount at a time. Yield: 8 servings.

Mrs. Gerald L. Short, Seattle, Wash., Favorite Recipes Food Fair

Saucy Shrimp Dip

1 lb. American cheese, diced
1 tbsp. butter
½ tsp. salt
½ tsp. paprika
1 tsp. dry mustard
1 c. beer
1 c. cooked diced shrimp
¼ c. chopped green pepper
1 tbsp. chopped onion
Bread croustades, crackers or chips

Melt cheese and butter in double boiler; add seasonings and beer, stirring constantly until smooth. Fold in shrimp, green pepper and onion; cook for about 3 minutes. Serve with croustades.

Mrs. Francis P. Jordan, Pres. Officers' Wives' Club, Norfolk, Va.

Kelly's Hors D'Oeuvres Fondue

2 c. champagne
1 lb. imported Swiss cheese
3 tbsp. flour
Salt and ground whole pepper to taste
Grated fresh nutmeg to taste
5 tbsp. Kirsch or brandy

Heat champagne in chafing dish; keep hot. Add cheese; sprinkle with flour, salt, pepper and nutmeg. Add Kirsch or brandy. May be served with squares of Italian bread.

Mrs. Grace Kelly, Kailua, Oahu, Hawaii

 ### Swiss Cheese Fondue

1 clove of garlic
½ tsp. salt
2 c. dry white wine
¾ lb. Swiss cheese, shredded
1 ½ tbsp. flour
⅛ tsp. cayenne pepper
Dash nutmeg
4 tbsp. Kirschwasser or 2 tbsp. Cognac
Cubes of crusty bread

Rub chafing dish with cut clove of garlic and a little salt. Heat wine in pan until bubbly. Add a handful of cheese at a time until melted. Add flour, seasonings and brandy. Stir well. Spear bread; dip into cheese mixture. Stir until well coated. Triscuit or thick chips may be substituted for bread cubes. If fondue becomes too thick, add a little preheated wine.

Mrs. Paul Dow McKinney, Pres. Officers' Wives' Club, Ansbach, Germany

Tuna-Cheese Dip

1 9½-oz. can light chunk albacore tuna, flaked
1 4-oz. wedge sharp or mellow cheese, grated
¼ to ½ c. mayonnaise
½ tsp. powdered or dried onion
1 tbsp. Worcestershire sauce
5 to 10 drops Tabasco sauce
Salt and pepper to taste

Combine tuna, cheese and mayonnaise; add onion, Worcestershire sauce and Tabasco sauce. Mix well. Season with salt and pepper to taste. Serve with crackers or melba toast rounds.

Mrs. Tom L. Holland, Officers' Wives' Club, Villefranche, France

Seafood Dip

1 can tomato soup
2 cans crab or lobster
2 lb. Velveeta cheese
1 sm. onion, grated
1 tsp. Worcestershire sauce
Dash of Tabasco sauce
Garlic
1 tsp. curry powder
Tomato juice (opt.)

Combine all ingredients, adding tomato juice if mixture is too thick. Cook for 2 to 3 hours in double boiler. Serve in chafing dish.

Mrs. Stello Taylor, Patterson, N. J.

 ### Velveeta Hot Dip

1 lb. block Velveeta cheese
1 4½-oz. can green chilies, chopped
1 sm. onion, finely chopped
½ fresh tomato or 2 tbsp. canned tomato, chopped
Garlic salt to taste (opt.)

Place cheese in top of double boiler. Add remaining ingredients. Heat over hot water until cheese is melted. Serve hot or cold with potato chips or corn chips. Yield: 2 cups.

Mrs. Paul E. Gilliland, Officers' Wives' Club, Hawthorne, Nev.

 ### Bleu Cheese Dip

2 lge. pkgs. cream cheese, softened
1 3-oz. pkg. Bleu cheese, softened
Garlic salt
Onion salt
Worcestershire sauce
Light cream
Raw vegetables

Blend cheeses. Season with garlic and onion salts to taste. Add few drops of Worcestershire sauce. Blend well. Add light cream until of desired consistency. Serve with raw cauliflowerets, carrot sticks, celery sticks, corn chips or crackers.

Mrs. Martin Barron, Meridian, Miss.

Chili Con Queso

2 tbsp. butter
1 clove of garlic, minced
¼ c. milk
½ lb. American cheese
¾ lb. Swiss cheese
1 onion, grated
1 c. canned tomatoes
½ sm. can green chili peppers
Salt to taste
Celery salt to taste
Dash of cayenne
Dash of paprika

Melt butter in top of double boiler. Add garlic; cook until soft. Add milk and cheese. Cook until cheese melts. Add remaining ingredients and heat through, stirring often to break up tomatoes and peppers. Serve in chafing dish surrounded with corn chips.

Mrs. James F. Ridley, Jr., Officers' Wives' Club, Grant Heights, Japan

Crab Mornay

Margarine
6 tbsp. flour
Liquid from 2 cans mushrooms
Chicken broth
1 ½ c. evaporated milk
1 onion, chopped
3 tbsp. chopped pimento
3 tbsp. chopped green pepper
⅓ lb. grated Gruyere cheese
¼ lb. grated Parmesan cheese
1 tsp. monosodium glutamate
Salt and black pepper to taste
Red pepper to taste
2 7-oz. cans King crab

Blend 6 tablespoons melted margarine and flour. Measure mushroom liquid; add chicken broth to measure 1½ cups. Combine with milk; stir into flour mixture. Cook until thickened, stirring constantly. Saute onion, pimento and green pepper in small amount of margarine; add to white sauce with all remaining ingredients. Cook until cheeses are melted and sauce has thickened. May be prepared in advance and refrigerated; heat to serve.

Mrs. W. E. Cummins, New York, N. Y., Favorite Recipes Food Fair

Jalapeno Cheese Dip

2 tbsp. flour
¾ c. cream
2 tbsp. margarine
2 lb. Velveeta cheese, cubed
1 pt. cottage cheese
1 medium onion, finely chopped
1 medium bell pepper, finely chopped
1 pod garlic, finely chopped
4 Jalapeno peppers

Mix flour and cream in double boiler. Add margarine and cheeses; melt. Add remaining ingredients and simmer 10 to 15 minutes or until thick, stirring occasionally. Serve warm as dip or as spread for crackers and sandwiches.

Mrs. Martha J. Barr, Home Economics Teacher, Fluvanna, Tex.

 ### Roquefort Cheese Dip

3 tsp. evaporated milk
1 c. cottage cheese
1 onion, thinly sliced
1 tsp. Worcestershire sauce
3 oz. Roquefort cheese, crumbled

Combine all ingredients in order given. Blend until smooth. Serve with crackers. Yield: 1¼ cups.

Eva Jane Schwartz, Home Economics Teacher, Gettysburg, Pa.

 ### Smoky Cheese Dip

2 3-oz. pkg. cream cheese
1 6-oz. roll smoky cheese
1 small clove garlic, minced
⅓ c. pineapple juice
¼ tsp. Tabasco sauce
1 tsp. Worcestershire sauce

Put all ingredients in blender and blend about 20 seconds or until smooth. Chill and serve. Yield: 1½ cups.

Mrs. Glenda Ballinger, Home Economics Teacher, Chattanooga, Tenn.

Clam Dip

1 pt. sour cream
1 flat can minced clams, drained
½ pkg. cream of leek soup mix
Dash of Worcestershire sauce

Combine all ingredients; let stand for at least 30 minutes.

Mrs. Howard Mellblom, Pres. Officers' Wives' Club, Los Alamitos, Cal.

Cocktail Sauce

½ c. chili sauce
⅓ c. catsup
2 to 4 tbsp. prepared horseradish
1 ½ tsp. Worcestershire sauce
¼ tsp. salt
Dash of pepper
2 tbsp. lemon juice
Few drops of Tabasco sauce

Combine all ingredients; chill thoroughly. Serve with seafood and vegetable cocktails. Yield: 1 cup.

Mrs. Donald Fuller, Charleston, S. C., Favorite Recipes Food Fair

 ### Coponati

2 medium eggplants, cubed
Salt
Cooking oil
1 can tomato sauce
1 lge. onion, finely chopped
2 celery stalks, finely chopped
1 clove garlic, finely chopped
10 green olives, quartered
1 tsp. vinegar

Sprinkle eggplants with 1 tablespoon salt and let set for about 30 minutes. Squeeze out lightly. Cook in 3 tablespoons hot oil until tender; add tomato sauce. Saute onion, celery, garlic and olives in a small amount of oil; add vinegar. Mix all ingredients together with sugar and salt to taste; cook until flavors are blended. Serve on crackers or with meats.

Mrs. Ted Trotter, Home Economics Teacher, Independence, La.

Crab And Cream Dip

½ pt. sour cream
½ c. crab meat
2 tbsp. chili sauce
½ tsp. Worcestershire sauce
Salt and pepper to taste
Chips or crackers

Combine all ingredients except chips. Chill if desired. Serve with chips or crackers.

Mrs. William T. Adams, Officers' Wives' Club, Enid, Okla.

 ## Hot Crab Dip

3 tbsp. melted butter
3 tbsp. flour
1 ½ c. milk
½ tsp. salt
1 tbsp. Worcestershire sauce
½ tsp. Tabasco sauce
¼ tsp. black pepper
¼ tsp. dry mustard
½ tsp. dried parsley
1 lb. crab meat
3 tbsp. cooking sherry

Combine butter, flour and milk to make a sauce. Add all remaining ingredients except cooking sherry. Just before serving, add sherry. Serve in chafing dish with melba toast squares or cocktail crackers.

Leona Woodling, Home Economics Teacher, Chesapeake, Va.

 ## Curried Mayonnaise Dip

1 c. mayonnaise
¼ tsp. salt
Dash of pepper
1 tbsp. minced onion
½ tsp. lemon juice
½ tsp. curry powder

Combine all ingredients; blend until smooth. Refrigerate until ready to use. Serve with raw cauliflower, crackers, potato chips, smoked oysters or boiled shrimp. Yield: 1 cup.

Mrs. S. J. Kremzar, Clearwater, Fla.

Curried Egg Dip

¼ tsp. Tabasco sauce
½ tsp. curry powder
¼ tsp. dry mustard
½ tsp. salt
½ c. mayonnaise
1 tbsp. minced onion
½ c. finely diced celery
4 hard-cooked eggs, finely chopped

Blend Tabasco sauce, curry powder, dry mustard, salt and mayonnaise. Stir in onion and celery; fold in eggs. Serve with carrot sticks, celery stalks, cauliflower clusters and green pepper strips. Yield: 2 cups.

Mrs. Fred Sanders, Lincoln, Neb., Favorite Recipes Food Fair

Dill Weed Dip

⅔ c. mayonnaise
⅔ c. sour cream
1 tbsp. shredded green onion
1 tbsp. parsley
1 tsp. dill weed
1 tsp. Beau Monde seasoning

Mix all ingredients; chill for 2 or 3 hours. Use as dip for raw vegetables.

Mrs. William C. Slattery, Officers' Wives' Club, Wurtsmith AFB, Mich.

Fruit-Mallow Dip

2 c. marshmallow creme
½ c. mayonnaise
3 tsp. grated orange peel
4 tsp. orange juice
3 tsp. lemon juice
2 c. strawberries
1 c. pineapple chunks
1 c. sliced bananas

Combine marshmallow creme, mayonnaise, orange peel, orange juice and lemon juice; blend until smooth. Arrange fruits on toothpicks; serve with marshmallow dip.

Mrs. Vincent P. Morreale, Newburgh, N. Y.

Green Goddess Dip

2 *cloves of garlic*
1 *tsp. dry mustard*
1 *tsp. salt*
¼ *c. anchovy paste*
2 *tbsp. meat sauce*
6 *tbsp. tarragon vinegar*
6 *tbsp. chives*
⅔ *c. minced parsley*
2 *c. mayonnaise*
1 *c. sour cream*

Put garlic through garlic press. Combine all ingredients; chill. Yield: 4 cups.

Mrs. Milton A. Hintze, Pres. Officers' Wives' Club, Otis AFB, Mass.

 ## Homas Bi Thineh

1 *19-oz. can garbanzos, well drained*
1 *tsp. salt*
1 *clove garlic, crushed*
½ *c. olive or salad oil*
1 *tbsp. lemon juice*
Chopped parsley
Paprika

Put peas, salt and garlic into blender and mash thoroughly. Add oil, a little at a time, until mixture is consistency of soft mashed potatoes. Add lemon juice. Garnish with parsley and paprika. Serve with crisp crackers.

Mrs. Jeanne Bundi, Home Economics Teacher, Van Buren, Ohio

 ## Liver Dip

1 *pkg. chicken livers or ½ lb. calves liver*
2 *lge. onions*
1 *c. butter*
5 *hard-cooked eggs*
1 *c. mayonnaise*

Fry livers and onions in butter. Put livers, onions and eggs through food chopper. Add mayonnaise; stir.

Catherine S. Bradley, Home Economics Teacher, Aliquippa, Pa.

Hot Mushroom Dip

1 lb. fresh mushrooms
1 clove garlic, crushed
1 sm. onion, grated
2 tbsp. butter
¼ tsp. Accent
⅛ tsp. mustard
½ tsp. soy sauce
⅛ tsp. paprika
⅛ tsp. salt
⅛ tsp. pepper
1 tbsp. flour
1 c. sour cream

Brown mushrooms, garlic and onion in butter. Combine Accent, mustard, soy sauce, paprika, salt, pepper and flour with a little cream to make a paste; add to mushrooms. Blend in remaining cream; stir over low heat until thickened. Do not boil. Serve with crackers or chips. Yield: 2 cups.

Annie Lillian Brewton, Home Economics Teacher, Pensacola, Fla.

Olive-Onion Dip

1 pt. sour cream with chives
1 4-oz. jar stuffed olives, chopped
1 pkg. onion soup mix
Dash of Worcestershire sauce
¼ tsp. celery salt
¼ tsp. garlic salt
Salt and pepper to taste

Combine all ingredients; mix well.

Mrs. Jorge Duque, Officers' Wives' Club, Chandler AFS, Minn.

Onion Dip

1 8-oz. pkg. cream cheese
1 c. sour cream
1 pkg. dry onion soup mix

Mix all together; beat until creamy.

Julia Golson, Montgomery, Ala., Favorite Recipes Food Fair

Peppy Seafood Sauce

⅓ c. chili sauce
⅓ c. catsup
3 tbsp. horseradish
¼ c. lemon juice
2 tsp. Worcestershire sauce
Dash of Tabasco sauce
Dash of salt

Combine all ingredients; chill thoroughly. Serve with chilled fresh cooked shrimp. Yield: 1 cup.

Mrs. Jerry K. Cunningham, Sault Ste. Marie, Mich.

 Raw Vegetable Dip

1 c. mayonnaise
½ c. drained chili sauce
1 clove of garlic, minced
½ tsp. dry mustard
⅛ tsp. cayenne pepper
1 tbsp. horseradish
2 or 3 drops of lemon juice

Mix all ingredients; let stand for several hours or overnight.

Mrs. Harold Hill, Portland, Ore.

 Remoulade Sauce For Shrimp

2 ½ tbsp. prepared mustard
2 ½ tbsp. creole mustard
2 tsp. horseradish
2 tsp. cider vinegar
½ tsp. paprika
½ tsp. chili powder
¼ tsp. salt
⅛ tsp. pepper
1 pt. mayonnaise
½ c. coarsely chopped celery
½ c. coarsely chopped green onions and tops
1 sm. clove of garlic, chopped
½ hard-cooked egg, coarsely chopped

Mix mustards, horseradish, vinegar, paprika, chili powder, salt and pepper; add mayonnaise and stir well. Add remaining ingredients and mix well.

Mrs. Franklin D. Waddell, Officers' Wives' Club, Bergstrom AFB, Tex.

Savory Shrimp Dip

2 4-oz. cans of shrimp
1 c. mayonnaise
4 tsp. grated onion
1 tsp. Tabasco sauce
Salt and pepper to taste
Sour cream

Mince shrimp; add mayonnaise, onion, Tabasco sauce, salt and pepper. Thin with sour cream; serve with potato chips.

Mrs. Frank R. Fusco, Madison, Wis.

 ### Shrimp Dip With Zip

1 4½-oz. can shrimp
1 tsp. minced onion
Dash of paprika
1 c. sour cream or cream cheese
Salt and pepper to taste
Few drops of Tabasco sauce
Few drops of lemon juice

Put all ingredients in blender for 15 to 20 seconds. Chill for 2 to 3 hours so flavors blend. If cream cheese is used, add a small amount of evaporated milk until of desired consistency.

Mrs. Joseph F. Burgess, Jr., Woods Hole, Mass., Favorite Recipes Food Fair

Smoky Seafood Dip

½ c. mayonnaise
½ c. sour cream
¼ tsp. hot mustard
¼ tsp. garlic powder
2 tsp. instant minced onion
1 tbsp. tarragon white wine vinegar
Dash of cayenne pepper.
1 tsp. hickory smoked salt

Blend mayonnaise, sour cream, mustard, garlic powder, onion and vinegar. Add cayenne pepper and smoked salt; mix well. Chill sauce for 1 hour for flavors to blend. Serve with cooked chilled shrimp, crab legs, small lobster tails or cubes of lobster. Yield: 1 cup.

Mrs. James R. Winn, Officers' Wives' Club, Jusmag, Philippines

Egg Monochina

3 tbsp. butter
Flour
1 c. milk
10 hard-cooked eggs, quartered and separated
½ c. chopped ham
3 tbsp. Parmesan or bleu cheese
Salt and pepper to taste
Dry mustard to taste
Dash of Tabasco sauce
Beaten eggs
Bread crumbs

Melt butter; blend in 3 tablespoons of flour. Gradually add milk; stir until thick and smooth. Shred hard-cooked egg yolks. Add yolks, ham, and cheese to white sauce. Season to taste with salt, pepper, mustard and Tabasco sauce. Chill. Refill quartered egg whites with filling. Roll in flour; dip in beaten eggs. Roll in crumbs. Refrigerate overnight. Fry in deep fat.

SAUCE:

1 c. mayonnaise
1 tsp. curry powder
Chopped chutney to taste

Mix ingredients. Serve with hot eggs.

Mrs. Charles D. Griffin, Hon. Pres., Officers' Wives' Club,
Allied Forces Southern Europe, Naples, Italy

 ## Avocado In Piquant Sauce

½ c. chili sauce
1 tsp. Worcestershire sauce
1 tsp. minced onion
½ tsp. salt
⅛ tsp. pepper
1 tbsp. vinegar
1 tbsp. horseradish sauce
1 tsp. celery salt
2 tbsp. sugar
2 avocados, peeled and cubed
Lemon juice

Combine all ingredients except avocados and lemon juice. Pour into jar; cover. Refrigerate overnight. To serve, pour sauce into bowl. Dip avocado cubes in lemon juice. Arrange on toothpicks around sauce. Yield: 15 servings.

Mrs. Bob D. Schuler, Boise, Idaho

Fruit Kabobs

½ Grapefruit
Fresh or frozen melon balls
Whole strawberries
Pineapple chunks
Bananas

Use half of grapefruit, cut side down, on a plate or tray to arrange kabobs. Place fruit on skewers or toothpicks and stick into grapefruit. Makes attractive centerpieces for breakfast or brunch.

Mrs. Ralph Shipman, Home Economics Teacher, Paris, Tex.

 ## Happy Peaches

4 1-lb. 13-oz. cans cling peach halves
2 whole cinnamon sticks
1 ½ c. brandy

Drain peaches, reserving syrup. Refrigerate. Add 1 stick cinnamon, broken in half, to peach syrup. Boil syrup over medium heat for 45 minutes or until syrup is reduced to about 3 cups. Pour into medium bowl; remove any scum. Stir in brandy; cool. Arrange peaches in a large jar or dish. Cover with syrup; add remaining cinnamon stick broken into pieces. Cover and refrigerate for 1 week to develop flavor. Yield: 32 servings.

Mrs. Edgar R. Kadel, Officers' Wives' Club, New Cumberland Army Dep., Va.

Pagoda Fruits

1 8-oz. can pear halves
1 8-oz. can cling peach slices
1 8-oz. can figs
1 8-oz. can Royal Anne cherries
1 5-oz. jar bleu cheese spread, well chilled
Bibb lettuce
½ c. mayonnaise
¼ c. honey

Drain fruits; reserve 2 teaspoons syrup. Shape cheese spread into small balls; chill fruits and cheese. Line a serving plate with lettuce, building up center slightly. Place 4 pear halves around center; fill pear hollows with cheese balls. Thread each of four kabob sticks with 2 peach slices, 1 fig and 1 cherry; stick into pears. Place remaining fruits around edge. Blend reserved syrup with remaining ingredients in a small bowl; serve separately.

Mrs. James Downs, Little Creek, Va.

Pineapple Mint

> 1 can frozen pineapple or 1 No. 2 can pineapple chunks
> ¼ c. creme de menthe

Place chilled pineapple and juice in bowl; add creme de menthe. Mix until fruit is green. Serve on toothpicks.

Mrs. Henry G. Victor, Officers' Wives' Club, Selma, Ala.

 ### Beef Teriyaki On Bamboo Sticks

> ½ lb. sirloin, flank or round steak, ½-in. thick
> ½ c. soy sauce
> ¼ c. wine vinegar
> 1 clove of garlic, chopped
> 1 tbsp. green onion, chopped
> ½ tsp. salt
> ½ tsp. powdered ginger
> ⅛ tsp. pepper
> 1 ½ tsp. sugar

Cut steak into 4 x ⅛-inch strips. Combine remaining ingredients; marinate steak in mixture for 1 hour. Thread 1 meat strip on each bamboo stick. Cook over hibachi or regular grill for 3 to 4 minutes, turning once.

Mrs. S. D. Ross, Officers' Wives' Club, Landsthul, Germany

 ### Dried Beef Roll-Ups

> 1 8-oz. pkg. cream cheese, softened
> 1 ½ tsp. prepared horseradish
> 1 tsp. Worcestershire sauce
> ⅛ tsp. onion salt
> 4 3½-oz. pkg. dried or smoked slice beef

Combine cream cheese, horseradish, Worcestershire sauce and onion salt. Separate slices of beef; spread ½ to ¾ teaspoon of cream cheese mixture on each slice. Roll up; slice each roll in half. Secure with toothpicks, if necessary. May be made a day in advance and stored in an airtight container. Yield: 40 servings.

Mrs. Frederick Meyerhoefer, Smyrna, Tenn.

Steak Bites

> 1 ½ to 2 lb. steak, ⅛-in. thick
> 1 c. soy sauce
> 1 c. cooking oil
> 2 tbsp. dry mustard
> 2 tbsp. sugar
> 2 oz. whiskey
> 2 tbsp. garlic salt
> 1 tsp. pepper
> 1 tsp. Tabasco sauce

Cut steak into bite-sized pieces. Combine remaining ingredients; pour over steak. Let stand for 5 hours at room temperature, stirring occasionally. Bring to a boil just before serving. Serve in chafing dish.

Mrs. Gerald H. King, Officers' Wives' Club, Coronado, Cal.

Stuffed Flank Steak

> 1 flank steak
> 2 slices white bread
> ½ lb. fresh mild Italian sausage
> 1 pkg. frozen chopped spinach, thawed and drained
> 2 eggs
> 2 tbsp. olive oil
> 2 cloves of garlic
> ¾ c. Parmesan cheese
> Salt

Have butcher cut pocket in steak, being careful to make no holes. Remove crusts from bread; moisten and squeeze dry. Break up bread. If sausage contains large number of pepper seed, remove some so pepper will not over power other seasonings. Mix all ingredients except steak. Stuff into steak. Lace opening together. Bake at 300 degrees for 1 hour and 30 minutes to 2 hours. Chill. Cut into ¼-inch slices; cut each slice into halves. Serve with crackers. Yield: 50 servings.

Mrs. F. C. Jackson, Las Vegas, Nev.

Texas Jerky

Lean eye of round roast
Garlic salt
Liquid smoke
Pepper

Cut meat into strips about 5 inches long and ¾-inch square. Generously coat strips of meat with garlic salt; let stand in covered dish for 24 hours. Hang meat in oven from highest rack, using paper clips straightened into an "s". Turn oven on warm; leave oven door slightly open. Let stand for 24 hours. Remove strips of meat; paint with liquid smoke. Coat with finely ground black pepper. Return to oven; leave for an additional 24 to 48 hours until meat is dried throughout. To eat, cut off slices or chunks.

Mrs. John Collins, St. Petersburg, Fla.

Cheese And Liverwurst Roll

1 8-oz. pkg. cream cheese, softened
1 8-oz. pkg. liverwurst, softened
1 tsp. minced onion
Dash of Worcestershire sauce
Minced parsley

Combine cheese and liverwurst; add onion and Worcestershire sauce. Roll in minced parsley. Slice and serve with crackers or party rye.

Mrs. Lewis Mason, Providence, R. I.

Chicken Wing Delights

2 lb. chicken wings
1 sm. onion
2 pieces of celery
1 tsp. salt
¼ tsp. pepper
6 tbsp. water
2 tbsp. honey
1 c. flour
2 c. shortening

Place chicken wings, onion, celery, salt and pepper in saucepan. Cover with water. Cook for 30 minutes; cool. Disjoint wing tips; discard. Disjoint remaining portion of wings. Cool. Combine water and honey. Dip wing pieces into water mixture; roll in flour. Let stand for 2 hours or until just before serving. Heat shortening; fry wing piece until brown. Yield: 4 servings.

Mrs. Robert B. Franks, Clearwater, Fla.

Barbecued Chicken Legs

18 broiler-fryer chicken legs
¼ c. unsulphured molasses
¼ c. prepared mustard
¼ c. catsup
2 tbsp. Worcestershire sauce

Place chicken legs in foil-lined shallow baking dish. Blend molasses and mustard; stir in remaining ingredients. Brush chicken legs with sauce. Bake at 350 degrees for 50 minutes, brushing occasionally with remaining sauce; turn legs once. Turn into chafing dish to serve. Yield: 18 servings.

Barbara Ames, Lansing, Mich.

Chicken-Nut Puffs

1 ½ c. cooked or canned chicken, drained and finely chopped
⅓ c. toasted almonds, chopped
1 c. canned or fresh chicken broth
½ c. salad oil or chicken fat
2 tsp. seasoned salt
⅛ tsp. cayenne
1 tsp. celery seed
1 tbsp. parsley flakes
2 tsp. Worcestershire sauce
1 c. flour
4 eggs

Mix chicken and almonds together. Combine chicken broth, oil, seasoned salt, cayenne, celery seed, parsley flakes and Worcestershire sauce. Bring to a boil. Add flour; cook over low heat, beating rapidly, until mixture leaves sides of pan and forms a smooth compact ball. Remove from heat; add eggs, one at a time. After each addition, beat with a spoon until mixture is shiny. Stir in chicken mixture. Drop ½ teaspoon of mixture at a time on greased baking sheet. Bake at 450°F. for 10 to 15 minutes. Serve hot. Yield: 20-25 servings.

Mrs. Mary A. Moore, Stephenville, Tex.

Chicken Liver Rollups

4 fresh chicken livers
4 water chestnuts
4 strips bacon

Roll chicken livers around chestnuts. Wrap with bacon strips; fasten with toothpicks. Broil until bacon is crisp. Yield: 4 servings.

Helena T. Martines, Home Economics Teacher, Los Angeles, Cal.

Curried Chicken Liver Pate

1 lb. chicken livers
6 tbsp. rendered chicken fat
1 tbsp. curry powder
Freshly ground pepper
Salt
Pinch of dried basil
Pinch of dried thyme
Pinch of dried marjoram
Pinch of dried cardamom
4 oz. dry Vermouth
1 tsp. dry Sherry
2 tbsp. sweet Sherry
3 tbsp. sour cream

Clean livers and cut into small pieces. Saute slowly in fat for 15 minutes, mashing constantly with fork. Reduce heat and mix in seasonings and spices. Remove pan from heat; add liquors. Mash to a fine paste. Stir in sour cream. Blend well. Place in covered crock; refrigerate for at least 3 days. Yield: 6-8 servings.

Mrs. Philip Thomsen, Officers' Wives' Club, North Bend, Ore.

Party Chicken Livers

1 ½ c. crushed barbecued potato chips
3 tbsp. melted butter
½ tsp. garlic powder
1 lb. chicken livers, cut into bite-sized pieces

Combine potato chips, butter and garlic powder. Roll livers in crumb mixture, coating well. Spread in 12 x 9 x 2-inch pan. Sprinkle any remaining crumb mixture over livers. Bake at 350 degrees for 20 to 25 minutes or until done. Serve immediately with toothpicks. Yield: 6-8 servings.

Mrs. John W. Freed, Albany, N. Y.

Pate' De Foie Gras Aspic

1 can Madrilene consomme
1 can pate'de foie gras
1 tbsp. unflavored gelatin
¼ c. water
Salt and pepper to taste
Pinch of tarragon
Parsley to taste

(Continued on next page)

Heat consomme; blend in pate. Dissolve gelatin in water; add to consomme. Add seasonings. Pour into oiled mold; chill for several hours. Serve with toast rounds or crackers. Yield: 8-10 servings.

Mrs. John Caldwell, Hon. Pres. Officers' Wives' Club, Sigonella, Sicily

 ### Spicy Frankfurter Appetizers

1 1½-oz. pkg. spaghetti sauce mix
1 8-oz. can tomato sauce
1 ½ c. water
2 tbsp. salad oil
1 to 2 lb. frankfurters, cut in 1-inch pieces

Prepare spaghetti sauce mix according to package directions, using tomato sauce, water and salad oil. Refrigerate sauce and frankfurters until serving time. Heat frankfurters in sauce. Serve in casserole over candle warmer at table. Or heat and serve from chafing dish. Serve with chunks of French bread, if desired. Yield: 8-16 servings.

Helen Smith, Home Economics Teacher, Galion, Ohio

 ### Beef-Burgundy Balls

½ lb. round steak, ground
1 egg
2 tbsp. flour
2 tsp. finely chopped onion
¼ tsp. Worcestershire sauce
1 tbsp. Burgundy wine
Salt and pepper to taste
Cracker crumbs

Combine all ingredients except crumbs. Mix well. Form into small balls. Roll balls in fine cracker crumbs. Fry in hot deep fat, heated to 375 degrees until brown. Serve hot on picks.

Mrs. John J. Becker, Charleston, S. C.

Cocktail Porcupines

> 1 c. uncooked instant rice
> 1 lb. ground chuck
> 1 egg, slightly beaten
> 2 tbsp. grated onion
> 2 tbsp. salt
> ⅛ tsp. marjoram
> ⅛ tsp. coarsely ground black pepper
> 2 ½ c. tomato juice
> ½ tsp. sugar
> 1 to 2 dashes of Tabasco sauce

Combine rice, meat, egg, onion, salt, marjoram, pepper and ½ cup tomato juice; mix lightly. Shape into 36 balls; place in large skillet. Add sugar and Tabasco sauce to remaining tomato juice; pour over meatballs in skillet. Bring mixture to a boil; reduce heat and simmer, covered for 15 minutes, basting occasionally. Yield: 12 servings. Two 8-ounce cans tomato sauce and 1 small can tomato paste may be substituted for tomato juice. May be made ahead and reheated; serve in chafing dish.

Mrs. James Craft, Pres. Military Officers' Wives' Club,
American Embassy, Rome, Italy

Individual Meatballs In Caper Sauce

> 1 lb. lean beef, ground
> ¾ c. wheat germ flakes
> ¼ c. minced onion
> 1 egg
> 1 ½ tsp. salt
> Dash of pepper
> 1 tbsp. Worcestershire sauce
> 1 ¼ c. milk
> 2 tbsp. oil
> 2 tbsp. flour
> 1 c. half and half
> 2 tbsp. drained capers

Combine beef, wheat germ, onion, egg, 1 teaspoon salt, pepper, Worcestershire sauce and ¾ cup milk; mix well. Shape into 36 small balls. Brown meatballs in hot oil; remove from pan. Stir flour into pan drippings. Add remaining milk, salt, half and half and capers. Cook slowly, stirring constantly, until thickened. Return meatballs to sauce. Cover; simmer for 10 minutes. Yield: 4-6 servings.

Mrs. Robert Smith, Beaufort, S. C.

Swedish Meatballs

SAUCE:

> 2 cans consomme
> 10 gingersnaps
> 4 tsp. brown sugar
> 1 ½ tsp. lemon juice

Combine all ingredients; simmer for 15 minutes.

MEATBALLS:

> 3 lb. ground beef
> Parsley
> Chopped onion
> ½ c. bread crumbs
> 2 eggs
> Salt and pepper
> 1 sm. potato, grated

Combine all ingredients; shape into tiny balls. Drop into sauce. Cook for 30 minutes. Yield: 20 servings.

Mrs. John F. Breslin, Madison, Wis.

Cheese-Meatballs

> 1 lb. ground beef
> 1 sm. can ham spread
> ⅓ tsp. salt
> Few grains of pepper
> 2 pkg. Bleu cheese, cubed
> 1 c. dry red wine
> ½ stick butter

Mix ground beef with ham spread. Season lightly with salt and pepper. Mold meat around cubes of cheese. Place in bowl; cover with red wine. Marinate in refrigerator for at least 3 hours. Melt butter in skillet; add small amount of wine from marinade. Panfry balls. Remove to hot platter or chafing dish. Yield: 8 servings.

Mrs. John F. Burgess, Warren, Mich.

Indian Chicken Balls

> ½ lb. cream cheese
> 2 tbsp. mayonnaise
> 1 c. chopped cooked chicken
> 1 c. chopped blanched almonds or pecans
> 1 tbsp. chopped chutney

(Continued on next page)

½ tsp. salt
1 tbsp. curry powder
½ coconut, grated

Beat cream cheese and mayonnaise; add chicken, almonds, chutney, salt and curry powder. Shape into walnut-sized balls; roll in coconut. Chill. Yield: 36 balls.

Mrs. Herman Tillman, Jr., Favorite Recipes Food Fair, Mountain Home, Idaho

 ## Poultry Meatballs

8 slices very dry bread
2 lge. onions
2 cloves garlic (opt.)
½ c. butter or margarine
6 c. cooked chicken or turkey, finely chopped
4 tbsp. Worcestershire sauce
½ tsp. ground cardamom
2 tsp. salt
1 tsp. black pepper
¼ tsp. red pepper
2 tbsp. flaked or fresh parsley, finely chopped
3 eggs, well beaten

Place bread, onions and garlic in blender; blend until very fine. Saute bread mixture in butter until light brown. Remove from heat; blend in remaining ingredients. Shape into meatballs the size of a walnut. Fry in deep fat at 375° until golden brown. Yield: 24 servings.

Mrs. Danis Hilliard, Home Economics Teacher, Adams City, Colo.

Sweet And Sour Meatballs

1 ½ lb. of lean pork, ground
1 lb. ground beef
1 c. bread crumbs
½ c. finely ground almonds
2 eggs
2 tbsp. soy sauce
2 cloves of garlic, finely ground
2 tsp. salt
Dash of Tabasco sauce
Nutmeg
Cornstarch

Mix all ingredients except cornstarch well; shape into meatballs the size of walnuts. Roll in cornstarch. Fry for 10 minutes.

(Continued on next page)

SAUCE:

    1 lge. can pineapple chunks
    ½ c. soy sauce
    2 c. vinegar
    1 ½ c. sugar
    4 tbsp. cornstarch

Drain pineapple, reserving 1 cup juice. Combine all ingredients. Cook for 10 minutes. Add sauce to meatballs; serve hot in a chafing dish. May be made ahead of time and frozen until ready for use.

Mrs. Thomas H. Cooper, Officers' Wives' Club, Sascom, Germany

Swedish Nuts

    ½ lb. blanched almonds
    ½ lb. walnut halves
    1 c. sugar
    ¼ tsp. salt
    2 egg whites, stiffly beaten
    ½ c. butter

Toast almonds and walnuts at 325 degrees until light brown. Fold sugar and salt into egg whites; add nuts. Melt butter in 15½ x 10½ x 1-inch jelly roll pan; spread nut mixture over butter. Bake at 325 degrees for about 40 minutes, stirring every 10 minutes or until nuts are coated with brown covering and no butter remains in pan. Cool; separate nuts if necessary. Store in air-tight container. Two cups of pecan halves can be substituted for walnut halves.

Betty Good, Fargo, N. D.

Oven-Toasted Pecans

    1 qt. pecans
    4 tbsp. Worcestershire sauce
    2 dashes of Tabasco sauce
    4 tbsp. butter
    Salt to taste

Combine all ingredients except salt; mix well. Bake at 250 degrees for 30 minutes, stirring frequently. Drain on paper towel; add salt to taste.

Mrs. Nelle Bireline, Urbana, Ill.

Abalone Appetizer

1 bottle soy sauce
4 to 5 tsp. brandy or sherry
1 can abalone, drained and cubed

Mix soy sauce and brandy; place in serving bowl. Add abalone; serve with toothpicks.

Mrs. Richard P. Scott, Hon. Pres. West Point Officers' Wives' Club,
US Military Acad., New York, N. Y.

Ripe Olive Appeteasers

1 lb. sirloin steak, 1 inch thick
1 lb. cleaned, cooked shrimp
1 c. canned pitted ripe olives
⅓ c. salad oil
2 tbsp. wine vinegar
⅛ tsp. garlic powder
1 tsp. Worcestershire sauce
½ tsp. coarsely ground black pepper
½ tsp. salt

Broil steak to rare. Cut into bite-sized pieces. Combine with all remaining ingredients. Marinate several hours. Alternate olives, steak and shrimp on skewers. Heat over small hibachi. Good hot or cold. Small lobster tails may be used in place of shrimp. Yield: 24 hors d' oeuvres.

Photograph for this recipe below.

Anchovy-Broiled Shrimp

24 fresh jumbo shrimp
24 anchovy fillets
12 slices bacon, halved lengthwise

Shell shrimp; split deeply down the back, removing sand vein. Insert a fillet of anchovy in each slit. Wind with a half slice of bacon; fasten with a pick. Broil over charcoal until bacon is crisp. Do not overcook; shrimp should be hot and juicy, never dry. Yield: 6 servings.

Mrs. Henry H. Wishart, Dover, N. J.

Caviar And Cream Cheese

1 8-oz. pkg. cream cheese
1 4-oz. jar black caviar
1 med. onion, finely chopped
2 hard-cooked eggs
Juice of ½ lemon

Place cream cheese on serving platter; cover completely with caviar. Surround cheese with chopped onion, a circle of sieved egg yolk and a circle of chopped egg white. Squeeze lemon juice over caviar just before serving.

Mrs. W. J. Maddocks, Coronado, Cal. Favorite Recipes Food Fair

Broiled Clams

12 medium-sized cherrystone or soft shell clams
Salt to taste
Paprika to taste
Cayenne pepper to taste
Green pepper, finely chopped
Red pimento, finely chopped
12 pieces bacon, cut the size of the clam
Lemon sections

Prepare a shallow baking pan with crumpled aluminum foil. Arrange clams on foil firmly to steady them while cooking. Season each clam with salt, paprika and cayenne pepper. Add a little green pepper, pimento and bacon pieces. Place pan about 4 inches from broiler; broil until bacon is cooked. Remove bacon; place in a warm dish. Broil clams 5 to 6 minutes longer. Serve in shell. Garnish with bacon and lemon sections. Yield: 4 servings.

Ruth Adams, Home Economics Teacher, Claymont, Del.

Clams, Liz Style

4 lb. clams
1 stick butter, softened
½ tsp. garlic powder or salt
1 tsp. chopped parsley
¼ c. grated cheese

Cover bottom of pan with water; add clams. Cover and steam until clams open. Remove each clam from shell, reserving half the shell. Wash clams and shells thoroughly. Place shells on cookie sheet; place 1 clam on each shell. Mix butter, garlic powder, parsley and cheese. Place a small amount on each clam. Broil until light brown. Yield: 2 servings.

Mrs. John G. Napier, Albany, Ga.

Walnut-Clam Rolls

½ lb. cream cheese
1 7½-oz. can minced clams
2 tbsp. lemon juice
2 tbsp. chopped onion
¼ tsp. salt
⅛ tsp. garlic salt
1 ½ c. chopped walnuts

Beat cream cheese and minced clams until smooth; blend in lemon juice, onion, salt and garlic salt. Stir in ½ cup walnuts; turn out onto waxed paper. Shape into 2 rolls; roll in remaining walnuts. Wrap in foil; chill for several hours or more. Serve with assorted crackers.

Mrs. Richard W. Dorff, Officers' Wives' Club, Canal Zone

Crab Rolls

1 6½-oz. can crab meat
1 egg
½ c. tomato juice
1 c. bread crumbs
½ tsp. salt
1 tsp. chili powder
2 tsp. prepared mustard
1 tsp. parsley

Combine all ingredients. Chill for 2 to 3 hours. Form mixture into finger-sized pieces. Broil 6 inches from heat for 5 minutes on each side. Serve plain or with hot mustard sauce. Yield: 2 dozen.

Mrs. Frank Hillman, Muncie, Ind.

Shrimp Arnaud

¼ c. vinegar
¼ c. salad oil
¼ c. chili sauce
¼ tsp. garlic salt
1 tsp. prepared mustard
1 lb. shrimp, cooked

Blend vinegar, oil, chili sauce, garlic salt and mustard. Add shrimp; toss to coat with sauce. Marinate overnight. Insert a toothpick in each shrimp before serving.

Elizabeth Woodward, Home Economics Teacher, New London, Ohio

 ## Shrimp Remoulade

½ c. oil
½ c. vinegar
1 c. finely chopped celery
½ c. finely chopped fresh parsley
2 tbsp. grated onion
½ c. creole or hot mustard
3 tbsp. paprika
1 tbsp. hot pepper sauce
½ tbsp. salt
2 tbsp. horseradish
½ tsp. pepper
3 lb. large boiled shrimp

Combine all ingredients; cover and refrigerate for 24 hours. Serve chilled on lettuce leaves. Yield: 6-8 servings.

Mrs. Geo. F. Warren, Quantico, Va.

Shrimp Scampi

¼ lb. butter
1 lb. shrimp
Dash of salt
Dash of pepper
1 tbsp. oregano

Melt butter. Clean shrimp and drain; add seasonings. After butter is melted; mix with shrimp until butter coagulates on shrimp. Marinate for 1 hour; broil for 20 minutes. Yield: 4 servings.

Mrs. George Little, Raleigh, N. C.

Artichokes Piquant

    2 carrots, sliced
    ½ c. water
    2 tbsp. olive oil
    2 tbsp. lemon juice
    1 sm. bay leaf
    1 tsp. salt
    ⅛ tsp. garlic salt
    1 9-oz. pkg. frozen artichoke hearts

Place carrots, water, oil, lemon juice, bay leaf, salt and garlic salt in saucepan. Boil for 5 minutes. Add frozen artichoke hearts; continue boiling for 5 to 10 minutes or until vegetables are tender. Chill artichoke hearts in seasoned liquid. Drain; serve as an appetizer. May also be served hot as a vegetable. Yield: 4 servings.

Mrs. John H. Fowler, Minot AFB, N. D.

 ## Asparagus In A Blanket

    Frozen asparagus
    5 slices boiled ham
    Grated Parmesan cheese

Cook frozen asparagus according to package directions; drain. Cut each spear crosswise into 2 pieces. Cut ham slices into 6 or 7 pieces. Place a piece of asparagus on each piece of ham; sprinkle with grated Parmesan cheese. Roll ham around asparagus; fasten with a toothpick. Broil for 5 minutes.

Mrs. George F. Patterson, Officers' Wives' Club, Point Arena AFS, Cal.

 ## Sprightly Sprouts

    30 sm. Brussels sprouts
    1 3-oz. pkg. cream cheese, softened
    1 tbsp. whipped cream
    1 ½ tbsp. freshly grated horseradish
    Salt

Cook Brussels sprouts for 3 minutes in boiling salted water; cook only long enough to obtain a brilliant green color. Mix cream cheese and whipped cream; add horseradish. Cut each sprout three-fourths of the way through the center. Stuff with cheese mixture; sprinkle with salt. Let stand at room temperature for 30 minutes before serving.

Mrs. L. W. Brauer, Hon. Pres. Officers' Wives' Club, Nellis AFB, Nev.

Cucumbers Au Jour Creme

½ tsp. salt
1 tsp. sugar
Pinch of cayenne pepper
1 tbsp. lemon juice
2 tbsp. vinegar
1 c. sour cream
3 med. cucumbers, sliced

Combine salt, sugar and cayenne pepper. Mix well; add lemon juice and vinegar. Stir in sour cream. Pour over sliced cucumbers. Chill. Yield: 6 servings.

Mrs. Irvin L. Klingenberg, Charleston, S. C.

 ## Hi-Hat Mushrooms In Wine Sauce

16 medium fresh mushrooms
½ lb. ground sausage
1 cup tomato sauce
1 c. white wine
½ clove garlic
⅛ tsp. oregano

Wash mushrooms; remove and chip stems. Add stems to sausage. Stuff caps, rounding meat mixture into a high crown. Bake in 350-degree oven for 30 minutes. Mince garlic; mash to a pulp. Heat tomato sauce, wine, garlic and oregano in a chafing dish. When blended, add mushrooms. Cover and let sauce bubble. Spear mushrooms with toothpicks and serve. Yield: 4-6 servings.

Mrs. Kathryn Chambers, Home Economics Teacher, Wayne, Neb.

Pepper Appetizer

12 green or red peppers
1 c. pickling onions, peeled
1 tbsp. salt
3 c. vinegar
1 c. salad oil

Wash peppers; remove seeds and centers and cut into serving pieces. Bring vinegar, oil and salt to a boil. Add a few peppers and onions at a time, turning in boiling liquid until peppers change color. Do not overcook, keep crisp. Cool and store in refrigerator if to be served within a few days. These peppers may also be canned.

Odessa L. Carlson, Home Economics Teacher, Wakefield, Mich.

APPETIZERS, 315-378

Beverages, 315-317
  Cranberry, 315
  Mixed fruit, 316
    Mock pink champagne, 316
    Pineapple-lemon foam cocktail, 316
  Tomato, 317
    Cocktail, 317
Canapes, 318-328
  Cheese, 318-320
    Surprise puffs, 319
    Toasted sandwich, 320
  Chutney and peanut butter, 320
  Meat, 320-323
    Bacon bits, 320
    Cocktail pizza, 321
    Dried beef spread, 321
    Hot ham, 322
      And cheese rolls, 322
    Liver, 321-322
    Mexican tostados tapatias, 323
  Seafood, 323-327
    Anchovy, 323
    Clam, 324
    Crab, 324-325
    Lobster, 325-326
    Shrimp, 326-327
  Vegetable, 327-328
    Artichoke, 327
    Eggplant spread, 328
    Hot onion, 328
Hors d'oeuvres, 328-378
  Cheese, 328-335
    Balls, 329-333
      Bleu, 329
      Brandied, 329
      Chili log, 331
      Cocktail, 331
      Cream, 330
      Garlic, 333
      Litpauer roll, 332
      Nut, 331, 333
      Roquefort rolls, 330
      Swiss, 330
    Cheddar chips, 333
    Cocktail biscuit, 334
    Pecan cheese roll, 333
    Pickle pineapple, 335
    Straws, 334
  Dips, 335-360
    Anchovy, 335
    Avocado, 336
    Black bean, 337
    Carrot, 337
    With cheese, 337-351
      Avocado-Roquefort, 337
      Bleu, 338, 351
        Shrimp, 338
      Chili con queso, 352
      Clam, 339
      Cottage, 339-340
        Caper sauce for cold lobster, 340
        Curry, 340
        Shrimp party, 339

      Crab, 340, 352
      Cream cheese, 341-348
        Anchovy, 341
        Avocado, 342
        Bacon, 342
        Chicken, 343
        Chutney, 343, 345
        Clam, 343
        Crab, 344
        Cucumber, 345
        Curried, 344
        Deviled, 345-346
          Ham, 346
        Green chili, 342, 346
        Raw mushroom, 347
        Sardine, 347
        Shrimp, 348-349
        Smoked oysters, 346-347
      Jalapeno, 353
      Roquefort, 353
      Seafood, 354-355
      Smoky, 353
      Swiss, 350
      Tuna, 350
      Velveeta, 351
        Seafood, 351
    Curried, 355-356
    Dill weed, 356
    Fruit mallow, 356
    Green goddess, 357
    Hot mushroom, 358
    Liver, 357
    Onion, 358
    Peppy seafood, 359
    Raw vegetable, 359
    Shrimp, 359-360
    Smoky seafood, 360
  Egg monochina, 361
  Fruit, 361-363
    Avocado in piquant sauce, 361
    Happy peaches, 362
    Kabobs, 362
    Pineapple mint, 363
  Meat, 363-371
    Beef, 363-365
      Dried roll-ups, 363
      Steak, 364
      Teriyaki on bamboo sticks, 363
      Texas jerky, 365
    Cheese and liverwurst roll, 365
    Chicken, 365-366
    Chicken livers, 366-367
      Curried pate, 367
      Rollups, 366
    Jellied appetizer cubes, 368
    Meatballs, 369-371
      Beef, 369-370
      Cheese, 370
      Chicken, 370-371
      Sweet and sour, 371
    Nuts, 372
    Pate de foie gras aspic, 367
  Seafood, 373-376
    Abalone, 373
    Anchovy-broiled shrimp, 374

Caviar and cream cheese, 374
Clams, 374-375
    Broiled, 374
    Walnut rolls, 375
Crab rolls, 375
Shrimp, 376
Spicy frankfurter, 368
Vegetables, 377-378
    Artichokes piquant, 377
    Asparagus in a blanket, 377
    Cucumbers au jour creme, 378
    Hi-hat mushrooms in wine sauce, 378
    Peppers, 376
    Sprightly sprouts, 377

CEREAL AND PASTA, 204-222

Macaroni, 204-217
        California sprout, 206
        With frankfurters, 207
    With poultry, 208-209
        Chicken, 209
    With seafood, 209-215
        Crab, 209
        Salmon, 210-212
        Shrimp, 211, 213-214
        Tuna, 209-210, 214
    With vegetables, 215-217
        Cabbage, 215
        Cucumber canoes, 216
        Sweet and sour, 217
Rice, 219-222
    Curried, 219
    Delicious chicken, 221
    With fruit, 219-221
        Strawberry, 221
    Gelatin, 219
    And meat, 221
    With seafood, 222
        Crab-wild rice, 222
        Shrimp deluxe, 222
Tomato and spaghetti, 222

CONGEALED FRUIT, 67-90

Apricot ring, 67
Avocado, 67
Bing cherry, 68
Blackberry delight, 68
Cranberry, 69
Melon, 69-70
    Watermelon delight, 70
Mixed, 74-90
    Applesauce-pineapple, 74
    Apricot, 75
    Avocado, 75
    Banana-pineapple, 75
    Blueberry, 76
    Cheese top, 77
    Cherry, 76
    Citrus, 77
    Cranberry, 78-79, 86, 90
        Orange, 78
        Pineapple, 86
        Strawberry, 79
    Fresh strawberry, 79
    Ginger, 79

    Gooseberry, 80
    Banana, 80
    Grapefruit, 83
    Grape supreme, 82
    Honeydew surprise, 80
    Lemon-cheese, 81
    Lime, 81
    Orange, 84-85
        Peach, 84
        Pineapple, 85
        Tangerine, 85
    Peach pickle, 86
    Raspberry, 88
        Melon ring, 88
    Strawberry, 89
        Banana, 89
        Grapefruit, 89
    Walnut jewel, 87
Orange, 70
Peach whip, 70
Pear, 71
Pineapple, 71-73
    Cheese, 72
Raspberry Bavarian, 74

CONGEALED VEGETABLE, 120-136

Artichoke, 120
Asparagus, 120
Beet, 121-122
Broccoli mold, 122
Carrots, 124
Cassel's spinach, 126
Cucumber, 124-125
    Ring with cottage cheese, 124
    Green onion, 125
Kidney bean, 121
Mixed, 128-136
    Beet-cabbage souffle, 129
    Cauliflower, 131
    Celery, 130
    Lime, 131-132
    Neapolitan, 133
    Onion, 130
    Tomato, 131, 133, 135-136
        Aspic, 133, 135-136
        And cheese, 131
        Soup, 135
One cup celery-nut, 124
Potato, 126
Slaw, 122-123
Tomato, 127-128
    Aspic, 127-128

EGG AND CHEESE, 224-244

Cheese, 224-235
    American, 224-225
        Pineapple, 224
    Camembert mousse, 225
    Cottage cheese, 227-229
        Date treat, 227
        Fruit, 227-228
        Lime delight, 228
    Cream cheese, 231
        Orange coke, 231
        Pineapple-nut, 231

380

Green ring, 232
Mold, 225
Mrs. Truman's ring, 232
Olive, 226
Pimento, 233-234
Royal frosted fruit mold, 234
Stuffed lettuce, 235
Swiss, 235-236
Egg, 236-244
Bacon, 236
And cheese, 237
With gelatin, 239-242
Seafood, 240
And shrimp, 241
And lettuce, 237-238
And peas, 238
Pennsylvania Dutch red beet, 242
Smoked, 242
Stuffed, 243-244
Curry, 244
Shrimp, 243
With wine, 243
With tomato, 238

FOREIGN, 296-312

Antigua, 296
Fruit, 296
Armenia, 296
Spinach, 296
Assyria, 296
Austria, 297
Hapsburg cucumbers, 297
Brazil, 297
Palmito, 297
China, 298
Crisp wun tun, 298
Egypt, 298
Salata bedingan—Eggplant, 298
England, 299
Dawson's pepper, 299
Finland, 299
Beet, 299
France, 299-301
Asparagus and shrimp, 299
Bouillabaisse, 301
D'endives, 300
Nicoise, 300
Germany, 301-302
Fleisch salat—Meat, 302
Potato, 301
Red cabbage slaw, 302
Greece, 302
Heart of palm, 302
Hawaii, 303
Chicken, 303
Holland, 303
Erwten sla—Pea, 303
India, 304
Peaches with curried chicken, 304
Tomato, 304
Indonesia, 304
Gado-gado, 304
Italy, 305
Ensalada Italiana, 305
Finocchio, 305
Japan, 306

Almond-sesame-lettuce, 306
Jordan, 306
Eggplant with yogurt, 306
Korea, 306
Bean Sprout, 306
Lebanon, 307
Tabbuli, 307
Mexico, 307-308
Ensalada de frijole—Bean, 307
Stuffed green chilies, 308
Norway, 308
Hummer smat—Lobster, 308
Panama, 309
Philippines, 309
Pineapple-tuna, 309
Poland, 309
Beet, 309
Puerto Rico, 310
Baked pepper, 310
Russia, 310
Summer, 310
Spain, 311
Combination de Aceitunas y cake pones—
Olive-shrimp mold, 311
Ensalada rusa, 310
Sweden, 311
Herring, 311
Syria, 312
Fruit, 312
Turkey, 312
Yalandgi dolmas—Stuffed grape leaves, 312

FROZEN, 246-270

Apple-orange frost, 246
Banana, 247-248
Charlene's apricot delight, 248
Sour cream jubilee, 247
Cheese coupe, 255
Cranberry, 252-253, 261
Pineapple cream, 253
Creamy, 249, 256
Tomato, 249
Crunchy apple-pineapple, 250
Date-cheese, 250
Delectable fruit, 250
Mallow fizz, 256
Mint, 253, 261
Pineapple, 261
Molded cottage cheese, 248
In orange shells, 254
Pear, 262
And cream cheese, 262
Peppermint, 253
Pineapple, 263, 266
Pink, 263-264
Raspberry whip, 263
Piquant, 256
Rainbow, 264
Raisin carnival snow, 265
Seafood supreme, 266
Spiced peach, 267
Ginger ale jumble, 257
Grapefruit-avocado, 258
Grape-pineapple treat, 258
Idaho cherry, 260
Strawberry, 249, 268

Cheese, 268
Pineapple delight, 268
Tomato, 249, 270
Creamy, 249
Zippy cheese, 270
Waldorf, 254

FRUIT, 45-64

Avocado, 45
Banana, 46
Coconut, 46
Nut, 46
Mixed, 49-64
Ambrosia, 49
In avocado boats, 56
Banana, 50
Cantaloupe, 51
Cherries and sour cream, 51
Citrus with lemon mayonnaise dressing, 52
Clara's grape, 52
Colorful quick fruit and melon, 53
Cranberry, 53-54, 63
Orange relish, 54
Stuffed-pear, 63
Fruit cocktail-marshmallow whip, 56
Grape, banana and cottage cheese, 58
Gumdrop, 58
Hawaiian papaya, 59
Orange, 60-61
And avocado, 61
Mandarin and grape, 60
Peanut butter, 61
Pear, 61-62
Pineapple sandwich, 55, 62
Stuffed honeydews, 63
Pear, 47-48
Marinated delight, 48
Pineapple, 49
Cranberry, 49
Stuffed apple, 45
Stuffed peach, 47

MEAT AND POULTRY, 154-176

Beef, 154-156
Ground beef, 155-156
Beefburger loaf, 156
Roast, 155
Soup, 155
Jellied, 154
Colorado lamb, 160
Corned beef, 157-159
Molded, 157-158
Frankfurter, 159-160
Luncheon meat, 161
Pepperoni and onion, 161
Potato, 161
Poultry, 162-168
Chicken, 162-165
Curried and grape, 163
With fruit, 163
Ginger-cream, 164
Jellied almond, 165
Mayonnaised, 164
Mousse, 162
Mrs. Eisenhower's jewel ring, 166

Pressed, 165
Turkey, 166-168
Almond, 167-168
Pineapple, 168
Baked, 166
Cranberry, 168
Pork, 169-173
Ham, 170-173
Aspic, 171
And cucumber, 170
Hot baked, 171
Kidney bean, 172
Pork, 169
And apple, 169
Party crown, 169
Rabbit, 173
Variety, 174
Chicken liver, 174
Tongue a la Peterson, 174
Veal, 175-176
Mold, 175

MIXED FRUIT AND VEGETABLES, 138-152

Apple, 138, 140-141, 147
Cauliflower, 140
Coconut and celery, 138
Sour cream slaw, 138
Beet and pineapple supreme, 139
Cabbage, 139, 141-142, 150
Banana, 139
Red orange, 150
Slaw, 139, 141-142
Carrot, 140
Cottage cheese-vegetable, 142
Cucumber, 142
Grapefruit, 143
Hearts of palm a la de Vera, 144
Lettuce, 145-146
Avocado delight, 145
And banana, 145
Lime, 146
Gelatin, 146
Velvet, 146
Millionaire's, 146
Orange, 148, 151-152
Olive plate, 148
And tomato tossed, 148
Tossed mandarin-avocado, 151
Watercress, 152
Pineapple, 149
And cucumber, 149
Spinach-avocado, 151
Tomato-grape, 151
Waldorf, 147-152
West Indian, 152

PARTY AND DESSERT, 272-294

Almond-peach cream, 272
Ambrosia in orange cups, 272
Angel hash, 272
Apple, 287, 291
Candlestick, 274
Canteloupe mold, 274
Cherry, 274-275, 278
In cream, 274

382

Lime crunch, 275
Chicken, 275-276
  In cheese shell, 275
Christmas, 276, 280, 287
  Candle, 280, 287
    Quick cranberry, 287
  Cheer, 276
  Eggnog, 279
Cucumber mousse, 277
Filled tomato cups, 280
Frozen berry-ice cream, 280
Fruit, 277, 281-282
  In avocado boats, 282
  Cheese loaf, 281
Fruit cocktail, 281, 288, 294
  Marshmallow whip, 281
  Waffles, 294
Grapefruit boats, 282
Green goddess seafood mold, 283
Gum drop, 283
Orange sherbet, 284
Pear, 273, 291
Pineapple, 273, 284-286
  Apricot ring mold, 273
  Coconut fluff, 285
  Ice cream delight, 285
Rainbow, 288
Ribbon, 288
St. Nick, 290
St. Patrick's Day, 290
Strawberry, 290-291
Thanksgiving cranberry, 292
Valentine, 293
Vanilla dream, 293
Whipped cream swirl, 294

SALAD DRESSINGS, 19-42

All-purpose, 19
Amish, 19
Avocado, 19
Bacon, 20
  Mayonnaise, 20
  Pennsylvania Dutch hot, 20
Bleu, 20-21
  Cottage cheese, 21
Buttermilk, 22
Cabbage, 22
Caesar, 23
Celery seed, 23
Chiffonade, 24
Condensed milk, 24
Dill, 25
French, 25-26
For fruit, 27-31
  Chutney, 27
  Cranberry, 27
    Ginger, 30
  Cream cheese, 28
  For grapefruit, 27
  Honey, 29
    Creme, 29
    Lime, 29
  Lemonade, 30
  Rum creme, 30
  Sherried, 31
Green goddess, 31

Greek, 31
Horseradish cream, 31
Italian, 32
Mayonnaise, 33-34
  One-minute, 33
  Soy, 34
Onion, 34
Paprika, low-calorie, 35
Parmesan, 34
For potato salad, 35-36
Roquefort, 36-37
Russian, 37-38
For seafood, 39-40
Sour cream, 40
Sweet, 40
  Mustard, 40
  Pickle, 40
Thousand Island, 41
Vinaigrette, 41-42
Waldorf, 42
Watercress, 42
Zippy for vegetable, 42

SEAFOOD, 178-202

Bayley's West Indes, 179
Clam, 178
Crab, 179-183
  Aspic, 180
  Bouillabaise, 183
  Grapefruit cocktail, 182
  King, 182
  Louis, 180
  Molded shrimp, 183
  Pear with hot vinaigrette dressing, 181
  Stuffed avocado, 181
Frozen, 178
  Fish, 178
  Tomato-caviar, 178
Halibut, 184-185
Lobster, 184-188
  Aspic Parisienne, 184
  Avocado, 188
  Egg, 186
  Melon with puffs, 185
  In pineapple shells, 187
  Potato, 186
  South African rock curry, 188
Mackerel, 188-189
Oyster, 189-190
Pecan-sardine, 193
Salmon, 190-192
  Cold with cucumber dressing, 190
  Mousse, 192
  Pepper, 192
Shrimp, 193-198
  Avocado, 193
  Curried, 194
    And melon, 194
  Mandarin, 196
  With peas, 198
Tuna, 198-202
  Apple, 200
  Bean bowl, 201
  Cabbage Hong Kong, 201
  Corn chip, 202
  Egg, 200, 202

Kidney bean, 199
Orange cups, 202

VEGETABLE, 93-118

Artichoke, 93
Asparagus, 94-95
 Radish, 94
 Vinaigrette, 94
Bean, 95-97
Broccoli vinaigrette, 197
Cabbage, 99-101
 Old fashion peanut, 100
 Slaw, 99, 101
Carrots, 98
Cauliflower, 101-102
Celery, 102-103
Corn, 104-105
Cucumber, 103-104
 In sour cream, 103
Dandelion, 105
Italian onion, 111
Jane's spinach, 116
Kraut, 116
Lettuce, 106-110
 Caesar, 106-108
 With hot dressing, 108
 Stuffed chilled, 110

Okra, 110-111
Parsnips, 111-112
Pea, 112-114
 And cheese, 114
 And zucchini, 113
Potato, 115-116
 Olive, 116
Tomato, 117-118
Zucchini and onion, 118

TITLE PAGE PHOTOGRAPHS, 20, 61, 70, 96, 121, 141, 160, 188, 220, 239, 248, 276, 311, 335

Aladdin's rice ring, 220
Blue cheese dressing, 20
Chicken salad ring, 276
Citrus apple salad w/lemon honey dressing 141
Colorado lamb salad, 160
Combination de aceitunas if cake pones— Olive shrimp mold (Spain), 311
Combination bean salad, 96
Egg crowned supper mold, 239
Molded cottage cheese salad, 248
Molded kidney bean salad, 121
Molded orange salad, 70
Orange-peanut butter salad, 61
Pickle cheese pineapple, 335
South African Rock lobster curry salad, 188

ACKNOWLEDGMENTS

We wish to express our appreciation for the use of photographs supplied us by the following: Cover—McIlhenny Co. (Tabasco) and Frontispiece—Western Iceberg Lettuce.

Color photographs were supplied by the following: International Tuna Fish Association; California Avocado Advisory Board; Florida Citrus Commission; Sunkist Growers; Evaporated Milk Association; Brussels Sprouts Marketing Program; and Knox Gelatin.

Title pages and half page photographs were supplied by the following: The Ruth Lundgren Company; Florida Citrus Commission; Keith Thomas Company; National Dairy Council; Diamond Walnut Growers, Inc.; General Foods Kitchen; Evaporated Milk Association; Knox Gelatin; Sunkist Growers; American Lamb Council; National Broiler Council; Tuna Research Foundation; National Banana Association; Carnation—Coffee Mate; National Macaroni Institute; R. T. French Company; Carnation Evaporated Milk; American Dairy Association; National Pickle Packers Association; and The Olive Advisory Board.